S0-CPS-586

Law in the Soviet Society

Law in the Soviet Society

Wayne R. LaFave, Editor

University of Illinois Press, Urbana, 1965

The essays in this volume were first published as a symposium on Soviet law in the University of Illinois Law Forum, *a legal periodical published by the College of Law, Vol. 1964, No. 1.*

© 1964, 1965 by the Board of Trustees of the University of Illinois. Manufactured in the United States of America. Library of Congress Catalog Card No. 65-19109.

ONULP

FOREWORD

"Late in the afternoon of Thursday, Oct. 15," reports Harrison Salisbury, "passers-by in Moscow's Manezhny Square saw half a dozen burly workmen taking down a great 40-foot canvas portrait of Nikita S. Khrushchev that had been put up a couple days earlier on the façade of the Moskva Hotel." [1] To these Soviet citizens, he adds, this was confirmation enough that the rumors sweeping the city were correct; Khrushchev had fallen. Khrushchev, who rose to party power within six months of Stalin's death in 1953, was now at age 70 replaced by the team of Alexei Kosygin and Leonid Brezhnev. The Khrushchev era, which had extended over more than a decade, had ended.

The Khrushchev period was one of dramatic change in the Soviet Union, and with Khrushchev now removed from power there will undoubtedly be renewed efforts by students of the Soviet society to assess the developments during this critical period. The essays in this volume, though prepared shortly before Khrushchev's downfall, may fairly be said to be a part of this assessment, for they are all concerned with *Law in the Soviet Society*. This is not to suggest that the Soviet legal system is purely a product of the Khrushchev era; clearly it is not. Yet, even those who are of the view that "the Soviet legal system remains Stalinist in its basic structure and its basic purposes" concede that "the reform movement in Soviet law is one of the most significant aspects of Soviet social developments in the . . . years since Stalin's death." [2]

It should also be noted that the articles appearing on the pages which follow are no less relevant to the post-Khrushchev era which has just begun. Khrushchev is gone, but the developments in Soviet law which occurred during his leadership remain a part of the existing system. As such, these reforms cannot be ignored by the Brezhnev-Kosygin team or their successors. The new leadership must seek to succeed where Khrushchev failed, both in domestic and foreign affairs, and in doing so there will inevitably appear the need for some further adjustments in the operation of the system. It remains to be seen whether the significant Soviet legal trends of the last decade [3] will continue in their present direction or will be diverted or reversed. However, it is unlikely that the legal and institutional changes described in this volume will be terminated; "they have acquired a momentum which is hard to stop." [4]

[1] Salisbury, *The Kremlin Plays Russian Roulette*, N.Y. Times, Oct. 25, 1964, § 6 (Magazine), p. 25.

[2] Berman, *The Dilemma of Soviet Law Reform*, 76 Harv. L. Rev. 929, 930 (1963).

[3] For an excellent statement of these trends, see Berman, *supra* note 2.

[4] Berman, *supra* note 2, at 951.

As an American lawyer who until recently was largely unaware of the workings of the Soviet legal system, I have found the essays in this volume a fascinating revelation. I am sure that other members of the legal profession will find the book equally rewarding. Lawyers and others concerned with the role of law in contemporary society have much to gain, of course, from study of other legal systems. As Professor Shimkin points out in his introductory article, the Soviet experience "exposes both useful plasticities and 'peril points' . . . that open the way to totalitarian and other evils," and thus "study of Soviet data can aid in the wise formulation of legal ways to meet the needs of developing nations and the solution of problems, such as slum violence, common to most nations." [5]

I do not mean to suggest that this is a book only for lawyers. It is not, and it should not be. Assessment of both the strengths and weaknesses of the Soviet legal system is a matter of critical importance to everyone. Professor Harold J. Berman has stated the point very well in the *Harvard Law Review:*

> "We have, strangely enough, a very great stake in the development of Soviet law. That stake is partly physical and partly spiritual. Physically, our very survival depends in part on the extent to which law can exercise a stabilizing influence on Soviet internal developments and on Soviet foreign policy. The fact that the Soviet people, including the Soviet leaders, believe in law is therefore a cause for us to rejoice. The fact that the law in which they believe differs sharply in certain essential features from the law in which we believe is, by the same token, a cause for us to be greatly concerned. Indeed, never before in our history has the study of a foreign legal system been of such crucial significance to us, for no other people has ever lived so close to us as the Soviets. We are less than half hour away from them by missile.
>
> "But even apart from the danger of atomic war, the destiny of the Soviet Union is intimately related to our own destiny. We are two revolutionary peoples in the world today—two peoples who have a world-wide mission. The struggle between us is only in part a power struggle. More basically, it is a spiritual struggle between two concepts —two developing concepts—of social order, each claiming universal validity. The spiritual struggle is more basic, for however the power struggle ends the spiritual struggle will remain. War would not settle the question of communism, no matter who is 'victorious.' The survivors of a war would still have to choose between something like the ideals reflected in Soviet law and something like the ideals reflected in American law." [6]

We have not attempted in this small volume to survey all aspects of the Soviet legal system. Rather, each of our contributors has been asked

[5] *Infra* at 36.

[6] Berman, *supra* note 2, at 929-30.

to pursue in some depth a topic of his own choosing. Each of these men is an established scholar in his own right, and it is therefore not surprising that each of them has made a significant and meaningful contribution to this symposium. This collection of essays, then, affords the reader an opportunity to explore certain important facets of Soviet law and to understand how that legal system affects relations between Soviet citizens, citizen-state relations, the operation of the planned economy, and Soviet foreign relations.

The introductory article in this volume, "Soviet Law and United States-Soviet Relations," is by Professor Demitri Shimkin of the University of Illinois. He has skillfully summarized the work which has been done heretofore outside the U.S.S.R. on Soviet law, with particular attention to prior analyses of law reform during the Khrushchev era. Shimkin points out why Soviet law merits serious attention for both intellectual and pragmatic reasons, and he emphasizes the importance of Soviet law in terms of United States-Soviet interaction. He concludes with a clear statement of the relevance of the essays which make up the balance of this volume.

My former colleague Dennis O'Connor, now on the law faculty at New York University, has written on "Soviet Procedures in Civil Decisions." In focusing upon the changing balance between public and civic systems of public order, O'Connor shows how organized nonjudicial groups serve to regulate human behavior in the Soviet society. Utilizing information obtained by interviews and field observations in addition to the traditional legal sources, he outlines the major decision methods and examines their relation to sanction policies, outlines the significant trends in both official and informal practice, and then presents an assessment of the impact of civic involvement and concerted sanctioning upon public order.

In "They Answer (to) Pravda," Colonel Bernard Ramundo discusses the Soviet press as a control mechanism supplementing the traditional police and judicial organs. His thesis is that a legal system intended to recast the individual in a new, more perfect image must, of necessity, supplement the traditional control organs in order to achieve the complete environmental control necessary for the recasting process. With documentation from cases reported in Pravda, he shows how the use of the press as an institutionalized form of criticism and self-criticism is an important device in this area.

Dr. D. A. Loeber, a West German authority on Soviet law and former editor of *Osteuropa-Recht*, has contributed the essay on "Plan and Contract Performance in Soviet Law." In contrast to civil law contracts, which have traditionally been viewed as free agreements between the parties, relations between socialist organizations are regulated by planned contracts, the essential conditions of which are predetermined by a planning act. Relying primarily upon Soviet legislative material and post-war practice in the settlement of contract disputes, Loeber analyzes how the performance of contracts occurs in and is affected by a planned economy.

In 1961, the U.S.S.R. Supreme Soviet adopted a skeleton code of fundamental principles of civil law, which will serve as the basis for individual civil codes to be adopted in each of the 15 union republics. Included in the code are tort provisions on the grounds of liability, recognized defenses, scope of compensable injury, workmen's compensation claims, wrongful death actions, and governmental liability. In "Soviet Tort Law: The New Principles Annotated," Whitmore Gray, professor of law at the University of Michigan, restates in the form of an annotation to these provisions the broad outlines of the contemporary Soviet law of tort.

"Law and the Distribution of Consumer Goods in the Soviet Union" is the subject explored by Professor Zigurds Zile of the University of Wisconsin. While greater concern for the consumer has been a significant characteristic of the Khrushchev era, Soviet theorists have at the same time stressed the need to restrain the growth of private property and to control and channel public demand. Zile undertakes to describe and analyze the organizational structure of Soviet trade in consumer goods, the transmission of consumer demand to producers, devices for shaping this demand, protection of buyers' interests with respect to the quality of service and merchandise, and the extent and function of illicit private trade.

A most appropriate conclusion to this series of essays is provided by Professor John Hazard of Columbia University. In "The Soviet Legal Pattern Spreads Abroad" he points out that what Inerius did for the civil law system at Bologna in the 12th century is now being done for the Soviet legal system. Thousands of law-trained communists are spreading around the world, taking with them definite concepts of what a legal system must be to effectuate the social change they desire. They have had to compromise with the culture patterns of the societies in which they have introduced the Soviet system, but the pattern is unmistakable. Hazard describes and analyzes this process, and concludes that "law has become a key weapon in the Soviet arsenal with which the Communists of the U.S.S.R. hope to influence the future of the world." [7]

I should like to express my thanks to our seven contributors, who so graciously responded to the invitation to participate in this symposium and who performed their tasks so well, and to Mrs. Zelda Derber, Associate Editor, and Mrs. Edith Shimkin, Consultant on Russian Bibliography, whose help was invaluable in the preparation of this volume.

WAYNE R. LAFAVE
Editor

Champaign, February 2, 1965

[7] *Infra* at 297.

TABLE OF CONTENTS

* Professor Gray's article constitutes a statutory annotation, and consequently cannot be broken down into sections in the same manner as the other articles. Listed above are the actual headings of the statutory sections being discussed beginning on the page cited.

ABBREVIATIONS AND GLOSSARY

The following abbreviations were used for Russian institutions, newspapers, periodicals, and legal collections.

Abbreviation	*Russian*	*English*
MISCELLANEOUS		
Inst. prav. Akad. nauk	Akademiya nauk, SSSR, Institut prava	Academy of Sciences of the USSR, Institute of Law
CPSU	Kommunisticheskaya partiya Sovetskogo Soyuza	Communist Party of the Soviet Union
LGU	Leningradskiy Gosudarstvennyy Universitet	Leningrad State University
MGU	Moscow Gosudarstvennyy Universitet	Moscow State University
RSFSR	Rossiyskaya Sovetskaya Federativnaya Sotsialisticheskaya Respublika	Russian Soviet Federative Socialist Republic
USSR	Soyuz Sovetskikh Sotsialisticheskikh Respublik	Union of Soviet Socialist Republics
VIYuN	Vsesoyuznyy institut yuridicheskikh nauk	All-Union Institute of Juridical Sciences
VYuZI	Vsesoyuznyy yuridicheskiy zaochnyy Institut	All-Union Juridical Correspondence Institute
NEWSPAPERS		
—	Izvestiya	News (Soviet government daily)
Kazakh. pravda	Kazakhstanskaya pravda	Kazakhstan Truth (Daily published in Alma Ata)
—	Pravda	Truth (Daily of the Central Committee of the CPSU)
Sov. Ross.	Sovetskaya Rossiya	Soviet Russia (Published daily)
Sov. torg.	Sovetskaya torgovlya	Soviet Trade (Published tri-weekly)
—	Trud	Labor (Daily of the All-Union Central Committee of Trade Unions)
PERIODICALS		
C.D.S.P.		Current Digest of the Soviet Press (Published weekly by the Joint Committee on Slavic Studies)
Sots. zakon.	Sotsialisticheskaya zakonnost'	Socialist Legality (Monthly of the Procuracy of the USSR and the Supreme Court of the USSR)
Sov. pechat'	Sovetskaya pechat'	The Soviet Press (Monthly of Union of Soviet Journalists)
Sov. yus.	Sovetskaya yustitsiya	Soviet Justice (Journal of the Supreme Court of the RSFSR and the Juridical Commission of the Council of Ministers of the RSFSR. Published biweekly)

Abbreviation	*Russian*	*English*
LEGAL COLLECTIONS		
Byul. verkh. suda RSFSR	Byulleten' verkhovnogo suda RSFSR	RSFSR Supreme Court Bulletin
Byul. verkh. suda SSSR	Byulleten' verkhovnogo suda SSSR	USSR Supreme Court Bulletin
Istoch. sov. grazh. prav.	Istochniki sovetskogo grazhdanskogo prava: Sbornik	Sources of Soviet Civil Law: A Collection
Pensionnoye obespecheniye	Pensionnoye obespecheniye v SSSR. Sbornik offitsial'nykh materialov	The Provision of Pensions in the USSR. A Collection of Official Materials.
Prav. reg. gos. torg. SSSR	Pravovoye regulirovaniye gosudarstvennoy torgovli SSSR	Legal Regulation of State Trade in the USSR
Sbornik	Sbornik instruktivnykh ukazaniy Gosudarstvennogo arbitrazha pri Sovete Ministrov SSSR.	Collection of "Instructive Letters" of the State Arbitration Agency of the Council of Ministers of the USSR.
Sbornik zakon.	Sbornik zakonov SSSR i ukazov Prezidiuma Verkhovnogo Soveta SSSR 1938-61 gg	Collection of Laws of the USSR and Edicts of the Presidium of the Supreme Soviet of the USSR, 1938-1961.
Sob. post. Prav. SSSR	Sobraniye postanovleniy Pravitel'stva SSSR (1938-1949, 1957-)	Collection of Decrees of the Government of the USSR (1938-1949, 1957-)
Sob. post. Prav. RSFSR	Sobraniye postanovleniy Pravitel'stva RSFSR (1939-1949, 1958-)	Collection of Decrees of the Government of the RSFSR (1939-1949, 1958-)
Sob. uzak.	Sobraniye uzakoneniy i rasporyazheniy Rabochego i Krest'yanskogo Pravitel'stva SSSR (1917-1938)	Collection of Legislation and Decisions of the Workers' and Peasants' Government of the RSFSR (1917-1938)
Sob. zak.	Sobraniye zakonov i rasporyazheniy Raboche-Krest'yanskogo Pravitel'stva SSSR (1924-1937)	Collection of Laws and Decisions of the Workers' and Peasants' Government of the USSR (1927-1937)
Sov. gos. i pravo	Sovetskoye gosudarstvo i pravo	Soviet State and Law (Monthly of the Institute of State and Law of the Academy of Sciences of the USSR)
Spravochnik sekretar.	Spravochnik sekretarya pervichnoy Partiynoy organizatsiyi	Handbook for Secretaries of Primary Party Organizations
Ved. verkh. sov. S.S.S.R.	Vedomosti verkhovnogo soveta S.S.R.	Gazette of the U.S.S.R. Supreme Soviet (Now published weekly)
Ved. verkh. sov. R.S.F.S.R.	Vedomosti verkhovnogo soveta R.S.F.S.R.	Gazette of the Russian Republic (R.S.F.S.R.) Supreme Soviet (Published weekly)
Zakon. akty (In some notes Zakon. akty narkhoz. SSSR)	Zakonodatel'nyye akty po voprosam narodnogo khozyaystva SSSR.	Legislative Acts on Problems of the National Economy of the USSR

The transliteration used is that of the United States Board of Geographic Names.

SOVIET LAW AND UNITED STATES — SOVIET RELATIONS

BY DEMITRI B. SHIMKIN *

I. The Scope and Value of Studies on Soviet Law

"LAW IN THE SOVIET SOCIETY" comprises a group of independent yet complementary studies. Dennis O'Connor and Bernard Ramundo analyze Soviet experiments in the use of organized nonjudicial groups and of the information-gathering and publicity mechanisms of mass communications media to effect behavioral conformity. In contrast, Dietrich Loeber and Whitmore Gray characterize the nature of familiar instruments of civil law —contracts and liabilities for torts—in the context of State capitalism. Zigurds Zile undertakes a thorough exposition of the legal aspects of retail trade in consumer goods, which correlates the interactions of civil law, administrative customs, and public attitudes to yield many insights on the environment as well as the procedures of Soviet law. Finally, John Hazard isolates stable and variable features in Soviet civil law by reviewing the continuities and changes evident in the diffusion of the Soviet legal system to Eastern Europe and Mainland China. He deals particularly with the characteristics of political authority, the scope of civil rights, the bounds of public and private property, and the codification of laws.

This collection contributes some new frameworks of reference and the review of selected new developments to the study of Soviet law. It constitutes a modest portion of a large and continuing international effort which, apart from those studies undertaken within the Soviet Union, has been largely concentrated in Germany, France, the United Kingdom, and the United States; recently, in the Netherlands, Belgium, India, and Japan, as well.[1]

**DEMITRI B. SHIMKIN. A.B. 1936, Ph.D. 1939, University of California; Professor of Anthropology and of Geography, University of Illinois; Visiting Professor of Anthropology at Harvard University for 1964-1965.*

[1] For Soviet publications prior to 1960, the most authoritative selected bibliography is the bilingual volume: ROMASHKIN, LITERATURA PO SOVETSKOMU PRAVU. BIBLIOGRAFICHESKIY UKAZATEL' (LITERATURE ON SOVIET LAW. A BIBLIOGRAPHICAL INDEX) (Moscow 1960). More complete bibliographical indices for individual areas of law, such as civil, family, state, criminal, and international law have also been published. The Academy of Science's law journal, *Sovetskoye gosudarstvo i pravo (Soviet State and Law)*, publishes regular but incomplete periodic and topical bibliographies which extend and render current this basic source. A fairly complete coverage of materials published in English, French, and German on Soviet law, up to the end of 1943, is HAZARD & STERN, BIBLIOGRAPHY OF THE PRINCIPAL MATERIALS ON SOVIET LAW (Am. For-

A. Pre-World War II Research

Prior to World War II, most foreign research on Soviet law took place in Germany, being centered especially at the Osteuropa-Institut (Eastern European Institute) in Breslau, and in Berlin. A monographic series, *Quellen ünd Studien (Sources and Studies)*, was published by the Institut from 1920 to 1933. Its journal, *Ostrecht*, which became *Zeitschrift für Ostrecht (Journal of Eastern Law)* in 1927, came out between 1925 and 1934, inclusive. In Berlin, another specialized periodical, *Zeitschrift für osteuropäisches Recht (Journal of Eastern European Law)*, lasted from 1925 to 1932, with a new series of the same name coming out in Hitler's day, 1934 to 1944.

Russian emigrés contributed significantly. They included L. Zaitseff and G. Soloweitschik on civil law, N. S. Timaschew on constitutional law, A. N. Makarow on international law, and others. However, leadership centered in German scholars. Among these, Heinrich Freund wrote most extensively (prior to Hitler's rise) on Soviet civil, commercial, labor, and criminal law, while Reinhart Maurach dealt with constitutional, international, family, and criminal law, as well as with legal procedure. Attention may also be drawn to E. Kelmann on legal theory; A. von Freytag Loringhoven and M. Langhans on constitutional law; M. Feitelberg and O. Serafinowicz on commercial law; G. Cleinow, H. Lorenz, C. Menzel, J. M. Rabinowitsch, and B. S. Graf von Stauffenberg on the legal aspects of foreign trade; and W. Gallas on criminal law.[2]

Overall, while policy implications were not neglected, the orientation of German work on Soviet law was commercial and consular. In the 1920's, most of the effort was concentrated on translating and collating the corpus of Soviet legislation.[3] In later works, greater emphasis upon the analysis of

eign Law Ass'n, Proceedings No. 27, 1945). Virtually comprehensive, carefully indexed, and partially annotated bibliographies on prerevolutionary Russian and on Soviet law, in English language materials only, are SZLADITS, A BIBLIOGRAPHY ON FOREIGN AND COMPARATIVE LAW, BOOKS AND ARTICLES IN ENGLISH 1953-1959 (1962); and SZLADITS, A BIBLIOGRAPHY ON FOREIGN AND COMPARATIVE LAW, BOOKS AND ARTICLES IN ENGLISH, SUPPLEMENT 1960-1961 (1963). The materials covered include translations of Soviet documents and monographs. Indian and a few other British Commonwealth reports come within the scope of these bibliographies.

No comprehensive bibliography for non-English publications has been found for 1943-53, but for 1954 on, see the periodic bibliographies by Dietrich Loeber and others in *Osteuropa-Recht (Eastern European Law)*, beginning with volume 1, at 75 (1955). On Japanese contributions, 1954 on, see Ushida, *Japanisches Schrifttum zum Recht der Ostblockstaaten (Japanese Writings on the Law of the Eastern Bloc Countries)*, in 6 OSTEUROPA-RECHT 295 (1960).

[2] For citations, see HAZARD & STERN, *op. cit. supra* note 1, at 24-43.

[3] For example, FREUD, DAS ZIVILRECHT SOWJETRUSSLANDS (THE CIVIL LAW OF SOVIET RUSSIA) (1924).

actual practice, on the social effects of particular laws, and on legal philosophy became evident.[4]

Significant French work was confined to two major compilations of Soviet law and three doctoral dissertations. Jules Patouillet's translation of the civil legislation of 1921-27, and Edouard Lambert's critical introduction thereto are still useful.[5] Other publications included a topical summary of civil and commercial law by B. Eliachevitch, Baron B. Nolde, and P. Tager; B. Mirkine-Guetzevich's dissertation on Soviet constitutions; A. Stoupnitzky's on the foreign-trade monopoly; and G. de Dolivo's on marriage laws.[6] The last represented a work, based on thorough use of the Soviet and German literature, which sought to establish the legal attributes and ethical problems of Soviet marital behavior.

In Great Britain, Samuel Dobrin alone produced substantive evaluations of Soviet law. Primarily a specialist in maritime and foreign-trade law, he also undertook competent analyses of legal practice and theory to counterbalance the uncritically pro-Soviet views of Harold J. Laski and Dudley Collard.[7] The reports of the latter, based on some direct observations but lacking in knowledge of the Soviet literature, were nevertheless influential politically.

In the United States, considerations of foreign policy and international law dominated views on Soviet legal developments. The primary vehicle of publication on Soviet law was the *American Journal of International Law*, which put out a continuing flow of articles and editorials, and a wide variety of book reviews, on Soviet matters. Several of the outstanding authorities on international law—Philip M. Brown, Charles C. Hyde, James B.

[4] See, for case data, Wirschubski, *Der Schutz der Sittlichkeit in Sowjetstrafrecht (The Protection of Morality in Soviet Criminal Law)*, 51 ZEITSCHRIFT FÜR DIE GESAMTE STRAFRECHTSWISSENSCHAFT (THE JOURNAL FOR GENERAL CRIMINAL JURISPRUDENCE) 317-28 (1931); on noncompliance by lower courts with Supreme Court decisions, Maurach, *Die Rechtsprechung des Obersten Gerichtshof der RSFSR in der Period des "sozialistischen Wiederaufbaus" (The Legal Opinions of the Supreme Court of the RSFSR in the Period of "Socialist Re-Construction")*, 53 *id.* at 333-47 (1934); on the public-health effects of legalized abortion, Kirstein, *Sowjetrussische Erfahrungen über lege artis ausgeführte Schwangerschaftsunterbrechungen (Soviet-Russian Experiences with Legal Medical Interruptions of Pregnancy)*, 52 *id.* at 459-76 (1932); and on the influence of Pashukanis and Krylenko on Soviet legal philosophy, Freund, *Strafrechtsreform im Zeichen der marxistischen Theorie (The Reform of Punishment in Regard to Marxist Theory)*, 51 *id.* at 301-16 (1931).

[5] LES CODES DE LA RUSSIE SOVIÉTIQUE (THE CODES OF SOVIET RUSSIAQ (Patouillet transl. Paris 1925-28); comprising vols. 9, 14, and 24, of Bibliothèque de l'Institut de Droit Comparé de Lyon. Études et Documents.

[6] For citations, see HAZARD & STERN, *op. cit. supra* note 1, at 15-23.

[7] See especially Dobrin, *Law and Justice in Soviet Russia* (pts. 1-3) 180 L.T. 277, 295, 373 (1935); Dobrin, *Soviet Jurisprudence and Socialism*, 52 L.Q. REV. 402 (1936); LASKI, LAW AND JUSTICE IN SOVIET RUSSIA (Day to Day Pamphlets No. 23 London 1935); and COLLARD, SOVIET JUSTICE AND THE TRIAL OF RADEK AND OTHERS (London 1937; Left Book Club. Topical Book, not for sale to the public).

Scott, and George G. Wilson—strongly opposed formal diplomatic relations with the USSR.[8] Even in 1934, a year after recognition, Philip M. Brown's judgment was that:

> "The acceptance of certain portions of the law of nations, such as the rights of diplomats and of sovereign states, must therefore be interpreted as a temporary opportunistic policy dictated by practical necessities until the rest of the world may have accepted Bolshevist principles and is under a new system of international law." [9]

Other authorities, notably Edwin M. Borchard and Edwin D. Dickinson, stressed pragmatic needs in recognizing *de facto* Soviet power, while the major protagonist of recognition, Chandler P. Anderson, emphasized potential contributions to peace and trade.[10]

This continuing debate stimulated a modest flow of excellent papers on Soviet law by Max Habicht, Malbone W. Graham, Lawrence Preuss, and Durward V. Sandifer.[11] These defined patterns and issues, such as the duality of State and Communist Party as sources of legal authority, which are relevant in United States-Soviet relations to this day. After the publication of *The Soviet Union and International Law* in 1935,[12] Timothy A. Taracouzio, a Russian emigré at Harvard, became the leading interpreter of Soviet affairs in the *American Journal of International Law.*

Prior to World War II, American work on Soviet domestic law was scattered in location, only fair in scale, but very good in quality. At the University of Chicago, Samuel N. Harper, a pioneer student of Russian government, devoted himself to work on the administrative structure and

[8] See Brown, *The Recognition of the Government of the Union of Soviet Socialist Republics,* 27 AM. J. INT'L. L. 290 (1933); Brown, *The Russian Soviet Union and the Law of Nations,* 28 *id.* at 733 (1934); Hyde, *Concerning a Russian Pledge,* 29 *id.* at 656 (1935); Hyde, *The City of Flint,* 34 *id.* at 89 (1940); Hyde, *International Law for Finland,* 34 *id.* at 285 (1940); Scott, *The Recognition of Soviet Russia,* 17 *id.* at 296 (1923); Wilson, *Diplomatic Relations and the U.S.S.R.,* 28 *id.* at 98 (1934).

[9] Brown, *The Russian Soviet Union and the Law of Nations,* 28 id. at 736 (1934).

[10] Borchard, *The Unrecognized Government in American Courts,* 26 AM. J. INT'L L. 261 (1932); Dickinson, *The Russian Reinsurance Company Case,* 19 *id.* at 753 (1925); Dickinson, *Recognition Cases* 1925-1930, 25 *id.* at 214 (1931); Dickinson, *The Case of Salimoff & Co.,* 27 *id.* at 743 (1933); Anderson, *Recognition of Russia,* 28 *id.* at 90 (1934); Anderson, *The Recent Trade Agreement With Russia,* 29 *id.* at 653 (1935).

[11] Habicht, *The Application of Soviet Laws and the Exception of Public Order,* 21 AM. J. INT'L. L. 238 (1927); Graham, *The Soviet Security Treaties,* 23 *id.* at 336 (1929); Preuss, *International Responsibility for Hostile Propaganda Against Foreign States,* 28 *id.* at 649 (1934); Sandifer, *Soviet Citizenship,* 30 *id.* at 614 (1936).

[12] See P. M. Brown's review in 29 AM. J. INT'L. L. 723 (1935); see also Taracouzio, *International Cooperation of the U.S.S.R. in Legal Matters,* 31 *id.* at 55 (1937); Taracouzio, *The Soviet Citizenship Law of 1938,* 33 *id.* at 157 (1939).

legal machinery of the Soviet Union.[13] His influence and that of James B. Scott, the international lawyer, induced John N. Hazard to study for three years, 1934-37, at the Moscow Juridical Institute. By the eve of World War II, Hazard had become a productive, recognized authority, especially on Soviet civil law.[14] In particular, his book, *Soviet Housing Law* (1939), was characterized by attention to the economic setting, by comprehensive documentation, and by elicitation of actual practice through case data.

In criminal law, Judah Zelitch's *Soviet Administration of Criminal Law* (1931), which represented the fruits of field inquiry as well as exhaustive documentary research in 1927-29, is still a landmark. Its merits derive not only from thoroughness and precision, but also from its apperception of basically contradictory attitudes toward law within the USSR. On the one hand, there is a theoretical denial of "the distinctiveness, not to say sanctity, of the judiciary"; on the other, the observable practice that "the Soviet courts are called upon to deal with judicial questions in a judicial way." [15] This contradiction has given rise to violent controversy, especially in postwar years, about the nature, even the actual existence, of Soviet law. The confusion rests in part on the differences between macro- and micro-analytical results, *i.e.*, those of the sociology of law (or legal policy) and of legal procedure. It also reflects the extraordinary, still unamalgamated and unstable configurations of power, values and concepts, the many unresolved pragmatic problems, characterizing the development of Soviet society.

Mary Callcott's book on Soviet criminal law, although naive, records many interesting observations.[16]

Finally, in the United States, as elsewhere, former Russian scholars did valuable research. Paul Haensel's analyses of Soviet public finance are still basic sources.[17] Aaron B. Holman's articles on inheritance and torts were significant, as were V. G. Olkhovsky's papers on patent law.[18] N. S. Timashev (Timaschew) and V. Gsovski, more recently arrived from Europe, also made noteworthy studies.[19]

B. Research During the First Postwar Decade

World War II virtually stopped Western investigations of Soviet law, and few of those hitherto prominent in the field were living or active professionally during the first postwar decade, 1945-54. Yet the need for re-

[13] For citations, see HAZARD & STERN, *op. cit. supra* note 1, at 6.

[14] *Id.* at 4-5, 8, 11-12, 14.

[15] ZELITCH, SOVIET ADMINISTRATION OF CRIMINAL LAW 363-64 (1931).

[16] CALLCOTT, RUSSIAN JUSTICE (1935).

[17] Especially, Haensel, *Public Finance in the U.S.S.R.* (pts. 1-4), 16 TAXES 517, 591, 659, 724 (1938).

[18] For citations, see HAZARD & STERN, *op. cit.* note 1, at 4.

[19] *Id.* at 7, 14.

search and teaching on Soviet law was intensified by the new legal problems which arose out of Soviet hegemony over Eastern Europe, the political challenge of socialism in Western Europe, and Soviet participation in the United Nations. Work revived and then expanded, particularly in the United States, with the participation of older emigrés, Soviet displaced persons, scholars drawn from other fields, and the young.

American efforts were more organized than in prewar days. In Washington, the Library of Congress developed a major program on Soviet and Eastern European law under the direction of V. Gsovski, the eminent legal scholar and former judge in Russia, Yugoslavia, and Czechoslovakia.[20] In New York, the temporary Research Program on the USSR utilized the talents of former Soviet citizens, especially G. V. Starosolski.[21] *De facto* chairs of Soviet law were established at Columbia, with John N. Hazard; Harvard, with Harold J. Berman; and California, with George C. Guins. Materials on Soviet law were published not only in separate volumes and mimeographed series, but widely as well in the law reviews (especially those of Columbia, Harvard, Michigan, and Washington), in the *American Journal of International Law*, in the *American Journal of Comparative Law*, and in the *American Slavic and East European Review* (then edited by Hazard). In 1949, the Joint Committee on Slavic Studies (appointed by the American Council of Learned Societies and the Social Science Research Council) initiated the publication of the *Current Digest of the Soviet Press*, an invaluable weekly source of translated legal and context materials. Outside of the legal profession, scholars such as Julian Towster (a student of Samuel Harper's), Merle Fainsod, Alex Inkeles, David Dallin, and Boris Nicolayevsky published usefully on Soviet constitutional law, on the Communist Party as a source of effective law, and on the use of mass communications and terrorism to augment the scope and effectiveness of legal sanctions.[22]

In France, René David of the University of Paris collaborated with Hazard in an extensive survey of Soviet law, *Le Droit Soviétique*.[23] Also,

[20] See particularly the mimeographed volumes, HIGHLIGHTS OF CURRENT LEGISLATION AND ACTIVITIES IN MID-EUROPE, vols. 1-8 (1953-60) and the numerous separate translations of codes and laws as well as compilations of the Law Library of the Library of Congress as listed in the three Szladits' bibliographies cited in note 1 *supra*.

[21] Starosolski, *Basic Principles of Soviet Criminal Law*, 28 N.C.L. REV. 359 (1950); STAROSOLSKI, THE PRINCIPLE OF ANALOGY IN CRIMINAL LAW: AN ASPECT OF SOVIET LEGAL THINKING (Research Program on the U.S.S.R., Mimeo. Series No. 55, 1954).

[22] TOWSTER, POLITICAL POWER IN THE USSR 1917-1947 (1948); FAINSOD, HOW RUSSIA IS RULED (1st ed. 1953); INKELES, PUBLIC OPINION IN SOVIET RUSSIA (1950); DALLIN & NICOLAYEVSKY, FORCED LABOR, IN SOVIET RUSSIA (1947).

[23] Vol. 1: DAVID, LES DONNÉES FONDAMENTALS DU DROIT SOVIÉTIQUE (FUNDAMENTAL ATTRIBUTES OF SOVIET LAW) (Paris 1954); Vol. 2: HAZARD, LE DROIT ET L'EVOLUTION DE LA SOCIETÉ DANS L'U.R.S.S. (LAW AND SOCIAL EVOLUTION IN THE USSR) (Paris 1954). The latter is a slightly edited translation of HAZARD, LAW AND SOCIAL CHANGE IN THE U.S.S.R. (London 1953).

the compact digest of P. Arminjon, Baron B. Nolde, and M. Wolff brilliantly isolated many of the logical regularities discernible in Soviet law.[24] Jean-Yves Calvez' monograph on international law and sovereignty in the USSR was most competent.[25] And beginning in 1949, Michel Fridieff extensively reviewed books on Soviet law and summarized Soviet legal developments, largely in the *Revue internationale du droit comparé.*

In the United Kingdom, Rudolf Schlesinger (at Glasgow) and Albert Kiralfy were among those writing professionally on Soviet law.[26] Many of the articles on this subject appeared in the *Modern Law Review.* In Germany, Lothar Schultz' *Russische Rechtsgeschichte (Russian Legal History)* was the most noteworthy contribution of this period.[27]

The western study of Soviet law in 1941-54 had many goals. Important assemblies of statutes, of Communist Party rules and pronouncements, and of legal cases were prepared by Gsovski, W. Gallas, J. H. Meisel and E. H. Kozera, Hazard and M. Weisberg, and Berman and B. Konstantinovsky.[28] Extensive descriptions of Soviet legal provisions and practices were undertaken, with varying degrees of ideological and social interpretation, by Arminjon, Nolde, and Wolff; Gsovski; Guins; David and Hazard; and Berman. These studies yielded remarkably divergent results, in part because of differences in coverage and the materials used, but fundamentally because of differences in approach to Soviet society.

Arminjon, Nolde, and Wolff dealt with the patterning of explicit legislation. In so doing, they showed, for instance, that while written statutes formed the basic source of law, recourse to general State policies and to analogy in types of contract as well as in criminal law widened judicial

[24] 3 Arminjon, Nolde & Wolff, Traité de Droit Comparé 227-398 (Paris 1951).

[25] Calvez, Droit International et Souveraineté en U.R.S.S. (International Law and Sovereignty in the U.S.S.R.) (Paris 1953).

[26] Schlesinger, Soviet Legal Theory (London 1945); Schlesinger, Changing Attitudes in Soviet Russia: The Family (London 1949); Kiralfy, *A Soviet Approach to Private International Law,* 4 Int'l L.Q. 120 (1951); Kiralfy, *The Juvenile Law-Breaker in the U.S.S.R.* 15 Modern L.R. 472 (1952).

[27] Schultz, Russische Rechtsgeschichte von den Anfängen bis zur Gegenwart einschliesslich des Rechts der Sowjetunion (Russian Legal History From the Beginnings to the Present Including the Law of the Soviet Union) (Schwarzwald 1951).

[28] 2 Gsovski, Soviet Civil Law (1948); Gallas, Strafgesetzbuch der Russischen S.F.S.R. vom 22 Nov. 1926 in der an 1 Jan. 1952 gultigen Fassung (The Penal Code of the Russian S.F.S.R. of November 22, 1926 in the Version Effective January 1, 1952) (Berlin 1953); Meisel & Kozera, Materials for the Study of the Soviet System (2d ed. 1953); Hazard & Weisberg, Cases and Readings on Soviet Law (1950); and Konstantinovsky, Soviet Law in Action: The Recollected Cases of a Soviet Lawyer (Berman ed. 1953).

options.[29] However, the very limited application of *stare decisis* sharply restricted the formation of judge-made law.[30] Another inductively derivable principle was that of the limitations of State liability: by the formation of State enterprises as separate, nonbudgetary legal entities, by the limitation of damages to excesses over the coverage of State insurance, by the exclusion of Comrades' Courts and allied institutions from State budgetary support, and by requirements of incorporation and registration which placed genuinely private associations and real-estate transactions beyond the scope of legal protection.[31] In the sphere of family law, Soviet jurisprudence systematically reinforced the ties of direct descent, sibling relation, and coresidence by inheritance rights and support obligations, up and down, but deprived consensual or dissolved marriage ties of virtually all force.[32]

Several authors sought to evaluate the broad relations between Soviet law and society. Gsovski and especially Guins emphasized the repressive aspects of Soviet law. Guins raised the question whether terror was the central mechanism of the Soviet State and law merely an expedient superstructure.[33] For David and Hazard the duality of explicit State goals, especially those of socio-economic development, and of the pragmatic resolution of work-a-day conflicts seemed more significant as interpretative guidelines. Although the fact of political repression was recognized, its relation to the system of Soviet law remained unclear.[34] In Berman's view

[29] 3 ARMINJON NOLDE & WOLFF, *op. cit. supra* note 24, at 260-61, 346-47. On the abuse of analogy in Soviet criminal law (up to 1960) see STAROSOLSKI, *op. cit. supra* note 21, and on a comparative basis, the anonymous article *The Use of Analogy in Criminal Law*, 47 COLUM. L. REV. 613 (1947).

[30] See also Hazard, *The Soviet Court as a Source of Law*, 24 WASH. L. REV. 80 (1949). Note that in Tsarist law, the principle of stare decisis applied only to officially published acts of cassation. 3 ARMINJON, NOLDE & WOLFF, *op. cit. supra* note 24, at 240 n.1.

[31] *Id.* at 251, 259, 278-79, 309-10, 315, 341, 360-63.

[32] *Id.* at 366, 369-71, 376, 380-81, 387, 392. This applies especially to the legislation of 1944-45, which in turn reflects many provisions of Russian customary law. See Shimkin & Sanjuan, *Culture and World-View: A Method of Analysis Applied to Russia*, 55 AMERICAN ANTHROPOLOGIST 329, 330-32 (1953).

[33] 1 GSOVSKI, SOVIET CIVIL LAW (1948); GUINS, SOVIET LAW AND SOVIET SOCIETY (The Hague 1954), especially 362-78. FAINSOD, *op. cit. supra* note 22, at 479, 500, shared this view:

" . . . The technique developed to enforce control represent a many-sided combination of indoctrination, incentives, and repression. . . . The governing formula of Soviet totalitarianism rests on a moving equilibrium of alternating phases of repression and relaxation, but its essential contours remain unchanged. The totalitarian regime does not shed its police-state characteristics; it dies when power is wrenched from its hands."

[34] DAVID, *op. cit. supra* note 23, at 2-4, 157-214; HAZARD, *op. cit. supra* note 23, at 104-07, 198. The pragmatic viewpoint is epitomized by Bodenheimer, *The Impasse of Soviet Legal Philosophy*, 38 CORNELL L.Q. 51, 67-68 (1952) as follows:

"While there are large areas in Soviet life in which political terror untempered by law is the order of the day, there exist fields of legal regulation, such as

of Soviet society, in Stalin's day at least, "Both law and terror are instruments through which the state accomplishes its objectives. Terror serves as an instrument of political and ideological discipline; law serves as an instrument of moral and social discipline, a means of promoting a sense of responsibility, a proper balance between inventiveness and restraint in the exercise of industry, initiative, honesty, and other 'legal virtues'."[35]

Apart from the complex, unresolved problems of Soviet legal reality, great interest developed in the critical examination of communist legal theory. In his pioneering exposition, Schlesinger hoped to identify features independent of Russia's stormy politics and usable for the development of democratic socialism. Although he found merit in specific aspects of the Soviet management of public property, he concluded that "under socialism, the rule of Law is granted by the public interest embodied in Public Law, and by nothing else."[36] Hugh Babb's translations made accessible a wide body of Marxist legal thought, from Lenin to Vyshinsky and Strogovich.[37] Critical analyses of these materials by Edgar Bodenheimer and Hans Kelsen[38] brought out the diversity, even confusion, of these views. The creative Soviet thinker, E. B. Pashukanis, espoused doctrines, until his recantation and liquidation, that identified "morality, law and state" as "forms of bourgeois society."[39] His successors recognized a distinctive Soviet socialist law "expressing the will of the worker class and of all the toilers; . . . guaranteed by the coercive force of the socialist state."[40] This definition, with its repressive class connotations, produced ideological dilemmas which have been attacked in later Soviet policy changes, especially since 1961. But it also justified a classification of international law, as a reflection of the class character of constituent States, into distinct "imperialist-reactionary" and "democratic-progressive" forms.[41]

Overall, the tenor of western studies was that the Soviet Union sought, by conduct and pronouncements, to mold international law simultaneously toward protecting the nation's political and socio-economic integrity, and

tort law, contract law, agency law, sales, negotiable instruments law, and non-political criminal law, which are governed by standards which the people in general would probably tend to regard as acceptable and reasonable. In fact, the legal principles in these fields are not very basically different from those prevailing in the countries of Western civilization, and the class-struggle interpretation of law contributes nothing to their understanding." (Footnotes omitted)

[35] Berman, *Soviet Justice and Soviet Tyranny*, 55 COLUM. L.R. 795, 807 (1955). For a fuller exposition, see BERMAN, JUSTICE IN RUSSIA (1950).

[36] SCHLESINGER, *op. cit. supra* note 26, at 271.

[37] 20TH CENTURY LEGAL PHILOSOPHY SERIES: VOL. V, SOVIET LEGAL PHILOSOPHY (Babb transl. 1951); VYSHINSKY, THE LAW OF THE SOVIET STATE (Babb transl. 1948).

[38] Bodenheimer, *supra* note 34; KELSEN, THE COMMUNIST THEORY OF LAW (1955).

[39] KELSEN, *op. cit. supra* note 38, at 106.

[40] *Id.* at 141.

[41] *Id.* at 187.

toward yielding privileges abroad for Communism and the Soviet State.[42] A central Soviet tenet was unlimited national sovereignty, without recognition of any but delegated powers to international organizations, and without any cognizance at all of individuals as subjects of international law.[43] In Soviet views, explicit national consent, especially that formulated in bilateral treaties, was the sole valid basis of international law. Binding principles and definitions were resisted, while the right to individual (even *post hoc)* reservations to multilateral agreements was avowed.[44] Concurrently, the Soviets recognized different standards for "nondemocratic" and "democratic" states. Thus, "guerrilla warfare is and remains one of the regular forms of the people's, that is, just, war and in this sense it is included in the collection of rules of international law directed to the prevention of any type of aggression." [45] In foreign trade and in private cases, the Soviet Union made effective use of foreign laws, *e.g.*, in choice of the vehicle of State trading, and in the pursuit of claims to land ownership, with minimal reciprocity.[46]

Past antecedents as well as current theory and practice concerned western analyses of Soviet law in the early 1950's. Guins attributed the "ease" with which the Soviets broke the old legal order to prior inadequacies:

> "The Russian nation was not familiar with the advantages of the 'rule of law' during the course of its history. . . . Russia could justly be proud of the judicial system organized in 1864, which produced many famous Russian judges, lawyers and law teachers, but the re-education of the masses of the population in understanding the significance of law and of legal methods of organizing social relations and protecting rights had not been achieved.
>
> . . . .

[42] For basic documentation see note 37 *supra* and Prince, *Current Views of the Soviet Union on the International Organization of Security, Economic Cooperation and International Law: A Summary*, 39 AM. J. INT'L L. (1945); Trainin, *Questions of Guerrilla Warfare in the Law of War*, 40 *id.* at 534 (1946); Korovin, *The Second World War and International Law*, 40 *id.* at 747 (1946). A careful exposition of Korovin's views is given by Chakste, *Soviet Concepts of the State, International Law and Sovereignty*, 43 *id.* at 21 (1949).

[43] CALVEZ, *op. cit. supra* note 25, at 265-66; Chakste, *supra* note 42, at 31; KELSEN, *op. cit. supra* note 38, at 177-82.

[44] CALVEZ *op. cit. supra* note 25, at 230-46; KELSEN, *op. cit. supra* note 38, at 187-92. At the Nuremberg trials, the initial Soviet position was to base Nazi guilt on the *Moscow Declaration of German Atrocities*, without reference to definitions or principles of international crimes. See Ivrakis, *Soviet Concepts of International Law, Criminal Law and Criminal Procedure at the International Conference on Military Trials*, London, 1954, 2 MERCER L. REV. 331 (1951).

[45] Trainin, *supra* note 42, at 562. See also CALVEZ, *op. cit. supra* note 25, at 270-74.

[46] Fensterwald, *Sovereign Immunity and Soviet State Trading*, 63 HARV. L. REV. 614, 631-33 (1950); Kiralfy, *A Soviet Approach to Private International Law*, *supra* note 26, at 120 (1951).

> ". . . . Because of the peasant village commune, the great majority of the population did not have private property. Other dark spots in the Russian legal order were the backward customs of the Asiatic tribes." [47]

Berman and following him, David, visualized Russia as "historically weak in lawgivers and jurists[,] . . . . strong in its sense of community, and strong in centrally directed energy, administrative initiative at the top. . . . [The Russians] have looked to spontaneous personal and administrative relationships rather than to the formality of law, with its time-consuming emphasis on due process and its rationalism." [48]

These conclusions are invalid, unjust, and dangerously misleading in their representation of popular reactions to State pressures, particularly in the areas of property rights and family law. Historically, as V. Sergeyevich's authoritative work makes clear, Muscovite legal institutions were by no means "backward," especially in the procedures of the civil courts.[49] Peter I's barracks-room ideology and the military power of the autocracy rather than a failing of the "Russian spirit" were responsible for the degeneration of law thereafter.[50] As it was, the florescence of Russian law after 1864 has aroused the admiration not only of liberal emigrés but even of today's Soviet jurists.[51] Many of the true reforms of the Soviet constitu-

[47] GUINS, *op. cit.* supra note 33, at 9, 15.

[48] BERMAN, JUSTICE IN RUSSIA at 157-58 (1950).

[49] SERGEYEVICH, LEKTSIYI I ISSLEDOVANIYA PO DREVNEY ISTORIYI RUSSKOGO PRAVA (LECTURES AND INVESTIGATIONS ON THE ANCIENT HISTORY OF RUSSIAN LAW) (3d ed. St. Petersburg 1903), especially 588-605. Muscovy law distinguished between civil courts *(sudy)* and criminal ones *(sysky)*, with markedly different procedures. Thus torture was prohibited in the former, and practised in the latter. The concept of Russian legal backwardness in this period has also been criticized on the basis of western data. See Schlesinger, *"Justice in Russia": A Dissent* 60 YALE L.J. 976, 980-81 (1951).

[50] Peter discarded Muscovite legal procedures as time-wasters, substituting therefor the inquisitorial, secret, and written processes then popular among the enlightened autocrats of Western Europe. The Military Regulation *(voinskiy ustav)* of 1716 set up a criminal code of extreme severity, enforced by a police organization headed by the Procurator General who was responsible to the Emperor alone. This police justice remained in effect for political crimes until 1917, the legal reforms of 1864 notwithstanding. Tsarist police practices, like many other elements of pre-Revolutionary governmental procedure, have persisted in the Soviet Union. A basic source on Petrine law is M. F. VLADIMIRSKIY-BUDANOV, OBZOR ISTORIYI RUSSKOGO PRAVA (SURVEY OF THE HISTORY OF RUSSIAN LAW) 641-43 (7th ed. Petrograd 1917). The standard work on Tsarist police law is BARON S. A. KORFF, ADMINISTRATIVNAYA YUSTITSIYA *v.* ROSSIYI (ADMINISTRATIVE JUSTICE IN RUSSIA) (2 vols. St. Petersburg 1910). The best non-Russian summary of Russian legal history is SCHULTZ, *op. cit. supra* note 27. The post-Revolutionary development of the procuracy and police law is surveyed in MORGAN, SOVIET ADMINISTRATIVE LEGALITY (1962).

[51] An outstanding work on this subject is KUCHEROV, COURTS, LAWYERS AND TRIALS UNDER THE LAST THREE TSARS (1953). On recent Soviet rehabilitation of past legal liberalism see ZAITSEV & POLTORAK, THE SOVIET BAR 93-100 (Moscow 1959).

tions reflect these liberal ideas.[52] Even more important is the fact, thoroughly attested to in the many volumes of legal norms and practices collected by the Imperial Russian Geographical Society and other agencies throughout the nineteenth century, that the Russian peasant developed and operated a sophisticated system of civil law even under serfdom.[53] The communalism of the Russian peasant was an official myth. On the contrary, his excellence as an entrepreneur, his keenness in preceiving equities, his ingenuity in forming economic organizations were realities which few Russian intellectuals other than Stolypin realized.[54] And assassination aborted his last minute reforms. The wealth of non-Russian legal traditions, Islamic, Turkic, Caucasian, Hebrew, and West European can scarcely be dismissed in a country ethnically only half Russian.[55]

The importance of these popular traditions in the Soviet Union explains the extreme bitterness of peasant resistance to agricultural collectivization in the 1930's, the consequences of which the demographer Frank Lorimer has assessed as costing fully 5,000,000 lives.[56] It has great relevance today, for the sharp social division of Soviet rural and urban societies has helped conserve the past within the former. So too have explicit legal concessions to traditional ways concerning the rural household and the private plot.[57] Moreover, half the present-day city population was born on the farm.[58] Among these persons as well as in rural areas, customary laws compete with codified standards and the moral injunctions of communist leadership in the rapidly expanding area of self-regulation, in part at least, which is governed by the Comrades' Courts.[59]

[52] See Korff, *The Future Russian Constitution as Seen by Russian Liberals,* 14 Am. Pol. Sci. Rev. 209 (1920).

[53] For a summary and bibliographical indications see Shimkin & Sanjuan, *supra* note 32, at 330-33, 347-48 and Shimkin, *National Forces and Ecological Adaptations in the Development of Russian Peasant Societies,* in Patterns and Processes in Culture 237-47 (Manners ed. 1964).

[54] On peasant entrepreneurship see Shimkin, *The Entrepreneur,* in Tsarist and Soviet Russia, 2 Explorations in Entrepreneurial History 24-34 (1949). The most perceptive account of peasant resistance to the imposed bonds of the commune, and of Stolypin's reforms is Treadgold, The Great Siberian Migration (1957).

[55] For a general review of this problem see 3 Arminjon, Nolde & Wolff, *op. cit. supra* note 24 at 232-33.

[56] Lorimer, The Population of the Soviet Union 120-21, 133-37, especially 136 (Geneva 1946).

[57] On elements of the legal position of the Soviet rural population see Shimkin, *Current Characteristics and Problems of the Soviet Rural Population,* in Soviet Agricultural and Peasant Affairs 79, 80-84 (Laird ed. 1963).

[58] On urbanization, see Shimkin, *Demographic Changes and Socio-Economic Forces Within the Union, 1939-1959,* in Milbank Memorial Fund, Population Trends in Eastern Europe, the USSR and Mainland China 231-35 (1960). Since 1959, the role of urban inmigration appears to have risen even more.

[59] In Soviet legal theory, custom is formally admissible only in rulings on title to, and the partition of, rural household property, and in certain practices of

C. Legal Trends and Studies in Khrushchev's Era

Provisions for expanded self-regulation under the close tutelage of the Communist Party have been part of the extensive legislation undertaken in the Soviet Union since Stalin's death on March 5, 1953, and especially since Khrushchev's rise to power in early 1955. This legislation has included new, revised, and repealed laws *(zakony)*, decrees *(ukazy)* and decisions *(postanovleniya)*, and has emanated from Supreme Soviets and Presidia of the USSR and the Union Republics, from the Council of Ministers of the USSR, from the Central Committee of the Communist Party, and from the All-Union Central Council of Labor Unions.[60] The net effects of this legislation may tentatively be grouped into nine areas of domestic and international law.

1. Between March, 1953, and late 1958, the Soviet government widened personal freedoms and work incentives. It promulgated reductions of most prison sentences, as well as amnesties and restorations of pension seniorities for lesser civil and military offenders.[61] It repealed labor conscription for adolescent boys and girls, and criminal penalties for breaches of labor

merchant shipping. However, the "rules of socialist community life" *(pravila sotsialisticheskogo obshchezhitiya)* mentioned in article 130 of the 1936 Constitution of the USSR, have developed considerable legal as well as moral force, particularly via Communist Party regulations. While the bulk of these rules is of imposed rather than popular origin, they are not unlikely to gain practice accretions from both traditional and emergent custom. See NOVITSKIY, ISTOCHNIKI SOVETSKOGO GRAZHDANSKOGO PRAVA (SOURCES OF SOVIET CIVIL LAW) 62, 82 (Moscow 1959).

[60] The basic outlet for legislation by the Supreme Soviet, including the Presidium of the USSR, is that body's *Vedomosti.* Important collections include SBORNIK ZAKONOV I UKAZOV PREZIDIUMA VERKHOVNOGO SOVETA S.S.S.R. 1938-61 gg (COLLECTION OF LAWS AND DECREES OF THE PRESIDIUM OF THE SUPREME SOVIET OF THE U.S.S.R. 1938-61) (Kalinychev ed. Moscow 1961); ROMASHKIN, LAPTEV & TORCHINSKIY, ZAKONODATEL'NYYE AKTY PO VOPROSAM NARODNOGO KHOZYAYSTVA S.S.S.R. (LEGISLATIVE ACTS ON PROBLEMS OF THE NATIONAL ECONOMY OF THE U.S.S.R.) 2 vols. (Moscow 1961); SPRAVOCHNIK SEKRETARYA PERVICHNOV PARTIYNOY ORGANIZATSIYI (HANDBOOK FOR SECRETARIES OF PRIMARY PARTY ORGANIZATIONS) (Yefremov, Storozhev & Churayev eds. Moscow 1960); and PENSIONNOYE OBESPECHENIYE V S.S.S.R. SBORNIK OFFITSIAL'NYKH MATERIALOV (THE PROVISION OF PENSIONS IN THE U.S.S.R. A COLLECTION OF OFFICIAL MATERIALS) (Borisov & Merkulov compilers Moscow 1958). For the continuous reporting, in English, of Soviet legislation, the most important source is the CURRENT DIGEST OF THE SOVIET PRESS, hereafter cited as C.D.S.P.

[61] Decree of March 27, 1953, [1953] Ved. verkh. sov. S.S.S.R. No. 4, SBORNIK ZAKON. 853-4. This decree released those convicted for less than five years; those convicted of abuse of military authority, AWOL, misuse of government property and dereliction of guard duty; the elderly; pregnant women, and those with children under 10 years of age. Other sentences, excluding those for "counter-revolutionary offenses," major embezzlements of State property, banditry, and intentional homicide were halved. This decree also required a start on new criminal legislation. "On the seniority of citizens, for whom penalties were decreased in the re-examination of criminal cases," Decision of Sov. Min. S.S.S.R., Oct. 4, 1956, PENSIONNOYE OBESPECHENIYE.

discipline.[62] It made use of the corvée for rural road work, which had been compulsory since 1936, a matter of local discretion.[63] It relegalized abortion, an important concession, given the parlous legal position of the unmarried mother and illegitimate child under the Decree of July 8, 1944.[64] And, in 1958, it prohibited the deprivation of voting rights as a punishment.[65]

Measures strengthening due process included the revival and reorganization, in 1955, of the procuracy as a comprehensive authority for ensuring legality in all government operations; the renewed requirement of normal judicial procedure as opposed to police justice for "terroristic" as well as other crimes; and general revisions introduced on December 25, 1958.[66] The last comprised basic principles of criminal legislation, of the organization of courts, and of criminal court procedures, which served as frameworks for detailed legislation by the Union Republics, and laws on state offenses, on military offenses, and on procedures of military tribunals.[67] The new meas-

[62] "On the induction (mobilization) of youths in craft and railroad schools," Decree of March 18, 1953, SBORNIK ZAKON. 563. "On the repeal of criminal responsibility of workers and employees for voluntary departure from enterprises and from agencies and for absence without satisfactory reasons," Decree of April 25, 1956 [1956] Ved. verkh. sov. S.S.S.R. No. 10, SBORNIK ZAKON. 566-68. Pension seniority was also alloted to former labor conscripts. "On the compulsory placement at work of Gypsies leading a roaming life," extract from Decree of Oct. 5, 1956, [1956] Ved. verkh. sov. S.S.S.R. No. 21, SBORNIK ZAKON. 569.

[63] "On the participation of kolkhozes, sovkhozes, industrial, transport, construction and other enterprises, and economic organizations in the construction and repair of automobile roads," Decree of Nov. 26, 1958, [1958] Ved. verkh. sov. S.S.S.R. No. 4, SBORNIK ZAKON. 171.

[64] "On the repeal of criminal responsibility of pregnant women for conduct of abortion," Decree of Aug. 5, 1954, [1954] Ved. verkh. sov. S.S.S.R. No. 15, SBORNIK ZAKON. 771. "Repeal of prohibition of abortion," Decree of Nov. 23, 1955, [1955] Ved. verkh. sov. S.S.S.R. No. 22, SBORNIK ZAKON. 724. On the Decree of July 8, 1944, and its effects see 3 ARMINJON, NOLDE & WOLFF, *op. cit. supra* note 24, at 378-87. On post-World War II legislation on abortions in Eastern Europe see Mauldin, *Fertility Control in Communist Countries: Policy and Practice*, in MILBANK MEMORIAL FUND, *op. cit. supra* note 58, at 179.

[65] "On the repeal of the deprival of voting rights as a punishment," extract from Law of Dec. 25, 1958, [1959] Ved. verkh. sov. S.S.S.R. No. 1, SBORNIK ZAKON. 772.

[66] "Procedures of procural surveillance in the USSR," Decree of May 24, 1955, [1955] Ved. verkh. sov. S.S.S.R. No. 9, SBORNIK ZAKON. 818-31. According to MORGAN, *op. cit. supra* note 50, at 133, the Soviets viewed this as the first comprehensive legislation defining the tasks, rights, and duties of the procuracy. "Repeal of regulations of the Presidium and the Central Committee of the CPSU, SSSR, Dec. 1, 1934, on terroristic acts, and of Dec. 1, 1934 and Sept. 14, 1937, on charges in criminal procedural codes of the Union Republics," Decree of April 19, 1956, [1956] Ved. verkh. sov. S.S.S.R. No. 9.

[67] "Basic principles of criminal legislation of the Soviet Union and the Union Republics," Law of Dec. 25, 1958, [1959] Ved. verkh. sov. S.S.S.R. No. 1, SBORNIK ZAKON. 727-45; "Basic principles of the legislation on the organization of courts of the Soviet Union and of the Union and Autonomous Republics." Law of Dec. 25, 1958, [1959] Ved. verkh. sov. S.S.S.R. No. 1, SBORNIK ZAKON. 779-87; "Basic principles of criminal court procedures of the Soviet Union and Union Republics," Law of Dec. 25,

ures retained much of the past, were harsher than before in some provisions, but afforded major gains. Particularly important, in Soviet as well as foreign views, were the guaranties against extra-judiciary repression, and for specifications of offense and responsibility in order to eliminate the uses of analogy and attainder as grounds for prosecution.[68] Closely allied to these reforms were provisions for the systematic publication of laws which, however, retained the possibility of legal secrecy by order of the USSR Presidium.[69] Protections against administrative evictions from homes, and arbitrary firings of workers and employees by management were also introduced.[70]

In 1956, workers and employees, military personnel, students in trade and in specialized secondary and higher schools, and other persons performing public (including party) duties were covered by new, more comprehensive social security.[71] Collective farmers, members of cooperatives, and the self-employed were excluded from this and allied protections of minimum wages, normal work hours, maternity leaves, protection for adoles-

1958, [1959] Ved. verkh. sov. S.S.S.R. No. 1, SBORNIK ZAKON. 798-816; "On criminal responsibility for State offenses," Law of Dec. 25, 1958, [1959] Ved. verkh. sov. S.S.S.R. No. 1, SBORNIK ZAKON. 749-57; "On criminal responsibility for military offenses," Law of Dec. 25, 1958, [1959] Ved. verkh. sov. S.S.S.R. No. 1, SBORNIK ZAKON. 758-68; "Procedures of military tribunals," Law of Dec. 25, 1958, [1959] Ved. verkh. sov. S.S.S.R. No. 1, SBORNIK ZAKON. 792-97.

[68] Kudrjacev, *Une Importante Etape dans l'Evolution de la Legislation Soviétique (An Important Step in the Evolution of Soviet Legislation)*, 11 REVUE INTERNATIONALE DE DROIT COMPARÉ 665-71 (1959); Ancel, *et. al.*, LA RÉFORME PÉNALE SOVIÉTIQUE, CODE PÉNAL, CODE DE PROCÉDURE PÉNALE, ET LOI D'ORGANISATION JUDICIARE DE LA RSFSR DU 27 OCTOBRE 1960 (THE SOVIET PENAL REFORM, THE CRIMINAL CODE, THE CODE OF CRIMINAL PROCEDURE, AND THE LAW OF JUDICIAL ORGANIZATION OF THE RSFSR OF OCTOBER 27, 1960) (Paris 1962), especially chs. 21-26. The discussion refers especially to the implementation of the 1958 Principles in subsequent Codes.

[69] "On the order of publication and placement into effect of laws of the USSR . . . ," Decree of June 19, 1958, [1958] Ved. verkh. sov. S.S.S.R. No. 14, SBORNIK ZAKON. 131-32.

[70] "On the supersession of administrative evictions from homes [owned] by State enterprises, offices and organizations of workers and employees having quit employment," Decree of Sept. 10, 1953, unpublished decree cited in SBORNIK ZAKON. 707-09; "Procedure on the sequence of examination of labor disputes," Decree of Jan. 31, 1957, [1957] Ved. verkh. sov. S.S.S.R. No. 4, SBORNIK ZAKON. 579-90.

[71] "On State pensions," Law of July 14, 1956, [1956] Ved. verkh. sov. S.S.S.R. No. 15, SBORNIK ZAKON. 590-608. Subsequent legislation provided the continuity of seniority essential for Soviet pension coverage to persons transferred from one establishment to another, and to certain categories of persons resigning voluntarily, *e.g.*, for reasons of illness, to attend school, etc. "Ensuring the unbroken length of service of workers transferred from one enterprise or establishment to another," Decision of Sov. Min. S.S.S.R., May 27, 1957, U.S. BUREAU OF LABOR STATISTICS, DEP'T OF LABOR, REP. No. 210, PRINCIPAL CURRENT SOVIET LABOR LEGISLATION 101 (1962); "On compensation for the temporary incapacity of workers and employees voluntarily leaving previous work," Decree of Jan. 25, 1960, [1960] Ved. verkh. sov. S.S.S.R. No. 4, SBORNIK ZAKON. 573-74. For a review of legislation see Kuypers, *Social Insurance in the Soviet Union*, 1 LAW IN EASTERN EUROPE 27 (Szirmai ed. 1958).

cents, and even limited possibilities of installment buying which the favored classes received.[72] Workers and employees paid less than 370 (later 450) old rubles per month were exempted from income taxes, while surtaxes were abolished on the incomes of all needy and dependent single adults.[73] Rural families now paid flat rates per square meter of private plot irrespective of income, but subject to satisfactory work in the public sector.[74] Credits for helping finance construction of private houses were made more readily available, albeit still on different terms to different classes.[75] In 1958, private citizens were given expanded rights to form year-round and summer housing cooperatives, subject to restraints on renting and speculative sales.[76]

2. Throughout the past decade, the Soviet Union has attempted, legislatively, to rationalize, control and economize in budgeted State operations and in State economic establishments. Between 1957 and 1960, it replaced the old system of centralized industrial Ministries and self-sufficient industrial manors by Economic-Administrative Regions which exercised decen-

[72] See "Minimum wage decision, Sept. 8, 1956," U.S. BUREAU OF LABOR STATISTICS, DEP'T OF LABOR, REP. NO. 210, PRINCIPAL CURRENT SOVIET LABOR LEGISLATION 84-85 (1962); "On implementing changeover in 1960 of all workers and employees to a 7- or 6-hour work day," Law of May 7, 1960, [1960] Ved. verkh. sov. S.S.S.R. No. 18, SBORNIK ZAKON. 565; "On increasing the length of leaves for pregnancy and birth," Decree of March 26, 1956, [1956] Ved. verkh. sov. S.S.S.R. No. 6, SBORNIK ZAKON. 573; "Six-hour day for 16-18 year-old adolescents," Decree of May 26, 1956, [1956] Ved. verkh. sov. S.S.S.R. No. 12, SBORNIK ZAKON. 564; "Leave and conditions of work for adolescents," Decree of Aug. 15, 1955, [1955] Ved. verkh. sov. S.S.S.R. No. 15, SBORNIK ZAKON. 564; "On strengthening labor protection for adolescents," Decree of Dec. 13, 1956, [1956] Ved. verkh. sov. S.S.S.R. No. 24, SBORNIK ZAKON. 564; "On the sale, on credit, of durable goods to workers and employees," Decision of Sov. Min. S.S.S.R., Aug. 12, 1959, No. 915, 2 Zakon. akty 529-30. Installment credits were allowed only for specific goods (radios, motor-scooters, etc.), required 20 to 25% downpayment, and were extended for 6 to 12 months.

[73] "On raising tax-free minimum wages for workers and employees," Decree of Sept. 8, 1956, [1956] Ved. verkh. sov. S.S.S.R. No. 18, SBORNIK ZAKON. 681; "On lowering the tax rate for workers and employees receiving wages up to 450 rubles a month," Decree of March 23, 1957, [1957] Ved. verkh. sov. S.S.S.R. No. 7, SBORNIK ZAKON. 681-82; "On supplementary taxes on bachelors, single persons and citizens with small families . . . ," Decree of Feb. 10, 1954, SBORNIK ZAKON. 680-81.

[74] "On the agricultural tax," Law of Aug. 8, 1953, [1953] Ved. verkh. sov. S.S.S.R. No. 7, SBORNIK ZAKON. 637-45.

[75] "Rules for credit for individual housing construction by commercial banks and agencies of the Agricultural Bank of the USSR," Min. finansov S.S.S.R. No. 320, May 16, 1955 2 Zakon. akty 349-56. Credits ranged from 7,000 rubles for ordinary persons to 25,000 rubles for generals, for periods of 7 to 10 years at 2% interest, and covered 50% of cost; except for physicians (70%) and rural school teachers (100%). Maximum house sizes, set in 1948, were two floors and five rooms; maximum lots, 300-600 square meters in cities, and 700-1200 square meters in rural areas. "On the rights of citizens to purchase and build individual homes," Decree of Aug. 26, 1948, and Decision of Sov. Min. S.S.S.R. No. 3211, Aug. 26, 1948, 2 Zakon. akty 547-49.

[76] "On home-construction and *dacha*-construction cooperation," Decision of Sov. Min. S.S.S.R. No. 320, Mar. 20, 1958, 2 Zakon. akty 542-43.

tralized control over operations, and by central planning and supply agencies responsible for coordinating interregional flows of materials, equipment and manpower.[77] Under these new conditions, inter-plant transactions and contracts assumed basic importance. To regulate them effectively, the authority of the State arbitration facility, Gosarbitrazh, was extended to all relevant disputes.[78]

Within enterprises, directors could now decide much previously prohibited to them, *e.g.*, the disposal of surpluses, pricing (within sharply restricted limits), the award of construction contracts, etc.[79] Piece-work rates, allocations to welfare, labor-law enforcement and allied responsibilities they shared with Labor-Union Committees.[80] In 1958, permanent production conferences of managers, technical persons, labor and party officials were established in larger plants to improve planning and innovation.[81] Concurrently, directors became liable to fines as high as three months' pay and

[77] "On the further perfection of the administrative organization of industry and construction," Law of May 10, 1957, [1957] Ved. verkh. sov. S.S.S.R. No. 11, SBORNIK ZAKON. 159-66; "On abolition of the All-Union Ministries of the USSR; aviation industry . . . and the transformation into State committees of the Council of Ministers," Decree of Dec. 14, 1957, [1957] Ved. verkh. sov. S.S.S.R. No. 27, SBORNIK ZAKON. 140-41; "Procedures for the Economic Councils of Economic-Administrative Regions," Decision of Sov. Min. S.S.S.R. No. 1150, Sept. 26, 1957, 1 Zakon. akty. 166-83; "On measures to improve the organization of the material-technical supply of the national economy of the USSR," Decision of Sov. Min. S.S.S.R. No. 432, April 17, 1958, 1 Zakon. akty 416-19; "On the sequence of material-technical supply of the National Economy of the USSR," Decision of Sov. Min. S.S.S.R. No. 87, Jan. 22, 1959, 1 Zakon. akty 419-20; "On further perfection of planning and directing the national economy," Decision of Sov. Min. S.S.S.R. No. 388, April 7, 1960, 1 Zakon. akty 333-36.

[78] "To remove from the people's courts suits in matters between State, cooperative (excluding kolkhoz) and other social organizations on sums up to 1,000 rubles," Decree of March 14, 1955, [1955] Ved. verkh. sov. S.S.S.R. No. 5, SBORNIK ZAKON. 817. "On the transferal for deliberation by *Gosarbitrazh* organs, all cases of disputes between State, cooperative (excluding kolkhoz) and other social organizations, establishments and agencies now brought to court," Decree of July 27, 1959, [1959] Ved. verkh. sov. S.S.S.R. No. 30, SBORNIK ZAKON. 817.

[79] "On Repeal of a decree . . . Concerning the prohibition of the sale, exchange and release of equipment and materials, and on responsibility to the courts for these illegal acts," Decree of May 13, 1955, [1955] Ved. verkh. sov. S.S.S.R. No. 8, SBORNIK ZAKON. 772; "On widening the rights of directors of enterprises," Decision of Sov. Min. S.S.S.R. No. 1430, Aug. 9, 1955, 1 Zakon. akty 185-90. Foremen also achieved limited rights of hiring, firing, and making incentive awards, as well as better job security. "On increasing the role of foremen," Decision of Sov. Min. S.S.S.R. [unnumbered], Sept. 20, 1955, 1 Zakon. akty 214-16.

[80] "On the rights of factory, plant, and local committees of labor unions," Decree of July 15, 1958, [1958] Ved. verkh. sov. S.S.S.R. No. 5, SBORNIK ZAKON. 609-14.

[81] "Procedure on permanent production conferences at individual enterprises, construction sites, in State farms, machine tractor stations and tractor repair stations," Decision of Sov. Min. S.S.S.R. and All-Union Central Council of Labor Unions, July 9, 1958, SPRAVOCHNIK SEKRETAR. 183-87.

to imprisonment for failure to meet economic plans; prison terms of up to three years could be imposed for falsifying reports.[82]

The provisions for increased managerial authority, improved administrative mechanisms and greater accountability have been offset by a continued proliferation of external controls. These include procuracy supervision over legality, that of *Gosarbitrazh* over contract fulfillment, that of the Labor-Union Committees over personnel matters, that of the State bank over all monetary dispersals and credits, with overall control by the primary party organization, especially in matters of plan fulfillment.[83] Paradoxically, the Soviets have sought to effect this proliferation with a paid State and party administrative apparatus which fell from 1.7 million persons in 1953 to 1.3 million in 1956, and stablized at that level thereafter.[84] Thus, both nominal execution of supervisory duties and much hidden administrative employment have unquestionably developed. The "withering away" of the State has served, however, to enhance the power of key party officials and of the quasi-voluntary groups under their supervision.[85]

The educational and agricultural reorganizations of 1958 provided extensive immediate and long-term economies for the State. For rank-and-file students, education beyond the eighth grade was to be in part-time trade schools which were to pay for themselves from their industrial production.[86] In higher education, part-time and correspondence work was to be stressed, while admissions would be "on the basis of references provided by Party, Labor Union, Komsomol and other social organizations, the directors of industrial enterprises and the administration of collective farms, so as to

[82] "On responsibility for nonfulfillment of plans and assignments in production," Decree of April 24, 1958, [1958] Ved. verkh. sov. S.S.S.R. No. 9, SBORNIK ZAKON. 846.

[83] See notes 66, 78, and 80 *supra*. "On the role and tasks of the State bank of the USSR," Decision of Sov. Min. S.S.S.R., Aug. 21, 1954, 1 Zakon. akty 154-63; "Charter of the State bank of the USSR," Oct. 29, 1960, 1 Zakon. akty 140-54; "On commissions in primary party organizations of production and trade enterprises for implementing by party organizations the right of control of the activities of enterprise administration," Decision of C.P.S.U., June 26, 1959, 1 Zakon. akty 211-14.

[84] JOINT ECONOMIC COMM., 88TH CONG. 2D SESS., ANNUAL ECONOMIC INDICATORS FOR THE U.S.S.R., 56-57 (Com. Print 1964).

[85] Restrictions have been placed on the extent of paid employment within both party and *komsomol* (Youth Auxiliary) organizations. "On fulltime paid secretaries of primary party organizations," Decision of C.P.S.U., May 27, 1957, SPRAVOCHNIK SEKRETAR. 148-50; "On the contraction of the paid apparatus and the development of volunteer work in the *komsomol*," Decision of the Central Committee of the Komsomol Aug. 28, 1957, *id.* at 157-60.

[86] "On strengthening ties between school and life and on the further development of the system of national education in the USSR," Law of Dec. 24, 1958, [1959] Ved. verkh. sov. S.S.S.R. No. 1, SBORNIK ZAKON. 177-92, especially arts. 3, 4, 7, 13-15.

enrol, by means of competitive selection, those most worthy, who have proven themselves in production to be prepared and competent people."[87]

Thus, the new legislation provided controls on social mobility concurrently with restraints on numbers. Between 1958 and 1962, enrolments in the day divisions of specialized secondary and higher schools in the USSR remained stationary, as did budgetary expenditures for secondary and higher education.[88]

In agriculture, the transfer of agricultural machinery operations and repairs to the collective farms relieved the government of pay and social security obligations for 2.6 million employees (1957) and exacted enormous levies upon collective-farm treasuries for equipment received. Subsequent difficulties in Soviet agriculture have been partially ascribable to these economies.[89]

3. Civilian economic sacrifices have been exacted explicitly to meet Soviet military demands.[90] Other security legislation has included a comprehensive law maintaining rigorous controls on frontier areas, which has been backed by treaties with several neighboring Communist and non-Communist states.[91] The loss of secret documents or secret equipment has been added to the disclosure of secrets as an especially dangerous State offenses for all persons.[92] Offenses of this type are investigated by agents of State security.[93] All cases involving State secrets are tried by military tribunals, which now also have jurisdiction over State security and prison

[87] Law of Dec. 24, 1958, art. 28, [1959] Ved. verkh. sov. S.S.S.R. No. 1, SBORNIK ZAKON. 177-92; article 36 requires graduates to be "models of fulfillment of State and social debts."

[88] JOINT ECONOMIC COMM., 88TH CONG. 2D SESS., ANNUAL ECONOMIC INDICATORS FOR THE U.S.S.R., 72, 75, 77 (Comm. Print 1964).

[89] FAINSOD, HOW RUSSIA IS RULED, 550-52 (2d ed. 1963).

[90] "Decree of the Presidium of the U.S.S.R. Supreme Soviet: On Postponing the Dates for Exempting Workers and Employees from Taxes on Wages, 14 C.D.S.P. No. 39, p. 3 (1962).

[91] "Decree of the Presidium of the U.S.S.R. Supreme Soviet on Approving the Regulations on the Protection of the State Border of the U.S.S.R." 12 C.D.S.P. No. 40, p. 3 (1960). This list of agreements includes only those formal international acts ratified by the Supreme Soviet of the USSR and recorded in its *Vedomosti.* These have been compiled in the SBORNIK ZAKON. as follows: frontier operations and co-operation with Rumania, at 302, and Poland, at 298 (also at 296 on sea frontiers); regulations of frontier incidents with Czechoslovakia, at 315, with Finland, at 311, and with Iran, at 27-72; on marine frontiers in Varanger Fjord with Norway, at 287.

[92] "On criminal responsibility for State offenses," Law of Dec. 25, 1958 arts. 12, 13, [1959] Ved. verkh. sov. S.S.S.R. No. 1, SBORNIK ZAKON. 749-57. Compare the 1926 R.S.F.S.R. CRIMINAL CODE arts. 58-3, 58-6. Gsovski, R.S.F.S.R. Criminal Code, 1956 Edition [of 1926 Code] and Supplementary Material 22, 23 (Mimeo n.d.).

[93] "Decree of the Presidium of the U.S.S.R. Supreme Soviet: On Granting Agencies for Safeguarding Public Order the Right To Conduct the Preliminary Investigation," 15 C.D.S.P. No. 18, p. 32 (1963).

personnel, and in areas wherever general courts are inoperative because of "exceptional circumstances."[94]

In other respects, Soviet security laws have changed little. Thus, flight abroad and refusal to return from abroad remain treason.[95] Military personnel must obey unconditionally, and may surrender only if fully incapacitated, on pain of 15 years imprisonment or a death sentence.[96] Military as well as civilian persons are now subject to criminal responsibility for traffic violations resulting in major accidents.[97] However, illegal use of military subordinates to perform personal services for oneself or others is no longer criminal.[98]

4. Strengthening the authority of the Communist Party over all spheres of Soviet life and the development of a new rationale for its special legal position have complemented increased military support and the proliferation and refinement of control agencies as reinforcements of national power. The tightening of party control over the State bureaucracy already mentioned has been augmented by provisions authorizing Communist Party organizations and their auxiliaries to initiate the recall of elected Deputies of the Supreme Soviet of the USSR.[99] Lay judges are now elected and recalled by voice vote in mass meetings, while professional judges are elected by, accountable to, and removable by, representative bodies also under party rule.[100] The practice of law, under the RSFSR law of 1962, is limited to

[94] "Procedures of military tribunals," Law of Dec. 25, 1958 arts. 9, 10, [1959] Ved. verkh. sov. S.S.S.R. No. 1, SBORNIK ZAKON. 792-97.

[95] "Decree of the Presidium of the U.S.S.R. Supreme Soviet: On Granting Agencies for Safeguarding Public Order the Right To Conduct the Preliminary Investigation," 15 C.D.S.P. No. 18, p. 32 (1963); Gsovski, R.S.F.S.R. Criminal Code, 1956 Edition [of 1926 Code] and Supplementary Material 21 (Mimeo n.d.), 1926 R.S.F.S.R. CRIMINAL CODE art. 58-la; "On criminal responsibility for State offenses," Law of Dec. 25, 1958, art. 1, [1959] Ved. verkh. sov. S.S.S.R. No. 1, SBORNIK ZAKON. 749-51.

[96] "On criminal responsibility for military offenses," Law of Dec. 25, 1958, arts. 2, 3, 27, [1959] Ved. verkh. sov. S.S.S.R. No. 1, SBORNIK ZAKON. 758-68; also "Decree of the Presidium of the U.S.S.R. Supreme Soviet on the Disciplinary Regulations and Service Regulations of the U.S.S.R. Armed Forces," 12 C.D.S.P. No. 39, p. 11, at 13-14 (1960). On earlier regulations, BERMAN & KERNER, SOVIET MILITARY LAW AND ADMINISTRATION 51, 83 (1955).

[97] "On criminal responsibility for military offenses," Law of Dec. 25, 1958, arts. 14-18, [1959] Ved. verkh. sov. S.S.S.R. No. 1, SBORNIK ZAKON. 758-68. Compare "On criminal responsibility for State offenses," Law of Dec. 25, 1958, art. 22, [1959] Ved. verkh. sov. S.S.S.R. No. 1, SBORNIK ZAKON. 749-57.

[98] Gsovski, *op. cit. supra* note 95, arts. 193-19; 1926 R.S.F.S.R. CRIMINAL CODE arts. 193-19.

[99] "On the order of recall of deputies of the Supreme Soviet SSSR," Law of Oct. 30, 1959, art. 2, [1959] Ved. verkh. sov. S.S.S.R. No. 44, SBORNIK ZAKON. 123-25.

[100] "Basic principles of the legislation on the organization of courts of the Soviet Union, Union and Autonomous Republics," Law of Dec. 25, 1958, arts. 19, 33-35, [1959] Ved. verkh. sov. S.S.S.R. No. 1, SBORNIK ZAKON. 779-87.

members of collegia subject to these formally representative bodies.[101] Finally, religious congregations, the sole voluntary groupings independent of the party's supervision have been subjected to renewed repression.[102]

The statutes of the Communist Party of the USSR of 1961 reinforced internal discipline, in comparison with those of 1952, by demanding detailed ideological commitment from its members. They have to "combat resolutely any manifestations of bourgeois ideology, remnants of a private-property psychology, religious prejudices and other survivals of the past, to observe the principles of communist morality and to place public interests above personal ones."[103] To communicate its policies, the Communist Party has decreed improved education for its members, the dissemination of appropriate printed and oral propaganda, and the systematic verification of its effectiveness by the elicitation of letters, complaints, and announcements from local volunteer correspondents and the public.[104] Conformity to party policies is required. As a current Soviet legal text states, "Judicial workers must be able, in the course of their work, not to let out of their sight as the most important [goal]—the policies of the Communist Party, which constitute the living basis of our society . . . . The directing and orienting role of the Communist Party is expressed in the selection and assignment of politically proven and prepared cadres, in care for their political education and in determination of the tasks set before them."[105]

At the same time, the party has sought to obscure its authoritarianism by new ideological rationalizations. It is no longer the instrument of proletarian dictatorship, but "the party of the entire Soviet people."[106] State

[101] "Statutes of the Bar," 14 C.D.S.P. No. 41, p. 5 (1962).

[102] "From the Ideological Commission of the C.P.S.U. Central Committee: On Measures for Intensifying the Atheistic Indoctrination of the Population," 16 C.D.S.P. No. 9, p. 3 (1964).

[103] The Statutes of the Communist Party of the Soviet Union, art. I.2 (d), 13 C.D.S.P. No. 47, p. 3 Dec. 20 (1961); compare "Statutes of the Communist Party of the Soviet Union," promulgated by the XIXth Party Congress with partial changes invoked by the XXth Party Congress, SPRAVOCHNIK SEKRETAR. 81-100.

[104] "On the tasks of party propaganda under contemporary conditions," Decision of the Central Committee of the CPSU Jan. 9, 1960, SPRAVOCHNIK SEKRETAR. 417-42; "On serious inadequacies in the review of letters, complaints and announcements of workers," Decision of the Central Committee of the CPSU, Aug. 2, 1958, SPRAVOCHNIK SEKRETAR. 193-98. The party has been anxious to eradicate illiteracy from among its members. See "On showing aid to communists in general educational study," SPRAVOCHNIK SEKRETAR. 268-69. Between 1956 and 1961 the proportion of members with an elementary education or less fell from 17 to 10% while the proportion of college graduates rose from 11 to 13%. "The Party in Figures (1956-61)," 14 C.D.S.P. No. 3, p. 3, at 4 (1962).

[105] ORGANIZATSYIA SUDA I PROKURATURY V SSSR (ORGANIZATION OF THE COURTS AND PROCURACY IN THE USSR) 8 (Karev ed. Moscow 1961).

[106] "The Statutes of the Communist Party of the Soviet Union: Preamble," 13 C.D.S.P. No. 47, p. 3 (1961).

coercion is now mediated, in many of its effects on the public, by voluntary organizations, and by persuasion as well as force; genuine popular government is defined as a long term goal. So too is a utopia of complete social welfare, which justifies immediate restrictions on private property, labor mobility, and leisure.[107] These restrictions have concurrently mobilized resources for the State and eliminated unwelcome inflationary potentials and consumer autonomy.

5. Public (or social) organizations, which Khrushchev viewed as the future heirs of the State, are basically the labor unions of particular enterprises and other occupational, technical, and public-service groups for sports, civil defense, etc. These groups are chartered legal entities with the right to hold properties, conclude contracts, take part in court actions as contestants, representatives, or third parties, and to engage in formal political activity.[108] Other organizations appear to be incorporated in this category by extension. For example not only labor unions but also collective farms, the student bodies of specialized secondary and higher schools, and the residents of "apartment buildings served by housing offices or apartment managements or united in street committees" and of rural settlements have been authorized to form Comrades' Courts.[109] Auxiliary police organizations must embrace an entire administrative district *(rayon)* or city, and "Party, State, Labor-Union and Komsomol organizations" with "independent commands."[110]

In adjudication and law enforcement the elements of public organizations taking part are mass assemblies, annually elected Comrades' Courts, auxiliary police and varied neighborhood inspectors.[111] In mid-1963, 200,000 Comrades' Courts and 130,000 detachments with a total of 5.5 million

[107] The best survey of the 1961 Program of the Communist Party, which develops these goals in detail, is RITVO, THE NEW SOVIET SOCIETY (1962). See especially 152-82.

[108] SHIPELEVA, OSNOVY SOVETSKOGO GOSUDARSTVENNOGO STROITEL'STVA I PRAVA (BASIC PRINCIPALS OF SOVIET GOVERNMENTAL ORGANIZATION AND LAW) 268-69, 322-23 (Moscow 1961). This is an official publication of the Higher Party School of the Central Committee of the CPSU.

[109] "Decree of the Presidium of the Russian Republic Supreme Soviet: On Approving the Statute on Comrades' Courts," art. 2, 13 C.D.S.P. No. 33, p. 8 (1961). "Decree of the Presidium of the Russian Republic Supreme Soviet: On Introducing Additions and Amendments to the Statutes on Comrades' Courts, 15 *id.* No. 47, p. 9 (1963) Compare Ramundo, *The Soviet State of the Entire People—Non-Marxist "Living Marxism,"* 32 GEO. WASH. L. REV. 315 (1963), for a different view on the reasons for this development.

[110] "On the participation of workers in defending the public order in the land," Decision of Central Committee of the CPSU, March 2, 1959, SPRAVOCHNIK SEKRETAR. 285-88, at 286.

[111] Mass assemblies are used to initiate the banishment of undesirables to work in remote areas under the "anti-Parasite" laws. The actions of these assemblies must be approved by the executive body of the city or administrative district. Decree of Presidium of Russian Republic Supreme Soviet: "On Intensifying the Struggle Against Persons Who Avoid Socially Useful Work and Lead an Anti-Social Para-

auxiliary police were operating.[112] Comrades' Courts have been particularly charged with the control of disorderly and offensive behavior, juvenile cases, nonsupport of dependent children or parents, and (with the consent of the parties) civil disputes between members of the group.[113] Since most offenses of violence in the USSR are associated with drunkenness and with the low levels of education characterizing recent urban in-migrants, these grass-roots organizations may indeed be effective in deterring more serious crimes.[114] Also significant has been their role in substituting reprimands and other pressures for the innumerable, often brutally exacted, fines levied for administrative offenses. These burdensome affairs took up 30 per cent of People's Court time in Moscow in 1958, prior to the advent of modern Comrades' Courts.[115]

Unpaid work conducted by Soviet public organizations comprises administration, fire protection, sanitation, gardening, street paving, plumbing repair, auxiliary educational and other services, in addition to adjudication and law enforcement.[116] In Vyborg, a city of 51,000, ten per cent of the entire population was enrolled, in 1961, in voluntary units. Free public labor totalled 200,000 man-days in 1960, or about 6 per year for every person aged 16 through 59 in the city.[117]

sitic Way of Life," May 4, 1961, 13 C.D.S.P. No. 17, p. 8 (1961). For a current illustration, see "Before Court of the Public—Banish Loafers From Moscow!," 15 *id.* No. 22, p. 28 (1963). See, on neighborhood inspectors, "Just and Comradely," 15 *id.* No. 22, p. 28 (1963).

[112] "Main Thing Is Prevention and Upbringing Work," 15 *id.* No. 22, p. 26, at 27 (1963).

[113] "Decree of the Presidium of the Russian Republic Supreme Soviet: On Approving the Statute on Comrades' Courts," 13 *id.* No. 33, p. 8, art. 5 (1961). "Decree of the Presidium of the Russian Republic Supreme Soviet: On Introducing Additions and Amendments to the Statutes on Comrades' Courts, 15 C.D.S.P. No. 47, p. 9 (1963). On the handling of juvenile problems see Piontkovsky & Tadevossian, *La lutte contre délinquance juvénile en URSS,* 16 REVUE INTERNATIONALE DE CRIMINOLOGIE ET DE POLICE TECHNIQUE 108 (1962).

[114] "On the Study and Prevention of Crime," 12 C.D.S.P. No. 41, p. 3, at 5 (1960); OSTROUMOV, SOVETSKAYA SUDEBNAYA STATISTIKA (SOVIET JUDICIAL STATISTICS) 267-79 (3d ed. Moscow 1962). On rural-urban differences in socio-economic characteristics see Shimkin, *Current Characteristics and Problems of the Soviet Rural Population,* in SOVIET AGRICULTURE AND PEASANT AFFAIRS 112-15 (Laird ed. 1963).

[115] "On the further limitation of the application of fines laid down by administrative fiat," Decree of June 21, 1961, art. 16, [1961] Ved. verkh. sov. S.S.S.R. No. 35, SBORNIK ZAKON. 837-43. Comrades' Courts may exact the heaviest allowable administrative fine, 10 new rubles. Decree of June 21, 1961, arts. 6, 7; and "Decree of the Presidium of the Russian Republic Supreme Soviet: On Approving the Statute On Comrades' Courts," 13 C.D.S.P. No. 33, p. 8, at 9 (art. 15(5) (1961). On conditions in 1958, see Subotskiy, *O poryadke vzyskaniya administrativnykh shtrafov (On Bringing Into Order the Extraction of Administrative Fines),* Sov. gos. i. pravo, No. 9 p. 115 (1958).

[116] "The Development of Soviet Democracy . . . ," 12 C.D.S.P. No. 46, p. 7 (1960).

[117] "The 5000 Mayors of Vyborg," 13 *id.* No. 38, p. 8 (1961).

6. Ideological drives, ambitious national plans, and economic setbacks have, since 1956, partly eroded the gains in freedom made after Stalin's death. Urban conscripts have been used to meet peak demands for agricultural labor.[118] More generally, long-term Soviet manpower plans rest on the explicit assumptions that the 10 million adults (largely women) engaged in private economic activity will be entirely absorbed by the public sector, and that the labor-force participation rates of others, especially mothers with young children, will rise significantly.[119] Moreover, the Soviets have become well aware of the greater economies in construction and operation (including fuel savings) of dense, multi-story housing.[120] Their petroleum export plans, which are crucial as earners of foreign exchange, are also predicated on continued stringent limitations in the use of private cars.[121]

The "anti-Parasite" laws have served to increase employment, tighten labor discipline and aid the execution of lagging plans for migration to Siberia.[122] Initiated in 1956 as controls upon gypsies, they have become universal measures permitting five-year sentences of exile and compulsory work imposed by mass rallies (ratified by executive authority) and by People's Courts.[123] The operation of private plots for commercial production has been severely hampered, national shortages of meat, milk, fruit and vegetables notwithstanding, by prohibitions on feeding purchased fodder to privately-owned animals, by restrictions on private livestock numbers, and by general attacks on "unearned" income.[124] The substance of the

[118] "On the Requests of Some Union Republics for Enlisting Urban Workers and Employees for Agricultural Work on Collective and State Farms"—Resolution of Party Central Committee and U.S.S.R. Council of Ministers, July 12, 1962, 14 C.D.S.P. No. 28, p. 15 (1962).

[119] Shimkin, *Resource Development and Utilization in the Soviet Economy*, in NATURAL RESOURCES AND INTERNATIONAL DEVELOPMENT 115, at 165-68 (Clausen ed. 1964).

[120] *Id.* at 194; "On the development of housing construction in the USSR," Decision of Sov. Min. S.S.S.R., July 31, 1957, 2 Zakon. akty 536-40, especially art. 30.

[121] See Shimkin, *supra* note 119, at 197-204, 218, 222-23.

[122] "Problems in the Territorial Redistribution of Labor Resources," 14 C.D.S.P. No. 26, p. 3 (1962).

[123] "On the compulsory placement at work of gypsies leading a roaming life," extract from Decree of Oct. 5, 1956, [1956] Ved. verkh. sov. S.S.S.R. No. 21, SBORNIK ZAKON. 569; "Decree of Presidium of Russian Republic Supreme Soviet: On Intensifying the Struggle Against Persons who Avoid Socially Useful Work . . . ," 13 C.D.S.P. No. 17, p. 8 (1961).

[124] "On Measures for Combatting the Expenditure From State Stores of Bread and Other Food Products To Feed Livestock," Decree of Sov. Min. S.S.S.R., Aug. 26, 1956, 8 *id.* No. 35, p. 9 (1956); "Decree of the Presidium of Russian Republic Supreme Soviet: On Increasing Liability for Feeding Livestock and Poultry Bread and other Grain Products Bought in State and Cooperative Stores," 15 *id.* No. 22, p. 25 (1963); "Place Legislation on Personal-Plot Land Tenure at the Level of New Tasks," 13 *id.* No. 21, p. 3 (1961); "On the Right of Personal Ownership of Housing," 13 *id.* No. 39, p. 3 (1961); "Decree of Russian Republic Supreme Soviet:

right of private rental, important not only for supplementary i pecially for the aged, but also to relieve chronic housing shortages, has re mained unchanged by the new Principles of Civil Legislation. However, the state now indicates a desire to check on these arrangements more closely, in the name of suppression of profiteering.[125]

Due process has been weakened once more. Sentences for "Parasitism" imposed by a People's Court may not be appealed.[126] "Malicious disobedience" of the orders of regular or auxiliary police is tried by a single people's judge. Sentences, which may be abrogated only on appeal by the procuracy, include pay deductions to be made to the State, of 5 to 20 per cent of wages, without stated maximum time duration. Pre-sentence incarceration, of undefined length, subjects the prisoners to work without pay.[127] Sentences for major economic crimes and crimes of violence have been drastically increased, with wide use of capital punishment.[128] Since 1961, deliberate harshness in living conditions, food, rations, and work requirements has been decreed for the treatment of major criminals.[129] Finally, published data indicate repression rather than relief to be the likely outcome for attempts to seek redress from libel by the Soviet press.[130]

7. Major legislative projects reported to be in progress in 1963-64 include the formulation of a new national constitution in accordance with the principles of the 1961 Program of the Communist Party; a modernization

On Norms of Livestock In the Personal Possession of Citizens Who Are Not Members of Collective Farms," 15 *id.* No. 22, p. 25 (1963); "Decree of Presidium of Russian Republic Supreme Soviet: On Monetary Tax on Citizens Owning Livestock Who Are Not Employed in Socially Useful Labor and on Citizens Maintaining Livestock for Purposes of Personal Enrichment," 15 *id.* No. 22, p. 26 (1963).

[125] PRINCIPLES OF CIVIL LEGLISLATION OF THE USSR AND THE UNION REPUBLICS arts. 25, 57 14 *id.* No. 4, p. 3 (1962); NAUCHNOPRAKTICHESKIY KOMMENTARIY K OSNOVAM GRAZHDANSKOGO ZAKONODATEL'STVA SOYUZA *SSR* I SOYUZNYKH RESPUBLIK (Scholarly and Practical Commentary on the Principles of Civil Legislation of the USSR and the Union Republics) 135, 238 (Moscow 1962). "On the rights of citizens to purchase and build individual homes," Decree of Aug. 26, 1948, Decision No. 3211 of Presidium U.S.S.R. of Aug. 26, 1948, 2 Zakon. akty 548-49.

[126] "Decree of the Presidium of Russian Republic Supreme Soviet: On Intensifying the Struggle Against Persons Who Avoid Socially Useful Work . . . ," 13 C.D.S.P. No. 17, pp. 8, art. 2 (1961).

[127] "Resolution of the Presidium of the U.S.S.R. Supreme Soviet: On Application of Measures of Influence for Malicious Disobedience . . . ," 14 *id.* No. 14, p. 18, (1962).

[128] "Decree of the Presidium of the U.S.S.R. Supreme Soviet: On Introducing Changes and Additions in arts. 22 and 44 of the Principles of Criminal Legislation," *ibid.*

[129] Yakovlev, *Ob effektivnosti ispolneniya nakazaniya (On the Effectiveness of the Execution of Punishment)*, Sov. gos. i pravo, No. 1, p. 99 (1964).

[130] On provisions for redress in libel, see "Principles of Civil Legislation of the U.S.S.R. and the Union Republics," 14 C.D.S.P. No. 4, p. 3, art. 7 (1962); On a case of repression aggravating libel, see "Follow-Up on Izvestia Reports," 16 *id.* No. 24, p. 28 (1964).

of family law mitigating present inequities in relation to unmarried mothers and illegitimate children; a codification of prison laws; and harsher laws against religious organizations and particularly against the religious education of the young.[131]

8. In international law, the basic development has been a full restatement, on the basis of multilateral and bilateral treaties, of the relations of the Soviet Union with the Eastern European and, to a lesser extent, Asiatic Communist states. Up to late 1961, the Soviet Union had established diplomatic relations with East Germany; concluded the Warsaw Pact of military alliance and joint command with the Eastern European states; legalized the status of its forces in Hungary, Poland, and Rumania; and made agreements on frontier, navigation, and fishing problems as relevant.[132] In 1959, the USSR and the Eastern European nations ratified a general convention on mutual aid in fighting plant and animal diseases; in 1960, the same partners activated a Council of Economic Mutual Aid (Comecon) established in 1949.[133] Bilateral agreements have established consular relationships, eliminated dual citizenship (except with East Germany), provided for extradition in civil and criminal cases and similar mutual legal aid, and set up reciprocity in social security with Bulgaria, Czechoslovakia, East Germany, and Rumania.[134] Soviet relations with the Mongolian People's Republic and North Korea are governed today by bilateral treaties of alliance, trade, plant and animal quarantine, consular relations, eliminations of dual citizenship, and mutual legal aid.[135] Khrushchev's treaties with China have embraced trade and navigation, frontier shipping, plant and animal quarantine, and consular relations.[136] Those with Vietnam have been limited to trade, navigation, and consular relations; those with Cuba, to trade, payments, and cultural cooperation.[137]

Soviet domestic legislation to reinforce these commitments is note-

[131] "Resolution of the U.S.S.R. Supreme Soviet On Working Out Draft of New U.S.S.R. Constitution," 14 *id.* No. 17, p. 8 (1962); "Humane and Just Principles.—In Legislative Proposals Commissions of Council of the Union and Council of Nationalities of U.S.S.R. Supreme Soviet," 14 *id.* No. 50, p. 24 (1963); Rudinskiy, *Sovetskoye pravo i preodoleniye religioznykh predrassudkov (Soviet Law and the Overcoming of Religious Prejudices)*, Sov. gos. i pravo, No. 2, p. 47 (1964).

[132] Diplomatic relations with East Germany, SBORNIK ZAKON. 266; Warsaw Pact, *id.* at 322; status of Soviet forces, *id.* at 262-63, 296, 300; frontier agreements, see note 91 *supra;* fishing and navigation, SBORNIK ZAKON. 327, 329.

[133] Quarantine, *id.* 329-30; Comecon, *id.* at 329. See Note, 1964 U. ILL. L. F. 301.

[134] Consular relations, *id.* at 262, 266, 283, 286, 297, 301, 316; dual citizenship, *id.* at 262, 283, 286, 297, 301, 316; mutual legal aid, *id.* at 263, 267, 284, 286, 297, 301, 316; reciprocal social security, *id.* at 267, 286, 302, 316.

[135] *Id.* at 278-89, 281-82.

[136] *Id.* at 276-77.

[137] *Id.* at 268, 280.

worthy. The law on grave crimes against the State includes "the assassination of representatives of foreign governments to provoke war or international complications," and extends to other "workers' governments" protection against hostile acts.[138] The 1961 Basic Principles of Civil Legislation provide, for the first time, an explicit priority for treaties and international agreements over domestic law in cases of legal conflict.[139] Special laws now provide for procedures in implementing extradition and allied acts, and in applying the terms of foreign arbitration decisions, the last being applicable to signatories of the New York convention and other countries on a reciprocal basis.[140]

9. Since Stalin's death, Soviet treaties with non-Communist countries have been largely multilateral. Three of these, the Austrian peace treaty, the declaration of neutrality for Laos, and the ban on nuclear tests in the air and under water, concerned military security.[141] Other areas of agreement have comprised international postal shipments, air flights, telecommunications, and standard measurements.[142] The Soviet government has agreed to participate in the stabilization of sugar, wheat and coffee marketing, albeit with reservations protecting its state foreign-trade monopoly; and in the regulation of whaling, sealing in the North Pacific, and fishing in the North-

[138] "On criminal responsibility for State offenses," Law of Dec. 25, 1958, arts. 4, 10, [1959] Ved. verkh. sov. S.S.S.R. No. 1, SBORNIK ZAKON. 749-57.

[139] "Principles of Civil Legislation of the U.S.S.R. and the Union Republics," 14 C.D.S.P. No. 4, p. 3, art. 129 (1962).

[140] "On the process of implementing the decisions of courts of governments with which the USSR has completed treaties of legal aid [extradition, etc.]," Decree of Sept. 12, 1958, [1958] Ved. verkh. sov. S.S.S.R. No. 23, SBORNIK ZAKON. 338-40; "Convention on recognition and execution of foreign arbitration," Decree of Aug. 10, 1960, [1960] Ved. verkh. sov. S.S.S.R. No. 32, SBORNIK ZAKON. at 341.

[141] Austrian State Treaty, May 15, 1955, T.I.A.S. No. 3298, SBORNIK ZAKON. 254; Neutrality of Laos, July 23, 1962, T.I.A.S. No. 5410; Treaty Banning Nuclear Weapon Tests in the Atmosphere, in Outer Space and Under Water, Aug. 5, 1963, T.I.A.S. No. 5433.

[142] Universal Postal Union. Convention and related documents, July 11, 1952, T.I.A.S. No. 2800, SBORNIK ZAKON. 320; Universal Postal Union. Convention, final protocol, regulations, air-mail provisions, and final protocol to the air-mail provisions, Oct. 3, 1957, T.I.A.S. No. 4202, SBORNIK ZAKON, 328; Protocol amending the Warsaw Convention of Oct. 12, 1929, for the unification of certain rules concerning international air transport, 35 U.S. DEP'T. STATE BULL. 128 (1956), SBORNIK ZAKON. 325; Telecommunications. Convention. Dec. 22, 1952, T.I.A.S. No. 3266 (U.S.S.R. reservations in re allocation of radio frequencies, at 1336), SBORNIK ZAKON. 322; Telecommunications. Telegraph regulations (Geneva Revision, 1958) and final protocol, Nov. 29, 1958, T.I.A.S. No. 4390; Telecommunications. Convention, with annexes, and final protocol (treaty), Dec. 21, 1959, T.I.A.S. No. 4892, SBORNIK ZAKON. at 331; Radio Regulations, With Appendices, and Additional Protocol, Dec. 21, 1959, T.I.A.S. No. 4893 (USSR reservations in re allocation of radio frequencies, at 2942-43), SBORNIK ZAKON. 331; Convention for the establishment of an International Organization of Legislative Metrology, SLUSSER & TRISKA, A CALENDAR OF SOVIET TREATIES 1917-1957, at 346 (1959); SBORNIK ZAKON. at 324.

east and Northwest Atlantic.[143] It has promised scientific cooperation in applying atomic energy to peaceful uses, in refrigeration, and in Antarctic research.[144] It has subscribed, with some reservations, to the International Convention on the Law of the Sea, to conventions for humanity in war (Geneva, Hague, United Nations on genocide), and to those on the citizenship of married women and on tourism.[145] And it has undertaken commit-

[143] International Sugar Agreement. Treaty, Oct. 1, 1953, T.I.A.S. No. 3177 (USSR reservations on limiting sugar production, reserves and subsidies and in re implied recognition of Republic of China, at 429), SBORNIK ZAKON. 320; International Sugar Protocol, Dec. 1, 1956, T.I.A.S. No. 3937 (USSR reservation on China, at 2013) SBORNIK ZAKON. 320; International Sugar Agreement, 1958. Dec. 1, 1958, T.I.A.S. No. 4389 (USSR reservations as for T.I.A.S. No. 3177), SBORNIK ZAKON. 328; International Wheat Agreement, 1962. Apr. 19-May 15, 1962, T.I.A.S. No. 5115 (USSR reservation on information to be supplied, at 1760); International Coffee Agreement, 1962. Sept. 28-Nov. 30, 1962, T.I.A.S. No. 5505 (USSR reservation on State foreign-trade monopoly, at 244-46); Whaling (amendments to the Schedule to the International Whaling Convention signed at Washington on Dec. 2, 1946), July 19-23, 1954, T.I.A.S. No. 3198; *ibid.*, July 18-23, 1955. T.I.A.S. No. 3548; *ibid.* July 16-20, 1956, T.I.A.S. No. 3739, SBORNIK ZAKON. 326; *ibid.*, June 24-28, 1957, T.I.A.S. No. 3944; *ibid.*, June 23-27, 1958, T.I.A.S. No. 4193; Whaling (Protocol to Convention of Dec. 2, 1946) Nov. 9, 1956, T.I.A.S. No. 4228; Whaling (amendments to the Schedule to International Whaling Convention, Dec. 2, 1946), June 22-July 1, 1959, T.I.A.S. No. 4404; *ibid.*, June 24, 1960, T.I.A.S. No. 5014; *ibid.*, July 6, 1962, T.I.A.S. No. 5277; *ibid.*, July 5, 1963, T.I.A.S. No. 5472; North Pacific fur seals Interim Convention, Feb. 9, 1957, T.I.A.S. No. 3948, SBORNIK ZAKON. 327. North Pacific Fur Seals. Protocol Between the United States of America, Canada, Japan, and the Union of Soviet Socialistic Republics Amending the Interim Convention of Feb. 9, 1957, Oct. 8, 1963 T.I.A.S. No. 5558; Northeast Atlantic Fisheries Convention. London, Jan. 24, 1959, SBORNIK ZAKON. 330; Northwest Atlantic Fisheries. Declaration of Understanding, Apr. 24, 1961, T.I.A.S. No. 5380.

[144] Statute of the International Atomic Energy Agency, Oct. 26, 1956, T.I.A.S. No. 3873, SBORNIK ZAKON. 325; Atomic Energy. Amendment to the Statute of the International Atomic Energy Agency, Oct. 4, 1961, T.I.A.S. No. 5284; International Institute of Refrigeration. Convention, Mar. 25, 1955, SLUSSER & TRISKA, *op. cit. supra* note 142, at 43, 325, SBORNIK ZAKON. 326; Anarctic treaty, Dec. 1, 1959, T.I.A.S. No. 4780, SBORNIK ZAKON. 330; Antarctica (Measures in Furtherance of Principles and Objectives of the Antarctic Treaty). Recommendations, July 24, 1961, T.I.A.S. No. 5094; *ibid.*, July 28, 1962, T.I.A.S. No. 5274.

[145] Law of the Sea: Convention on the High Seas, Apr. 29, 1958, T.I.A.S. No. 5200 (U.S.S.R. reservations for absolute sovereignty of government vessels and on piracy, at 2383); Final Act of the International Conference on Safety of Life at Sea, with related documents, April 19, 1954, SLUSSER & TRISKA, *op. cit. supra* note 142, at 310; International convention for the prevention of pollution of the sea by oil. Treaty, May 12, 1954, T.I.A.S. No. 4900; Protection of War Victims [Geneva Convention], Aug. 12, 1949—(Armed Forces in the Field), T.I.A.S. No. 3362; *id.* (Armed Forces at Sea), T.I.A.S. No. 3363, *id.* (Prisoners of War), T.I.A.S. No. 3364, (Civilian Persons), T.I.A.S. No. 3365 (USSR reservations in all asserting invalidity of neutral actions without the consent of the Government of which the protected persons are nationals, *e.g.*, No. 3362, at 3206-07), SBORNIK ZAKON. 321; Protection of cultural property in the event of armed conflict. Convention with regulations and protocol, 36 U.S., DEP'T. STATE BULL. 289 (1957), SBORNIK ZAKON. 325; The Crime of Genocide and Punishments for It, UN General Assembly Convention, Dec. 9, 1948 (U.S.S.R. reservation), SBORNIK ZAKON. 321; Citizenship of Married Women, Sept. 6, 1957, SBORNIK ZAKON. 327; Customs Facilities for Touring. Convention, June 4, 1954, T.I.A.S. No. 3879.

ments affecting domestic practices through adherence to numerous clauses of the International Labour Organisation's Convention, and to conventions on political rights for women and on the outlawing of slavery.[146]

Bilateral treaties of nonagression have been signed with Finland and Afghanistan; mutual military security has also been enhanced by the unofficial "hot line" agreement with the United States.[147] Conversely, the Soviet Union annulled nonaggression pacts with France and the United Kingdom after the creation of NATO.[148] Other types of agreements have included loans, economic and technical aid (Finland, Yugoslavia, United Arab Republic, Ceylon, Ghana, India, Indonesia, Iraq, Mali, and Yemen), consular relations (Austria, West Germany, and Yugoslavia), elimination of dual citizenship (Yugoslavia), trade (Austria, Canada, Cambodia, Finland, West Germany, Ghana, Iraq, Japan, Lebanon, Somalia, and the United Arab Republic), air navigation (Afghanistan, Yugoslavia), and cultural and scientific cooperation (Afghanistan, Cambodia, India, Iraq, Italy, Ghana, United

[146] Date, number, short title, and source on Soviet ratifications of International Labour Organisation Conventions: April 4, 1956, ILO Convention No. 100, Equal Pay for Men and Women; June 4, 1956, *id.* No. 29, Forced Labor; July 6, 1956, *id.* No. 10, Minimum Age in Farm Labor; *id.* No. 11, Labor Unions in Agriculture; *id.* No. 15, Minimum Age for Stokers; *id.* No. 16, Medical Examination of Youths on Vessels; *id.* No. 52, Annual Paid Vacations; *id.* No. 58, Minimum Age for Work at Sea; *id.* No. 59, Minimum Age for Work in Industry; *id.* No. 60, Minimum Age for Other Work; *id.* No. 77, Medical Examination of Youths in Industry; *id.* No. 78, Medical Examination of Youths in Other Work; *id.* No. 79, Limits on Non-Industrial Night Work for Youths; *id.* No. 87, Freedom of Organizations; *id.* No. 90, Night Work of Youths in Industry; *id.* No. 98, Collective Agreements, *id.* No. 103, Maternity Protection; Jan. 31, 1961, *id.* No. 45, Women in Underground Mining; *id.* No. 95, Protection of Pay; No. 111, Discrimination; No. 112, Minimum Wage for Fishermen, SLUSSER & TRISKA, *op.cit. supra* note 142 at 352, 357, 360-63, 10 OSTEUROPA-RECHT 119-20, (June 1964), SBORNIK ZAKON. at 323-24, 331. Slavery Protocol, Dec. 7, 1953, T.I.A.S. No. 3532, SBORNIK ZAKON. 326.

[147] SLUSSER & TRISKA, *op. cit. supra* note 142, at 336-37, 344-45, SBORNIK ZAKON. 257, 309. Memorandum of understanding between the United States and the Union of Soviet Socialist Republics', regarding the establishment of a direct communication link, with annex, June 20, 1963, 49 U.S. DEP'T STATE BULL. 50-51 (1963). Other significant bilateral United States-Soviet agreements, all at the ministerial or unofficial level, made since Stalin's death include: Lend Lease Settlement: Return of Certain U.S. Naval Vessels, Mar. 26, 1954, T.I.A.S. No. 2990; *ibid.*, Dec. 22, 1954, T.I.A.S. No. 3168; *ibid.*, May 26, 1955, T.I.A.S. No. 3384; Germany: Boundary Between United States Sector of Berlin and the Soviet Zone of Occupation, June 25, 1955, T.I.A.S. No. 3378; Exchange of Medical Films. Agreement, Mar. 17 and Sept. 5, 1955, T.I.A.S. No. 3409; Cultural, Technical, and Educational Exchanges, Jan. 27, 1958, T.I.A.S. No. 3975; Scientific, Technical Educational and Cultural Exchanges, Nov. 24, 1959, T.I.A.S. No. 4362; Cultural Relations: Exchanges in the Scientific, Technical, Educational and Other Fields in 1962-1963, Mar. 8, 1962, T.I.A.S. No. 5112; Passport Visas, Mar. 26, Aug. 11 and 20, 1958, T.I.A.S. No. 4134; Memorandum of Understanding To Implement the Bilateral Space Agreement of June 8, 1962, 49 U.S. DEP'T STATE BULL. 404-10 (1963).

[148] SBORNIK ZAKON. 332-35.

Arab Republic, and Yugoslavia).[149] Overall, Soviet bilateral treaties outside the bloc have established relations with many states but only limited ones, with neutralist countries.

Khrushchev's legislative program appeared in a context both of profound political, economic, and technological change in the Soviet Union and of highly variable international relations dominated by the danger of thermonuclear war. These facts and the program itself have aroused much interest, especially in West Germany, in work on Soviet law and its implications for foreign and domestic affairs.

In the United States, the major development over the past decade has been the rapid expansion of teaching, in law schools and departments of political science, of Soviet legal institutions and practices. Currently, perhaps 20 institutions offer a course on one or more of these subjects. An incomplete inventory of schools and teachers follows: California (J. Towster, J. A. Cohen), Columbia (Hazard, O. J. Lissitzyn), Connecticut (E. Margolis), George Washington (B. Ramundo), Harvard (Berman), Illinois (P. Maggs), Indiana (D. P. Hammer), Iowa (G. Ginsburgs), Kansas (O. Backus), Michigan (W. Gray), New York (D. O'Connor, I. Shapiro), San José State College (G. Morgan), Santa Clara (R. G. Meiners), Stanford (J. Triska), Syracuse (W. W. Kulski), Wisconsin (Z. Zile), and Yale (L. Lipson).

American research on Soviet law has progressed at a moderate pace. At the Library of Congress, investigations culminated in 1939 in a broad survey of communist law, with special attention to the problems of labor and of the peasantry.[150] Thereafter, especially following Vladimir Gsovski's retirement and death, the effort declined; work at other government institutions, such as the Department of Labor, has compensated only in part for this loss. Private researches have led to selected collections of current Soviet laws, case data and related materials by Hazard and Shapiro, Berman, and Zile.[151] Triska and Slusser's comprehensive compilation and analysis of Soviet agreements with foreign governments, 1917-1957, deserves attention.[152] Since 1955, important monographs have been published by Hazard,

[149] References in SBORNIK ZAKON. to bilateral agreements: loans, economic and technical aid, at 264, 268-71, 274, 281, 290-92, 305, 308, 310, 313; consular, at 255, 303, 306; dual citizenship, at 305; trade, at 255, 264, 269, 274-75, 280-81, 291, 303, 308, 310-12, 318, 908; air navigation, at 258, 304; cultural and technical cooperation, at 258, 265, 268, 270, 273-74, 289, 305.

[150] GOVERNMENT, LAW AND COURTS IN THE SOVIET UNION AND EASTERN EUROPE (Gsovski & Grzybowski eds. London 1959), 2 vols.

[151] HAZARD & SHAPIRO, THE SOVIET LEGAL SYSTEM (1962); BERMAN, MATERIALS FOR COMPARISON OF SOVIET AND AMERICAN LAW (Mimeo 1958); ZILE, READINGS ON THE SOVIET LEGAL PROCESS (Mimeo, 1962). See the excellent bibliographies in HAZARD & SHAPIRO, *supra*, and HAZARD, THE SOVIET SYSTEM OF GOVERNMENT (3d ed. 1964).

[152] TRISKA & SLUSSER, THE THEORY, LAW AND POLICY OF SOVIET TREATIES (1962); SLUSSER & TRISKA, *op. cit. supra* note 142 (1959).

on the structure of Soviet administration and law, and on the early history of Soviet law; Morgan, on the procuracy; Berman and Kerner, on military law and disciplinary regulations; George Carson, on electoral practices; F. D. Holzman, on taxation; and R. W. Davis, on State budgets. Berman's *Justice in Russia* appeared in a revised and enlarged form.[153] Fainsod's remarkable presentation of hitherto secret Communist Party materials on Smolensk Oblast' in the 1920's and 30's yields unique data on Soviet criminal law and extralegal repression.[154]

The periodical literature includes many useful articles on legal trends since Stalin's death. Among those are Berman's insightful discussions of qualitative gains, and of areas threatened by reaction, in the substance and procedures of Soviet criminal law. Also noteworthy are Ginsburgs' writings on the shift from socio-political threat toward objective offense as a basic criterion in Soviet legal decisions; Ginsburgs and Rusis' on the intensified protection of State secrets; and Kucherov's on the decline of private rights in real property; and a study by Friedman and Zile of the present developments relative to the Soviet legal profession.[155] Grzybowski has critically examined the application of the Soviet criminal-law reforms of 1958 in the Powers trial, coming to a negative view of Soviet justice in practice. George Feifer, summarizing 150 cases observed by him in the courts of Moscow, came to more favorable conclusions; these data and interpretations were previewed in magazine articles but are more fully expounded in a book which appeared as this issue was going to press.[156]

In international law, Lissitzyn and Margolis have written broad, temperate reviews of recent Soviet positions and practices; Zile's unflattering sketch of the views and ethics of a former Soviet member of the Court of

[153] HAZARD, THE SOVIET SYSTEM OF GOVERNMENT (1957 2d ed. rev. 1960); HAZARD, SETTLING DISPUTES IN SOVIET SOCIETY (1960); MORGAN, SOVIET ADMINISTRATIVE LEGALITY (1962); BERMAN & KERNER, SOVIET MILITARY LAW AND ADMINISTRATION (1955); BERMAN & KERNER, DOCUMENTS ON SOVIET MILITARY LAW AND ADMINISTRATION (1958); CARSON, ELECTORAL PRACTICE IN THE USSR (1955); HOLZMAN, SOVIET TAXATION (1955); DAVIES, THE DEVELOPMENT OF THE SOVIET BUDGETARY SYSTEM (1958); BERMAN, JUSTICE IN THE USSR (rev. ed. 1963).

[154] FAINSOD, SMOLENSK UNDER SOVIET RULE (1958). The entire volume is immensely relevant, but see especially 132-237, 343-408.

[155] Berman, *The Dilemma of Soviet Law Reform*, 76 HARV. L. REV. 929 (1963); Berman, *The Role of Soviet Jurists in the Struggle To Prevent a Return to Stalinist Terror*, Harv. L. School Bull., Dec. 1962, p. 3; Ginsburgs, *Objective Truth and the Judicial Process in Post-Stalinist Soviet Jurisprudence*, 10 AM. J. COMP. L. 53 (1961); Ginsburgs & Rusis, *Soviet Criminal Law and the Protection of State Secrets* in 7 LAW IN EASTERN EUROPE 3-48 (Szirmai ed. 1963); Kucherov, *Property in the Soviet Union*, 11 AM. J. COMP. L. 376 (1962); Friedman & Zile, *Soviet Legal Profession: Recent Developments in Law and Practice*, 1964 WIS L. REV. 32.

[156] Grzybowski, *The Powers Trial and the 1958 Reform of Soviet Criminal Law*, 9 AM. J. COMP. L. 425 (1960); Feifer, *Crime in Moscow*, Sat. Eve. Post, May 9, 1964, p. 36; Feifer, *Moscow: A Day in the People's Court*, Reporter, May 21, 1964, p. 29; FEIFER, JUSTICE IN MOSCOW (1964).

International Justice is also iluminating.[157] Studies of more specialized problems include those by Hazard and Edward McWhinney of Toronto on the validity and utility of "peaceful coexistence" as a concept in international law; B. A. Ramundo's on the weakness of the claim that the Soviet state has fully implemented in its criminal legislation the Hague and Geneva conventions; and Samuel Pisar's on Soviet contracts and arbitration practices in foreign trade.[158]

Today's West German work on Soviet law retains links with the past through the continued efforts of R. Maurach at Munich and A. N. Makarow at Tübingen. However, its rapid growth since 1955 has largely represented a recruitment of new scholars. In that year, the Deutsche Gesellschaft für Osteuropakunde (German Society for East European Studies) founded a journal, *Osteuropa-Recht (Eastern European Law)*, as an international vehicle for articles, reports of research in progress, and bibliographies on Soviet law, under the editorship of Dietrich Loeber from 1955 to 1960. Another scholarly journal, carrying articles, reviews and abstracts of important law cases in the USSR and Eastern Europe was founded in 1957. *Recht in Ost und West: Zeitschrift für Rechtsvergleichung und Interzonale Rechtsprobleme (Law in East and West: Journal of Comparative Law and Interzonal Legal Problems)* is edited by Hermann Mirbt and published by the Vereinigung Freiheitlicher Juristen (Union of Free Jurists) of Berlin and the Institut für Ostrecht (Institute for Eastern Law) of Munich. The Institut für Ostrecht also publishes *Jahrbuch für Ostrecht.* In addition, several local monographic series have been founded, *e.g., Dokumente zum Ostrecht (Documents on Eastern Law)* at Cologne. Finally, by 1962-63, regular teaching in Soviet law had been established at the Free University of Berlin (W. Meder, R. Löwenthal), and at the universities of Göttingen (L. Schultz), Hamburg (G. Geilke), Kiel (B. Meissner), and Munich (R. Maurach).[159]

A cross fertilization in theory between Roman and Common Law, a widened appreciation of law as policy as well as technique, extensive docu-

[157] Lissitzyn, *International Law in a Divided World*, International Conciliation, March 1963 p. 3, at 14-36; Margolis, *Soviet Views on the Relationship Between National and International Law*, 4 INT'L & COMP. L.Q. 116 (1955); Zile, *A Soviet Contribution to International Adjudication: Professor Krylov's Jurisprudential Legacy*, 58 AM. J. INT'L. L. 359 (1964).

[158] Hazard, *Codifying Peaceful Co-existence*, 55 *id.* at 109 (1961); McWhinney, *"Peaceful Co-Existence" and Soviet-Western International Law*, 56 *id.* at 951 (1962); Ramundo, *Soviet Criminal Legislation in Implementation of the Hague and Geneva Conventions Relating to the Rules of Land Warfare*, 57 *id.* 73 (1963); RAMUNDO, THE SOCIALIST (SOVIET) THEORY OF INTERNATIONAL LAW (1964) Pisar, *Soviet Conflict of Laws in International Commercial Transactions*, 70 HARV. L. REV. 593 (1957); Pisar, *The Communist System of Foreign-Trade Adjudication*, 72 HARV. L. REV. 1409 (1959).

[159] For details on German courses in Soviet law see the notices in 8 OSTEUROPA-RECHT 264 (1962).

mentary research, numerous conferences with Commuist-bloc lawyers, and use of the background of recent refugees and other direct experiences with Soviet law have provided the base for many diverse investigations, often of excellent quality, in West Germany. At present, their volume runs close to a hundred monographs and articles annually, comprising over a third of worldwide publication in this field outside of the communist bloc.

Recent reports of interest and merit include selected, annotated collections of legal documents on the Soviet constitutions of 1918-36, the Warsaw Pact, the European Communist Economic Alliance (Comecon), and on European communist treaties affecting persons.[160] Among noteworthy analyses of domestic law are those of Meder on State budgets; W. Rzepka, on the semantics and logical construction of Soviet laws; A. Bilinsky, on presumptions in criminal law and on the Comrades' Courts; Maurach, on the treatment of juveniles; F. C. Schroeder, on the antecedents of the "anti-Parasites" law in Soviet and Tsarist police justice back to 1762; and A. Hastrich, on current issues in Soviet civil law.[161] Theory, armaments, and trade have been issues discussed, respectively, by Meissner, C. Gasteyger, and G. Joetze in the considerable German literature on Soviet public international law.[162] Work in private international law is also in progress.[163]

[160] Maurach, *Handbuch der Sowjet-Verfassung (Soviet Constitutional Handbook)*, 14 Veröffentlichungen des Osteuropa-Instituts (Munich 1955); *Der Warschauer Pakt (The Warsaw Pact)*, 1 Dokumente zum Ostrecht (Meissner ed. Cologne 1962); Uschakow, *Der Rat für gegenseitige Wirtschaftshilfe (Comecon) (The Council for Mutual Economic Aid (Comecon)*, 2 Dokumente zum Ostrecht (Cologne 1962); Makarov, Recueil de Textes Concernant le Droit International Privé 2d ed. en Francais et en Allemand. t II. Texts des Traités Internationaux (Collection of Texts on Private International Law, 2d ed. in French and German. vol. 2, Texts of International Treaties) (Tübingen 1960).

[161] Meder, *Das Haushaltsrecht der Sowjetunion (The Budgetary Legislation of the Soviet Union)*, 7 Osteuropa-Recht 149 (1961); Rzepka, *Sowjetische Gesetztechnik (Soviet Legal Technique)*, 5 Recht in Ost und West 177-80 (1961); Bilinsky, *Die Präsumption der Unschuld in der sowjetischen Rechtslehre (The Presumption of Innocence in Soviet Jurisprudence)*, 6 Recht in Ost und West 55-62 (1962); Maurach, *Das neue sowjetische Jugendstrafrecht (The New Soviet Law on Juvenile Criminal Punishment)*, 7 Recht in Ost und West 137-52 (1963); Bilinsky, *Kameradschaftsgerichte in der UdSSR (Comrades' Courts in the USSR)*, 8 Osteuropa-Recht 306-30 (1962); Schroeder, *Gesellschaftsgerichte und Administrativjustiz im vorrevolutionären Russland (Social Courts and Administrative Justice in Pre-revolutionary Russia)*, 8 *id.* at 292-305 (1962); Hastrich, *Die öffentliche Diskussion um die Gestaltung der Grundlagen der Zivilgesetzgebung der UdSSR (The Public Debate on the Formulation of the Principles of Civil Legislation of the USSR)*, 8 *id.* at 242-56.

[162] Meissner, *Völkerrechtswissenschaft und Völkerrechtskonzeption in der UdSSR (The Science and the Conception of International Law in the USSR)*, 5 Recht in Ost und West 1-5 (1961); Gasteyger, *Abrüstung and Völkerrecht. Zur sowjetischen Völkerrechtsdoktrin über die Abrüstung (Disarmament and International Law. On Soviet International Law Doctrine on Disarmament)*, 7 *id.* at 89-95 (1963); Joetze *Völkerrechtliche Probleme des Ost-West Handels (Problems of International Law in East-West Trade)*, 6 *id.* at 141-147 (1962).

[163] For example, Rzepka, *Die Rechtsstellung der Ausländer in der UdSSR (The Legal Status of Foreigners in the USSR)*, 8 *id.* at 49-55 (1964).

In the Netherlands, the University of Leyden has been a focus, via its Documentation Office, of studies on Soviet law. In 1957, it founded an international series, *Law in Eastern Europe*, publishing documents and original research. The editor, Z. Szirmai, also teaches Soviet law. Other work is being conducted at Amsterdam (G. Kuypers), and at Utrecht (W. P. J. Pompe), which published F. J. M. Feldbrugge's outstanding treatise on Soviet legal theory in 1959.[164] This volume deals with the concept of guilt in criminal law, historically and currently, with reference to the definition of crimes, criminal casualty, intent, nonimputability and the politics of law. Feldbrugge concludes that guilt, in today's Soviet law, "is the hostile and nonconforming stand taken by an individual in his act, against the will of Soviet authority. . . . The present situation carries a danger of strong conservatism and legal positivism. The Soviet concept of guilt is rejected by us, because—notwithstanding its merits—it is ultimately aimed at subjugating the individual completely to the state."[165]

French work is still concentrated in Paris, largely in conjunction with the Centre Français de Droit Comparé (French Center of Comparative Law). The *Revue International de Droit Comparé (International Review of Comparative Law)* and the monographic series *Librairie Générale de Droit et de Jurisprudence (General Collection on Law and Jurisprudence)* are the major outlets. French publications have been qualitatively uneven. Noteworthy recent studies include reviews of Soviet civil liability and judicial organization by M. Fridieff, the law of the sea by F. de Hartingh, the functions of public organization by G. Langrod, and the nature of Soviet federalism by M. Mouskhely of Strasbourg.[166] Jean Bellon's attempt to view the Soviet reforms in criminal law stressing prevention and education as part of a general European legal modernization, the *Défense Sociale Nouvelle*, has been very controversial.[167] The work has, in Marc Ancel's judgment, ignored the central role of the judge in Western, as opposed to the social collective in Soviet, practice.[168] Yet despite this methodological

[164] FELDBRUGGE, SCHULD IN HET SOWJET STRAFRECHT (GUILT IN SOVIET CRIMINAL LAW) (Utrecht 1959). (English summary at 183-87.)

[165] *Id.* at 187.

[166] Fridieff, *La Responsibilité Civile en Droit Soviétique (Civil Liability in Soviet Law)*, 10 REVUE INTERNATIONALE DE DROIT COMPARÉ 574 (1958); Fridieff, *L'organisation Judiciarie Soviétique (Soviet Judicial Organization)*, 14 *id.* at 725 (1962); DE HARTINGH, LES CONCEPTIONS SOVIÉTIQUE DU DROIT DE LA MER (Paris 1960); Langrod, *Les Formes de la Participation des Masses dans le Gouvernement et l'Administration de l'URSS (Forms of Mass Participation in Soviet Government and Administration)*, in 1 L'URSS DROIT, ECONOMIE, SOCIOLOGIE, POLITIQUE, CULTURE 101-40 (1962); Mouskhely, *Les Contradictions du Federalisme Soviétique (The Contradictions of Soviet Federalism)*, in *id.* at 19-34 (1962).

[167] BELLON, DROIT PÉNAL SOVIÉTIQUE ET DROIT PÉNAL OCCIDENTAL (SOVIET AND WESTERN CRIMINAL LAW) (Paris 1961). See especially 187-99.

[168] *Id.* at 7-10.

difference and despite the coercive reality expressed in much recent as well as Stalinist legislation, Bellon's work appears to have much validity as an apperception of the hopes of liberal Soviet jurists.

In Great Britain, Schlesinger and R. Beermann at Glasgow, I. Lapenna and A. K. R. Kiralfy at the University of London, and E. L. Johnson at Durham, are the principal workers on Soviet law. *Soviet Studies*, the *Modern Law Review*, and the *International and Comparative Law Quarterly* constitute the media of publication. The work done is modest in scale, but valuable. Kiralfy's penetrating paper on the use of law as a dynamic instrument of social change in Communist Europe justifies special note.[169]

Finally, attention is drawn to the *Review of Contemporary Law* (formerly *Law in the Service of Peace*), the journal of the International Association of Democratic Lawyers, made up of Soviet and Eastern European representatives and nonbloc communist sympathizers. Edited currently by Pierre Cot of France, and published in Brussels, the periodical carries many Soviet translations, some apologia, and occasional articles expressing communist heterodoxy.[170] One of these was an early (1956) defense of objectivity in Soviet legal thinking, in opposition to Vyshinsky's then-dominant stress on the subjective protection of the Soviet social system. Another, by a Czech jurist, has identified borrowings from United Nations statutes and practices in the basic concepts of Comecon. He has also clarified Comecon's limitations, especially in the extent of authority delegated to it by the sovereign member states.[171]

In all, the past decade has transformed work on Soviet law into a multinational effort of significant size.

D. *Intellectual and Pragmatic Values in Studying Soviet Law*

Over 40 years of work by many scholars has produced several hundred monographs and several thousand articles and reviews on the theory, institutions, practices, and personnel of Soviet law, international and domestic, civil and criminal. These studies have encompassed the wide range of conditions under which Soviet law has operated—revolution, economic nationalization, war and recovery. They have considered the application of Soviet law to different social strata—private tradesmen, nomads, peasants, workmen, soldiers and party élite. But they have also been unified by the

[169] Kiralfy, *The Rule of Law in Communist Europe*, 8 INT'L & COMP. L.Q. 465 (1959); LAPENNA, STATE AND LAW, SOVIET AND YUGOSLAV THEORY (1964).

[170] The Foreign Languages Publishing House, Moscow, is an important source of official English-language translations of Soviet legal works. See especially DENISOV & KIRICHENKO, SOVIET STATE LAW (Moscow 1960); INTERNATIONAL LAW: TEXTBOOK (Moscow 1960); and ROMASHKIN, *et al.* FUNDAMENTALS OF SOVIET LAW (Moscow 1962).

[171] Rakhounov, *Value of the Confession of the Accused in Soviet Criminal Procedure*, Law in the Service of Peace, Dec. 1956, p. 13 (1956); Kalensky, *The Council for Economic Co-operation and International Law*, Rev. Contemp. L., June 1962, p. 42.

political continuity of the Soviet Union and the unceasing insistence of Soviet leadership, since 1917, upon one-party supremacy, State control of all large-scale economic activities, forced-draft industrialization for maximum military-economic power, and ideological conformity. The studies have varied greatly in the data examined, and in the legal schools, hypotheses, and political biases represented This variation itself has helped to isolate uncertainities in theory and practice, and to develop insights through the clash of ideas.

At the same time, the body of research on Soviet law is subject to marked limitations. Unquestionably practice often varies from theory, for access to legal materials is incomplete even for Soviet lawyers, let alone the vast body of informal decision makers and police.[172] Yet the case data available for independent study are less than adequate. Since the 1920's only scraps of judicial statistics have even been indicated. Many legal questions, such as the actual legal positions of non-Rusians, especially Moslems, in the USSR have received only superficial treatment. Legal studies have, in general, taken little account of social, demographic, economic, and military contexts, and of administrative as well as juristic motivations for given practices. Conversely, sweeping psychological, social, and historical interpretations of an ill-defined aggregate of Soviet law have been too frequent. Moreover, even the wisest foreign observers have been able to anticipate few changes in the content or operation of Soviet law. Above all, the largely derivative nature of Soviet law, its frequent incompleteness, crudity and inconsistency, and its many inequities, deprive its study of much strength as a source of legal inspiration.

Nevertheless, Soviet law merits serious attention for both intellectual and pragmatic reasons:

It constitutes a record of experience of the adaptability of Roman law, essentially, to particular policies. This record exposes both useful plasticities and "peril points," in Hazard's words,[173] that open the way to totalitarian and other evils. Thus, study of Soviet data can aid in the wise formulations of legal ways to meet the needs of developing nations and the solution of problems, such as slum violence, common to most nations. Its study also contributes to an understanding of Soviet culture which, both in its own right and as the heir of Russian history, forms a significant

[172] In 1959, Soviet legal personnel totalled 78,700, including 1,000 without complete university educations; 23,000 of these lawyers served in the courts and procuracy, leaving only 55,700 to serve all other legislative, commercial, and administrative needs. These numbers should be compared to those of the Comrades' Courts and auxiliary police (see note 112 *supra*) and to the copies of legal reports published: 30,000 for *Sbornik zakon.*, 22,000 for a new text on the courts and procuracy (see note 105 *supra*), and 20,000 for the Higher Party School's volume on State organization and the law (see note 108 *supra*). See also "On Distribution of the Population of the U.S.S.R. by Social Groups, . . ." 13 C.D.S.P. No. 6, p. 25, at 28-30 (1961).

[173] Hazard, The Soviet System of Government 192 (2d ed. rev. 1960).

part of the scientific, musical, literary, and ethical (viz., Tolstoy, Dostoevsky, and Lenin) components of today's world civilization. And it provides an institutional basis upon which measures to avoid or limit thermonuclear war, and to further international legality and beneficent cooperation between East and West, must build.

The indispensable focus of these measures is the stabilization of relationships between the United States and the Soviet Union, currently and in the foreseeable future. These two countries are the world's primary ideological antagonists and the sole holders of potentially decisive military, economic, and technological capacities. Soviet law, explicit or customary, enters into four aspects of United States-Soviet interaction.

First is reciprocal military security. This requires information, to avoid surprise, and counterbalancing strength. Such information is abetted by communications media to transmit to the opponent urgent issues and limits of accommodation, and to permit negotiation. Under current conditions, the quickness and magnitude of possible military action, on one hand, and the technical complexity of issues, on the other, have made many channels essential: the "hot line," embassy contacts, the United Nations and various unofficial means. The mutual recognition of unacceptable hazards has come, in part, unilaterally; in part, from exchanges arising from the Geneva Conference of 1955. Least progress has been made in the reciprocal recognition of legitimate rights; the web of multi-lateral agreements (*e.g.*, the Charter of the United Nations) and bilateral pacts (*e.g.*, on the boundary of Berlin) provide crucial guaranties, but faith in these remains limited because of untoward incidents, such as the Kasenkina affair, the U-2 and RB-47 crises, and the Soviet resumption of nuclear testing in 1961.

Second is the strengthening of relations with third powers based upon cognizance and exploitation of their changing relationships with the Soviet Union. The limitation of Soviet controls upon Eastern Europe has presented the most significant opportunities of this type. Conversely, the rise of Soviet trade relations with NATO countries, especially West Germany and Italy, has restricted United States efforts. In the United Nations, a quasi-independent entity in world power relations, a comprehensive balance of U.S. - U.S.S.R. participation prevails, excepting for those local security operations (Palestine, Congo, Cyprus) and economic agencies (World Bank, I.M.F., F.A.O.) from which the Soviet Union chooses to abstain.[174] Soviet legal influence upon the domestic policies of non-Communist countries has, thus far, been most evident in the widespread adoption of limitations upon foreign property.

Third is the gain of economic, technical, and cultural benefits through the development of appropriate trade, exchanges, and cooperation. Here the weather information exchanges inaugurated during World War II and

[174] 1962 YEARBOOK OF THE UNITED NATIONS 570-682 *passim* (1964).

maintained through the United Nations have been outstandingly important. In the long term, the magnitude of problems in worldwide economic development, in the control of marine and air pollution, and the regulation of weather modification are likely to require extensive cooperation to avoid general disasters. Build-ups of the necessary systems of agencies (specialized organizations, consulates, etc.), the pertinent technical regulations, and the safeguards for persons and property involved in conflicts, are still rudimentary. Conflicts in Soviet domestic laws, which recognize the priority of treaties, on one hand, and insist upon foreign conformity with the rules of Soviet public organization, on the other,[175] cannot be minimized.

Fourth is the favorable estimation of trends in internal stability and acceptable intent. With the extreme dangers of modern weapons of mass lethality, reciprocal concern in United States-Soviet political stability is manifest. Consequently, the identification of areas of serious legal conflict, *e.g.*, in relation to Soviet private property, religion, and ignored aspirations, such as those of the rapidly-growing Turkic minority, should counterbalance the recognition of positive trends. Strategic uncertainities arise from the continuing lack of provisions for orderly succession to Khrushchev, and the immensely favored position of the Soviet military establishment, as manifest by the secrecy and other defense laws, the absence of military prosecutions for high living, and heavy military pressure on Soviet resources which has imperiled the hard won gains in living standards and liberties effected since Stalin's death.

II. The Relevance of the Essays

A. General Observations

The six essays on Soviet civil law encompassed by this symposium deal with specific, distinct problems of significance for comparative law, Soviet society, and international relations. These studies have not attempted to be exhaustive, either in their scope or in their documentation. Instead, they have emphasized concepts, issues, decision-making mechanisms, legal environments, and socio-political predispositions.[176] Nevertheless, much of the factual material presented in them has either been previously unavailable in the Western literature or unanalyzed from a legal standpoint.

[175] "Regulations on Foreign Citizens Studying in Higher and Specialized Secondary Educational Institutions of the U.S.S.R." (Order No. 6 of the U.S.S.R. Ministry of Higher and Specialized Education, Jan. 7, 1964), 16 C.D.S.P. No. 16, p. 24 (1964).

[176] On the methodology of modern comparative legal studies see McDougal, *The Comparative Study of Law for Policy Purposes: Value Clarification as an Instrument of Democratic World Order*, 61 Yale L.J. 914 (1952) and McDougal & Lasswell, *The Identification and Appraisal of Diverse Systems of Public Order,* 53 Am. J. Int'l L. 1 (1959); Loeber, *Rechtsvergleichung zwischen Landern mit verschiedener Wirtschaftsordnung (Legal Comparisons Between States With Different Economic Systems),* 26 Rabels Zeitschrift fur auslandisches und internationales Privatrecht 201-29 (1961).

In particular, B. A. Ramundo's examination of mass communications and Z. Zile's of retail trade are new explorations in Soviet law. These institutions have hitherto been dealt with from the standpoints of sociology and psychological operations, and economics, respectively.[177] John Hazard's paper contributes, on one hand, a refinement and updating of evidence on the Sovietization of Eastern Europe; on the other, it opens new questions in the study of developing nations. Other insightful papers on the former problem have been written by Kiralfy and Grzybowski, while extensive basic data have been published in Gsovski and Grzybowski's survey, and continuously in *Recht in Ost und West*.[178] Dennis O'Connor synthesizes and analyzes evidence hitherto partially available of forms of decision-making in the resolution of civil disputes.[179] Dietrich Loeber enriches with analyses of cases and Arbitrazh instructions, the topic of contracts in State economic institutions, which has been handled in previous work largely on the basis of statutory provisions.[180] Finally, Whitmore Gray examines the recent codification of tort concepts which had been reviewed at earlier development stages by several Western writers.[181]

The relevance of the studies for problems of Soviet socio-political development and international relations, especially those with the United States, may be summarized as follows:

1. They consistently indicate a trend toward the multiplication and diversification of legal means during the past decade. Social relationships, capacities, and actions have been given revived legal emphasis, but much more so in the field of behavioral regulation than that of economic management. The expanded means are incomplete, often ambiguous and even offsetting in their effects. Yet as an aggregate they seem to present expanded

[177] INKELES, PUBLIC OPINION IN SOVIET RUSSIA (1950); Inkeles, *Mobilizing Public Opinion in Soviet Russia*, in 1 L'U.R.S.S. DROIT ECONOMIE, SOCIOLOGIE, POLITIQUE, CULTURE 61-72 (1962); BARGHOORN, THE SOVIET CULTURAL OFFENSIVE (1960); Goldman, *The Cost and Efficiency of Distribution in the Soviet Union*, 76 Q.J. ECON. 437-53 (1962).

[178] Kiralfy, *supra* note 169; Grzybowski, *Reform of Civil Law in Hungary, Poland, and the Soviet Union*, 10 AM. J. COMP. 253 (1961); GSOVSKI & GRZYBOWSKI, *op. cit. supra* note 150.

[179] Berman & Spindler, *Soviet Comrades' Courts*, 38 WASH. L. REV. 842 (1963); Bilinsky, *supra* note 161; Langrod, *supra* note 166; Schroeder, *supra* note 161.

[180] 3 ARMINJON, NOLDE & WOLFF, TRAITÉ DE DROIT COMPARÉ 257-58, 281-89 (Paris 1952); Berman, *Commercial Contracts in Soviet Law*, 35 CALIF. L. REV. 191 (1947); 1 GSOVSKI, SOVIET CIVIL LAW chs. 11-13 (1949); Johnson, *State Arbitration in the USSR*, in 1 L'U.R.S.S. DROIT, ECONOMIE, SOCIOLOGIE, POLITIQUE, CULTURE 185-91 (1962); Krynski, *Management Problems in Soviet Public Enterprise as Indicated by Arbitration Awards*, 12 AM. SLAVIC & EAST EUROPEAN REV. 175 (1953).

[181] 1 GSOVSKI, *op. cit. supra* note 180, chs. 14-15; Hazard, *Personal Injury and Soviet Socialism*, 65 HARV. L. REV. 545 (1952); Holman & Spinner, *Bases of Liability for Tortious Injury in Soviet Law*, 22 IOWA L. REV. 1 (1936). Also relevant is the discussion of criminal liability for abuses of power by Bruggmann, *Amtshaftung in der Sowjetunion (Official Liability in the Soviet Union)*, 8 OSTEUROPA-RECHT 236 (1962).

ves in role to Soviet groups and persons, with reduced opportunities for arbitrary, inescapable coercion. By limiting central bureaucratic powers,[182] they give other social elements—partly ideologists, local interests, legal liberals—increased effectiveness. Because of the inaccessibility of detailed and precise legal information, this diversification of means and the participation of millions of persons untutored in legal matters brings dangers of caprice, but also promotes the widened use of administrative practices and especially of traditional and emergent customs as sources of law.

2. Pragmatic reasoning, rather than dogma, appears to underlie the basic innovations pursued: the seriousness of alcoholism and violence among poorly educated young in-migrants into urban slums, the fear of all-encompassing centralized bureaucracies, the desire for the political consolidation and support of Soviet urban workers, the reluctance to expand social welfare unduly, and so forth. At the same time, the innovations fall far short of an abrogation of party dictatorship, being fully consistent with explicit provisions of the 1936 Constitution and the 1961 Party Statutes.[183]

3. Several possibilities exist for the future development of political and economic decentralization as exemplified by the roles of Soviet social organizations and contracting firms. These are reintegration with central bureaucracies as subsidiary or atrophied elements, growth to the point of genuine pluralism, or conflict and instability. Important factors in what may happen are the future intensity of pressures on manpower and other economic resources, which are in part self-generated and in part reflect the course of military-technological competition, and the effective penetration of new institutional ideas, such as liability insurance. Today, the fundamental accepted source of conceptual progress is Eastern Europe, which also transmits concepts from the West.

4. The Eastern European communist states, excluding Albania, have profoundly modified Soviet institutions, although critical features such as party hegemony over the State have been carefully maintained. These modifications affect both early and recent borrowings from the USSR, such as the codes of agricultural law and the Comrades' Courts. Soviet lawyers follow these developments through participation in joint agencies, such as the standing Agricultural Commission of Comecon at Sofia, Bulgaria; through formal visits; and through reports in Soviet legal books and periodicals.[184]

[182] For example, the auxiliary police are juridically independent of the regular police establishment, being coordinated with them at a political level. Evidence of friction between the two may be found, *e.g.*, "The Soviet Militia as an Agency for Safeguarding Public Order" 15 C.D.S.P. No. 7, p. 7, at 7-8 (1963).

[183] Especially articles 9, 11, 14, 125-26, 130-31 of the Constitution. See Hazard, THE SOVIET SYSTEM OF GOVERNMENT 208 (2d ed. rev. 1960).

[184] On agricultural legal cooperation in Comecon see Kikot', *Pravovyye voprosy sotrudnichestva sotsialisticheskikh stran v oblasti sel'skogo khozyaystva (Legal Questions in the Cooperation of Socialist Countries in the Field of Agriculture)*, Sov.

The published reports on Eastern European law are selective. They reinforce self-esteem by noting adaptions of Soviet ways and, while avoiding very controversial developments such as the Hungarian codification of customary law, do use Eastern European, especially Polish, materials as suggestions for Soviet legal improvement.[185]

For example, a Soviet delegation lauded Polish judicial organization, especially the novel features of strong educational requirements for judges, appointment, and indefinite tenure for judges, one-judge courts, and courts specializing in divorce, juvenile, and other demanding work.[186] Polish efforts to transfer administrative law-making to legislative control and hence to promote greater consistency, better drafting, and better legal protection have also gained favorable Soviet attention.[187] A description of Hungarian Comrades' Courts stressed the institution's fully official nature, its protective requirements (a member must be from the accused's work group; no intermediaries are permitted to testify except relatives in case of the absence of the accused), its stress on medical treatment for alcoholics, and the high levels of restitution allowable for private injuries.[188] A similar report for East Germany brought out three-year tenure, procedural safeguards, and emphasis upon conciliation in Conciliation Councils (Comrades' Courts) there.[189] In the economic sphere, Rumanian practices of coordinating entire flows of production, involving as many as 34 legal entities, in joint master contracts setting the framework for sets of bilateral ones, seemed a clear

gos. i pravo No. 1, p. 64 (1964); on legal exchanges see Anashkin & Kalenov, *U Pol'skikh druzey (Among Polish Friends)*, Sov. yus. No. 9, p. 14 (1962) and Kirichenko, *Mezhdunarodnoye soveshchaniye v Budapeshte kriminalistov sotsialisticheskikh gosudarstv po voprosam ugolovnogo prava (International Conference in Budapest of Socialist State Criminologists on Questions of Criminal Law)*, Sov. gos. i pravo No. 3, p. 131 (1961); a typical textbook survey of Eastern European courts may be found in ORGANIZATSIYA SUDA I PROKURATURY V SSSR (ORGANIZATION OF THE COURTS AND PROCURACY IN THE USSR) 245-71 (Karev ed. Moscow 1961).

[185] Illustrative is the report on the adoption of People's Guards and Comrades' Courts in Bulgaria, Hungary, and Outer Mongolia in Bobotov & Luk'yanov, *Trudyashchiyesya sotsialisticheskikh stran na okhrane obshchestvennogo poryadka (The Workers of the Socialist Nations in Defense of Public Order)*, Sov yus. No. 12, p. 20 (1960); for a development unreported in the Soviet legal press see Leh, *La Codification du Droit Coutumier Hongrois (The Codifications of Hungarian Customary Law)*, 12 REVUE INTERNATIONALE DE DROIT COMPARÉ 559 (1960).

[186] Boldyrev, *Sovetskiye yuristy v Pol'skoy Narodnoy Respublike (Soviet Jurists in the Polish People's Republic)* Sov. yus. No. 5, p. 36 (1960).

[187] Rozmarin, *O rabotakh po uporyadocheniyu administrativnogo zakonodatel'stva v Pol'skoy Narodnoy Respublike (On Regulating Administrative Law-Making in the Polish People's Republic)*, Sov. gos. i pravo No. 3, p. 87 (1962).

[188] Vorozheykin, *Tovarishchskiye sudy VNR na novom etape (The Comrades' Courts of the Hungarian People's Republic at a New Stage)*, Sov. yus. No. 20, p. 24 (1963).

[189] Bobotov, *Primiritel'nyye kamery v GDR (Conciliation Councils in the German People's Republic)* Sov. yus. No. 6, p. 32 (1960).

advance on Soviet usage. So too did extensive leeways for technical mutual aid and even resource transfers within the contracting group.[190]

5. Outside of Eastern Europe, the most intense Soviet legal influence is apparently being exercised on Outer Mongolia, North Vietnam (whose institutions, as reported, are far more Soviet than Chinese),[191] and Cuba. By 1962, in the last-named country, 90 per cent of all industry and transport, and 41 per cent of all agricultural land had been nationalized. Economic legal entities of the Soviet type, contractual relations within the framework of a State plan, and Arbitrazh were then introduced.[192]

In Africa, Soviet data indicate some influence upon Ghana, Guinea, Dahomey, and Mali through the institution of "right to work" laws, workers' brigades, and in Mali, a one-party system. Yet all of these countries continue to manifest strong relations with Western law, especially via the declarations and conventions of the United Nations.[193]

Recent developments in China, North Korea and Albania appear to be largely ignored by Soviet legal publications, in contrast to the situation between 1956 and 1961 when Chinese influence was appreciable. The recent investigations of Professors Jerome Cohen and Dennis O'Connor, as yet unpublished, strongly suggest Chinese priority in the development or revival of several legal institutions, including auxiliary police, anti-parasite procedures, lay Comrades' Courts, and the prophylaxis campaign to abort civil disputes. The frequent articles on law in the major Western powers are comically grotesque, but do serve as media for indicating advances in legal and law-enforcement techniques, propaganda notwithstanding.[194]

6. In the conduct of direct relations with the USSR, several practices covered in this symposium would adversely affect American nondiplomatic visitors. The general problem has been excellently reviewed by Rzepka, who notes as a principle that foreigners in the USSR enjoy no wider rights than do Soviet citizens.[195] Under such circumstances, response to Soviet

[190] Eminescu, *Kooperirovanyye postavki v Rumynskoy Narodnoy Respublike (Coordinated Production Flows in the Rumanian People's Republic)* Sov. gos. i pravo No. 2, p. 108 (1964).

[191] For example, Nguen Dinh Lok & Bobotov, *Sudebnaya reforma v Demokraticheskoy Respublike Vyetnam (The Reform of Judicial Organizations in the Democratic Republic of Vietnam)*, Sov. yus. No. 2, p. 20 (1961).

[192] Olteanu, *Arbitrazhnyye komissiyi v revolyutsionnoy Kube (Arbitration Commissions in Revolutionary Cuba)*, Sov. yus. No. 15, p. 26 (1963).

[193] Ivanov, *O pravovom regulirovaniyi truda v molodykh suverennykh gosudarstvakh Afriki (On the Legal Regulation of Labor in the Young Sovereign States of Africa)*, Sov. gos. i pravo No. 1, p. 86 (1962); Ikonitskiy, *Konstitutsiya Respubliki Mali (Constitution of the Republic of Mali)*, *id.* No. 9, at 132 (1961).

[194] Shraga & Eminov, *Rost prestupnosti v kapitalisticheskikh stranakh i izpol'zovaniye tekhnicheskikh sredstv bor'by s neyu (The Rise of Crime in Capitalist Countries and the Use of Technical Means of Combatting It)*, Sov. yus. No. 6, p. 28 (1964).

[195] Rzepka, *supra* note 163, at 50.

propaganda might entail liability to punishment under articles 70 and 130 of the 1960 RSFSR Criminal Code.[196] As mentioned earlier, foreign students must accept in writing the disciplinary jurisdiction of Comrades' Courts at their institutions.[197] Traffic accidents resulting in any injury could lead to 2 years of imprisonment, with 10 years the maximum punishment for accidentally-inflicted death.[198] Conversely, the absence of liability insurance for other than foreign drivers and the poverty of Soviet citizens practically eliminate recovery for damages to Americans.

B. The Authors' Findings

In *Procedures in Civil Decisions*, Dennis O'Connor analyzes Soviet theory and practice in the social regulation of lesser crimes, general misbehavior, and personal disputes. He distinguishes two ways of generating legal standards and decisions. One is the public order system, which is bureaucratic in organization, formal in procedure, and supported by the full authority, the entire range of sanctions, of the society. The other is the civic order system, which is based on local institutions, and has looser procedures, limited authority, and use of expressed public disapproval as its main, but not sole, sanction. The balance between public and civic order systems in current Soviet law is the central question discussed in the paper.

Jurisdictional boundaries between the two overlap markedly, which permits State and Communist Party agencies to shift cases to given tribunals for maximum exemplary effects, and allows private persons to have recourse to regular courts, albeit with difficulty. Current Soviet ideology anticipates the increasing use of civic order systems to replace the coercive "law" of the proletarian dictatorship by the consensual "non-law" of the classless utopia. However, today's dangers of serious miscarriages of justice and, conversely, of the frustration of party and State intents, are so great that the procuracy continues to intervene often and at all stages in cases handled by the civic order system.

The Soviet system of public order has grown out of prerevolutionary institutions adapted to new policies. It has been augmented by special boards, Gosarbitrazh, to handle litigation between legal entities of the State, especially in the economic sector. To meet the specialized demands of priority military-technological planning goals, and to avoid dependence upon the artificial Soviet price system, Gosarbitrazh stresses specific compliance rather than substitute compensation in decisions. In contract failures, particularly, it seeks culprits on whom to impose individual sanctions. "Social" or collateral penalties affecting reputations, livelihoods and careers may

[196] La Réforme Pénale Soviétique *(The Soviet Penal Reform)* 42, 52, (Ancel ed. Paris 1962).

[197] See note 175 *supra*.

[198] La Réforme Pénale Soviétique 68-69 (Ancel ed. Paris 1962).

augment or substitute for these. This punitive viewpoint places a high premium on devices to shift blame, and tends also to limit liabilities for remote responsibility and for personal injury (in establishments other than those where hazardous conditions lead to strict liability). Another reflection of the limited involvement of the Soviet public order system in truly civil law is its neglect of personal legal needs and conflicts.

Even in civic order, the primary Soviet concern is not restitution of injured personal rights but the mitigation of "social injury." Hence, the boundary between civil and criminal law is hazy; civic order procedures attempt simultaneously to satisfy the injured party, coerce the injurer, and educate the community. The sanctions authorized in the laws of 1958-61 for use by social organizations via Comrades' Courts and mass rallies, range from adverse publicity and fines to petitions to empowered bodies to invoke paycuts, demotions, dismissals and, for those stigmatized as "parasites," up to five years of exile at compulsory labor.

Soviet agencies of public order, the procuracy and the People's Courts, utilize civic means in adjudicating nonsupport, public nuisances and allied misbehavior. By informal surveys or from authorized representatives of social organizations, they elicit data on reputations and other qualifying evidence, suggestions as to appropriate decisions, and acceptance of responsibility for individuals paroled to groups or communities. Circuit trials at the sites of disputes promote spectator participation and mass indoctrination. Legal standards receive some protection by the off-time use of lay judges, who also serve on the bench two weeks a year, for supervising implementing actions delegated to local groups; and by rudimentary instruction in law via mass media and spare-time lectures by lawyers.

Civic order agencies, especially Comrades' Courts, may assume full responsibility, subject only to confirmation by regional executive organs (Soviets) and to review by the procuracy. They seek particularly to handle lesser infractions with minimum sanctions, and to resolve in-group disputes, especially through mediation, reconciliation, and claim-quieting. Experimentation with procedures is still continuing, but it is clear that the rise of an effective and equitable system will involve substantial educational and supervisory efforts, by unpaid community leaders, lawyers, and officials. Thus the social services that may be realized by civic order means will require significant true costs, the long term acceptability of which by the party and State remains uncertain.

Soviet mass communications comprise an essential mechanism of central policy control by the Communist Party over national administration, the public and civic order systems of law, and the population directly. Bernard Ramundo's survey, *They Answer (To) Pravda*, succinctly identifies the operational characteristics of this control mechanism, especially as it is related to justice.

In essence, the mass communications organization of the Soviet Union, particularly the press, constitutes, for most public purposes, the eyes, ears, and mouth of the Communist Party. It undertakes to amass volunteered and elicited information (supplemented by data gained from coercive inquiry and even provocation and fabrication) by means of which developments in Soviet society needing corrective action or meriting approbation from the standpoint of party policies can be identified. It reports a selected body of news and general information, designed especially to promote correct ideology. It also transmits and backs by selected evidence, the policies, directives, and criticisms emanating, or purporting to emanate, from high political authority. The scope of this guidance is protean, from industrial technology to artistic canons. It includes explicit, detailed, and peremptory interventions into alleged misconduct and into judicial actions at every stage, including the Supreme Court of the USSR. The responses achieved serve to correct some abuses, but also to interfere gravely with due process, judicial independence, and legal certainty. They dramatize the subordination of justice to party policy.

To fulfill its assigned roles, the Soviet system of mass communications is supported by party and state authority, particularly in post-Stalin Russia. The Central Committee of the Party and the Council of Ministers of the USSR directly govern its affairs. Press representatives may demand access to all persons and matters, apart from the topmost leadership and areas of party and military secrecy. Regular reporting is reinforced by networks of unpaid auxiliary correspondents, drop-boxes for volunteered news and complaints, and surprise "raids" by party, komsomol and labor-union teams upon sites of suspected ill-doing. Press and radio findings must be attended to by officials as well as ordinary citizens; failure to do so and, above all, recalcitrance, may evoke not only more savage attacks but party and criminal sanctions. Yet mass communications constitute an auxiliary rather than primary device of Soviet authority. Their power is limited by inevitable discordances between the media of varying hierarchical levels, regions, and functional groups; by competition with other plenipotentiary agencies (the Party-State Control Commissions, the procuracy, the K.G.B. or security police); and by an absence of means for physical sanctions.

Soviet experimentation with unusual legal, quasi-legal and extralegal institutions and procedures in the field of social regulation has been accompanied by marked conservatism and incomplete development in legal ways to govern economic operations. Apart from the fundamental constitutional and code provisions defining the scopes of State, cooperative, and private property, and the establishment of State planning as an obligatory system, and apart from family and peasant-household legislation on inheritance and support obligations, administrative decisions rather than legal relations have predominated in economic management. Nevertheless, the roles of contract and tort law have always been necessary ones both in the State and private sectors, and it is certain that economic rationalization, the development of a true calculus of advantage and choice, would vastly extend their use.

For 40 years, State economic enterprises have been legal entities, with accountable managements, defined properties, and capacities for contract. These concepts were necessary in a period of mixed State, cooperative and private, domestic and foreign, economic activity. They also permitted concentration of State planning on broad strategic objectives, with wide leeway in the details of implementation. However, from the rise of Hitler in 1933 onward to this day, Soviet economic policies became increasingly dominated by exacting, urgent, and massive military requirements. Furthermore, the enormous human and physical losses caused by collectivization, World War II, and Stalinist postwar political consolidation transformed the Soviet Union into an economy of chronic scarcity. Command priorities and resource allocations, insistance upon the reliable execution of key missions regardless of other effects, and direct coercion characterized State economic operations, while the private sector survived as best it could. Under these circumstances, legal relations and managerial options atrophied, but shady arrangements and hoarded reserves won leeway to offset command errors. Since Khrushchev's rise, allocation procedures have been tightened and illegalities reduced. Counterbalancing managerial freedoms have been only partly invoked; contractual possibilities remain tightly constrained by administrative planning directives, especially in production and supply commitments, probably less so in the poorly reported areas of research and development, and construction.

Yet contracts between links in a production chain are developed very extensively. While they cannot affect the choice of partners, production, and transfer quantities, or prescribed specifications, they do allow arrangements for detailed scheduling, details of payments, packing, and allied matters. What is most important, as is shown by the case data and analyses of Dietrich Loeber's article on *Plan and Contract Performance in Soviet Law,* is that the contract relationship permits appeal, negotiation, and settlement by a legal board, Arbitrazh, of features such as the delivery of unwanted goods, that may be highly detrimental to a partner in a production transaction. The system of State arbitration has risen to special significance in dealings between administratively unrelated entities, wherein a common command decision is difficult. Moreover, it eases corrections and changes in plans by introducing reciprocal lateral cross-checks into the operation of industrial hierarchies. It stimulates a shift from specific obligations to monetary liabilities, at least for some defaults. Thus, it represents a step toward a more autonomous economy within the framework of State ownership; further development may take place should there be the diversification of permissible, independently valued goals upon which meaningful prices and economic choices depend.

In *Soviet Tort Law: The New Principles Annotated*, Whitmore Gray provides an exposition and interpretation, based on the examination of spe-

cific laws, court decisions, judicial instructions and legal writings, c
88 through 93 of the 1961 Basic Principles of Civil Legislation of t
Union and the Union Republics. These articles replace code provisions of the early 1920's through the incorporation of intervening judicial experience, and with some cognizance of the opinions of the bar. They cover grounds of liability and defenses recognized, the scope of compensable injury, employers' and general State liability, and actions taken in cases of wrongful death.

The concepts of tort law which the articles indicate may be briefly summarized.

The basis of compensation for injury to persons or property is a finding of fault on the injurer's part. Absence of fault, *i.e.*, of a crime, an unjust deliberate infliction of injury, and failure to exercise reasonable care, must be demonstrated by the injurer to avoid liability. In fact, strict or absolute liability pertains to injuries to others than employees which are caused by the operation of hazardous equipment, such as automobiles. In cases of strict liability the only permissible defenses are causation by irresistible force or gross negligence on the part of the injured. Employee injuries from the use of hazardous equipment are covered only by social insurance and by normal liability based on finding of fault, with the compensation negotiated with the employer and subject to appeal to the pertinent labor-union committee and the courts, if unsatisfactory.

The absence of liability insurance in the Soviet Union intensifies the severity of liability provisions, particularly for persons and financially weak legal entities. The owners or renters of equipment are liable, but may press claims on hired operators. Personal liability, in the absence of crime, is limited to one-third of the injurer's pay.

Compensation to individuals is almost always monetary. It is limited to the value of the actual loss in property, to costs and pay losses incurred net of social insurance benefits, or to a future maintenance equal to past earnings. No added compensation for unavailability of the property, for income lost thereby, for pain, or for disablement not affecting earning capacity appears to be given. Contributory negligence on the part of the injured normally cuts compensation awards in half. Only those payments in excess of social insurance benefits go to the injured, with the remainder returning to the State. Dependents alone may receive compensation in cases of wrongful death.

Finally, despite the strong representations of the Soviet bar, the liability of the government for acts committed by officials is still poorly defined. In particular, no means of compensation for false arrest, illegal imprisonment, and other police abuses has yet been established by law.

Since World War II, the Soviet Union has become a largely urban society, in which retail trade is the source not of tools, raw materials, and specialty goods, but of daily necessities and major luxuries. Improvements in consumer-goods supply as material incentives have also been sought by Soviet leaders, although only to the degree that they did not hamper State military-economic objectives. Moreover, Soviet economic and technological development brought both increases and diversifications in consumer goods, rapidly up to 1958, and more slowly thereafter. Yet Soviet capacity to consume remained limited, because of poverty, especially in rural areas, lack of living and storage space, shortages and high costs of electricity, and high use taxes for mechanical equipment.[199] In addition, Soviet ideologists have frowned, as in the 1961 Party Program, on "private property" psychology. They have espoused "rational" plans over witless public demand, and they have banned private profits from trade as criminal "speculation." These paradoxes have resulted in a strange amalgam of timid experiments in marketing, small survivals of free enterprise, mistreatment of the consumer, and repression of black marketeering described by Zigurds Zile in *Law and the Distribution of Consumer Goods in the Soviet Union.*

Soviet trade today is overwhelmingly in State hands, either directly, or via the nominal cooperatives serving mainly rural areas. The free markets run by urban authorities provide outlets for the sale of produce from rural private plots and the manufactures of licensed handicraftsmen. Individuals may also contract with persons or the State to do odd construction work, alter clothing, or repair goods, but always with the customers' materials so that "speculation" is obviated. Cooperatives also undertake sales on commission, under standard terms, of produce from farmers' private plots. In addition, State Commission stores resell second-hand goods, but always at less-than-new prices.

State stores serving the general public[200] are subordinated to local political authorities, and grouped into networks covering the corresponding areas. The legal entities in trade vary from large single establishments to local chains; vertical integration with wholesalers or service shops is not evident. Central trade organizations, which culminate in the State Committee on Trade of the USSR Council of Ministers, are, among other things, charged with the coordination of inter-regional adjustments in supplies.

State stores, in common with other economic entities, must operate on a funded basis, to yield planned profits; employee bonuses reflect gains in the gross values of sales; and, especially, the State's revenues depend heavily

[199] Article 30 of the decree cited below prescribes graduated rates per horsepower of motor vehicles and motor boats ranging from 25 (old) rubles per horsepower-year in large cities to 10 (old) rubles in workers' settlements; the rates for motorcycles went from 15 to 5 (old) rubles per horsepower-year in corresponding fashion. "On local taxes and levies," Decree of April 10, 1942, [1942] Ved. verkh. sov. S.S.S.R. No. 13, SBORNIK ZAKON. 657.

[200] Closed stores, so-called ORS (*Otdeleniya rabocheskogo snabzheniya*, or Departments of Workers' Supply) account for a substantial part of all retail trade. They are managed by the corresponding industrial or administrative organization.

upon hidden sales taxes averaging 40 per cent of retail prices. For these reasons, sales promotion has developed to include some advertising and marking down of prices for slow-moving goods. Mail order operations have also helped sell surplus goods to distant customers. Credit buying has expanded; in 1961 it comprised 1.5 per cent of all retail sales, with 63 per cent of this total being clothing.[201] Its further growth is hampered by the limited range of goods (usually surpluses) which may be purchased in this way and by harsh restrictions protecting the State. Credit is available only to those local residents certified as having regular incomes. Down payments of at least 20 per cent, employer withholding, restraints upon job changes by debtors, and civil actions or authorizations of compensatory seizures of property guarantee low default rates even though title passes in the first transaction. Rentals have also been introduced for very scarce expensive durables, especially automobiles. Large deposits, indorsements, and special guaranties may all be required. Delays in returning the borrowed object subject the renter to double-time penalties, while damages or losses lead to liabilities of 50 to 450 per cent beyond the State's replacement costs, a device adjusting for the difference between nominal and black-market values.

Soviet laws carry severe penalties for the production of unacceptable and unwanted goods. These and other protections for consumers are enforced by local authorities, supported by the periodic "raids" of public organizations and Party-State Control Commissions. Yet abuses abound. Manufacturers, loath to adjust output to demand, force tie-in sales upon retailers and, ultimately, consumers. Procedures for repairing or replacing defective goods are grossly inadequate. At the same time, consumer choice is restricted by small store sizes,[202] uneven flows of supply, immobile populations, and sharp restrictions on legal private trade. Black marketeering has consequently been most profitable; many large operations integrating cultivation or manufacturing, wholesaling and rapid distribution have been uncovered in recent years. The State has curbed these undertakings by draconic penalties against offenders, but with short-term detriment at least to consumers.

The final essay, *The Soviet Legal Pattern Spreads Abroad*, by John Hazard, develops three theses. The first is that in Soviet eyes the adoption of a communist political system is both facilitated and consolidated by an appropriate pattern of law. For this reason, training in Soviet law is an important part of the indoctrination of foreigners, especially those from

[201] NARODNOYE KHOZYAYSTVO SSSR V 1961 G (NATIONAL ECONOMY OF THE USSR IN 1961) 637 (Moscow 1962).

[202] In 1961 the average number of employees per store was 4.1 for all State and cooperative stores; 5.7 for the former and 2.7 for the latter, separately. *Id.* at 650, 655, 661.

developing nations. The second is that the essential core of this politically productive legislation comprises measures ensuring, simultaneously, the effective control of the Communist Party over governmental electoral and administrative machineries; governmental control over all large-scale economic operations, with a maximum feasible development of State-owned, centrally directed establishments; and universal indoctrination in the ethical supremacy of a socially homogeneous, altruistic, welfare State, the promotion of which justifies all measures expedient to the party. Thirdly, the dissemination of Soviet law to Eastern Europe and the Far East has engendered both tolerated and heretical variations in secondary aspects of the pattern. Significant among the former are the maintenance of subsidiary political parties as spokesmen of special interests and symbols of national consensus, and the legalization of private productive property, without hired labor, in agriculture and handicrafts. The worst heresies are Leninist hyper-orthodoxies. They include Chinese insistence upon leaving revolutionary expediency free of procedural restrictions in criminal law, upon governing disputes between State enterprises by command rather than adjudication, and upon pressing economic equalitarianism, at least experimentally, even to the total abolition of personal property.

SOVIET PROCEDURES IN CIVIL DECISIONS: A CHANGING BALANCE BETWEEN PUBLIC AND CIVIC SYSTEMS OF PUBLIC ORDER

BY DENNIS M. O'CONNOR *

I. Introduction

ALL MAJOR LEGAL SYSTEMS have provided an official forum for adjudication of citizens' disputes, and have maintained public order by the provision of clearly defined formal procedures for dealing with the multivaried conflicts which occur in any complex pattern of social organization, as well as for regulation of such coercion as is authoritatively prohibited.[1] Even totalitarian experiments in social organization which employ legal and extra-legal sanctions in the alternative to achieve policy objectives use defined and orderly procedures of an official legal process to resolve a great variety and number of the disputes between subjects. Despite diverse forms of social and political organization prevalent in the world conventional

* *DENNIS M. O'CONNOR. A.B. 1954, LL.B. 1957, Yale University; Associate Professor of Law, New York University.*

This article is based in part upon interviews and field observations made possible by a research grant from the Center for Russian Language and Area Studies of the University of Illinois, for which grateful appreciation is expressed. The article is adapted from an address delivered by the author at the American Political Science Association Annual Meeting in New York on September 7, 1963.

[1] Civil disputes are those in which restoration of a value is sought, regardless whether the state or its agent is a party in interest. Criteria which have been advanced to distinguish "private" legal relations from the constitutive order of society usually suggest classification according to the type of prescriptive rules which are applicable, the entity issuing them, or their form. Recognized more in the civil law tradition than in the common law such distinction was categorically rejected by Soviet jurists, who refer to Lenin's statement that all law is "public" and hold that governmental and party perspectives do and should pervade any application of law. 29 Lenin, Socheneniya (Works) 419 (Moscow 1928-37). For purposes of comparative study of law in Soviet society one focus has been "legal relations between Soviet citizens." Hazard, Settling Disputes in Soviet Society viii (1960) [hereinafter cited as Hazard]; Hazard & Shapiro, The Soviet Legal System pt. 3 (1962) [hereinafter cited as Hazard & Shapiro]. Another approach is taken by Grzybowski, who discerns that as official "social intervention" and new social conditions prevail "private law has declined as a regulator of basic social functions." Grzybowski, Soviet Legal Institutions ch. 1 (1962) [hereinafter cited as Grzybowski].

institutions of the legal process are easily distinguishable from informal procedures by which individuals and groups resolve disputes which concern local legal relations or the discipline of members of an organization or of the community. Non-official groups and associations may easily be observed to possess a role in various societies, in some relative degree of conformity to general community standards, for making effective decisions enforced by a variety of persuasive and sometimes coercive sanctions.[2] The feature which distinguishes the *civic* order systems of modern societies from their *public* order systems is absence of official governmental prescription as an authority base and of severe value deprivations as a consequence of the non-official decisions. Recently a Soviet jurist has urged greater attention to non-legal "norms" so that the lawmaker, possessed of the necessary knowledge, may select the proper form for legal regulation in order to achieve the maximum effect on social relations. The following is the description given of "social norm-creation":

> "From the emergence of the state social norm-creation became relegated to the sphere of social relations which were beyond the bounds of state regulation. But even in their domain social norm-making relations are not homogeneous and do not pursue a single social course. They may be subdivided into norm-creation: 1) by different classes, 2) by different social groups, delimited both by intra-class and extra-class features: status, professional, territorial, national, etc., and 3) by different non-state organizations. The result of the first two types of norm-creation is moral, customary, ritual, etc. norms, and the third, the charters and provisions of diverse types of organizations, is associational norms. In substance this latter type of norm-creative activity is adjoined to one of the first two and is the consequence either of classes or social groups. But its distinctive characteristic is a certain formalization of the process of elaboration and adoption of legal acts, and in this respect it is possible to observe a resemblance of the norm-creative activity of nonstate organizations with lawmaking by the state."[3]

Recent elaboration of civic forms to supplement or displace the fully official public order institutions in Soviet societies has thus far received little

[2] Legal scholars have devoted little attention to nonofficial decisions. For some examples of traditional practices in China and Russia, see Hu Hsien-chin, The Common Descent Group in China and Its Functions (1948); and Boysman, Sbornik ukazaniy i rasporyazheniy pravitel'stva o pravakh i obyazannostyakh sel'skikh obyvateley (Collection of Legislation and Directives of the Government on the Rights and Duties of Rural Inhabitants) (2 vols. St. Petersburg 1861).

[3] Antonova, *Nekotoryye voprosy teoriyi pravotvorchestva (Some Problems in the Theory of Norm-Creation)*, Pravovedeniye No. 3, pp. 14-15 (1963).

scholarly attention either within or without the Soviet Union. One reason for this is the easy conceptual dichotomy between "legal" and "social" decisions and sanctions. Legal scholars who in their analysis rely upon uncritical use of conventional legal terminology are inadequately equipped to discuss the procedures and effects of decisions taken with a high degree of informality. In the Soviet legal system, as in any other, conventional legal terms have a meaning as understood by jurists within the system and which is primarily suitable for discussion of the *formal* decisions which are made in the official legal process. In contrast, the *informal* decisions which are made by organizations, groups, associations and by individuals acting in other than an official capacity are not regarded as fully incorporated into the prevailing system of authoritative prescription. When examined in context informal decisions made by nonofficials may prove to be in fact dominated by official or semi-official agencies. Or they may in a particular context be self-directed, as when the decision is made independently of official control.[4] In Soviet society the party acts as a semi-official decision-maker, as its decisions are outside the system of official authoritative prescriptions though it possesses a fully protected constitutive role and its policies are controlling and authoritative. Observers of Soviet type societies are interested in whether or not investigation will show that scope is being given to an enlargement of pluralistic choices. Party support of the general revision of decision procedures raises questions as to the weight given autonomous local group and individual action under changing patterns of authority.

Civic autonomy or direction is obviously not determined by law alone, and a distinction between law and regulation is posed by Soviet jurists:

> "In our view it is not proper to identify the realization of law with a broader category—the legal regulation of social relationships. The latter are the forms of influence of the law on social life: publication of norms of law, securing the fulfillment of these prescriptions, i.e. the conduct itself governed by law, and also everything which creates the bases and prerequisites for such conduct and which secures it. The realization of law is that part of legal regulation which amounts to the fulfillment of the demands of legal norms by the activity of the participants in social relationships."[5]

[4] Classification of decisions as formal or informal depending upon the degree of official prescriptive support, with subsidiary classification depending upon the degree of official control, has not hitherto been elaborated but is indispensable in study of the public order systems of those societies in which official governmental decisions have a limited role. This is a further elaboration of the distinction proposed by Professor Harold D. Lasswell in *The Public Interest: Proposing Principles of Content and Procedure*, 5 Nomos 54 (1962).

[5] Pigalkin, *Formy realizatsiyi norm obshchenarodnogo prava (Forms of Realization of the Norms of General Law)*, Sov. gos. i pravo No. 6, p. 26 (1963).

Latent to the question is distinction between the constitutive process viewed as the allocation of effective decision-making authority on the one hand, and as the exercise of authority over activities which are less directly relevant to the power process on the other. Informal resolution of civil disputes may be seen as the allocation of authority for permitted decision functions or as social action regulated into permitted patterns. Thus this part of the civic action program is a convenient one with which to measure current Soviet perspectives of authority and practice.

Soviet official civil procedures as borrowed from European civil procedural forms, adapted to the estimated requirements of Soviet policy and expressed in the Civil Codes of the 1920's and further qualified in practice, were viewed by Soviet jurists for more than a decade as a direct borrowing from "capitalist" law.[6] The adaptations in codified provisions and qualifications by directives and in practice did result in significant differences.[7] However, a non-Soviet scholar was able to draw analogy to "a new building erected of old bricks,"[8] as the principles which in fact governed administration of the legal process merely outweighed similarity in a multitude of details to non-Soviet official procedures. The basic conception of civic order as distinct from the formal legal order was perpetuated in Soviet jurisprudence for several more decades. Experimentation with the civic disposition of certain types of civil disputes during the 1930's was not reflected in changes in civil legislation. Instead it was considered a sui generis mode of social decision-making.[9] During the last decade in Soviet societies, and in the Soviet Union particularly after the 20th Party Congress in 1956, the qualified acceptance of non-Soviet methods for resolving civil disputes in Soviet society, and the dichotomy of official and informal decision-making, has been challenged.[10] Perhaps less dramatic than the parallel trends in criminal law administration, and the emergence of distinctive methods for dealing with antisocial activity, the experimentation with new methods for resolving civil

[6] Civil Procedure (Textbook) (Moscow 1938).

[7] See 1 Gsovski, Soviet Civil Law ch. 23 (1948) [hereinafter cited as Gsovski].

[8] *Id.* at 856.

[9] The informal decisions were not considered either as civil or criminal legal decisions. The most recent Soviet general bibliography on law continues to omit the literature on them, but contains a chapter on "judicial law." Akademiya nauk SSSR—Institut gosudarstva i prava, Literatura po sovetskomy pravu (Academy of Sciences—Institute of State and Law, Literature on Soviet Law) (Moscow 1960).

[10] See notes 206 and 214 *infra* for reference to the practices in Communist China. Ideological considerations which affect Soviet classification of decisions are reflected in such statements as the following: "Law, as the state, will disappear under full communism . . . this disappearance will be expressed on the norms of socialist law developing into unitary rules of communist community life, together with other norms of socialist society, gradually losing the specifically legal character expressed in their sanctions." Leyst, *O prirode i putyakh preobrazovaniya sanktsiy sotsialisticheskogo prava (On the Nature and Paths of Transformation of Sanctions in Socialist Law)*, Sov. gos. i pravo No. 1, pp. 44, 45 (1963).

disputes is no less significant. Two factors have influenced tl
adaptation of methods of civic disposition. The recent leadersh
to render law and other institutions in Soviet society more efi
struments of social change. And the present recodification c ...aw
principles and rules governing methods for resolving disputes has highlighted a demand to fashion truly unique Soviet patterns of decision-making to serve as a model for emulation abroad.[11]

Disputes which in most societies would be justiciable are dealt with in many instances by social organizations or local groups acting in relative conformity to official policies, either with or without formal involvement of officials or civic representatives.[12] An inquiry suitable for comparative study must begin with examination of the expectations which are actually held regarding sanction deprivations with respect to civil disputes in Soviet society. It is then possible to examine the official adjudicatory and informal decision-making practice, and to observe that there are multiple processes of decision governed in substantial degree by official perspectives and incorporated into comprehensive sanctions policies administered by officials, the party, and civic entities. When a given dispute may be dealt with either by informal procedures or by an official adjudication in court the concurrent "jurisdiction" is usually resolved informally; the case may be selected as suitable for exemplary treatment and the relevant supporting action coordinated by officials such as judges or procurators, or by semi-officials such as party secretaries or members, or by nonofficials such as civic representatives. Such reconciliation of parallel but differing decisions and sanctions is roughly analogous to the matters usually dealt with in conflicts of laws or jurisdiction. Finality of outcome may in a given dispute occur in the less formal process of decision. And the conventional exclusivity of the legal process when invoked in a dispute where prescriptions of law are applicable may not be assumed, since practice accords recognition of and regular deferral of authority to certain informal decision-making institutions.[13]

An understanding of the features and significance of these innovations in decision-making procedures, and their impact upon public order and law in Soviet society, may be attained only by examination of the methods by which such decisions are taken in practice. Some stabilization both of procedural practices and of the theories which relate them to law, appears to have been achieved in the Soviet Union. But practice and theory as developed in recent years have been factors in procrastination of new legislation on civil law and procedure, and the current informal decision procedures

[11] *Id.* at 53, 54.

[12] See HAZARD 436. A general reference on administrative and party coordination in Soviet society is FAINSOD, HOW RUSSIA IS RULED (1963).

[13] See text accompanying notes 99-131 *infra*.

must be considered subject to further change and experimentation before viable patterns are successfully integrated into both a general practice and theories of jurisprudence and social action. The Soviet perspective on diminution of the role of law is expressed in such statements as the following:

> "The process of internal transformation of legal regulation reduces itself . . . to the following.
>
> *First,* in the period of accelerated building of communism particular qualities of legal norms are developed, expressing their moral and directly social influence.
>
> . . .
>
> "*Second,* during the transition to communism the participation of the working masses in the execution of law-making and law-applying activities of the socialist state will grow and broaden. Particularly important here is the role of social organizations of the workers, among them such specific social formations as the People's Guards, Comrades' Courts and others.
>
> . . .
>
> "*Third,* the period of accelerated building of communism is characterized by qualitative changes in the very legal form of social regulation (*i.e.* that which relates to the "purely legal" content of the norms of socialist law).
>
> . . .
>
> "In time the accumulated changes in legal regulation will lead to deeper qualitative changes— to the transition from law to a system of norms of communist community life. In its present form Soviet law is not completely prepared for this transition. There is still necessary a definite process of internal development of Soviet law, gradually drawing it nearer the system of norms of communist community life to such a distance that the transition from law to nonlaw (if the respective internal and external conditions permit) will appear possible and necessary." [14]

Were the innovations deemed to relate only to disputes regarding criminal activity they could be considered as an extension or supplementation of the laws regulating such conduct. But the evidence of practice and jurists' commentaries which are available reveal that an underlying assumption of the present program is that not only may criminal and quasi-criminal conduct be regulated by law, but that *all* infractions of legal and social norms, whether "criminal" or "civil," may effectively be sanctioned. Statistical data is generally unavailable, but such information as is available makes it possible to outline briefly the major decision methods and to examine

[14] Alekseyev, *O pererastaniyi sovetskogo prava v sistemu norm kommunisticheskogo obshchezhitiya (On the Development of Soviet Law Into a System of Norms of Communist Community Life)*, Sov. gos. i pravo No. 5, pp. 18, 19-20 (1962).

their relation to sanction policies, to outline significant t official and informal practice, and to make a preliminary the impact of civic involvement and concerted sanctioning upon order.[15]

II. Civil Decisions in Soviet Society

Early Soviet experimentation with virtual elimination of legal institutions of Tsarist Russia was brief. Among the first types of disputes for which judicial activity was revived shortly after the October 1917 revolution were actions brought by peasants for damage to crops caused by stray cattle.[16] Despite some suggestions that the social order which was to be established in the future society should not include governmental institutions for the maintenance of internal public order, it was early resolved in practice that courts were to deal with many types of civil disputes in a manner roughly similar to prerevolutionary practice, despite the fact that formal prescriptions were not officially permitted to be traced to the earlier period.[17] Legislation on civil law and procedure enacted during the period of brief experimentation with limited private entrepreneurial activity in the early 1920's was patterned after codes of the civil law tradition,[18] and such modifications as were introduced to provide for estimated unique Soviet policies of public order did not result in more than a few legislated provisions appearing radically different from their non-Soviet counterparts.[19] Adaptation of some substantive law provisions permitted easy access to official and semiofficial policy determinations in particular cases. The judicial support of civil claims was limited to those situations in which this conformed to officially recognized social purpose,[20] agreements were unenforceable which although not illegal were clearly prejudicial to the state,[21] and there were other similar provisions.[22] Adaptations of civil *procedures* were less apparently significant, but they included emphasis upon the discretion and ex officio powers of the bench and some distinct procedures of review and modification of judgments.[23] The pattern of procedure which was formally legislated was in most features unmistakably similar to European civil law. The character-

[15] The current program thus far has not been the subject of published general studies. It may constitute a revival of the "unresolved contest" between methods of regulation favored by policy-makers and those preferred by lawyers. See Hazard 490.

[16] See Hazard & Shapiro pt. 3, at 72; Hazard ch. 1.

[17] On discontinuity of prerevolutionary prescription and "judicial vacuum," see 1 Gsovski 273-86; also Hazard ch. 1.

[18] See 1 Gsovski 21-24.

[19] See *id.* ch. 9; Hazard chs. 11, 12.

[20] R.S.F.S.R. Civil Code art. 1 (1922) [hereinafter cited Civil Code].

[21] *Id.* art. 30.

[22] See, for example, *id.* art. 5; Hazard ch. 12; 1 Gsovski 344.

[23] 1 Gsovski ch. 23.

,tically Soviet features of the legal system fashioned on the basis of this legislation were broad access to general policy determinations in particular disputes, and relatively flexible availability of alternative procedural forms.[24] Much of the legislative and directive activity during the next decade dealt with political and criminal regulation by decision methods only in a limited manner employing judicial processes of law. Attention to civil disputes was secondary in importance and was focused largely on displacement of the traditional institutions considered to serve as bearers of customary practices sought to be eliminated.[25]

As official policies began to assume functions of comprehensive regulation in an effort to transform Soviet society into an urban industrial model, the conception of social processes as autonomic and amenable only to party direction was replaced by the view that official administrative intervention was necessary to hasten development. While official and semi-official pronouncements were still used to stabilize interpretations of policy, including legal policy, the accompanying programs of industrialization and collectivization were seen to require a multiplicity of legal norms in the form of edicts, decrees, ordinances, regulations, instructions, and decisions for the regulation of social transactions and governmental administration.[26] Requirements of predictability in interpretation and application of norms also increased, and the role of the party was supplemented by increased organization and activity of the revived official prerevolutionary Russian procuracy institutions for verification and control of compliance with official directives.[27] Yet the profusion of legal norms dealing with administrative programs and conduct of citizens posed serious enforcement problems in that the prescribed conduct and social changes often could be fully achieved only at substantial expense in enforcement activities, while on the other hand prescriptions maintained at a limited level of effectiveness would cause respect for institutions of law and government to suffer.[28]

Parallel to the major programs of administrative action designed to promote development of an urban industrial society, there occurred substantial changes in the forms of civil decision-making. Attempts to employ courts to adjudicate the much larger volume and complexity of commercial litigation between state enterprises were unsuccessful and state arbitration boards were established as specialized official tribunals for resolution of practically all disputes between enterprises.[29] Decisions of these tribunals were unlike arbitration decisions, and features such as limited selection of

[24] See HAZARD 463-76; GRZYBOWSKI 66-78.

[25] Compare HAZARD & SHAPIRO pt. 2, 1 GSOVSKI chs. 3 and 4, and GRZYBOWSKI 10-27.

[26] See, *e.g.*, GRZYBOWSKI 177-78.

[27] See HAZARD ch. 7; MORGAN, SOVIET ADMINISTRATIVE LEGALITY (1962).

[28] See HAZARD 463-76.

[29] See HAZARD & SHAPIRO pt. 2, ch. 13; GRZYBOWSKI 85-103.

decision-makers by the claimants and the finality of the proceedings without appeal to courts have caused some commentators to conclude that they are specialized commercial courts.[30] In disputes where state enterprises were not claimants informal decisions were sometimes employed, particularly for cases concerning tenant conduct and nonsupport or nonpayment of alimony, and the infraction was dealt with by comrades' courts or residential or occupational groups. Infractions of labor safety or discipline rules usually were handled in committee or group decisions at the appropriate enterprise level.[31]

These innovations placed emphasis upon corrective rather than compensatory resolution of civil disputes. For the productive sector enterprise disputes were "resolved" in the state arbitration boards, but such extra-dispute consequences as effects of performance on compensation, promotion, and career assumed increased importance. The formal decision sanctions were but one of several significant consequences.[32] The civic innovations as they applied to individual parties to disputes provided decision forms as alternatives to the official adjudicatory jurisdiction of courts and administrative agencies. Yet availability of the new forms was not reflected in comprehensive revision of legislation or directives on civil procedures, though there were formal implementing prescriptions which authorized comrades' court decisions and the civic resolution of certain labor disputes.

Concentration of Soviet administrative priorities on urban and industrial problems resulted in limited effective enforcement of Soviet-type prescriptions in rural agricultural areas. While some major programs were consequential with respect to agriculture, much rural nonproductive activity was left unchanged through Soviet action except insofar as political, collectivization, and planning programs affected the social structure. Civil matters such as equities in land use, dower, inheritance, and many types of personal claims were in fact dealt with by the traditional rural households.[33] Soviet legislation accorded effect to some types of value exchanges executed in accordance with customary traditions, and offered limited protection to the household as a legal person in enforcement of claims against other households or persons. There is reason to believe that an accurate measure of the extent and value consequences of effective decisions of these traditional

[30] See GRZYBOWSKI 85-103. On the Foreign Trade Arbitration Commission similarly established to resolve foreign trade disputes, see Pisar, *Soviet Conflicts of Laws in International Commercial Transactions*, 70 HARV. L. REV. 593, 607-08 (1957).

[31] See GRZYBOWSKI 100-03.

[32] For a conclusion that these decisions serve primarily a liaison function and may be made exclusively in terms of economic policy, see GRZYBOWSKI 97-100. Some of the extradispute consequences are indicated in HAZARD & SHAPIRO pt. 2. On the general role of incentives, see BERLINER, FACTORY AND MANAGER IN THE U.S.S.R. (1957). On criminal responsibility for production and shipment deviations, and for falsification in official and planning records, see the R.S.F.S.R. CRIMINAL CODE arts. 152, 152(1) (1960).

[33] See text accompanying notes 142-49 *infra*.

institutions has not been available to Soviet administrators. However, the policy of acquiescing in continuation of traditional forms of civil decision-making has permitted official administrative effort to be directed to urban and industrial problems considered more urgent.[34]

A perspective on civil transactions in urban areas is similarly not fully reflected in the recorded official litigation. With their recognized social function diminished it has been asserted that such transactions are reduced to "insignificant proportions." [35] Certainly the concentration of property in public ownership has relatively reduced the frequency of citizens' disputes. But it is clear from numerous reported cases that there exists a preference for private barter or sale, executed transfers of wealth, and extrajudicial settlement, often to avoid exposure of civil transactions to official scrutiny.[36] Transfers of interests in land and buildings not infrequently have gone unrecorded, and imaginative and diverse concealment procedures have been occasionally revealed in recent enforcement campaigns directed against illegal economic activity.[37] Periods and areas of concentrated emphasis have been alternated with relaxed enforcement when the given type of activity assumes low priority in administrative policy. Resulting fluctuations in the effectiveness of official prescriptions depending upon policy interpretations and attention to enforcement in administrative programs has been termed "oscillation" by one Soviet judge.[38]

Civil decisions require the allocation of resources for effective administration of decisions. Attention has been directed in Soviet societies to the costs of the legal process in terms of public funds. And the "social self-regulatory" features of civic decisions have been noted.[39] But Soviet jurists

[34] See Shimkin, *Current Characteristics and Problems of the Soviet Rural Population*, in SOVIET AGRICULTURAL AND PEASANT AFFAIRS 79 (Laird ed. 1963): FAINSOD, SMOLENSK UNDER SOVIET RULE ch. 13 (1958).

[35] See GRZYBOWSKI 97.

[36] See, *e.g.*, several of the cases translated in HAZARD & SHAPIRO.

[37] See the *Current Digest of the Soviet Press* for translations of some of these cases.

[38] Izvestiya, Nov. 22, 1961, p. 4; 13 C.D.S.P. No. 47, p. 41 (1961). See also GRZYBOWSKI 215.

[39] Following is a typical Soviet formulation:

> "In connection with the tasks of strengthening the socialist legal order and the perfection of legal norms posed by the Program of the C.P.S.U. the matter of the method of resolution of property and other disputes between citizens and socialist organizations, and the protection of their rights and legally protected interests possesses a particular significance. The correct and quick resolution of legal disputes, and the effective protection of rights and interests of the participants in civil and other legal relations and the prevention of infractions of the law require every possible improvement and perfection of the procedural activity of those organs which by law have the task of resolving legal disputes, and the implemention of measures which have the aim of protection of the violated or disputed right and legally protected interest."

Zeyder, *Predmet i sistema sovetskogo grazhdanskogo protsessual'nogo prava (The Subject and System of Soviet Civil Procedural Law)*, Pravovedeniye No. 3, p. 69 (1962).

are unable to be fully articulate in examining the changes in the legal system which tend to emphasize civic order. "Public participation" is claimed to have an immediate value as constituting a democratization of the legal process.[40] But particular patterns of official and semi-official action remain fully protected, as Soviet jurists do not explicitly interpret their ideal as an effective sharing of power so as to leave open for continuous apprisal the manner in which particular institutions contribute to autonomous civic action. The basic objective of the involvement of lay persons in decisions and of the concerted use of both formal and informal sanctions is to facilitate social change, and in the short run this is apparently held to require sharp reduction in the amount of civil litigation resolved in an official forum. For the longer run the question of permanent displacement of some official adjudicatory functions, or their total elimination for some types of disputes, is left open.[41]

III. Decision Procedures and Comprehensive Sanctions Perspectives

In non-Soviet legal systems the methods of resolving civil disputes upon an alleged infraction of civil prescription include procedures designed primarily for restoration of the *status quo ante* for the injured claimant to the extent feasible, either in kind or through substitute compensation. Only occasionally are sanctions employed for other purposes than restoration, and such "punitive" damages as are available in some types of disputes invariably are conditioned upon especially reprehensible conduct of the defendant. Contempt sanctions of course do not have a primarily compensatory purpose, but they are employed to maintain orderly legal processes or to obtain compliance with a specific judicial dispositive order. Civil infractions are considered in and of themselves to have but limited relevance to public order, and the state or society is not an essential adversary participant in their adjudication although the government provides the official forum and enforcement procedures and the views of society may be reflected in the decision functions of a jury or other trier of fact. Civil claimants are able to control initiation of the official legal processes; they provide the information upon which the decision is to be based, they promote the judicial or other decision through use of complaints and other procedural forms, they suggest the relevant legal prescriptions to be invoked and applied in the decision and present arguments on the consequences of these in the particular dispute, and they have virtually unlimited capacity to terminate official adjudicatory action at any time by indicating their settlement upon terms mutually agreed upon or through withdrawal of

[40] Civic involvement in official functions through approved social organizations is discussed in Luk'yanov & Lazarev, Sovetskoye gosudarstvo i obshchestvennyye organizatsiyi (The Soviet State and Social Organizations) (Moscow 1962).

[41] *Cf.* notes 14 and 53.

the affirmative claims. The official decision-maker does not have facilities for continuous supervision of the execution of the decision and its consequences, nor is this considered a proper function except for the instances where specific or injunctive relief is available and where the claimants themselves generally have the option of bringing information on noncompliance to the decision-maker and using formal procedures to obtain an additional, supplementary decision.[42]

In Soviet societies the distinction between "public" and "private" interest has been drawn with predominant weight given the former, so that the conventional bases of the public-private distinction in civil law jurisprudence and common law countries is virtually absent. The qualifications on borrowed procedural forms for official civil decisions have for many years reflected several unique procedures. The procuracy could intervene in any civil matter at any stage of the dispute, either prior to or subsequent to formal judicial action, as well as during the process, and appear to represent the interests of society and the state.[43] Once the procuracy had intervened in the dispute, or judicial action had been invoked, the claimants had limited control of the disposition of their claims and were not free to settle the dispute independent of procuracy and judicial supervision.[44] And the broad functions of review possessed by the procuracy, together with the collaboration of public and social organizations, permitted continuous post-decision supervision of the consequences of official action.[45] The Western model of civil procedures was profoundly altered in effect by the Soviet prescriptive limitations on settlement and the availability of the party, the procuracy and informal agencies to perform functions supplementary to official adjudicatory action. Yet in many disputes these supplements were not employed, and official adjudication in fact occurred much as it would in a civil law system.[46]

When informal decision-making was established in civic groups or organizations and comrades' courts during the 1930's it was conceived that this amounted to "social" action which, although coordinated by government or party or civic representatives and applying sanctions for other purposes than

[42] The relationship of particular civil procedures to the objective of restoration of values through voluntary use of official decision procedures has received scant scholarly attention.

[43] CODE OF CIVIL PROCEDURE arts. 2, 2a; BASIC PRINCIPLES OF CIVIL PROCEDURE OF THE SOVIET UNION AND THE UNION REPUBLICS art. 14 (1962) [hereinafter cited as BASIC PRINCIPLES OF CIVIL PROCEDURES], translated in 7 LAW IN EASTERN EUROPE 299 (Szirmai ed. 1963). See 1 GSOVSKI 855-66; and HAZARD 235-36, 406.

[44] *Ibid.* See also the several enactments on the procuracy, and CIVIL CODE art. 6.

[45] See MORGAN, *op. cit. supra* note 27; also enactment on the procuracy, art. 23 and ch. II (1955).

[46] See several of the cases translated in HAZARD & SHAPIRO pt. 3. For a statement of the Soviet perspective on professional counsel in civil cases, see ZAYTSEV & POLTORAK, THE SOVIET BAR ch. 3 (Moscow 1959).

restoration of the loss of an injured claimant, did not require comprehensive revision of the formal rules governing civil procedures.[47] The contemporary revival and intensification of these procedures, coupled with exposure of Soviet jurists to domestic and foreign appraisal in shaping a new and novel jurisprudence in the post-Stalin era has made necessary consistent and comprehensive legislated prescription and practice. There is evidence that some Soviet jurists have not enthusiastically supported some of the more novel features of the current innovations.[48] And the Criminal Code provision that only a court may apply punishment,[49] and as well the provision in the Basic Principles of Civil Procedure that trials in civil cases may be conducted only by courts,[50] appear not irrelevant to the informal procedural innovations. The uniform response of Soviet officials and jurists has been that coordinated informal decisions and sanctions do not violate such provisions.

Discussions of the nature of the informal decisions at first continued the earlier position that they constituted "social" and not "legal" decisions.[51] The simplicity of this view was soon affected by emphasis upon revision of sanction policies following the 21st Party Congress.[52] Persuasive sanctions were held to increase relatively to coercive ones with the transfer of some governmental functions to civic organizations and lay committees, and a parallel was seen in the resolution of civil and criminal disputes. Some suggestions that this amounted to early symptoms of "withering" of the state, with imminent advent of communistic social organization remained

[47] See note 9 *supra;* and GSOVSKI ch. 23.

[48] For an expression of the view that nonofficial organizations and groups when applying official prescriptions and supporting them with effective sanctions are invoking state authority and exercising governmental functions, see ALEKSANDROV, PRIMENENIYE NORM SOVETSKOGO SOTSIALISTICHESKOGO PRAVA (APPLICATION OF NORMS OF SOVIET SOCIALIST LAW) 9, 13 (1958); and for a conclusion that this view is "not completely justified," see Gorshenev, *O roli obshchestvennykh organizatsiy v sovetskom pravotvorchestvye (On the Role of Social Organizations in Soviet Law-Creation)*, Sov. gos. i pravo No. 8, p. 115 (1962). See also STROGOVICH, KURS SOVETSKOGO UGOLOVNOGO PROTSESSA (COURSE IN SOVIET CRIMINAL PROCEDURE) pt. 1 (1958).

[49] BASIC PRINCIPLES OF CRIMINAL PROCEDURE OF THE USSR AND THE CONSTITUENT REPUBLICS, art. 3 (1958), translated in 7 HIGHLIGHTS OF CURRENT LEGISLATION AND ACTIVITIES IN MID-EUROPE 69, 71 (1959); R.S.F.S.R. Criminal Code, art. 3 (1960).

[50] Article 7, which is interpreted to apply only to forensic disposition of disputes concerning other than production activities.

[51] See *ibid.* Also the editorial, *Bol'she vnimaniya razbiratel'stvy grazhdanskikh del (Greater Attention to the Trial of Civil Cases)*, Sov. yus. No. 2, p. 1 (1958). The duality is expressed in article 6 of the BASIC PRINCIPLES OF CIVIL LAW (1958):

> "The protection of civil rights is effectuated in the established procedure by a court, by arbitration panels or by a court of arbitration . . . .
>
> "The defense of civil rights is also exercised by Comrades' Courts, professional unions and other social organizations in cases and according to procedure established by USSR and Union Republic laws . . . ."

[52] See, *e.g.*, Fedkin, *Resheniya XXI c''yezda KPSS—osnova dal'neyshego sovershenstvovaniya sovetskogo prava (Decisions of the 21st Congress of the CPSU—The Foundation for Further Perfection of Soviet Law)*, Sov. gos. i pravo, No. 5, p. 12 (1959).

officially unaccepted, and the question of whether the role of law was "expanding or contracting" as a result of employment of civic institutions for decision-making was not given a direct answer.[53] The generic term adopted to describe the application of informal sanctions was "measures of social influence," and jurists were assigned the task of relating this term to the theories and prescriptions of law. During the last several years both the practice and theoretical justifications which have been offered have undergone significant modification.[54]

The dominant theme has been the expansion of sanctions objectives from the traditionally accepted purpose of *restoration* in civil disputes to include with respect to some types of civil disputes the full range of sanctioning goals: deterrence, restoration, rehabilitation, prevention, and reconstruction.[55] "Social injury" is expressed as the foundation for informal party and official decision-making,[56] and prevention of such injury by use of "social influence" sanctions includes compensation to the injured claimant as but one of the desired sanction consequences. In the formulation of a Soviet writer:

1. Measures of social coercion displace coercion applied by organs of the state;
2. In the legal process persuasive practices increase and coercive practices are reduced;

[53] Discussion of "contraction of the sphere of law," not without some irony, has stimulated Soviet writings on jurisprudence. See Keyzerov, *O vzaimodeystviyi prava i nravstvennosti v kommunisticheskom stroitel'stve (On the Interaction of Law and Morality in Communist Construction)*, Pravovedeniye No. 4, pp. 3, 11-13 (1962). The more pragmatically directed writing has reserved conclusion in the manner of the following statement on criminal law:

> "Is the domain of criminal and criminal procedural law expanding or contracting in connection with the transfer of a given category of criminal cases for decision by workers' collectives or Comrades' Courts? It would seem that this question may not arise, as the basic paths of the transfer from legal regulation to social which we have considered lead to an obvious conclusion concerning the natural contraction of the sphere of law with the development of social self-regulation."

Galkin, *O sochetaniyi sudebnogo prinuzhdeniya i obshchestvennogo vozdeystviya vbor'be s pravonarusheniyami (On the Combination of Judicial Action and Social Influence in the Struggle Against Law-Breakers)*, Sov. gos. i pravo No. 10, pp. 126, 133 (1961).

[54] An early perspective on the current program is stated in an editorial, *Sovetskaya obshchestvennost'—reshayushchaya sila v bor'be za ukrepleniye sotsialisticheskogo pravoporyadka (The Soviet Community—The Decisive Force in the Struggle for Strengthening the Socialist Legal Order)*, Sov. gos. i pravo No. 10, p. 16 (1959); *cf.* criticism of "subjective and unilateral approaches to the matter" by Mironov, *Glavnoye—profilaktika, vospitatel'naya rabota (The Most Important Things Are Prophylaxis and Educational Work)*, Izvestiya, June 2, 1963, p. 2.

[55] This categorization of the goals of sanctioning is elaborated in McDougal, Lasswell & Vlasic, Law and Public Order in Space 404-06 (1963). A more comprehensive statement is made in Arens & Lasswell, *Toward a General Theory of Sanctions*, 49 Iowa L. Rev. 233 (1964).

[56] See the quotation and interpretation of Khrushchev in Mironov, *supra* note 54.

3. Some matters formerly dealt with by coercive methods are treated by simple persuasion.[57]

This emphasis upon the sanction consequences of decisions extended to the *methods* for resolving civil disputes, with suggestions that the purpose of restoration of injured private rights be displaced by attention to a stimulus-response relationship. Substantive law provisions necessitated some procedural changes. With fault as a general basis, civil liability was to be reduced in some cases and also increased in others—those where fault is found but no material injury to a particular claimant has yet occurred. And neither the limiting nor extensive consequences of fault as a general prescriptive measure for civil infractions were neglected in the discussions.[58] Implications for procedures were clear. In particular cases increased attention was to be given to procedural forms which facilitated "correction" of the defendant and "education" of others in society in contrast to traditional procedures designed for compensatory relief of claimants. Procedures as well as substantive provisions were held to be relevant to stimulation of law-abiding conduct and the deterrence of similar violations, and the proponents of this emphasis upon the full sanction potential of civil decisions have stated the objectives of civil procedure to be:

1. Satisfaction of the injured party, whose material rights and interests were violated by the conduct of another person, through placing an obligation on the violator to restore the damaged right or to make proper compensation;
2. Influence on the person who through his illegal conduct violates the material-rights and interests of another person; and
3. Education of others in society to habits of compliance with civil law norms.[59]

The sanctions policies in civil decisions in the Soviet Union thus presently range from prevention and deterrence of particular infractions, and compensation and rehabilitation where infractions occur, to especial emphasis upon the "corrective" or reconstruction effects upon both individuals and local groups. This fusion of the sanctions policies designed to influence

[57] See Shargorodskiy, *O roli i sootnosheniyi prinuzhdeniya i ubezhdeniya v prave v period razvyornutogo stroitel'stva kommunizma (Concerning the Role and Relationships of Coercion and Persuasion in Law in the Period of Accelerated Building of Communism)*, Sov. yus. No. 14, pp. 3-4 (1961).

[58] Argument is made that even the forms by which an obligation to compensate is placed upon the infractor "must serve as a stimulus to law-abiding conduct and assist in eliminating the violation of rights and interests of other persons."

Khalfina, *Vospitatel'naya rol' grazhdansko-pravovoy otvetstvennosti v period razvyernutogo stroitel'stva kommunizma (The Educational Role of Civil Legal Liability in the Period of Accelerated Building of Communism)*, Sov. gos. i pravo No. 6, p. 73 (1963).

[59] Shargorodskiy, *supra* note 57.

conduct with the more conventional sanctions objective of restoration has rendered distinction between criminal and civil decisions difficult in some cases.[60] Development of suitable and distinctive civil procedures would be difficult enough if satisfaction of both general civic and individual claimant interests was sought in a single judicial proceeding. But the availability of informal as well as semi-official decision institutions adds another dimension of complexity. The civic action program requires considerable supervisory effort and it has been proposed that a new special entity be created "to organize, coordinate and control the activity of the police, procuracy, courts and community action," but this implicit challenge to adequacy of the party has been rejected:

> "It is necessary to activate, upgrade and perfect the work of those autonomous organizations already existing and in one form or another now participating in the struggle against criminality and violations of socialist legality. As far as coordination and control over the activity of administrative organs and social organizations is concerned this should be done by local Party organs, which are the organizers in the struggle for strict and undeviating observance of Soviet laws and which direct all their efforts towards the communist education of workers."[61]

That the sanctions applied under the heading of "social influence" may be severe is attested by reported instances of persons requesting criminal prosecution in lieu of application of sanctions by a social organization or local group. Presently Soviet writers are uniform in recognizing that "social influence" measures are in fact coercive in many situations. Less specific are the discussions of the methods by which the relevant informal decisions are initiated and the necessary procedural steps coordinated. Consequently distinction between official and informal action is often difficult. For example, without official invocation of either the Criminal Code provision[62] or the civil law provisions[63] governing nonsupport or nonpayment of alimony, a residential or occupational group may decide to apply certain sanctions either with or without intervention of procuracy, party, or social organization representatives. The sanctions applied in a particular case may in

[60] See, *e.g.*, the cases illustrated at notes 137 and 151 *infra*. Much of the administrative activity intended to produce behavior in better conformity to the official economic perspectives is directed to prohibition of the use of property to obtain "unearned income." "This means that in the struggle against private-property tendencies, court agencies can now draw not only from the norms of criminal and administrative law but from the norms of civil law as well." Bratus', *Pravo, sovremennost' i chelovek (Law, Modern Times and the Individual)*, Izvestiya, Jan. 20, 1962, p. 3.

[61] Editorial, *Obshchestvennost'—reshayushchaya v bor'be s pravonarusheniyami (The Community—The Decisive Force in the Struggle Against Violations of Law)*, Sov. yus. No. 24, p. 1 (1963).

[62] R.S.F.S.R. CRIMINAL CODE art. 158 (1956).

[63] R.S.F.S.R. CODE OF LAWS ON MARRIAGE, THE FAMILY AND GUARDIANSHIP arts. 14-16, 42 (1926 as amended).

fact be coercive, but in Soviet conception they are not criminal law sanctions "although they possess certain aspects of state character."[64] The action of the civic collective is similarly held not to be a civil legal decision, even though elements of a decision process and a high degree of expectation of effective enforcement of legal or social norms is often present.[65]

Discussions of replacement of rules of law by principles of morality and social conduct, through establishing and making effective a "moral code" and "rules of life in a socialist community," [66] have produced an effect on the theoretical justifications offered for informal decisions. Since civic groups in all societies are considered to possess competence to deal with membership problems, the decisions of groups applying "social influence" measures to members have been classified as "moral" as well as "social" by some Soviet jurists in order to distinguish them from official legal action. But distinction between sanctions applied on the basis of membership in the group and sanctions applied on the basis of delegated authority from the state is only vaguely elaborated.[67] And in most of the relevant decisions "membership"

[64] Gorshenev, *Vozrastaniye roli obshchestvennykh organizatsiy i kollektivov trudyashchikhsya v primeneniyi norm sovetskogo prava na sovremennom etape (Growth of the Role of Social Organizations and Collectives of Workers in the Application of Norms of Soviet Law in the Present Stage)*, Pravovedeniye No. 1, p. 3 (1963). See note 137 *infra* for illustration of cases where informal sanctions were applied although criminal and civil provisions were inapplicable.

[65] See note 50 *supra*. See Golunskiy, *K voprosu o ponyamiyi pravovoy normy v teoriyi sotsialisticheskogo prava (On the Question of the Conception of Legal Norms in the Theory of Socialist Law)*, Sov. gos. i pravo No. 4, p. 21 (1961).

[66] See GRZYBOWSKI 122. Soviet writers have had difficulty distinguishing the "moral code" (incorporated in the Program of the CPSU 1961) and "rules of life" (ordinances, administrative decisions, and interpretations of unlegislated norms by officials and the party) from law. See Keyzerov, *supra* note 53, at 3-4, where legal norms are distinguished from moral norms solely by the "comparatively greater concretization of their demands, prohibitions and permissions." Compare contemporary Western discussions which emphasize as the function of law the protection of third persons: HART, LAW, LIBERTY AND MORALITY (1962); ROSTOW, THE SOVEREIGN PREROGATIVE: THE SUPREME COURT AND THE QUEST FOR LAW ch. 2 (1962).

[67] See, *e.g.*, Igitov, *O prirode mer vozdeystva, primenyayemykh obshchestvennost'yu v oblasti okhrany obschchestvennogo poryadka (On the Nature of Measures of Influence Applied by the Community in the Area of Preservation of Public Order)*, Sov. gos. i pravo No. 11, pp. 109, 111 (1963):

> "Measures of influence applied by a social organization with respect to its members are distinct from measures applied by it in execution of powers delegated by the state. . . .
>
> "The internal organizational activity of social organizations is founded fully on moral bases. This condition also characterizes the nature of powers delegated by the social unit within its organization. On the other hand, the delegated powers transferred by the state to workers' collectives must not be fully identified with powers determined by the intra-union competence of these collectives since in such cases there are preserved individual elements of state authority."

Sometimes technical distinctions are drawn to support the difference. See, *e.g.*, Gorshnev, *supra* note 64, who considers inappropriate the designation of union inspectors to impose "administrative fines" but deems acceptable their designation to impose equivalent "monetary fines."

in the group is only tangentially involved; only for a small number of the civil disputes is there an expectation of expulsion from the residence or occupational group.[68]

On the other hand, where more conventional legal concepts are relevant to the problem, actions of social organizations or groups with respect to nonmembers are somewhat more clearly perceived in Soviet discourse. It is held that external civic group application of sanctions may occur only if: 1) there has been a delegation by the state to the organization of appropriate authority with respect to nonmember citizens or other organs, and 2) the requisite action of the civic group may be secured legitimately under state authority.[69]

The four types of "social influence" categorized in a recent statement may be summarized in order to suggest the present Soviet specification of sanction perspectives:

The first type consists of sanctions applied "externally," as well as for group membership matters, and which are considered to have merely a "moral" effect. These include "a comradely warning, a social condemnation, a social warning, obliging the violator to apologize publicly, a warning with establishment of a period of good behavior, and the obliging of attendance at a lecture on the rules of the road during after work hours."[70]

The second type of sanction may be applied in connection with compensation for a particular property or material injury. These include fines imposed by comrades' courts or committees on juvenile affairs, and the "obliging" of a violator to compensate for an injury. The issuance of fines by social or administrative organizations is said to be a "state" sanction for which specific authority is needed. But the designation of an obligation to compensate is deemed "moral," as is a policeman's warning.[71]

The third type consists of petitions made by social organizations to official organizations for transfer of a person to employment at lesser pay, reduction in rank, dismissal, eviction from housing accommodations, deprivation of parental rights, and the imposition of responsibility for administrative infractions. These petitions are considered to have a particular "educational" effect, and are reported often to be effective in influencing conduct prior to the recommended official governmental action.[72]

The fourth type consists of public order sanctions such as the transfer of a violator to the parole or custody of a group, and the exile of "parasitic elements" upon sentence of the group. Both of these measures involve direct

[68] See, *e.g.*, note 163 *infra*.
[69] Igitov, *supra* note 67, at 111.
[70] *Id.* at 112.
[71] *Ibid.*
[72] *Ibid.*

supporting action by judicial or administrative agencies, and the view appears increasingly held that they are not simply "social-moral" sanctions.[73]

While the second of these categories of "influence" appears at first glance most appropriate to civil decisions, in practice the broad sanctioning objectives leave none of the measures irrelevant in perceived extreme cases of infraction of some civil law prescriptions. Those prescriptions which are relevant to "correction" of the violator and members of the group are the ones which most frequently in practice result in deferral of official authority, either formally or tacitly, to informal decisions and sanctions. Once it became clear to Soviet jurists that the emergence of comprehensive sanctions perspectives was not entirely, but only partially, to displace judicial and other official decisions problems such as the adaptation of official adjudicatory practice to these new objectives in civil decisions, regularization of the appropriate civic group action and providing some procedures for distributing the competence of official and nonforensic decisions became paramount.[74]

IV. Trends in Official Adjudicatory Practice

Objectives of exercising "social influence" on persons whose conduct violates civil law provisions, and of social reinforcement of approved behavior and attitudes towards norms in groups, have produced significant trends in the methods by which disputes are resolved in the formal adjudicatory institutions—courts, state arbitration boards, and enterprise administration and union tribunals. Some of the innovations have been legislated, some have been reported in practice which is at variance with prescribed procedures, and some have been merely discussed and tested in pilot experimentation. The trends differ sharply in form depending upon whether production activities are involved. Discussion of innovations of procedure in contract disputes between state enterprises, and actual innovations in the procedures for litigation of personal injury disputes are obviously relevant to economic theories as well as to the "corrective" effect of the procedures upon individual and social conduct. The substantive law trend of placing upon the enterprise liability for those infractions which could have been avoided through proper administrative practice is reflected also in procedures designed to bring to the attention of the enterprise administration the facts and consequences of an infraction for which it is responsible. Disputes which concern nonproduction activities are still often adjudicated in the courts, but present trends include the involvement of the relevant organization or local group in the judicial process at various stages of the proceeding. Significant trends in the emergence of a practice of judicial deferral

[73] *Id.* at 113.

[74] See text accompanying notes 205—18 *infra*.

of decision functions and of authority to informal decisions, and judicial approval of concerted use of informal sanctions, may be observed.

A. Disputes Regarding Production Activities

1. Where Expectations Interests Are Involved

The major Soviet gloss on borrowed substantive civil law prescriptions adapted from civil law countries for contractual liability between state enterprises has been the added requirement of fault.[75] This is related to the various extra-dispute consequences which have for many years reinforced the effect of an award for damages in the appropriate case and have been assigned major roles in the encouragement of conformity to the planned expectational interests of enterprises. In cases of defective performance the social interest in production was deemed more important than substitute compensation, hence a comprehensive "corrective" decision policy was suitable. However, evidence which was offered to prove absence of fault in litigation between bilateral contract parties often proved difficult to evaluate, and the rapid and efficient trial of these cases was virtually impossible if precise appraisal of the degree of fault of the defendant was required.[76] Consequently two basic and mutually inconsistent types of damage remedies were developed.

One damage remedy, roughly analogous to ordinary contract damages as supplemented by an added requirement of fault, was based upon provisions of the Civil Code as supplemented by planning decrees of the 1930's and by the practice of the state arbitration boards. This system of damages did not work well with respect to losses which were transmitted along the vertical line of production—those caused as a result of defective performance by an enterprise early in a chain of several. Official plans projected requirements designed to tax fully the capacity of economic enterprises, with the result that a seriously defective performance in most instances was reflected in serious deviations by successive economic units. Agreements between state enterprises, to the extent that they were enforceable, were shaped in terms of quantity, quality, and time of delivery without regard to many contingencies usually reserved against in societies where volition of autonomous civic entities is the basis for contractual obligation. This combination of the civil law premise of volitional contract obligation with Soviet administrative requirements of decreed obligation necessitated either the elaboration of conditions of excuse, such as absence of "fault," or procedural innovations,

[75] See GRZYBOWSKI 85-110; HAZARD & SHAPIRO pt. 2, ch. 13; 1 GSOVSKI ch. 12.

[76] See, *e.g.*, Novitskiy, *Pravovyye voprosy tovarooborota i planovogo raspredeleniya* produktsiyi *(Legal Problems in the Exchange of Goods and the Planned Distribution of Production)*, in PROBLEMY SOVETSKOGO GRAZHDANSKOGO PRAVA V SUDEBNOY PRAKTIKE I V ARBITRAZHE (PROBLEMS OF SOVIET CIVIL LAW IN JUDICIAL PRACTICE AND ARBITRATION) 281, 331 (Moscow 1960).

such as suits between remote contract parties or joinder of privy and remote parties in a single proceeding. Realistic distribution of the economic loss was impossible using conventional substantive and procedural forms, as an intervening enterprise conducting its affairs without "fault" would insulate a defaulting enterprise from a successor sustaining actual damages. Consistent application of absence of "fault" as an excuse for defective performance of contract resulted, through a series of bilateral disputes, in the damages (to the extent not diminished through relative absence of fault or lesser damage in intervening parties) being transmitted through regressive litigation until the loss rested at the enterprise whose supplier was able successfully to prove absence of fault.[77] An alternative would permit an enterprise not at fault to serve as a conduit to transmit liability to a supplier who should bear the loss.[78] This system of general damage remedies placed a premium upon the preparation and adducing of exculpatory evidence, and complaints regarding the burden and consequences of this method have been voiced.[79]

A second system of damage remedies was fashioned in response to these problems. At the time of making contracts enterprises stipulated damage specifications relating to defective quantity, quality, or time of performance, and when this was done "fault" was not to constitute an additional requirement for liability. Regressive suits between enterprises sustaining actual damages and their suppliers, or the relevant transportation enterprises, would direct the loss back along the chain of production and distribution depending exclusively upon the formal stipulations of damage, usually in standard form contracts.[80] The stated loss was simply reflected to any predecessor unit linked in a chain of contracts with stipulated damage provisions, and which had breached the formal provisions of its agreement (assuming the contract was not subsequently rendered unenforceable in whole or part by later inconsistent planned obligations). Damages were measured according to advance and standardized predictions of the amount of loss caused

[77] Lack of managerial care is the usual measure of fault. See Grossfeld, *Money Sanctions for Breach of Contract in a Communist Economy*, 72 YALE L.J. 1326 (1963).

[78] See GRZYBOWSKI 85.

[79] See Novitskiy, *supra* note 76, at 358-70; and 2 SOREK LET SOVETSKOGO PRAVA (40 YEARS OF SOVIET LAW) 254-61 (Shargorodskiy ed. Moscow 1957).

[80] Grossfeld, *supra* note 77, demonstrates the relevance of monetary damages for production deviations in a Soviet society, and, at 1340-42, indicates some features of this supplementary system of "compensatory" remedies. In 1960 a summary report of a state arbitration board decision excusing a supplier from payment of the stipulated "fine" since he had not received the necessary raw materials, was shortly followed by an announcement of the board that this "was not a general rule of Soviet law." Sots zak. No. 10, p. 87 and *id.* No. 12, p. 77 (1960). The necessity of maintaining the stipulated damage provisions free from the fault rules is argued by Fleyshits, *Obshchiye nachala otvetstvennosti po osnovam grazhdanskogo zakonodatel'stva Soyuza SSR i Soyuznykh Respublik (General Bases of Liability According to the Basic Principles of Civil Law of the USSR and the Union Republic)*, Sov. gos. i pravo No. 3, pp. 34-43 (1962).

by a particular type of breach, and this damage remedy was crude, and often did not result in realistic compensation for economic loss.[81]

Discussions on whether fault should be a general ground for civil liability are critical to the remedial resolution of contract disputes between production enterprises. The Basic Principles of Civil Law as adopted in 1961 did not contain the provision which was in its proposed draft that an exception to fault as a basis for civil liability is made where defective contract performance is caused by a supplier's breach.[82] The provisions governing penalties and stipulated damages will in effect be reversed if the pattern of the enacted Basic Principles survives, since enterprises will in no case be liable if they are successful in proving absence of managerial fault. The conflicting demands of theoretical consistency on the one hand and realistic distribution of the economic loss on the other have provoked considerable discussion by Soviet jurists.[83] The proposals which appear to offer the best method of reconciling the problem are those which provide for new departures in procedure, permitting joinder of parties in state arbitration board proceedings.[84] This would permit claimants to trace actual damages through all predecessor economic units with the relevant intermediaries before the tribunal. Then the total actual damages would be allocated among the various parties according to their particular degree of fault. Such an approach undoubtedly would involve great complexity in adjudication, but it at least meets the demand for theoretical consistency with prescribed grounds for liability. The alternatives which are discussed constitute variations of the present system of penalties and stipulated damages.[85] It is likely that until a fully adequate mechanism for distributing the loss caused by breach of contracts between production enterprises is developed the present emphasis upon extradispute consequences will continue to be utilized to influence the conduct of factory managers and officials for the foreseeable future, since these serve as rough alternatives for accurate adjudication where declared losses reflect somewhat arbitrarily assigned values and prices. Yet the experimentation on a pilot scale with the proposal of a Kievan economist to evaluate performance of factory management according to profitability of the enterprise as measured by realistic assignment of values suggests that a trend toward enterprise liability may be possible in Soviet law, with an enterprise bearing responsibility in monetary terms for all losses it (and its management) have occasioned.[86] Such a trend may not

[81] See Khalfina, *supra* note 58, and sources cited therein.

[82] Article 42 of the Draft, published in Sov. gos. i pravo No. 7, p. 3 (1960).

[83] See the Fleyshits and Khalfina articles, *supra* notes 58 and 80 and sources cited therein.

[84] Khalfina, *supra* note 58, at 79-82.

[85] Fleyshits, *supra* note 80.

[86] See Liberman, *Plan, pribyl', premiya (The Plan, Profit and Bonuses)*, Pravda, Sept. 9, 1962, p. 3.

be predicted at this early date, but were it to occur methods of decision-making for enterprise disputes may be modified to permit more accurate computation of damages resulting from defective performance of contracts.[87]

2. Where Deprivations Are Involved

Production activities which have caused personal injury, and situations in which injury is likely to be caused, are placed under increased administrative scrutiny in enterprises as a result of a 1961 decree covering industrial accidents,[88] and of the developing practice of judicial issuance of special rulings concerning infractions of safety rules. Special rulings may be issued by courts regardless of whether injury has been caused or the relevant offender is before the court.[89] Damage to production-related property has for some time been dealt with by administrative decisions,[90] as well as by a number of criminal law provisions.[91] Prior to the 1961 decree in industrial accident cases an injured person was permitted to claim in court under provisions of the Civil Code for the amount of loss in earning capacity not reimbursed by monthly payments from the social insurance agency or other benefit fund, where social insurance benefits were not prescribed as the exclusive form of compensation. The interrelation of administrative social insurance and judicial remedies provided for preemptive priority of the administrative remedies for most production-related injuries where social insurance provisions were applicable.[92] Determinations of the social insurance agency were based upon formal rules which resulted in relatively little involvement of managerial personnel. The proof of injury to an employee covered by social insurance and medical evaluation of the degree of permanent injury required little active interest of the enterprise. Accident prevention was sought to be effected through the availability of criminal and administrative sanctions for infractions of the labor safety rules,

[87] See Andreyev, *Plany i prava predpriyatiy (Plans and Rights of Enterprises)*, Pravda, July 23, 1962, p. 2. *Cf*. Grzybowski 93-97.

[88] Decree of the Presidium of the Supreme Soviet of the USSR, Concerning the Resolution of Cases of Compensation by Enterprises, Institutions and Organizations for Injury Suffered by Workers and Employees Where the Damage or Other Injury to Health Is Connected With Their Work, Oct. 2, 1961, [1961] Ved. verkh. sov. S.S.S.R. No. 41. The prior Soviet position is discussed in Hazard, *Personal Injury and Soviet Socialism*, 65 Harv. L. Rev. 545 (1952).

[89] See text accompanying notes 138-41 *infra*.

[90] Decree on the Material Liability of Workers for Materials, Merchandise and the Property of the Enterprise or Institution Placed in their Use, Svod zakonov No. 40, 1932, Grazhdanskoye pravo Soyuza SSR i Soyuznykh Respublik (Civil Law of the USSR and the Union Republics) 154 (Moscow 1957).

[91] R.S.F.S.R. Criminal Code arts. 99, 100 (1960).

[92] See 1 Gsovski 543; Hazard, *supra* note 88.

and in most instances supervision by the superior administrative agency and the procuracy were the main techniques for directing official attention.[93]

A major trend in resolution of disputes concerning production injuries is represented by the 1961 decree which deals with "work-related injuries occurring as a result of fault of the enterprise." Such injuries are adjudicated and compensation determined in the first instance by the enterprise administration. If the employee is not satisfied with this decision he may appeal the dispute to a shop or factory union committee for further decision, following which either the employee or enterprise management are permitted to take the dispute to a court. The accumulated prescriptions for fault as a basis for liability in judicial determinations have been incorporated in the regulations issued to govern application of the fault requirement of this decree.[94] The Basic Principles of civil substantive and procedural law enacted several months subsequent to the decree make no provision regarding its application and offer no rules to govern questions of its exclusivity or priority. Exclusive application of the decree, which provides only for compensation of injuries occurring as a result of fault of the enterprise, would decrease liability for situations of extrahazardous activity where the Civil Code and Basic Principles provide for absolute liability. Priority of the procedures specified by the decree precludes recourse to the courts by injured employees covered by the decree until both the enterprise administration and union committee have acted. The reports and appraisals of experience under the decree thus far indicate that decisions by these tribunals are seldom taken to courts. And comments uniformly indicate that the initial enterprise-administration decision is relatively seldom taken by the injured employee to the union committee for a redetermination.[95] Official policy is reported to encourage adequate and final resolution of the claim in the first administrative decision. And it appears that informal sanctions employed on both the enterprise administration and injured employee are designed to discourage inadequate administrative resolution in the first instance and likewise unnecessary employee continuation of the dispute. Formal evidence of injury and fault of the type usually presented in Soviet courts must be

[93] Current concerted use of mass propaganda as a supplement contrasts with earlier employment of administrative and criminal sanctions. Knip, *Posle prigovora (After the Sentence)*, Trud, Apr. 19, 1963; YABLOKOV, METODIKA RASSLEDOVANIYA UGOLOVNYKH DEL O NARYSHENIYAKH PRAVIL TEKHNIKI BEZOPASNOSTI (METHOD OF INVESTIGATION OF CRIMINAL CASES ON VIOLATION OF THE RULES OF SAFETY PROCEDURES) (Moscow 1958).

[94] Regulations of the State Committee of the Council of Ministers for Matters of Labor and Wages and the All-Union Central Union of Labor Unions, Dec. 22, 1961. See Sov. yus. No. 2, p. 15 (1962).

[95] See Savitskaya, *Otvetstvennost' gosudarstvennykh uchrezhdenniyi za vred, prichinynnyy deystviyami ikh dolzhnostnykh lits (The Obligation of State Institutions for the Causing of Injury by Their Employees)*, Sov. gos. i pravo No. 8, p. 48 (1962); Maleyin, *Pravovoye regulirovaniye obyazatel'stv po vozmeshcheniyu vreda (Legal Regulation of Obligations To Compensate for Injury)*, Sov. gos. i pravo No. 10, p. 68 (1962).

presented to the enterprise administration, which presumably also has other knowledge and information relating to the accident.[96] The injured employee and the management are thus acting in a situation where the direct and vicarious primary parties in interest in the dispute are expected to resolve it through use of adjudicatory forms.

The general pattern of this innovation in procedure—casting disputants in the role of decision-makers—is intended to produce an educational effect on the persons best able to prevent recurrence of the accident through requiring a full hearing of the facts of the dispute, and issuance of a reasoned opinion on these facts and the relevant legal rules, which decision later may be challenged in court.[97] Reported applications of the new procedure do not reveal the extent to which negotiation by the parties preceeds "adjudication" by the enterprise or union. And there has been experimentation in the composition of the committee tribunals convened by enterprise directors as well as variations in procedures of preparation and receiving of evidence.[98] In instances of official judicial decision upon "appeal" substantial weight is given to the earlier enterprise and union decisions. Certainly an element of impartiality is not present at the earlier decision levels, and to the degree that such decisions displace or render unnecessary judicial determination it may be said that nonadjudicatory methods of decision-making assume increased importance in the resolution of personal injury disputes, and that the procedures actually employed are designed to further other sanctions objectives as well as the conventional one of restoration.

[96] See Lopukhin & Maksimov, *Kak my organizovali rassmotreniye zayavleniy o vozmeshcheniyi ushcherba (How We Have Been Organizing the Hearing of Cases for Compensation of Injury)*, Sov. yus. No. 18, p. 22 (1962); and letters by Usov and Soloveychik respectively, under heading *Praktika razzmotreniya zayavlemiy o vozmeshcheniyi ushcherba (Experience in Hearing Complaints for Compensation for Injury)*, Sov. yus. No. 6, p. 23 (1963).

[97] See Soloveychik, *supra* note 96. For the contrary conclusion that the 1961 decree "suggests that the deterrent value of tort law is losing its paramount nature in Soviet minds," see HAZARD & SHAPIRO pt. 3, at 76.

[98] For three variants in procedures for the enterprise decision see:

a) Lopukhin & Maksimov, *supra* note 96, who relate the experience of the Dinamo factory, where the safety department assumes charge of preparing the case, consults with the factory lawyers and other persons, and holds a hearing. The factory director must approve an award before it becomes effective;

b) Usov, *supra* note 96, who relates the practice of the Lenin factory, where the legal bureau prepares the materials of the case and issues its opinion on the responsibility of the enterprise for approval of the factory director; and

c) Soloveychik, *supra* note 96, who recounts the method used at the Dzerzhinskiy factory, where a committee was formed composed of the chief engineer, the assistant director in charge of safety procedures, the head of the department of labor and wages, and the legal consultant. A procedure was also established whereby the factory lawyer prepares the case and drafts the opinion after the hearing, at which time the entire record of the case is transferred to the accounting office if there is no "appeal."

B. Disputes Regarding Other Than Production Activities

Disputes which are not directly production-related have been subject to quite different procedural trends than contract and tort disputes in which a state enterprise is a party. Judicial practice has permitted involvement of the party and civic groups at various stages of the official proceeding. There is also judicial deferral of competence to civic decisions in a relevant organization or group, and judicial insistence on party settlement of the dispute or reduction of its scope. Finally, there is a tendency towards judicial approval of the concerted use of informal sanctions to support official decisions.

1. Trends in the Judicial Process

Involvement of local groups in the judicial proceeding may occur at various stages. While adjudicatory decisions invoking official public authority remain the outcome of the decision process, the consultation and participation of local groups for purposes of initiating, promoting, and invoking judicial action qualifies the usual remoteness of official sanctions from the relations of the litigants with their colleagues or neighbors. Through the involvement of fellow-workers and neighbors the views of persons who have a substantial connection with the claimant's social activities are obtained, and conversely the successful involvement of such small groups is expected to result in reinforcement of approved behavior patterns in society.[99]

a. Survey of local opinion prior to promoting judicial action. Opinion of the relevant residential or occupational group, both on the facts of the dispute and on the character and general conduct of the litigants, is sometimes sought for the purpose of obtaining information on local attitudes prior to the judicial trial of first instance, and sometimes prior to appellate review.[100] The usual instance is when the procuracy has intervened in the civil dispute because of its significance to local law enforcement or its po-

[99] See, *e.g.*, *Povyshat' vospitatel'nuyu rol' suda (Raise the Educational Role of the Court)*, Sov. yus. No. 11, p. 57 (1959).

[100] See Murav'yeva, Nikitinskiy & Chechiva, Uchastiye obshchestvennosti v rassmotreniyi sudami grazhdanskikh del (Participation of the Communy in Judicial Trials of Civil Cases 15-23 (1963). A useful source on practices of civic involvement in judicial decisions is by a procurator of the Department of Audit of Judicial Decisions in Civil Cases of the R.S.F.S.R. procuracy: Kichatov, *Formy privlecheniya obshchestvennosti k uchastiyu v razresheniyi grazhdansko-pravovykh sporov i v preduprezhdeniyi grazhdanskikh pravonarusheniy (Forms of Involvement of the Community in Participation and Decision of Civil Law Disputes and in the Prevention of Civil Law Infractions* [hereinafter cited as *Kichatov*], Sov. gos. i pravo No. 12, pp. 76-85 (1961). A more conventional perspective is given in LOGINOV, PREDVARITEL'NAYA PODGOTOVKA GRAZHDANSKIKH DEL K SLUSHANIYU V SUDE (PRELIMINARY PREPARATION OF CIVIL CASES FOR HEARING) (Moscow 1960).

tential as an exemplary case.[101] The immediate purpose of the polling of opinion often is to provide information on whether the group itself or a comrades' court which it has constituted would be a suitable forum for direct resolution of the dispute without invocation of judicial action. But it is reported that often the procedure is employed to ascertain attitudes on a judicial trial in order to guide procuracy action at the appellate level.[102] In most instances the subject matter of the dispute is directly concerned with conduct, such as tenant eviction, nonsupport or nonpayment of alimony, and the like. Where the judicial decision was issued in a conditional form, for example the judicial stay of administrative eviction conditioned on future tenant conformity to housing regulations, information on subsequent conduct is necessary for verification of compliance with the decision. Often the officially recognized representatives of the group inform the court or procuracy on compliance or the necessity to revise the sanction specified in the decision. The survey and use of local opinion by the procuracy in the promotion of official action is considered to be governed by formal rules which admit of considerable flexibility in practice, and specific rules have not been promulgated to govern this procedure.[103]

b. Representative participation. Sometimes officially recognized representatives of local groups participate in judicial trials conducted at the official place of business of the court. Presently this procedural innovation is discouraged and direct on-site judicial trials conducted at the litigants' place of employment or residence are preferred.[104] Representative participation by collectives is still practiced, however, and the procedural status of the representatives, which vicariously involves their organization or group, presents a perplexing problem for Soviet jurists. Interest of the group in the usual

[101] Kichatov states that many procurators and people's judges invoke "discussions" at the relevant local group as a preliminary procedure. In order to retain judicial control "until the final resolution of the dispute" a procurator invariably is present and often "lectures at the meeting." *Kichatov* 83-84. For a more conventional view, compare Salingin, *Some Proposals for Improving Pre-Trial Preparation of Civil Cases,* Sov. yus. No. 9, p. 39 (1953).

[102] Kichatov gives as an example the case of a petition by a dismissed worker for reinstatement. At the group meeting a number of fellow workers "spoke on the possibility of correction of N. in the collective" and requested the enterprise management to reinstate him. It is reported that the management, "taking community opinion into account," reinstated N. *Kichatov* 83-84.

[103] Kichatov states that article 2 of the Civil Procedure Code, which simply authorizes procuracy participation in civil disputes, serves as the prescriptive basis for this practice. *Ibid.*

[104] *Kichatov* 78-81. The Civil Procedure Code, in article 16(b), permits participation of authorized union representatives in cases concerning members. Kichatov notes that law does not specifically provide for other types of representative participation, but observes that "practice indicates that any type of civil case may be heard with participation of representatives of social organizations and worker's collectives." *Id.* at 80. See also Edelman, Shakaryan & Volozhanin, *The Community in Civil Procedure,* Sov. yus. No. 1, p. 18 (1960).

sense of the term is not a requirement, since the continuing conduct of the litigants rather than material interest in the outcome of the civil decision is what is considered relevant.[105] Clearly such representatives do not fit the typical pattern of a party to the civil dispute. Nor do they appear as witnesses by the prevailing Soviet view, since they offer opinion as well as testimony of facts, and also perform functions of advocacy. However, in judicial practice courts are reported regularly to advise such representatives of a duty to testify fully, and of the penalties for perjurious testimony. A novel status such as that of an amicus curiae with capacity to inform the court not only on legal issues but primarily on matters of fact and opinions in the local group has been suggested.[106] Not infrequently appearing before courts in civil matters are recognized representatives of such organizations as committees on apartment affairs of housing administrations, women's councils, pensioners councils, and other specialized organizations.[107] Their opinions and comments are deemed not formally to bind the court, but rather to be facts which are considered along with other evidence and arguments in the case. Invariably cases in which there is representative participation are those in which conduct reform can be expected, and many are cases of judicial stay of an administrative sanction. Usually representative participation follows thorough investigation of the circumstances of the case by the relevant group or organization and the participating representatives recommend to the court a decision which is adopted.[108] Often the desirability of representative participation is weighed by the procuracy and court, and the general nature of the outcome is coordinated prior to a judicial hearing commemorating a decision which conditions a sanction on successful future conformity of the offender to the officially approved pattern of conduct.[109]

[105] The participation of third persons without independent claims in conventional Soviet civil decisions may be compared. See RING, VOPROSY GRAZHDANSKOGO PROTSESSA V PRAKTIKE VERKHOVNOGO SUDA SSSR (PROBLEMS OF CIVIL PROCEDURE IN THE PRACTICE OF THE SUPREME COURT OF THE USSR) 68-78 (Moscow 1957).

[106] Article 36 of the BASIC PRINCIPLES OF CIVIL PROCEDURE (1961) provides that representatives of organizations and groups may be permitted to participate for the purpose of placing their "opinions" before the court. This provision and articles 80(g) and 172 of the CODE OF CIVIL PROCEDURE (1923) have been used to authorize participation on the basis of civic interest. See Faustov, *Uchastiye obshchestvennosti v rassmotreniyi grazhdanskikh del (Participation of the Community in the Trial of Civil Cases)*, Sov. yus. No. 13, p. 16 (1963).

[107] See *Kichatov;* Faustov, *supra* note 106; and *Privlekat' obshchestvennost' k passsmotreniyu grazhdanskikh del (Involve the Community in the Examination of Civil Cases)*, Sov. yus. No. 5, p. 53 (1960).

[108] See *Kichatov* 81; and note 128 *infra* for an example of party participation in which a letter from the local party secretary averring resolution of the dispute with consent of the parties served as the basis for terminating the judicial proceeding.

[109] The Basic Principles provision, *supra* note 106, has been criticized for insufficient specificity. The draft Civil Procedure Code provides that representative participants may acquaint themselves and cross examine, and to "present their views and opinions on all matters arising in the course of the judicial trial." See *K itogam obsuzhdeniya*

c. Judicial survey of fact and local opinion. Removal of the bench to the physical locus and social site of the dispute is reported to be relatively common, particularly in accident cases. During trials the proceedings may be suspended while there is a visitation of the site of the events of the dispute, or a survey of opinion in the relevant local group. It is also reported that in many cases this permits resolution of the dispute or settlement by the parties without the court reconvening and issuing a formal decision.[110] A mediative role by the judicial bench in such cases is suggested but not discussed in Soviet commentaries. A variant of visitation is the transfer of the record of the case for discusion in the relevant local group with a request that the court be notified of the conclusion of the group. Polling of opinion regarding the evidence of the case is often done prior to trial, and it may even be used as a preliminary procedure by the procuracy before a complaint is filed. Often the judge or procurator is present, and such consultations frequently commemorate an agreement by the defendant to reform his conduct. Cases are also temporarily transferred for a subsidiary decision of a group or a comrades' court to be prepared and reported to the court. Those often selected for such procedures include disputes on eviction, cases on paternal rights and removal of children from home, nonsupport of spouse or children, and improper behavior. Neither civil legislation nor the comrades' court enactments specifically provide who may request such a temporary transfer. The procedural practice is a result of broad adaptation of existing civil procedure provisions.[111] While consent of both complainants is required for comrades' court jurisdiction for purposes of compensatory disposition in minor civil matters, the temporary judicial transfer to a local group, or comrades' court is not so limited.[112] If compensatory relief is not required in the particular case and it is judicially determined that informal decision is appropriate, the consent of the claimants is not required and the procedure may be invoked directly by the court or procuracy. The civil complainant though notified of the decision to transfer may not be heard to object.[113]

d. Trials in circuit at local groups. Where considered appropriate for sanctions purposes judicial trials are conducted at the defendant's place of residence or work with the relevant group of neighbors or colleagues assembled under conditions calculated to "correct" the defendant as well as the group. As a rule a procurator is reported to be present at such trials to assist in "exposing the civil violation," and participation in the process by

proyekta Grazhdanskogo protsessual'nogo kodeksa RSFSR. (A Summary of the Discussion of the Draft Civil Procedure Code of the R.S.F.S.R.), Sov. yus. No. 2, pp. 13, 14 (1963).

[110] See *Kichatov* 82.

[111] See *Privlekat' obshchestvennost' k rassmotreniyu grazhdanskikh del (Involve the Community in Examination of Civil Cases)*, Sov. yus. No. 5, p. 53 (1960).

[112] *Kichatov* 82-84.

[113] *Ibid.*

group representatives and members as spectators is encouraged in order to assist in such exposure and the civic condemnation of the legal infraction.[114] Many of the trials conducted in this manner are tenant evictions, which are heard at the housing unit with participation of neighbors. If the offender expresses repentance and promises to reform his conduct the outcome frequently is merely the issuance of a warning or a conditional sanction.[115] Under Soviet housing conditions, with limited tenant selection and mobility, housing disputes formerly crowded the civil calendars of courts. At present nearly all housing disputes regarding tenant conduct are resolved locally with neighbor participation, either in circuit judicial trials or in residence group or comrades' court decisions. Nonsupport, nonpayment of alimony, and property, debt and tort actions between citizens, also are not infrequently heard in judicial trials at the offender's place of work with the participation of fellow workers.[116] And where the offender is identifiable as an "idler" concerted action by several official agencies is often arranged so as to create a climate of intolerance towards his conduct within the relevant local group. Yet Soviet commentary offers little discussion of the requisite procedures of coordination and planning by the court, civic representatives, the party and the procuracy.[117]

e. Spectator participation. Although neither the Civil Procedure Code nor the Basic Principles provide for spectator participation in judicial trials, persons present are regularly given permission to speak in conduct-related cases.[118] Observers have commented on the informality of Soviet trials, and have noted that occasionally a spectator interjection has been heard without critical judicial comment.[119] Trials on local circuit are expected regularly to

[114] This is "one of the most widespread forms of involvement of the community" according to Kichatov. *Id.* at 73.

[115] Kichatov gives as an illustration a case on eviction on the ground of incompatible joint apartment tenancy in which on local circuit trial neighbors of the parties "assisted the court in examining the circumstances of the case and in establishing the incorrect conduct of S." The court issued him a "strict warning," and it is reported there were no further complaints against S. *Id.* at 79.

Kichatov's example of a labor dispute suitable for local circuit trial is that of an employee dismissed because of a foreman's grudge. Fellow workers assisted in establishing the facts and, following the advice of the deputy procurator present at the trial, the court reinstated the employee and issued a special ruling on the foreman's conduct. See text accompanying note 138 *infra*.

[116] See Bel'skiy, *Delovyye suvazi ukreplyayutsya (Operating Ties Are Strengthened)*, Sov. yus. No. 3, p. 18 (1964), which deals with the coordination of state control, the courts, the procuracy, and the police.

[117] For a discussion of some problems in organizing local circuit trials in criminal cases, see Baskov, *Pravil'no organizovyvat' vyyezdnyye sessiyi sudov (Correctly Organize Judicial Circuit Sessions)*, Sov. yus. No. 2, p. 4 (1963).

[118] See Murav'yva, *et al., supra* note 100, and *Kichatov* 79-80.

[119] See the report of an American sociologist on the spectator role in a criminal case: Azrael, *Murder Trial in Moscow*, Atlantic Monthly, May 1962, pp. 63, 68. See also the case illustrated note 137 *infra*.

involve active participation of some if not most of those present as spectators. Such participation is not limited to comment on questions of fact on which the spectator has personal knowledge, nor to comment on the character of the defendant. It extends to fact statements conventionally classifiable as hearsay in the common law and to nonexpert opinions on the best methods for producing reformed conduct.[120] Spectators' formal status in the proceeding has not yet been established, and comments on judicial practice reveal that in some instances persons present have been heard as representatives of the local group. But this is discouraged, as only officially recognized representatives of a group are considered to have the capacity to present its opinions.[121] Spectator status as witnesses is also considered inappropriate, since their comments are expected to extend beyond the factual circumstances immediately involved in the dispute. Nonetheless, prevailing judicial practice is to advise those present of the penalties for false testimony as to matters of fact.[122] The participation of spectators in local circuit trials combines condemnatory and testimonial features, and an element of "incrimination" through association or cooperation is often also present. Conventional categories of participation such as interested claimant, prosecutor or complaining witness, witness, codefendant or advocate are inadequate to describe their role, since elements of any or several of these roles may be present in a particular case depending upon the complex of circumstances and the procedures actually employed in the particular trial for regulating participation.[123]

f. Continuous supervision of the outcome of the decision. Decisions which concern defendant's conduct, and also property division, boundary problems, distribution of land and property use, and a variety of other civil matters often require some supervision of the execution of the decision. Official court agents are supplemented, and sometimes displaced, by lay volunteers, by authorized local group representatives, and not infrequently by the lay judges who have issued the decision in the case together with the professional judge.[124] These lay judges under present venue practice are likely to be citizens from the locale of the parties, and may even be members of the same residence or occupational group. Such lay judges have been appointed to examine and report compliance with the decision, and occa-

[120] See authorities cited in note 107 *supra*. Kichatov concludes that although existing procedure provisions do not offer "any specific guidance," courts legitimately may permit persons present to "speak on the substance of the dispute being resolved by the court." *Kichatov* 79-80.

[121] *Ibid.*

[122] See *Kichatov* 80.

[123] Discussions on the Draft Civil Procedure Code fail to reveal support for incorporation of this novel category of participation. See note 115 *supra*.

[124] See *Kichatov* 85.

sionally to take an active part in its execution.[125] This practice constitutes a deprofessionalization of the enforcement component of judicial decisions, and also offers a supplementary channel for continuous judicial supervision over the effects of the decision. In cases where the decision is issued in the form of a conditional sanction this social, geographic, and sometimes professional, proximity of the supervisory arm of the court appears likely to render the decision more effective. To the extent that the parties to the civil dispute do not have control over invocation and application of sanctions where compensation is not the exlusive objective, some person or agency must be charged with responsibility for reopening the case if revision of the formal decision or imposition of the conditioned sanction is necessary. The procuracy is sometimes employed, but presumably more serious matters regularly involve its attention. Lay judges and civic representatives are assigned either active or passive supervisory roles rather frequently in present practice.[126]

2. Judicial Emphasis Upon Extrajudicial Settlement

In contrast to the express provisions of the Civil Code, which require judicial regulation of the settlement or withdrawal of claims by the parties once judicial procedure has been initiated,[127] the policies of encouraging the involvement of civic groups in judicial decisions and direct informal decisions require restriction of the adjudicatory functions of the court. The supervisory component of the legal process is exercised only in part by courts when party and civic representatives, and local groups render decisions which sanction conduct. An example is the following report:

When Mrs. Kalashnikov filed a complaint against her husband in the Ribinskiy City People's Court requesting support funds for their two children the judge sent a letter to the Chairman of the factory shop committee of which the husband was a member, and a copy to a representative of the shop in which the wife worked stating the following:

> "The Ribinskiy City People's Court is sending you the complaint of K. A. Kalashnikov (who works in shop no. 13) in which she requests support and maintenance for her two children from her husband K. P. Kalashnikov who works in the main mechanical department.
>
> "Since the Kalashnikovs have two children and the family is breaking up, and they both work in the same enterprise, I consider this matter suitable to be discussed at a meeting of the shop committee in an effort

[125] *Ibid.*

[126] Kichatov indicates that lay judges in Voronezh Province sometimes singly hear and resolve claims about the execution of judgments. *Ibid.* See also Valeyeva, *Uchastiye obshchestvennosti v stadiyi ispolneniya sudebnykh resheniy (Participation of the Community at the Stage of Execution of Judicial Decisions)*, Sov. yus. No. 2, p. 42 (1960).

[127] CODE OF CIVIL PROCEDURE art. 2 (1923).

to preserve the family, and for you to take measures to resolve the family dispute. Return the enclosed material to me together with the decision of the shop committee."

The secretary of the Party Bureau of shop no. 16 later informed the court that "the matter has been heard in a joint meeting of shop committees 16 and 13 with the parties present, and it also has been heard in the Party Bureaus of the main mechanical department and shop no. 16 . . . . Kalashnikov promised to change his conduct and his wife consented to withdraw the nonsupport claim. Kalashnikov was warned by the Party Bureau of the strict Party responsibility for unnormal and incorrect personal conduct and attitudes towards the family. The decision was issued with the consent of both parties."

The court terminated the case on receipt of the party secretary's letter.[128]

Provisions of the Basic Principles offer general standards to govern judicial limitation, requiring that if preliminary settlement procedures are not complied with or a decision of a comrades' court has been issued within the limits of its competence a court may not accept a complaint or must terminate its action.[129] Since group involvement and informal decisions are coordinated by judicial, procuracy, civic or party representatives the conformity of extrajudicial settlement to official policy and prescriptions may be expected with some regularity. When it appears the conduct of civil disputants will conform to the approved pattern and the conclusion of an official decision becomes unnecessary the judicial action is terminated, either with or without issuance of a formal judgment.[130]

Civil parties are encouraged to present to the court a minimum divergence in claims and to propose an agreed solution which the court will accept.[131] There is meager specification of the types of disputes which may be resolved extrajudicially and there has been until recently some uncertainty of the procedures for review of a comrades' court decision.[132] While the

[128] Faustov, *Uchastiye obshchestvennosti v rassmotreniyi grazhdanskikh del (Participation of the Community in the Trial of Civil Cases)*, Sov. yus. No. 13, pp. 16-17 (1963).

[129] THE BASIC PRINCIPLES OF CIVIL PROCEDURE arts. 31 and 41 (1961).

[130] See *Kichatov* 82.

[131] The Basic Principles of Civil Procedure of 1961 provides in articles 41(2) that failure to utilize an established nonforensic preliminary settlement procedure may constitute grounds for terminating the judicial proceeding.

[132] THE PRACTICAL GUIDE FOR COMRADES' COURTS 73 (1961) states: "Decisions of Comrades' Courts are executed voluntarily. The violator is obliged to fulfill his promise, and the obligation he has assumed, which are consolidated in the decision." The 1963 revision and the comrades' court statute provide that for cases of nonfulfillment of a decision within the stated time the record is reviewed by a single professional judge who in appropriate cases employs the enforcement powers of the official court. See [1963] Ved. verkh. sov. R.S.F.S.R. No. 43, pp. 843-46, translated in 15 C.D.S.P. No. 47, pp. 9, 10 (1963).

self-regulated judicial limitation is analogous to forum non conveniens rules in non-Soviet countries, the result of the judicial action leaves the dispute usually to be resolved by nonadjudicatory as well as by non-official means. Dissatisfaction has been expressed with the evolution of a practice of judicial self-restraint, even when comparatively specific provisions govern the decision of the civic group.[133] The problems in evolving useful procedural standards are due in some measure to selectivity. Only conduct-related disputes and not all civil cases are effected, and specific coordination of civic action by procuracy or professional legal personnel is effected mainly for selected exemplary cases within this group. Difficulties with decisions made by persons without legal training and who have social if not material interests in the dispute sometimes require resumption of the judicial process even after informal decisions have been made in exemplary cases of the appropriate type.[134] The practice of judicial deferral to informal decisions, and the promotion of party settlement in civil cases is not without significant practical consequences. It is reported that in one district in Leningrad at present only 10 per cent of the civil complaints which are filed remain unsettled or unresolved and go to trial.[135] This practice of judicial deferral to informal decisions appears to have been influenced by experimentation with such measures and the prevention of civil disputes in Communist China. But the practice in the Soviet union has not been explicitly related to diffusion of the forms in the other Soviet societies.[136]

3. Concerted Use of Informal Sanctions in Conjunction With Forensic Decisions

Judicial support of concerted use of informal sanctions is a feature of present Soviet practice. Different from the "show trial," in which the judicial process is exposed to mass observation through attendance and the use of communications media so as to utilize an exemplary effect for deterrence purposes, the concerted use of informal sanctions involves judicial approval

[133] See Nedbaylo & Bersheda, *Primeneniye pravovykh norm kollektivami i samodeyatel'nymi organizatsiyami sovetskikh grazhdan (Application of Legal Norms by Collectives and Autonomous Organizations of Soviet Citizens)*, Sov. gos. i pravo No. 5, pp. 30-38 (1961). A 1960 ruling of the Plenum of the Supreme Court of the USSR required the administrative authorities of collective farms first to designate a defendant in property damage suits rather than request procuracy or police assistance in selecting the person to be sued. A judge subsequently complained that the farm administrators sometimes indifferently designated defendants, and has recommended greater judicial supervision. Tikhov, *A kto-zhe otvechik? (But Who's the Defendant?)*, Sov. yus. No. 4, p. 25 (1963). See also Shepelev, *V posleduyushchey vashey rabote sleduyet soblyudat' . . . . (Next Time Take Care in Your Work)*, Sov. yus. No. 18, p. 32 (1963).

[134] See *Kichatov* 78-80.

[135] See Sov. yus. No. 22, p. 30 (1963).

[136] See notes 206, 214 *infra*.

of sanctions applied to defendants or nonparties and which are not prescribed officially and are not within conventional powers of the court. Such sanctions as are applied in Soviet practice include various "social influence" sanctions when they are judicially recommended or are approved in subsequent judicial action. The following report illustrates the practice as employed in an alimony case where the defendant was not liable on the grounds of criminal or civil law provisions, apparently because there was no registered marriage:

> "The hall was filled with anger. The spectators disrupted the normal conduct of the hearing and made the judge nervous. The courtroom itself was putting Volkov on trial, deriding him when he lied, acted indignant or slandered Rita. Although the judge in carrying out his duty tried to sift the facts, only the facts, without emotion in order to weigh them with a dispassionate hand on the scales of justice, the courtroom suddenly became a public trial of the scoundrel who had deceived a girl and had betrayed his own son. Volkov turned from "respondent" to "defendant." What was on trial was a terrible human vice—meanness.
>
> "Meanness cannot be forgiven. Many people had come to expose it and to defend Rita's honor and the future of little Yuri. They came from the hotel where Rita lived, from the hospital where she worked, from the cafeteria where she ate. Fatima Bzhasso, secretary of the city Y.C.L. committee, also came to support Rita. The young defense lawyer Babichev dropped urgent cases and gladly counselled Rita without a fee, doing everything in his power to obtain success. The Procurator Strelnikova saw in the case more than the simple decision of a question 'Should Volkov pay or not?'—and with her speech she helped impart social significance to the case.
>
> "The Maykop City Court resolved against the complaint of Citizenness Mitenijece. The judge did not yield to his emotions. Sifting the facts he found it impossible to match them with the relevant article of the law. The legal provision was clear enough, and the decision of the court came in conflict with social morality. An amazing case! But jurists assert that it isn't such a rare case. The article on alimony is too vague and probably should be revised. The decision of the court states: 'The court strongly condemns defendant Volkov from a moral standpoint, and from the standpoint of his unworthy behavior as a Y.C.L. member.' But the decision itself is in favor of Volkov.
>
> "But is it in his favor? The court excused him of any obligation to assist his son. But Volkov lost the case. He left the courtroom a convicted man and bore his great shame on stooped shoulders."[137]

Exemplary cases are also communicated by various media to audiences of laymen and jurists. But the main focus in current trends is upon discussion in the form of a "hearing" in the relevant social organizations and local groups.

[137] Pochivalov, *Tvoy gorod (Your City)* Pravda, Dec. 19, 1963, p. 6.

In appropriate cases where trials are not conducted at local group meetings trial courts often dispatch a copy of the official opinion to the defendant's residence or occupation group with a recommendation that his conduct be discussed at a meeting.[138] Special rulings also are intended to produce "corrective" consequences beyond the formal sanctions competence of the court. One recent ruling in a trial of a student for theft was directed to the school administration and criticized "poor organization of cultural education work in the school dormitory." [139] Even in cases where the infraction is merely technical and no material injury has been caused to the claimant or another person special rulings may be issued. This may be done even when the person who has violated a civil prescription is not a party before the court, usually in industrial accident cases where a collateral infraction of the labor safety rules was discovered during the course of a personal injury trial.[140] Use of such rulings extends the sanction consequences of judicial action to matters for which the court does not have competence to issue compensatory sanctions, and for which the conventional judicial enforcement functions would be inadequate.[141]

V. Semi-Official and Informal Decision Trends

Decisions taken by other than the official adjudicatory institutions most directly involve reciprocal features of civic participation and official regulation. Legal prescription is applied in decisions in which official policies and small group action influence the conduct of a violator with the objective of producing social reinforcement of approved attitudes towards norms. Systematic survey of the current innovations must include examination of civic group decision-making both in traditional culture groups and in the Soviet model for group civic action, the specialized local group comrades' courts which in some degree mirror procedures of the legal

[138] See *Kichatov* 79.

[139] *From the Practice of the People's Court of the Petrograd District of Leningrad*, Sov. yus. No. 23, p. 29 (1963).

[140] See *Kichatov* 84. It has been suggested that special rulings, issued in accordance with article 38 of the Basic Principles of Civil Procedure (1961), be used to commemorate "noble deeds" as well as to sanction "shortcomings." Volkov, *Opredeleniye chastnoye, interes obshchiy (The Ruling Is Special, The Interest Is General)*, Izvestiya, July 26, 1963, p. 3.

[141] Difficulties have been reported with enforcement of the rulings:

> "But how does the court control the enforcement of its rulings? This is not an idle question. Most often copies of the rulings are kept by consultants, sometimes by senior secretaries. After sending the ruling to an organization, the court waits a month. If there is no answer, it sends a reminder. Then it waits again.
>
> "This system must be changed: Judges and the people's assessors themselves must keep track of the implementation of their rulings. After all, no judge will write 'for the archives' on a case folder until the sentence is executed. This is what should be done with rulings: Keep them under your control until they are carried out."

Volkov, *supra* note 140, at p. 3. See Murav'yeva, *et al.*, *supra* note 100.

process, the supplementary employment of propaganda of law norms and exemplary cases, and the concerted use of informal sanctions for the purpose of prevention of particular civil disputes.

A. Local Group Decision-Making

1. Traditional Culture Institutions

Dichotomy of urban and rural institutions long prevalent in Russian and Soviet societies continues to be represented in divergent methods for resolving civil disputes.[142] Official policy priorities, geographic and economic remoteness, cultural differences and class distinctions sometimes promoted through actions of local party and government officials have been major factors in perpetuating rural differences.[143] Discussions of the imperfect extension of the Soviet legal system to regulate rural nonproductive activity are usually cast in terms of problems of effectiveness of the Model Collective Farm Charter.[144] Even absent adequate statistical information, the disputes concerning ownership, division, and equities in property, land use, and other civil matters for which traditional customary laws were applied are seen to be resolved in many instances without recourse to official adjudicatory institutions by the rural population. While the number of rural households has been reduced and the number of persons living within households has decreased even more sharply, the traditional institution remains viable while functioning under adverse social and political conditions. Recognition of its viability is found in occasional recommendations of Soviet jurists, for example in the suggestion that the right to use land plots be recorded in the household name rather than in the name of an individual as a member of a collective farm in order to render land records more realistic.[145]

Continuance of the rural household may be attributed to threatened loss in production and morale, and the institution retains substantial protection in official legal prescription, enjoying capacity as a legal person for

[142] For a historical summary of the function of the traditional Russian household in civil matters, see Shinn, *The Law of the Russian Peasant Household*, 20 SLAVIC REVIEW 601 (1961). For the Soviet perspective of the role of the civic action program in effecting rural social change, see Kolomiyets, *Sovety i obshchestvennost' v kul'turnom stroitel'stve na sele (The Soviets and the Community in Cultural Construction in the Village)*, Sov. gos. i pravo No. 4, p. 109 (1962).

[143] See Shimkin, *Current Characteristics and Problems of the Soviet Rural Population*, in SOVIET AGRICULTURE AND PEASANT AFFAIRS (Laird ed. 1963).

[144] See, *e.g.*, Sedugin & Shirshikov, *Nekotoryye voprosy sudebnoy praktiki po grazhdanskim kolkhoznym delam (Certain Questions on Judicial Practice in Civil Collective Farm Cases)*, Sov. gos. i pravo No. 7, p. 115 (1959); Levchenko, *Vnytrikolkhoznyy obshchestvennyy kontrol' (Intra-Collective Farm Social Control)*, Pravovedeniye No. 1, p. 78 (1963).

[145] See Pozubenko, *Selu—novyy zhilishchnyy zakon (A New Housing Law for the Village)*, Sov. yus. No. 16, p. 9 (1963).

the purpose of property ownership, access to courts and administrative agencies for the protection of ownership and possessory rights, and possessing substantial authority in devolution and division of community property.[146] The two main limitations imposed in Soviet legislation are that earned income of members becomes community property only in the event of a specific transfer by a member to the group, and that property disputes, including division of community property, are governed by official legislation.[147] Depending upon the effectiveness with which these limitations are enforced, the households would have their proprietary interests gradually dispersed to the point of their legal personality becoming a vestigial form. But the distinctly lesser effectiveness of Soviet legal policy in rural areas has delayed the advent of such fate.

Reports of practice in dealing with conduct-related civil disputes indicate that there is some use of officially directed informal decisions in rural areas, but mainly through the use of comrades' courts rather than whole-group civic decisions.[148] Availability of the traditional institutional patterns in areas where the household remains viable suggests that the effort and expense of coordinating civic action may be greater in rural than in urban areas. Inheritance and a large number of other civil disputes are still often resolved in practice in the traditional households as self-directed informal decision-makers.[149]

2. *Soviet Social Reinforcement Models*

Actions of social organizations and civic groups as Soviet institutional models are officially conceived to be harmonious, usually spontaneous, and fully in conformity with both official prescriptions and prevailing authoritative policy perspectives.[150] Organizations and groups assume decision-making capacity in civil disputes either through internal initiation of pro-

[146] See, *e.g.*, Dobrovol'skiy, *Grazhdanskiye kolkhoznyye dela v sude (Civil Collective-Farm Cases in Court)*, Sov. yus. No. 8, p. 53 (1959); Gusev, *Sudebnaya praktika po grazhdanskim kolkhoznym delam (Judicial Practice in Civil Collective-Farm Cases)*, Sov. yus. No. 9, p. 16 (1960).

[147] The Basic Principles of Civil Law arts. 26 and 27 (1961) continue earlier legislative provisions.

[148] See Kolomiyets, *supra* note 142.

[149] See Trukhin, *Property Division and Apportionment in the Collective Farm Household*, Sov. yus. No. 7, p. 43 (1960); Liskovets, *Novoye grazhdanskoye zakonodatel'stvo i pravovoye regulirovaniye imushchestvennykh otnosheniy v kolkhoznom dvore (New Civil Law and Legal Regulation of Property Relations in the Collective Farm Household)*, Sov. yus. No. 7, p. 13 (1962); Kovalenko, *Iz sudebnoy praktiki po delam o razdelakh i vydelakh v kolkhoznykh dvorakh (Court Practice in Cases of Division and Apportionment in Collective-Farm Households)*, Sov. yus. No. 20, p. 13 (1963).

[150] See Nedbaylo & Bersheda *supra* note 133.

cedures or as a result of transfer of a case by the court or procuracy, or upon party initiative. Their application of informal sanctions is reported often to produce substantial effect. The effects of an informal decision on foreign participants were reported in *U.S. Tour Leader Censures Soviet*, N.Y. Times, Aug. 8, 1962, p. 3, col. 1. Dr. Wickwire, who was conducting a group of Americans visiting the U.S.S.R., related that members of his group:

> "Were unofficially 'tried' before an international youth camp council for three hours and forty minutes on charges that they had distributed anti-Soviet literature.
>
> "Were accused by Russian students they had thought to be their friends of acts of unfriendliness, including attempts to photograph the seamy side of Soviet life and efforts to get militarily useful information.
>
> . . .
>
> "Were given a warning by the camp council to halt unfriendly behavior.
>
> "Became the subject of a Moscow radio broadcast telling the world they had broken the 'rules of friendship' at the camp.
>
> " 'They had no business to do this,' Dr. Wickwire said. 'It was a painful experience, rather shocking, and perhaps an eyeopener.' "[151]

The prevailing view is that even though civil legal prescriptions are applied, so that "legal regulation" is involved, such decisions are merely "preliminary" despite any actual sanction effects upon the person whose conduct is condemned and a substantial probability that any necessary subsequent judicial action will affirm them.[152] Judicial deferral to such decisions is formally analogous to exhaustion of remedies rules in non-Soviet legal systems, but essential points of difference include official or semi-official direction, involvement of lay persons who possess social if not material interest in the dispute, possible personal prejudice, and the informality of procedures which are not easily amenable to the sifting of relevant and appropriate evidence and arguments.[153]

In cases where a dispute is transferred by a court some defined standards govern the submission to an organization or group. Petition to the court by recognized "social" representatives expressing a wish to assume disposition of claims against the offender and to "take charge over his conduct" is required. Also necessary is an expression of repentance and a promise to reform by the defendant.[154] The practice has been mixed on whether the presence of claims for compensatory relief which are officially justiciable

[151] See also Zinatulin, V domkh stalo spokoyno *(It Has Become Quiet in the Houses)*, Sov. yus. No. 4, p. 9 (1960).

[152] See note 51 *supra*.

[153] See cases cited in notes 115, 128, 137, and 151 *supra*.

[154] See *Kichatov* 81-82.

will prevent the transfer, but it is reported that usually such claims are absent where informal decisions are judicially approved.[155]

Decisions of social organizations are governed by diverse rules. More or less regular procedures have been developed for the union committees which render determination on eligibility for social insurance benefits, labor discipline, and safety disputes.[156] On the other hand, pensioners' councils and other specialized organizations informally elaborate their procedures, usually coordinating them where necessary with those of the administrative agencies with which they deal.[157] While complaints have been voiced concerning lack of uniformity, there are differences of opinion on whether official administrative agencies or the relevant organizations should prescribe procedural rules.[158]

Civic groups in rendering decisions in which criminal, labor, family law, and civil law provisions are applied are sometimes considered to execute public functions and in other instances to exercise civic functions.[159] When civic participation in processes of official authority is emphasized the former rationale is preferred, and when informality of sanctions is emphasized the decisions are said to constitute autonomous civic action.[160] Whole-group decisions in civil disputes occur primarily in conduct-related cases. But sometimes the conduct which is condemned is resort to the legal process by a litigious person or the filing of a complaint on a totally unfounded claim, in which case action is taken against the "complainer." [161]

B. Specialized Decision-Makers in Local Groups: Comrades' Courts

The best known decisions of comrades' courts are those in cases of antisocial infractions, administrative violations, and minor criminal offenses.[162] But their array of sanctions and the provision that with consent of parties civil compensatory decisions may be issued on small claims permits their resolution of a significant percentage of civil disputes.[163] When decisions are issued within their competence, a court may not assume jurisdiction for purposes of adjudication or review, and formal procedures for

[155] See Gorshenev, *Vozrastaniye roli obshchestvennykh organizatsiy i kollektivov trudyashchikhsya v primeneniyi norm sovetskogo prava na sovremennom etape (Growth of the Rule of Social Organizations and Collectives of Workers in the Application of Norms of Soviet Law in the Present Stage,* Pravovedeniye No. 1, p. 3 (1963).

[156] *Id.* at 11.

[157] *Ibid.*

[158] *Id.* at 10-11.

[159] See note 67 *supra* and accompanying text.

[160] *Ibid.*

[161] See, *e.g.*, Zinatulin, *supra* note 151.

[162] See, *e.g.*, Editorial, *Novyy etap v deyatel'nosti tovarishcheskikh sudov (The New Stage in the Activity of Comrades' Courts)*, Sov. yus. No. 23, p. 1 (1963).

[163] See THE PRACTICAL GUIDE FOR COMRADES' COURTS ch. 12 (Moscow 1961).

party appeal of the comrades' court decision are absent.[164] The decision must be approved by the executive committee of the local soviet before becoming "effective," and this allows official administrative review without the presence of the local group.[165] Procuracy review of administrative action offers still further possibility for modification of the decision independently of party claims.[166]

Although the Criminal Code provides for transfer of some types of cases to a comrades' court for decision, no comparable provisions exist in the Basic Principles of Civil Law.[167] There are provisions governing nonreception of a complaint and termination of civil trials when a comrades' court has issued a decision within its competence, but such details as whether administrative confirmation is necessary for a decision to be recognized and whether the competence of a comrades' court may be challenged collaterally in a judicial proceeding are not specified.[168] Some Soviet writers have concluded, however, that the absence of legislative provisions prohibiting judicial transfer of a case to a comrades' court implies authority for judicial execution of such a transfer in appropriate cases.[169] But most comrades' courts civil decisions appear to be matters of original jurisdiction.[170]

The civil jurisdiction of comrades' courts is concentrated in four areas of the law: violation of labor discipline provisions,[171] illegal use of state and social property,[172] disputes between citizens requiring compensatory resolu-

[164] See the criticism in Bul'varov, *Zhaloby net (There Is No Appeal)*, Pravda Vostoka, July 8, 1962. See note 132 *supra* and article 19 of the comrades' court statute [1961] Ved. verkh. sov. R.S.F.S.R., No. 26, Sbornik zakon. 401-405; translated in 13 C.D.S.P., No. 33, pp. 8-9 (1961).

[165] See, *e.g.*, Lunyev, Soviet Administrative Law 449 (Moscow 1960).

[166] See, *e.g.*, Morgan, Soviet Administrative Legality (1962).

[167] *Cf.* R.S.F.S.R. Criminal Code art. 51 (1960). The provision that failure to utilize an established nonforensic preliminary settlement procedure appears to be inadequate as authority for a judicial transfer order. See note 13 *supra.*

[168] See note 164 *supra.*

[169] See, *e.g.*, *Kichatov* 82-83.

[170] See The Practical Guide for Comrades' Courts (Moscow 1961).

[171] Cases of violation of labor discipline in which restoration sanctions may be applied are of course concentrated in the occupation-based Comrades' Courts, and matters of the following types are heard: late arrival to work, early departure, and loss of working time as a result of simple fault of the worker; absence without proper cause, appearing for work while drunk; willful working in the wrong shift or leaving equipment in operation before arrival of the worker in the next shift; unconscientious work or tolerance of waste; failure to obey orders or instructions of the enterprise administration; failure to comply with the rules and instructions on the protection of labor, technical safety, production sanitation, or fire protection; careless use of state or social property; unproductive waste of electrical energy; deviation from established production techniques. *Id.* at 97-120.

[172] Decisions on illegal use of state or social resources include such matters as improper use of material or equipment for the asserted interests of the enterprise; illegal use of materials for personal gain; production of objects for personal gain from equipment and materials of the enterprise; illegal use of the labor of subordinate workers; and illegal use of means of transport. *Id.* at 120-23.

tion,[173] and family relations disputes.[174] The procedures which are employed in initiating the proceedings are flexible, and usually involve considerable collaboration between the chairman of the court, who is often a trained jurist, and party and civic group representatives, administrative officials, and sometimes procuracy, police and court personnel.[175] Handbooks and short courses on laws relevant to their activity are made available to comrades' court judges, and procedures for the conduct of their hearings are specified in some detail. But the very significant operations of gathering and preparing evidence and arguments prior to the hearing are given rather limited attention in Soviet publications.[176] Complaints of misapplication of law, and of decisions exceeding competence not infrequently have been made.[177]

C. Propaganda of Norms and Exemplary Cases

For full effectiveness the procedural trends are considered to require mass propaganda of norms and of exemplary cases. These are promulgated

[173] Disputes between citizens frequently result in application of provisions of the civil code or relevant decrees, and comrades' court judges are instructed to consult law judges, procurators, lawyers, and other professional jurists when they are uncertain as to the applicability of particular rules. Most of the civil matters handled by these tribunals are contract disputes: contracts of sale particularly or personal property; contracts of barter; gift contracts; transfer of property to another for use during his life; leases; contracts of repair, storage, or hire; and contracts of free use of property. Next in frequency appear to be disputes concerning the obligation to return property in kind. Tort cases involving compensation for intentional or accidental property damage, and some auto accident cases, are occasionally adjudicated in comrades' courts. Cases of unjust enrichment, usually involving the return of an erroneous overpayment, are also resolved by comrades' courts. *Id.* at 124-58.

[174] Family relations disputes in the comrades' courts are mainly of two types: nonfulfillment of the obligation to educate children; and nonsupport of spouse, children of parents, or nonpayment of alimony. *Id.* at 159-68.

[175] See *id.* at 78-80; Vorozheykin, *Kak organizovat' rabotu tovarishcheskogo suda (How To Organize the Work of a Comrades' Court)* (Moscow 1961); and the review by Filippov in Sov. yus. No. 18, pp. 25-26 (1962). See also note 70 *supra.* It is also reported that despite the absence of legislative authorization they issue "special rulings" on infractions observed in the group "in cases where necessary." Gorshenev, *supra* note 155.

[176] See THE PRACTICAL GUIDE FOR COMRADES' COURTS, 23-25 (Moscow 1961) for an outline of the recommended abbreviated law courses for comrades' court judges.

[177] *E.g.*, a case is reported where, subsequent to a decision of a people's court awarding custody of a child in a separation case to his mother, a comrades' court assumed jurisdiction and decreed transfer of the child to the father and cancellation of the mother's urban residence permit. The decision was reversed after procuracy protest. Velichkin, *Povysit' uroven' rukovodstva tovarishcheskimi sudami (Increase the Caliber of Control of Comrades' Courts)*, Sov. yus. No. 12, p. 14 (1963). Several other cases are reported in Savitskiy, *Uchastiye obshchestvennosti v bor'be s pravonarusheniyami i garantiyi sotsialisticheskoy zakonnosti (Participation of the Community in the Struggle Against Violations of the Law and for Guarantees of Socialist Legality)*, Sov. gos. i pravo No. 5, pp. 80, 90 (1963).

in news media, and jurists are instructed to propagandize the law.[178] Some of this propaganda serves mainly to overcome earlier limited publication of Soviet laws. But the value of knowledge of civil law by citizens was pointed out at the opening of the propaganda campaign by publication of a letter from a Leningrad engineer who wrote that he was constantly beseiged by requests to explain wage rates, rules on transfer and dismissal, the proper forms for documents, and the like. The inclusion of a labor law course in vocational schools was suggested.[179] Law journals carried the suggestion further, urging that real property and collective farm law be taught in agricultural schools, that the fundamentals of Soviet law should be a required course in schools for party and government administrators, and that teachers and doctors should be given training in the law because their knowledge is disseminated to others through conduct of their professional activities. Proposals for introducing courses on legal subjects into curricula have produced some changes, but the burden of the program was carried by the mass media. Newspapers published an increasing number of articles on law for the layman; jurists lectured on the law in local auditoriums, and the campaign of propaganda was intensified.[180]

The development of a propaganda program of large proportions could not be expected to continue without some redirection of activity. Since 1960 two significant trends may be observed. There appears an increase in relative emphasis on civil as compared to criminal matters, and there is increased emphasis upon courses, coordinated lecture series, and journal and newspaper publication of exemplary cases as compared to volunteered individual lectures by jurists.[181] "Civic Universities of Legal Knowledge" have been established in many of the larger cities as institutes for lecture series on law for the layman.[182] Propaganda of the law is also urged for individual consultations, as judges and procuracy employees are expected to insist on compliance with the law, and to discourage litigation, when counselling

[178] See, *e.g.*, Lukasheva, *O vospitaniyi pravosoznaniya i pravovoy kul-tury v period razvyornutogo stroitel'stva kommunizma (On the Inculcation of Consciousness of Law in the Period of the Accelerated Building of Communism)*, Sov. gos. i pravo No. 7, p. 35 (1962); *Sovety i propaganda zakonodatel'stva (Soviets and the Propaganda of Legislation)*, Sovety deputatov trudyashchikhsia (Soviets of Working-Peoples' Deputies) No. 8, pp. 3-5 (1963); Editorial, *Propaganda yuridicheskikh znaniy—obshchestvennyy dolg kazhdogo yurista (Propaganda of Legal Knowledge Is the Social Duty of Every Jurist)*, Sov. yus. No. 2, p. 1 (1959); Petrenko, *Yuristy—obshchestvenniki (Jurists Are Actors in the Community)*, Sov. yus. No. 8, p. 10 (1961).

[179] Raskokokha, *V etom nuzhdayetsya molodoy spetsialist (The Young Specialist Needs This)*, Pravda, June 10, 1960, p. 2.

[180] See Editorial, *Pravovyye znaniya—v massy! (Legal Knowledge to the Masses!)*, Sov. gos. i pravo No. 8, p. 3 (1960).

[181] See *Kichatov;* and also Lopukhov, *Vazhnyye formy pravovoy propagandy (Important Forms of Legal Propaganda)*, Sov. yus. No. 11, p. 23 (1963).

[182] See, *e.g.*, *V obshchestennyh universitetakh pravovykh znaniy (In the Civic Universities of Legal Knowledge)*, Sov. yus. No. 17, p. 20 (1962).

citizens who may become parties to litigation and when responding to letters and formal complaints.[183] Another development in the propaganda program is emphasis upon discussion in small group meetings of those official decisions and rulings which have particular local significance.[184]

D. Prevention of Disputes

Not the least interesting of the Soviet civil procedural trends is the development of techniques for prevention of disputes through direct action upon prospective or actual claimants.[185] One of the main functions of residentially based comrades' courts has been to cause the resolution of disputes between tenants without their resort to the official legal process. This is often accomplished with assistance of prospective or applied informal sanctions.[186] If an alternative forum is unavailable for resolution of the dispute it may be said that the claim itself is regulated as a procedural form without adjudication on its particular merit. This policy of quieting claims is valid according to Soviet sanctions objectives only if it affects the conduct of disputants and leaves their demands unsatisfied only to the degree that private coercive vengeance does not appear as an alternative to the official and informal decisions.[187] In Soviet judicial practice there are elements of prevention of official civil litigation in the varying degrees of persuasion applied by judges, lawyers and procurators to reduce the amount of civil litigation; the practice of judicial emphasis upon extrajudicial settlement; and judicial deferral to informal decisions.[188] And social organizations, civic groups, and comrades' courts practice "prophylaxis" of civil claims with the aid of "social influence" sanctions.[189] This Soviet practice has apparently

[183] See, *e.g.*, *Prusakov, Profilaktika pravonarusheniy i organizatsiya raboty narodnogo suda (Prophylaxis of Law Violations and Organization of the Work of the People's Court)*, Sov. yus. No. 14, p. 4 (1963); and *Legal Consultation for the Population provided by the Lawyers' Associations*, under heading *Rostki novogo* (Seedlings of New Ways) Sov. yus. No. 1, p. 25 (1964).

[184] For a discussion of some of these features of the propaganda program, see Grozdev, *Rabota seminarov na mestakh (The Work of Seminars in Localities)*, Sov. yus. No. 2, p. 53 (1960). See also *Kichatov* 84.

[185] See, *e.g.*, *V nogu s zhizn'yu (Abreast of the Times)*, Sov. yus. No. 3, p. 25 (1964).

[186] See, *e.g.*, Lyass, *Voprosy profilaktiki prestupnosti v SSSR (Questions of Prophylaxis of Criminality in the USSR)*, Sov. gos. i pravo No. 7, p. 182 (1960); and on administrative "prophylaxis," see Kravchenko, *Ob administrativno-pravovom regulirovaniyi v svyazi s povysheniyem roli obshchestvennosti (On Administrative-Legal Regulation in Connection with the Increase in the Role of the Community)*, Sov. gos. i pravo No. 4, pp. 116, 117 (1963).

[187] See, *e.g.*, Potashnikov, *Vyyezdnoy priyom (Hearing Citizens on Circuit)*, Sov. yus. No. 8, p. 17 (1960); and notes 127-36, and 139 *supra*.

[188] See text accompanying notes 127-41 *supra*.

[189] See note 115 *supra*.

been influenced by the earlier Communist Chinese experimentation.[190] And similarly enthusiastic appraisal is offered of success of the program, with the allegation that it has resulted in fewer cases being litigated, fewer complaints being filed, and that therefore there has been a smaller number of civil law infractions.[191]

VI. Public and Civic Systems of Public Order in Soviet Law

As to the consequences of the civil procedural trends for law and public order, the posing of the question as Soviet writers have done in terms of querying whether the "sphere of law" is expanding or contracting is spurious.[192] Response to the question is affected by practical considerations. Internally Soviet administrators seek to offer the semblance of a transition from the severity and arbitrariness of pre-1953 administrative coercion. For foreign audiences attuned to more conventional concepts of public order the semblance of either a conventional or a novel approach to law is appropriate to be presented,[193] depending upon whether similarity to other societies is stressed for diplomatic purposes or a unique form of social organization is claimed for ideologic or propaganda purposes. Futhermore, the conceptual difficulties with the posed formulation are substantial.[194] Depending upon the support of particular civic decision practices by official prescription, and the degree of prescriptive formality defined as appropriate to "law," differing answers may be given as to whether informal decisions in the civic action program are "legal" ones. The conception that decisions attendant to the innovations were "social" has been a factor contributing to present limited and vague elaboration of procedures.

Major differences in the procedures actually employed in resolution of civil disputes, depending upon whether the dispute is related to production activities or is resolved in a rural household, continue to exist in Soviet practice.[195] Procedures in decisions which concern production activities are de-

[190] See Tretyakov, *Profilaktike grahdanskikh pravonarusheniy bol'she vnimaniye (More Attention to Prophylaxis of Civil Legal Violations)*, Sov. yus. No. 14, p. 8 (1961); Pechnikov, *Raznoobrazit' formy profilakticheskoy raboty (Diversify the Forms of Prophylactic Work)*, Sov. yus. No. 9, p. 4 (1962).

[191] See *Kichatov* 85.

[192] See note 53 *supra*.

[193] See notes 46 and 5 *supra*. The Soviet publications translated for Western audiences to date, however, deal with the more conventional aspects of Soviet civil decision-making. See Tadevosyan, *Civil Procedure*, in Fundamentals of Soviet Law (Romashkin ed. Moscow 1962).

[194] See Keyzerov, *O vzaimodeystviyi prava i nravstvennosti v kommunisticheskom stroitel'stve (On the Interaction of Law and Morality in Communist Construction)*, Pravovedeniye No. 4, pp. 3, 11-13 (1962).

[195] In the expression of a leading Soviet civil lawyer the "differentiation" of production disputes is "diversity amid a unity." Bratus', *Vazhnyy etap v razvitiyi sovetskogo grazhdanskogo zakonodartel'stva (A Major Stage in the Development of Soviet Civil Law)*, Sov. gos. i pravo No. 2 pp. 3, 9 (1962).

signed to be employed within a framework of administrative perspectives and sanctions, with the resolution of a particular civil dispute serving as a basis for other decisions on administrative performance. Presently contract disputes between state enterprises are the subject of experimentation, the result of which will determine whether they will be excepted from the principle of fault as a general ground for civil liability or whether innovations in procedure will be used to permit litigation between remote parties or the joinder of multiple parties in cases where the claim is contested on grounds that supply has been inadequate.[196] Personal injuries which are work-related are, as a result of recent trends, usually resolved by an enterprise or union decision, with the court serving as a passive mediator. Prior judicial decisions, and the expectations of the parties regarding the official judicial decision which may be taken in the particular case, undoubtedly influence the resolution of the dispute. But the court does not assume to act in the particular dispute until a formal complaint is presented.[197]

For the civil disputes which are not production-related the dominant trend in procedures has been a shift away from public and towards a civic order system. Civic involvement in official adjudication and the use of informal decisions and sanctions largely unsupported by existing civil substantive and procedural legislation have become major features of present practice. The difficulties of incorporating such procedural forms into new legislation on civil procedure appears to be a factor in the delay in enacting such legislation.[198] And there are some significant countertrends towards bringing some of the practices of the civic action program under increasing official regulation. The comrades' court, a nonofficial decision-maker, has evolved as a result of a few years of recent experience, and appears more in the role of a secondary legal process possessing substantial jurisdiction and relatively regularized procedures.[199] The tendency towards procedural regularity is also reflected in increased emphasis upon comrades' courts as compared to social organization and civic group decisions.[200] This regularization has been facilitated by redefinition of Soviet concepts of public order

[196] See text accompanying note 84 *supra.*

[197] See text accompanying note 95 *supra.*

[198] See, *e.g.*, the assertion that use of defined procedural forms by social organization is "superfluous legalization." Bazhenov, *V. I. Lenin o sotsialisticheskom pravosudiyi (Lenin on the Socialist Legal Process)* in 90 LET SO DNYA ROZHDENIYA V. I. LENINA (90TH ANNIVERSARY OF LENIN'S BIRTHDAY) 54 (Kazan' 1961); Gorshenev, *supra* note 155, questions whether "social initiative" would be bound by defined procedural rules.

[199] See note 132 *supra.* Gorshenev, *supra* note 155, urged greater regularization of comrades' court procedure.

[200] See Kaznin, *Sud tovarishchey (Court of Comrades)*, Pravda, Nov. 13, 1963, p. 1; Editorial, *Spravedlivyy, obshchestvennyy (Just and Social)*, Izvestiya, Nov. 20, 1963, p. 1.

to include the application of informal sanctions which have some basis in official prescription.[201]

Soviet jurists appear presently to consider many of the informal decisions and sanctions as relevant to public order, regardless of whether they are effected by public or civic agencies. The "external" applications of sanctions by organizations and groups are said to have official aspects, and these are distinguished from decisions which delimit civic organization and group membership obligations.[202] However, this distinction is difficult to draw in Soviet society, as it does not reflect an actual difference in the degree of administrative influence upon civic action. It remains to be seen whether in Soviet law there will appear an adequate specification of a distinction between membership matters and "governmental function" sanctions.[203]

A. Features of the Nonforensic Decisions

Extensive use of nonofficial decisions in civil disputes in current Soviet practice renders appropriate a brief survey of their features. Nonforensic decisions may by definition be considered to be informal decisions effected in patterns different from official processes of law. Nonforensic decisions in diverse societies may either support or be in conflict with official decisions, and may or may not possess tacit or express official approval. In the Soviet context many of the decisions of local party representatives, either on the direct disposition of a civil dispute or in coordination of the relevant informal decisions, may be considered nonforensic decisions.[204] The decisions taken in rural households, and social organizations and civic groups are of course within the scope of the definition. So are comrades' courts save to the extent that their enabling legislation can be said to constitute them inferior courts in the official judicial system. Much of the sanctions consequence of comrades' court decisions, however, occurs during the prehearing or hearing stages of a case, and for many disputes the assistance of official agencies in enforcement of a dispositive order is not required. With a substantial role in the prevention of civil disputes, as contrasted with their

[201] See Igitov, *O prirode mer vozdeystva, primenyayemykh obshchestvennost'yu v oblasti okhrany obshchestvennogo poryadka (On the Nature of Measures of Influence Applied by the Community in the Area of Preservation of Public Order)*, Sov. gos. i pravo No. 11, p. 109 (1963).

[202] See notes 64-67 *supra* and accompanying text. Igitov, *supra* note 201, includes as "extra-authoritative" those sanctions applied to nonmembers of an organization or group and those applied to members but exceeding "moral" effect and requiring governmental delegation of authority.

[203] *Ibid.*

[204] See note 61 *supra*, and *Kichatov*. Relations between participants are asserted to be "one of the least resolved problems in the science of Soviet civil procedure." Ivanov, *Grazhdanskiye protsessual'nyye pravootnosheniya (Legal Relations in Civil Procedures)*, Vestnik Mosk. Univ. No. 2, p. 26 (1963). Aside from representative participation, however, Soviet jurists have given little attention to the participation features of the innovations in official adjudicatory practice.

disposition, and with limited regulation by official prescription, comrades' courts only partially simulate forensic decision procedures.[205]

The nonforensic decisions introduce major qualifications on adjudicatory decision procedures. The conventional pattern of civil adjudication is well known. It includes decision-maker acquisition of facts and attendance to arguments presented largely through party initiative, priorities of official prescriptions and sanctions over informal ones, and the use of appropriate supporting institutional structures. The Soviet pattern of limited party control of procedures in the official forum has been amplified with respect to civil disputes involving disapproved conduct. In such cases presently there is substantial limitation on party initiative. There are even more significant departures in institutional structure. Current Soviet practice must be distinguished from nonforensic decision institutions in Western industrial societies, where arbitration, conciliation, and some organization and group decisions are engaged at party choice and with official adjudicatory review available for errors which contravene formal prescription. The possible institutional structures may range from the usual forensic one of adjudication, in which there is full hearing and disposition of claims by an independent decision-maker, to the imposition of limitations on the mere issuance of a claim without any hearing on its merits. Infinite variations are of course possible, depending upon the degree to which a decision-maker "hears" and "disposes" of claims. But four decision structures which have discernible counterparts in many societies are adjudication, mediation, reconciliation, and claim quieting or mere prevention. The Soviet informal decision procedures provide qualifications on official hearing and disposition of claims,[206] and a survey may be made in terms of these institutional forms:

1. Adjudication

Official adjudicatory institutions are usually courts, although administrative decisions may be adjudicatory as may informal decisions. In the common law tradition nonofficial adjudicatory institutions such as manorial, professional and commercial tribunals were displaced with the expansion of jurisdiction of the official courts. The Soviet trends in official adjudicatory prac-

[205] Soviet jurists have directed little attention to these features of nonforensic decisions. See Gorshenev, *supra* note 155.

[206] Prior to the prevention program a Soviet jurist reported favorably on the experience with a similar program in communist China. He cited Chinese publications for the assertion that in July 1958 in one district there were fewer than 10% of the civil claims filed a year earlier and that all were resolved by people's adjudicatory committees without official adjudication, while in another area no civil complaint was filed: Ostroumov, *Novaya forma privlicheniya obshchestvennosti k bor'be za soblyudeniye pravil sotsialisticheskogo obshchezhitiya v KNR (The New Form of Involvement of the Community in the Struggle for Conformity to Rules of Socialist Community Life in the [Chinese Peoples' Republic])*, Sov. gos. i pravo No. 5, pp. 73, 78 (1960).

tice qualify adjudication through dispersal of judicial attention to matters beyond the substance of claims presented for compensation and judicial emphasis upon civic or party disposition. Both interest and the use of extra-dispute evidence and opinion may be noted for the civic decisions.

2. Mediation

When party settlement of claims is induced by strategies of the decision-maker who "hears" but does not himself resolve the dispute, the pattern may be classified as mediation. A mediator is in substantial degree independent of the parties in the particular dispute, and his distinctive role is to induce a settlement rather than to dispose of the claims. Many of the decision institutions of traditional societies conform to this pattern, particularly where developed official adjudicatory institutions exist and cultural or social predispositions reject their use. Where family or village elders assume charge of preservation of traditions they often utilize their power to confine and reduce civil claims, and in the successful case induce party settlement rather than devolve directly upon themselves the functions of disposition and enforcement. Remnants of traditional institutions in Soviet society in some measure effect mediation, and it may be asked whether the decision innovations constitute a modern parallel. The procedures for personal injury disputes in industry often produce party settlement outside official courts, but no clearly defined mediator role of courts is apparent, though the modifications in official adjudicatory practice may in some cases have a mediation effect.[207] And the actions of comrades' court judges, civic representatives, party and procuracy officials may also constitute mediation.[208]

3. Reconciliation

The withdrawal of claims or abstention from their prosecution, when induced by strategies of a decision-maker, may be distinguished from adjudication, as the action of the decision-maker is not dispositive, and from mediation, as mutual cessation of assertion of claims rather than their settlement is the outcome. Reconciliation through active intercession of a decision-maker is effected through procedures which usually include a temporal delay and sometimes a stipulation of conditions intended to maintain the reconciliation process. Traditional institutions in many societies and official procedures, particularly for family relations disputes, may employ this pattern. The new Soviet procedures for resolving personal injury disputes in industry may be noted in some degree to conform to this pattern. Other

[207] For an example of combination of official authority and informal procedures, see note 128 *supra*.

[208] For a discussion of the similarity of comrades' court procedure to that of the official legal process, see Zeyder, Pravovedeniye No. 3, pp. 69, 76-79 (1963).

of the procedural trends are also analogous. Personal reconciliation of quarreling neighbors, often prior to official or informal decision in the dispute, is regularly reported in tenant conduct cases.[209] Elements of reconciliation may be present, though such decisions do not have regular specified procedures which provide for temporal delay or other conditions for mutual party termination of the dispute. In the prevention program the actions of officials, jurists, civic representatives, and the party informally may effect a reconciliation of civil disputants, but the program is designed broadly for reduction in the amount of civil litigation, in the number of civil claims filed and in the incidence of civil violations. Whatever reconciliatory effects occur are the product of local practice rather than institutional structure.[210]

4. Claim Quieting

Direct action by a decision-maker upon a claimant or prospective claimant so as to prevent the maintenance or assertion of a claim may be distinguished from adjudication, mediation and reconciliation. It differs from adjudication and mediation as there is no hearing or party settlement, and from reconciliation, as the decision-maker does not provide a preliminary hearing on the merits of the claims and does not necessarily offer reciprocity or procedural parity to the adverse parties. Institutions of this type are sometimes found in primitive and folk communities but are virtually absent in more developed societies. The Soviet prevention program appears to possess certain of these features, as official direction emphasizes reduction in civil litigation as well as the resolution of disputes in the precomplaint stage.[211]

B. Public Order Consequences of the Current Trends

Current practice in civil decisions challenges Soviet officials and jurists to develop viable informal procedures and institutions for civic decision-making while simultaneously maintaining them distinct from official public order structures. The declared objective of long range diminution of the activity of official power structures has not been demonstrated to be furthered by the practice thus far with an increased number of participants in civil decisions. The more immediate goal of reconstruction of civic action has resulted in difficulties with the recodification of civil procedure legislation. Many of the adaptations in official adjudicatory practice defy formulation in conventional legal terminology, and it is unlikely that new legislation will contain provisions authorizing and regulating official survey of local group opinion, spectator participation, continuous supervision of decisions by civic agents, and the use of informal sanctions as supplements to

[209] See, *e.g.*, *ibid.*

[210] See, *e.g.*, the cases cited herein and in the Soviet literature which indicate party (or Youth League) or procuracy coordination. See also note 61 *supra.*

[211] See, *e.g.*, note 72 *supra.*

formally prescribed ones. Of particular importance is the manner in which competence is distributed between official and informal decisions, yet on this question Soviet discussion is absent regarding the conflicts which are possible. Provision for summary judicial review of comrades' court decisions appears to offer a practical compromise. Less official action than formal adjudication authorizes official enforcement of the decision, while dispositive comrades' court decisions are subjected to official judicial review if the parties decline compliance.[212] Similar trends appear less likely for the other civic group and organization decisions, particularly where defined procedures are absent and the decision is made by nonprofessionals and with unconventionally structured participation. For such decisions the procuracy and party continue to have key roles in supervising the administration of the informal decisions and their coordination of them with official practice, largely unregulated by formal prescription.[213]

In the decade since Stalin's death there has been significant experimentation with law and other forms of social regulation in Soviet society. The central—and often administrative—application of coercion has been reduced, while the generalization of the sanctions objectives of regulation of conduct has extended even to the methods for resolving civil disputes. The shift towards a civic system of order is associated with comprehensive "corrective" sanctions applied to civil disputants and is influential in shaping the conduct of others in proximate social groups. This geographic decentralization and social integration of civil decisions has been accompanied by some specialization according to professional, organizational, and local social competence and by some multiplication at the local level of structures which perform equivalent decision functions. But the present quest for uniquely Soviet procedures in civil decisions has only a limited history. Nonforensic practices for dealing with civil disputes were established in Communist China in the early 1950's in adaptation of the Soviet informal decision practices which had lapsed during the 1930's. The recent Soviet practice has in turn been influenced by the Chinese experience.[214] Dissemination of the trends to

[212] See note 132 *supra*.

[213] See Shchebanov, *O vozdeystviyi prava na obshchestvennoye razvitiye v usloviyakh obshchenarodnogo gosudarstva (On the Influence of Law on Social Development Under Conditions of a State of the Whole People)*, Sov. gos. i pravo No. 12, p. 12 (1963).

[214] See, *e.g.*, the discussion of the use of local circuit trials and some other innovations in Communist China in civil and cirminal cases. Gudoshnikov, *Sudebnaya reforma 1952-1953 gg i dal'neyshaya demokratizatsiya sudebnoy sistemy Kitayskoy Narodnoy Respubliki (The 1952-53 Law Reform and the Further Democratization of the Judicial System of the Chinese People's Republic)*, Sov. gos. i pravo No. 8, p. 56 (1954). Information on the Chinese experience with people's reconciliation committees (later changed to people's adjudicatory committees) was also available to Soviet officials and jurists prior to Soviet intensification of the civic action program. See THE CONSTITUTION AND BASIC LAWS OF THE C.P.R. (Moscow 1955); and for 1954-58 (Moscow 1959); and Ostroumov, *supra* note 206.

East Europe was accompanied by particular emphasis upon occupational group specialized decision-makers which are roughly parallel to the Soviet comrades' courts.[215] This diffusion of the general pattern within various Soviet societies during the past decade has been accompanied by variations which may be traced to differing administrative policies and possibly also diverse cultures.

Matters of effectiveness and economy appear critical to Soviet evaluation of the efforts to establish a civic system of order which parallels the public one. The supervisory costs of the civic decision practices and their effects on productivity are important. The use of unpaid "social obligation" time of officials and professional jurists can be expected to require some form of compensating inducements and rewards.[216] Certainly limited achievement of the assigned sanctions objectives could be expected to result in lower administrative priority for the civic action program.[217] Yet it is clear for the present that not only has a general structure of civil procedures been adapted to Soviet policies but that its components are not solely "old bricks." For certain types of decisions informal procedures supervised largely by officials and the party supplement or displace legal institutions which have been modified from Western social systems.

[215] See, *e.g.*, a summary of the Hungarian comrades' courts, which are administered through union organizations and deal mainly with occupational infractions. Vorozheykin, *Tovarishcheskiye sudy VNR na novom etape (Comrades' Courts in the Hungarian People's Republic in the Present Stage)*, Sov. yus. No. 20, p. 24 (1963).

[216] It has been reported that "some court officials do not understand that involvement of the community in the work of the organs of justice is not a campaign but an ongoing achievement." Editorial, *Shire privlekat obshchestvennost' k deyatel'nosti organov yustitsiyi (More Broadly Involve the Community in the Activity of the Organs of Justice)*, Sov. yus. No. 1, p. 1 (1963). It has also been suggested that "lukewarm persons" not punishable under the criminal code be "judged by the strict court of the community." Speech by Pavlov at the 14th Congress YCL Central Committee meeting, Pravda, April 17, 1962. But the newspaper *Izvestiya* in response to a letter replied that social influence sanctions should not be applied to persons merely because they refrain from regular participation in civic activity. *Pochtovyy yashchik "Izvestiy" (The "Izvestiya" Mail Box)*, Izvestiya, May 16, 1963, p. 4.

[217] Soviet officials often emphasize that law and other social regulatory measures will be used to the fullest extent. See, *e.g.*, KHRUSHCHEV, REPORT OF THE CENTRAL COMMITTEE TO THE 22ND CONGRESS OF THE CPSU 101 (Moscow 1961). But appraisal of the relative utility of official and informal sanctions in regulating criminal conduct has been reported. See Mironov, *Nasushchnyye voprosy dal'neyshego ukrepleniya sotsialisticheskoy zakonnosti (Urgent Questions for the Further Strengthening of Socialist Legality)*, Kommunist No. 1, pp. 49, 53 (1963). More recently production disputes and adaptation of the official legal process have been assigned particular importance. Editorial, *Yuridicheskaya nauka v usloviyakh kommunisticheskogo stroitel'stva (The Science of Law Under Conditions of Communist Construction)*, Kommunist No. 16, p. 26 (1963).

THEY ANSWER (TO) *PRAVDA*

BY BERNARD A. RAMUNDO *

AS EARLY AS 1918, Lenin stated the need to "transform the press from an organ which primarily reports the political news of the day to an organ earnestly educating the masses, teaching them how to live the new life and work in a new way." [1] The Soviet press, honored each 5th of May on "Press Day," [2] has been given an important role in the building of a communist society.[3]

> "The Soviet press founded by V. I. Lenin has its own special aspect: Its unique character is determined by one key factor—it is the spokesman for the fundamental interests of the people, the true and closest helper of the Party, the propagandist and organizer in the building of communism." [4]
>
> "The Soviet press actively assists the party, and fulfills well its important role of shock force on the ideological front. It struggles for achievement of the party program and, during the creation of communist forms of social organization, contributes in all ways to the even deeper and stronger confirmation of communist principles in life, labor and relations between people, so that there will be developed the skill to utilize wisely the blessing of communism." [5]

* *BERNARD A. RAMUNDO. A.B. 1947, College of the City of New York; LL.B. 1949, M.A. 1957, Certificate-Russian Institute 1958, Columbia University; Lieutenant Colonel, Judge Advocate General's Corps, U.S.A.; Office of the Assistant Secretary of Defense for International Security Affairs; Lecturer in Soviet Law, George Washington University.*

[1] *Pechat' (The Press),* 50 BOL'SHAYA SOVETSKAYA ENTISKLOPEDIYA (LARGE SOVIET ENCYCLOPEDIA) 412, 413 (2d ed. Moscow 1955). The transformation of the press into a weapon for the building of communism is said to have been accomplished shortly thereafter by the CPSU. *32 id. at 636.*

[2] Since 1922, Press Day is celebrated on May 5 in commemoration of the founding of *Pravda* by Lenin on May 5, 1912. 32 *id.* 635, 636.

[3] The press occupies a similarly important place in the East European countries of the Soviet bloc. See, for example, the speech of Antonin Novotny, First Secretary of the Central Committee of the Communist Party of Czechoslovakia and President of the Czechoslovak Soviet Socialist Republic, delivered in Brno on Sept. 22, 1963 (Czechoslovak Press Day) and printed in Pravda, Sept. 25, 1963, p. 3 (*S sovetskim soyuzom—na vechnye vremena (Forever With the Soviet Union)*).

[4] Report of L. F. Ilyichev, Secretary of the CPSU Central Committee on June 18, 1963, at the Plenary Session of the CPSU, transl. from Pravda, June 19, 1963, p. 1, in 15 C.D.S.P. No. 24, p. 7, at 12-13 (1963).

[5] *Vsenarodnaya pechat' (The Press of the Entire People),* Pravda, Nov. 16, 1963, p. 2.

Past and present participation in this economic and social engineering effort, *i.e.*, in the "construction of the material and technical basis of communism" and "rearing of the new [Soviet] man," [6] requires the press to be "a collective organizer" in addition to its more conventional role of "propagandist" and "agitator." [7]

> "In the center of interest of the press of Uzbekistan as is the case with the press of the entire country—are the tasks of creating the material-technical base of communism, political education of the toilers, instilling in them a communist attitude towards work, and rearing the man of the future." [8]
>
> "For the workers of the Soviet press there is no more important task now than to inspire and organize the Soviet people to fulfill the great program of communism. What can be more important and a greater honor for the journalist than the devotion of his zeal, efforts and talent to that noble cause." [9]

In 1950, a comprehensive study of the Soviet press in terms of the stated roles of agitator, propagandist, and collective organizer was included in a work devoted to the use of media of mass communication in the Soviet Union.[10] The author demonstrated that the Soviet press is "an instrument of the party for mobilizing public opinion and executing the national economic, social, and political plans," [11] with its control or supervisory function an important aspect of the execution of these plans.[12] This paper will, in

[6] "Comrades! The building of communism entails not only the creation of its material-technical base, but also provision for the rearing of the new man." Grishin, *Otchyot o rabote VTsSPS i zadachi profsoyuzov SSSR v periode razvyornutogo stroyitel'stva kommunisticheskogo obshchestva (Report of the Work of the All-Union Central Council of Trade Unions and the Tasks of the Trade Unions of the USSR in the Period of the Intensive Building of a Communist Society)*, Pravda, Oct. 29, 1963, pp. 2, 5. The text of the report was concluded in the following issue of *Pravda*. See also, *V tsentre vnimaniya—vospitaniye novogo cheloveka (All Attention on the Rearing of the New Man)*, *id.*, July 9, 1963, p. 2, and *Chelovek i kollektiv (Man and the Collective)*, *id.*, Sept. 12, 1963, p. 1.

[7] 50 BOL'SHAYA SOVETSKAYA ENTSIKLOPEDIYA 412 (2d ed. 1955), and Pravda, May 15, 1963, p. 1.

[8] Pakhimbabayeva, *S dobrym slovom k lyudyam (With a Kind Word for the People)*, Pravda, May 5, 1963, p. 3.

[9] *Ibid.*

[10] INKELES, PUBLIC OPINION IN SOVIET RUSSIA (1950).

[11] *Id.* at 147. Further on he states:

> "It is clear that in every aspect of its work, the Soviet press is expected to make some contribution to the effective rule of the nation by the Communist Party and to the attainment of those goals which the party has set for the nation and its component parts. But such an over-all statement cannot take account of the various specific ways in which the press plays its role in Soviet society. One can, however, subsume under the three broad categories provided by Lenin —agitation, propaganda, and organization—all of the relevant activities of the Soviet press." *Id.* at 164.

[12] *Id.* at 194-96.

effect, revisit the Soviet press in 1963 and discuss its current inspirational and organizational roles, with particular emphasis upon those of its activities which reflect a function of societal control.

I. Press Techniques

In discharging its broad responsibilities in the building of communism,[13] the Soviet press must supplement traditional operational techniques with those not generally associated with the work of a medium of mass communication. It must propagate the party line; eulogize the active builder of communism; criticize, and where necessary seek the punishment of, those who impede the march towards communism; and help ferret out and correct deficiencies in the building effort.[14]

In propaganda and agitational work, the "campaign" approach, evidenced by the repetition of themes with a constancy and upon a scale reflecting the importance attached to them, is the technique employed. For example, the recent sustained emphasis upon the benefits to be derived from a highly developed chemical industry in connection with the Plenum of the Central Committee of the CPSU [15] represents a major agitational effort of immediate urgency. In contrast, the less intensive, continuing exhortation to increase labor productivity [16] typifies a propaganda effort in a lower key. The commitment of the Soviet press to service as a "transmission belt" rather than a news media [17] permits, when needed, full attention and resources to agitational and inspirational work. The extent of this commitment is a distinguishing characteristic of Soviet press activity.

[13] The press is "to discern and sharply pose fundamental questions of the development of economics and culture, to reveal the true beauty of free labor, to criticize all that hinders Soviet people from living and working in a communist way." Report *supra* note 4, at 13.

[14] *On the Current Tasks of the Party's Ideological Work,* Resolution of the Plenary Session of the CPSU Central Committee on the Report of Comrade L. F. Ilyichev, adopted June 21, 1963, transl. from Pravda, June 22, 1963, p. 1, in 15 C.D.S.P. No. 25, p. 12 (1963).

[15] See, *e.g., Pravda* editions for Oct., Nov., and early Dec., 1963. The Plenum lasted from Dec. 9-13, 1963. Pravda, Dec. 8-16, 1963. On Dec. 21, 1963, *Pravda* noted that:

> "The Soviet people will not spare any effort in successfully completing, under the leadership of the Leninist Party, the task of the accelerated development of the chemical industry and the achievement of the widespread use of chemicals in the economy, thereby making a new, important contribution to the building of communism." *Za boevuyu rabotu (For Determined Work)*, p. 1.

[16] For example, *Neotlozhnye zaboty zhivotnovodov (The Urgent Concerns of Those Who Raise Livestock)*, Pravda, July 18, 1963, p. 1; *Zhatve—udarnyye tempy (Crash Tempos for the Harvest), id.*, July 9, 1963, p. 1; and *Navstrechu 46-oy godovschchine oktyabrya proizvodstvennye rekordy prokhodchikov Donbassa (For the 46th Anniversary of October: The Production Records of the Drifter Team Workers of the Donbas Region), id.*, Aug. 24, 1963, p. 1.

[17] Inkeles, *op. cit. supra* note 10, at 141, 156.

A more unique aspect of the work of the Soviet press is its functioning as an organ of criticism and a clearing house for criticism and self-criticism.[18] "The Party-Soviet press is a mighty means of expanding criticism and self-criticism. . . ." [19] Through editorial criticism of conditions uncovered by the press through its own investigative action and editorial comment upon criticism and self-criticism in the form of oral complaints registered at newspaper "points," [20] letters to the editor, and reports received from local newspapers acting as "collective correspondents" of the larger ones,[21] the press attempts to influence and shape societal development in the direction of communism. As a consequence, press criticism is purposeful or, in Soviet terminology, "principled."

> "[T]he Party always teaches us that criticism is not an end in itself, that it should help our people, the builders of communism, to scale new heights. We will never imitate those writers who think that to criticize means, as Nikita Sergeyevich put it, to behave like the rooster who digs in the garbage and has claws and spurs on his feet to scratch in the dung heap. . . . Criticism must be constructive." [22]

Press criticism is routinely directed against all quarters and all elements in society except those who sit in the highest Party circles.[23] For example, recently criticism has been directed at a minister of the USSR (The Minister of Higher and Secondary Specialized Education),[24] the council of ministers of a republic,[25] a republic ministry (The Ministry of Construction of the Kazakh Soviet Socialist Republic),[26] Gosplan of the USSR, and republican

[18] The Soviet institution of criticism and self-criticism is said to insure progress by eliminating remnants of the past and accelerating new developments and trends. The Soviet claim is that the effectiveness of the institution demonstrates the vitality and strength of the socialist public order. *Kritika i samokritika (Criticism and Self-Criticism)*, in POLITICHESKIY SLOVAR' (DICTIONARY OF POLITICAL TERMS) 297-98 (2d Ponomarov ed. Moscow 1958). See also, INKELES, *op. cit. supra* note 10, at 196-203.

[19] 32 BOL'SHAYA SOVETSKAYA ENTSIKLOPEDIYA 636 (2d ed. 1955).

[20] See, for example, *Po signalu zheleznodorozhnikov (The Signal of the Railroad Workers)*, received at a "Punkt Pravdy" (Pravda Point, *i.e.*, complaint desk), Pravda, Dec. 25, 1963, p. 2.

[21] See, for example, *Popustitel'stvo spekulyantam (Winking at Speculators)*, *id.*, Aug. 23, 1963, p. 4.

[22] Adzhubei, *The Party's Fighting Weapon*, Sov. pechat', No. 5, p. 1 (1963), transl. in 15 C.D.S.P. No. 25, p. 18 (1963). See also INKELES, *op. cit. supra* note 10, at 198-99.

[23] FINN, EXPERIENCES OF A SOVIET JOURNALIST 17 (Research Program in the U.S.S.R., Mimeo. Series No. 66, 1954).

[24] *Pochemu ne khvatayet uchebnikov dlya vuzov i tekhnikumov? (Why Are There Insufficient Textbooks for Institutions of Higher Education and Technical Schools?)*, Pravda, Sept. 30, 1963, p. 2.

[25] *Oshibki priznayutsya . . . polozheniye ne menyayetsya (Mistakes Are Acknowledged . . . The Situation Doesn't Change)*, *id.*, July 26, 1963, p. 2.

[26] *Stroyka ez zabotlivogo khozyayna (Construction Without a Careful Manager)*, *id.*, July 24, 1963, p. 2.

and regional administrative and Party officials.[27] The press itself is the object of self-criticism for its failure to perform its tasks in the building of communism. At the June Plenum of the Central Committee of the CPSU, the press in general was criticized for "departmentalism" and "its inevitable products—narrow field of vision, insufficient militancy, duplication [and] irrational use of forces and means." [28] A more effective system was said to be necessary to insure "the opportunity for sufficiently complete coverage . . . of questions of economic and cultural construction." [29] Towards this end, the State Committee for the Press (attached to the USSR Council of Ministers) was established by the Presidium of the Supreme Soviet on August 10, 1963.[30] Major responsibility for supervising the press, however, rests with the Ideological Department of the Central Committee of the CPSU.[31] The "leading central newspapers" exercise a measure of supervision over the press by criticizing or praising the work of individual publications. For example, local newspapers have been criticized for printing stereotyped materials of low ideological quality [32] and for attempts at frivolity instead of "striving to make a newspaper for youth more militant and interesting." [33] *Sovetskaya kul'tura* [34] has been criticized for its failure to influence the development of Soviet culture.[35] On the other hand, *Literaturnaya gazeta* [36] was commended for a new feature, "Institute of Readers Interests," which, as a vehicle for readers' statements of literary interests and preferences, "convincingly shows that readers are most interested in books which deal

[27] *Avralom delu ne pomozhesh' (The Matter Will Not Be Helped Even by an All-Out Effort)*; *Tak zavedyono (It Has Been So Ordered)*, *id.*, July 4, 1963, p. 2; *Pochemu gigant khimii rabotayet na polsilu? (Why Does a Giant Chemical Plant Operate at Half Its Capacity?)*, *id.*, Sept. 3, 1963.

[28] Report, *supra* note 4, at 13.

[29] *On the Current Tasks of the Party's Ideological Work*, *supra* note 14, at 15.

[30] Pravda, Aug. 11, 1963, p. 2, transl. in 15 C.D.S.P. No. 32, p. 24 (1963).

[31] Senate Comm. on Government Operations, *Staffing Procedures and Problems in the Soviet Union*, 88th Cong., 1st Sess. 14 (1963). The Ideological Department has a separate Department for *Pravda*. *Ibid.* The Department of Agitation and Propaganda (AGITPROP) formerly supervised the press and other media of mass communication. McCLOSKY & TURNER, THE SOVIET DICTATORSHIP 548 (1960).

[32] *Mery prinyaty (Measures Taken)*, Pravda, Nov. 14, 1963, p. 2, referring to original criticism contained in *Obshchiye frazy i nenuzhnye podrobnosti (Generalities and Unnecessary Details)*, *id.*, Sept. 24, 1963, p. 2.

[33] *Lishnye kavychki (Unnecessary Quotation Marks)*, *id.*, Nov. 18, 1963, p. 4, transl. in 15 C.D.S.P. No. 46, p. 31 (1963). *Cf.* praise of *Komsomol'skaya pravda*, another youth paper, for its regular feature *Institut obshchestvennogo mneniya (Institute of Public Opinion)*, Pravda, Dec. 27, 1963, p. 4.

[34] *Sovetskaya kul'tura (Soviet Culture)* is the official organ of the Ministry of Culture.

[35] *Bez chuvstva otvetstvennosti, bez znaniya dela (No Sense of Responsibility, No Understanding of the Cause)*, Pravda, Nov. 20, 1963, p. 4.

[36] *Literaturnaya gazeta (Literary Gazette)* is the official organ of the Soviet Writers Union.

with today's vital problems, recount tales of the hero-creator of a new society, and assist the Soviet man to comprehend life more deeply, to find his place, his sector in the building of Communism." [37]

Letters to the editor are an important part of the work of the press.[38] "[These letters] inform the paper of the achievements of the collectives, of their factories and collective farms, raise vital questions concerning all aspects of our life, and disclose shortcomings." [39] "The newspaper mailbag is a wellspring of themes, of bright and interesting material, of many newspaper campaigns. . . . "The Central Committee of our party ascribes great importance to work with readers' letters." [40] Published figures indicate that the newspaper mailbag is a heavy one. "The Soviet press belongs to the people. Millions of public correspondents actively participate in it." [41] Specifically, it is said that in 1956, the central newspapers received more than one million letters to the editor; [42] for the first four months of 1963 the editors of *Pravda* received 141,450 letters and comments from its readers.[43] By the end of the year, the figure was over 400,000.[44] Not all of this correspondence can be published; that which is not, is disposed of by reference to the appropriate agency for corrective or other action [45] or at meetings set up by the press at which the letter writers and representatives of the Party, press, and appropriate administrative agencies consider the criticisms or suggestions (proposals) contained in the letters.[46] To coordinate the activities of the press in acting upon letters to the editor, all-union seminars of those who head the letters to the editor departments of republic, territorial, and regional newspapers are held from time to time "to exchange experiences," a euphemism for dissemination of the Party line. On August 27, 1963, such a seminar was organized by the Union of Journalists of the USSR and participated in by 120 representatives of the largest newspapers of the 15 constituent republics.[47]

[37] *Forum chitateley otkryt (A Readers Forum Has Been Opened)*, Pravda, Oct. 2, 1963, p. 4.

[38] See INKELES, *op. cit. supra* note 10, at 207-15.

[39] *Pochta pravdy (Pravda's Mail)*, Pravda, May 5, 1963, p. 4.

[40] Adzhubei, *supra* note 22.

[41] *Vsenarodnaya Pechat, supra* note 5.

[42] 50 BOL'SHAYA SOVETSKAYA ENTSIKLOPEDIYA 413 (2d ed. 1955).

[43] *Pochta pravdy, supra* note 39.

[44] *Kchitatelya pravdy (To the Readers of Pravda)*, Pravda, Dec. 31, 1963, p. 6.

[45] MCCLOSKY & TURNER, *op. cit. supra* note 31, at 548; see also *Mery prinyaty (Measures Taken)*, Pravda, Aug. 23, 1963, p. 4, and *id.*, Oct. 4, 1963, p. 4, reporting the corrective measures taken in connection with unpublished letters referred by the editors of *Pravda* to appropriate agencies for action.

[46] *Pochta pravdy, supra* note 39.

[47] *Pis'ma trudyashchikhsya v gazete (Letters of the Workers in the Newspaper)*, Pravda, Aug. 28, 1963, p. 4.

Frequently editorial criticism and comment appear to be based solely upon the correspondence received by the press. In such cases, the letter to the editor is published together with the editorial comment evoked by it.[48] The editorial staff, however, does not merely comment upon the letters it receives. These "signals" (*signaly*) that all is not well in a given sector of the economy or society frequently form the basis for investigative action or a so-called "raid" by representatives of the press with subsequent publication of the findings of those representatives confirming the situation criticized.[49]

In all of its activities, the press is assisted by workers' correspondents, the *rabsel'kory, rabkory (rabochiye korrespondenty)* and *sel'kory (sel'skiye korrespondenty)*, who act as the eyes and ears of the press and the frequent source of "signals." [50] *Rabsel'kor* personnel, recruited primarily from the ranks of party members, Komsomols and activists at state enterprises, constitute "a network of non-professional correspondents," [51] who assist Soviet press work by disseminating the current line through enterprise wall newspapers and other agitational work [52] and participating in press investigations.[53] The work of the *rabsel'kory* is coordinated and harnessed to the effort to build communism through Party-sponsored large scale assemblies of such personnel: [54] Their organ, *Rabochiy-krest'yanskiy korrespondent (Worker-Peasant Correspondent)*, published by *Pravda*, which organizes and reports the results of local meetings and activities of activists of the press, "conducts on its pages 'Zaochnye kursy redaktorov stengazet' (Correspondence Courses for Editors of Wall Newspapers) and 'Shkola obshchestvennykh foto-korrespondentov' (School for Public Photo Correspondents)," and prints and discusses examples of the literary work of *rabsel'kor* personnel; [55] a network of "*rabkor* posts" sponsored by the central

[48] See, for example, *Opyat' svodkomaniya (Again Reportomania)*, Pravda, Aug. 19, 1963, p. 2, where the editors of *Pravda* agreed that the multiplicity of reports required by local party organs is not good management but bureaucratism, a serious sin of Soviet officialdom; also, *Predpriyimchivye styazhateli (Resourceful Grabbers)*, *id.*, Sept. 13, 1963, p. 2, where editorial comment is made in connection with the reprinting in *Pravda* of local press criticism of collective farmers who spend most of their time working on their private garden plots.

[49] FINN, *op. cit. supra* note 23, at 15-19.

[50] *Id.* at 9-16. See also, INKELES, *op. cit. supra* note 10, at 203-07.

[51] FINN, *op. cit. supra* note 23, at 9.

[52] See *Obshchestvennyye rasprostraniteli pechati (Public Distributors of the Press)*, Pravda, Sept. 1, 1963, p. 6.

[53] FINN, *op. cit. supra* note 23, at 15.

[54] *Id.* at 11. See also, *Iz odnogo kresla v drugoye (From One Arm Chair to Another)*, Pravda, Oct. 12, 1963, p. 2.

[55] *Aktivisty pechati pomogayut svoyemu zhurnalu (The Activists of the Press Help Their Magazine)*, Pravda, Sept. 28, 1963, p. 4. See also, *Pereklichka rabkorov-khimikov prodolzhayetsya (The Roll Call of Rabkor Chemical Personnel Continues)*, *id.*, Dec. 18, 1963, p. 6, describing the results of a raid conducted jointly by *rabkor* personnel of neighboring enterprises.

press;[56] and study in universities and schools for *rabsel'kor* personnel where "tired after work and sacrificing their leisure hours, they [activists of the press] rush, sometimes 10 kilometers or more, in all kinds of weather, to learn how to write comments, correspondence, and satire and to improve the format of their wall newspaper."[57]

II. The Press as an Organ of Education

The Soviet press is said to be "a weapon of political education of the masses . . . a mighty means . . . of communist education of the broadest mass of the population . . . [and] propagandist of the ideas of Marxism-Leninism. . . ."[58] "Our press should become a means for pulling along those who lag behind by educating them for work, labor discipline and organization."[59] The immediate goal of educational work is transmission of the current party line or decision to the masses.[60] The longer range goal of political education is inextricably connected with the concept of the new man—"the conscious builder of communism."[61]

> "Comrades! The demands our society makes on each person are embodied in the moral code of the builder of communism. The [ideological] task is to transform the norms of the moral code into guidelines of life, into the personal convictions of all Soviet people."[62]
>
> "The party attributes great importance to the rearing of the new man, who will have a communist attitude towards labor and his societal obligations. This requires great and tireless work. We should not expect communist consciousness to come to people automatically as a result of the growth of our economic successes. The party teaches that it is necessary to wage an active battle on all fronts of communist construction, and the ideological front is one of the most important in the struggle for communism."[63]

[56] For example, from time to time the criticism of local conditions originating from "rabkor posts" of *Pravda* is printed under the caption *Rabkorskiy post Pravdy soobshchayet (Rabkor Post of Pravda Informs) (e.g., Trevogi balakhninskikh bumazhnikov (The Alarms Sounded by the Workers of the Balakhninskiy Paper Combine)*, Pravda, Sept. 27, 1963, p. 2).

[57] *Aktivisty pechati uchatsya (Activists of the Press Study), id.*, Aug. 18, 1963, p. 2.

[58] 32 Bol'shaya sovetskaya entsiklopediya 636 (2d ed. 1955).

[59] Pravda, May 5, 1963, p. 1.

[60] The headline "Informatsionnoye soobshcheniye" (Official Communication) is used to report important policy decisions (see, *e.g.*, Pravda, June 19, 1963, and Dec. 10-14, 1963, for coverage of the June and December Plenary Sessions of the Central Committee of the CPSU).

[61] Report of L. F. Ilyichev, Secretary of the CPSU Central Committee on June 18, 1963, at the Plenary Session of the CPSU, transl. from Pravda, June 19, 1963, p. 1, in 15 C.D.S.P. No. 23, p. 5, at 10 (1963).

[62] Report, *supra* note 61, 15 C.D.S.P. No. 24, at 9.

[63] *Mogucheye oruzhiye leninskoy partii (The Mighty Weapon of the Leninst Party)*, Pravda, May 5, 1963, p. 1.

"The chief task in the ideological-upbringing work of the Party in present-day conditions is to ensure ideologically the implementation of the Party Program, the creation of the material and technical base for communism, the formation of communist social relations and the rearing of the new man; to enhance political vigilance and to wage a broad offensive against imperialist ideology, against survivals of the past in the consciousness of people.

. . .

"Under present-day conditions the *press, radio, films and television*—shock forces of the ideological front—have especially great significance in the ideological education of the people." [64]

The new man is one who will work selflessly for society and instinctively conform to the moral code of communism.[65] The press is to assist in the educational process by inspiring greater labor productivity, Marxist-Leninist morality, and better understanding of the work of the Party, and the encouragement of "sharp and principled criticism and self-criticism." [66] To enhance the effectiveness of criticism and self-criticism, there is "widespread dissemination of positive examples." [67] True to this mandate, the Soviet press conducts its educational work along the three lines of inspirational exhortation, glorification of those who have demonstrated in their actions the ideals of communist behavior, and criticism of certain personal shortcomings.

Labor productivity and overfulfillment of the plan are usually treated together. The primacy of plan fulfillment is constantly stressed.[68] In addition, major holidays, *e.g.*, May Day or the Anniversary of the October Revolution, or plenary meetings of the Central Committee of the CPSU are used as occasions to exhort a spurt of productivity from all sectors of the Soviet economy.[69] Further, "positive examples" in the form of regional

[64] *On the Current Task of the Party's Ideological Work,* Resolution of the Plenary Session the CPSU Central Committee on the Report by Comrade L. F. Ilyichev, adopted June 21, 1963, transl. from Pravda, June 22, 1963, p. 1, in 15 C.D.S.P. No. 25, pp. 12, 15 (1963). (Italics in original.)

[65] AKADEMIYA NAUK SSSR—INSTITUT GOSUDARSTVA I PRAVA, FUNDAMENTALS OF SOVIET LAW 13-14 (Romashkin ed. Sdobnikov transl. Moscow 1961) [hereinafter cited as ROMASHKIN].

[66] *On the Current Tasks of the Party's Ideological Work, supra* note 64, at 15.

[67] *Ibid.*

[68] See *Vse sily na vypolneniye planov kommunisticheskogo stroitel'stva (All Efforts for Fulfillment of the Plans of Communist Construction),* Pravda, Dec. 21, 1963, p. 1.

[69] *E.g., Vstretim pervoye maya novymi trudovymi pobedami (We Shall Meet the First of May with New Labor Victories), id.,* April 9, 1963, p. 1, and *V chest' plenuma TsK KPSS (In Honor of the Plenum of the Central Committee of the CPSU), id.,* Dec. 6, 1963, p. 1.

and individual successes in agricultural [70] and industrial [71] work in fulfillment of the plan are glorified by the press.[72] The immediate, tangible goal is plan fulfillment; the more distant, and less measurable, end is development of a "love for labor," a trait of the new man.

> "By propagandizing the experience of our innovators and developing in our youth a love for work, the newspaper assists the working collectives, party, trade-union and Komsomol organizations in reaching each individual." [73]
>
> "The heart of ideological work of the party, soviets, trade-unions and Komsomol . . . should be the instilling in each Soviet man, love and respect for socially useful labor." [74]

The other aspects of the character of this new man are not neglected by the press, which "in all its coverage actively expresses communist morality and assists the instilling in Soviet people a Marxist-Leninist outlook, ideological conviction and devotion to the cause of communism." [75] Specifically, the press was praised recently for its effective educational work in support of atheism.[76] In addition, lead articles continually extol adherence of the builder of communism to communist morality which "triumphantly proclaims: 'man is to man—a friend, comrade and brother—one for all and all for one' [and] . . . teaches collectivism, comradely assistance, honesty, truthfulness and moral purity." [77]

Principled criticism and self-criticism in the educational effort is, at the present time, "directed against sluggishness, bureaucratism, extrava-

[70] *Uborke urozhaya—vysokiye tempy (High Speed to the Gathering of the Harvest), Ukrainskiye milliony (The Millions of the Ukraine),* and *Vysokiy urozhay gorokha (The High Yield of Peas), id.,* July 18, 1963, p. 1; see also, *Primer sovkhoza "Belaya dacha" (The Example of the State Farm "White Dacha"), id.,* p. 2.

[71] *S pobedoy, tovarishchi moskvichi i Leningradtsy! Trudyashchiyesya Moskvy i Leningrada dosrochno vypolnili plan pyatogo goda semiletki (Congratulations on Your Victory, Comrades of Moscow and Leningrad! The Workers of Moscow and Leningrad Have Fulfilled the Plan of the Fifth Year of the Seven Year Plan Ahead of Schedule), id.,* Dec. 26, 1963, p. 1. *Trudovoy uspekh shakhtyorov (The Labor Success of the Miners), ibid. Godovoy plan—dosrochno (The Annual Plan is Ahead of Schedule), id.,* Dec. 25, 1963, p. 1. *Krupnyy uspekh uzbekskikh khimikov (The Great Success of the Chemical Workers of Uzbekistan), id.,* Dec. 24, 1963, p. 1. "Dnevnik vsenarodnogo sorevnovaniya" (Diary of National Competition) is a regular feature of *Pravda* which reports accomplishments in the industrial sector. See, for example, *id.,* Aug. 24, 1963, p. 1, and *id.,* Oct. 5, 1963, p. 1.

[72] *V tsentre vnimaniya—chelovek truda (In the Center of Attention—the Man of Labor), id.,* Aug. 11, 1963, p. 4.

[73] *Ibid.*

[74] *Vospityvat' lyubov' i uvazheniye k trudu (Instill Love and Respect for Work), id.,* Aug. 29, 1963, p. 1.

[75] *V tsentre vnimaniya—chelovek truda, supra* note 72.

[76] *Svet pobezhdayet (Light Conquers [Darkness]),* Pravda, Dec. 23, 1963, p. 2.

[77] *V tsentre vnimaniya—chelovek truda, supra* note 72.

gance, sponging and other antisocial phenomena." [78] The approach here is to demonstrate the survival of these negative characteristics as a part of the continuing struggle against them.[79] Recently, campaigns have been conducted against the improper use of grain and bread to feed personally-owned livestock,[80] defective workmanship and poor quality of manufactured goods,[81] speculation,[82] improper management of wage and other enterprise funds,[83] poor attitude towards the conservation of state resources,[84] crop neglect on state and collective farms,[85] and personal shortcomings ranging from putting on airs [86] to dishonesty.[87] The technique is to publicize the fate of the perpetrators and other persons involved (*i.e.*, subjection to criminal or administrative penalties) in an attempt to deter similar conduct.[88]

The expressed hope in all of the educational work of the press is that: (a) "the Soviet people . . . [will] not lose a single day and [will] use all its reserves and potential in order to move more quickly and on a broad front towards our great goal—the building of a communist society"; [89] and (b) the undesirable "survivals of the past" will be eradicated from the Soviet man of the future. In performing this educational work, the press serves as "one of the major instruments of social education" *(obshchestvennoye vospitaniye)*.[90]

III. The Press as an Organ of Investigation

The Soviet press acts as "one of the most powerful means of discovering deficiencies, particularly in the field of controlling the execution of laws

[78] *On the Current Tasks of the Party's Ideological Work, supra* note 64, at 15.

[79] See *Pouchitel'naya istoriya (An Instructive Story)*, Pravda, Oct. 5, 1963, p. 2.

[80] *Mery prinyaty (Measures Taken), id.*, Oct. 5, 1963, p. 2. In *Berech' zerno! (Conserve Grain!), id.*, Aug. 18, 1963, p. 2, the press was exhorted to "increase its efforts in the struggle for bread." See also, *Berech' khleb—narodnoye dostoyaniye (Save Bread [grain]—Wealth of the Nation), id.*, Aug. 29, 1963, p. 2.

[81] *Khalturnaya rabota (Shoddy Work), id.*, Oct. 18, 1963, p. 3; "*O shakhtyorskoy kaske (Concerning Miners' Helmets), id.*, July 24, 1963, p. 2; *Mery prinyaty (Measures Taken), ibid.*

[82] *Nashlas' uprava na spekulyantov (Justice Was Found for the Speculators), id.*, Oct. 18, 1963, p. 3.

[83] *Tak rukovodit' khozyaystvom nel'zya (The Economy Must Not Be Managed That Way), id.*, Oct. 18, 1963, p. 4.

[84] *Yakutskiye mastera otpisok (The Yakutsk Masters of Formal Replies), id.*, June 26, 1963, p. 3.

[85] *Zabytyye plantatsiyi (Forgotten Plantations), id.*, July 17, 1963, p. 2.

[86] *Zabyv o skromnosti (Modesty Has Been Forgotten), id.*, Aug. 12, 1963, p. 2, containing criticism of a local official who insisted on the use of a black sedan as a prestige symbol.

[87] *Vygorazhivayut zhulika (A Swindler Is Shielded), id.*, July 12, 1963, p. 2.

[88] See materials cited in notes 80-87 *supra*.

[89] *Vdokhnovlyayushchiy primer (A Stirring Example)*, Pravda, Dec. 27, 1963, p. 1.

[90] *Vsenarodnaya pechat' (The Press of the Entire People)*, Pravda, Nov. 16, 1963, p. 2.

and the fulfillment of decisions of local organs of state authority." [91] The impetus to investigations by the press may stem from the needs of a party-inspired campaign to overcome a particular problem or condition, letters to the editor reporting deficiencies and shortcomings, or participation by the press as a formal member of party-state control committees.[92] The foregoing are not mutually exclusive, as all three frequently are factors in a given investigation. For example, the campaign may be instituted as a result of letters to the editor or the work of the control commissions. On the other hand, the campaign may employ letters to the editor [93] or the party-state control commissions as vehicles for the accomplishment of its purposes. In any case, the investigative activities of the press, "the organ of all the people," are represented as the work of the masses.

The results of investigative work are usually printed in the form of a report upon an unsavory situation or condition.[94] In *Pravda,* these results frequently appear as part of a column entitled "Pod ogon' kritiki" (Under the Fire of Criticism).[95] A special forum for the work of the committees of party-state control, "Listok partiyno-gosudarstvennogo kontrolya" (Leaflet of Party-State Control) was established by *Pravda* on March 22, 1963,[96] and by *Izvestiya* on March 26, 1963.[97] *Izvestiya* described the Leaflet as follows:

[91] McCLOSKY & TURNER, *The Soviet Dictatorship* 391 (1960), quoting a Soviet textbook, YEVTIKHIYEV & VLASOV, ADMINISTRATIVNOYE PRAVO SSSR (ADMINISTRATIVE LAW OF THE USSR) 133 (Moscow 1946).

[92] "In accordance with the Program of the CPSU, the November (1962) Plenum of the Central Committee of the CPSU revived the Leninist principles of effecting control. Committees of Party and State control, composed, in particular, of representatives of the trade-unions, the Komsomols, the press, and workers, collective-farmers and intelligentsia, were established. These organs assist the Party and the State in fulfilling the Program of the CPSU, in organizing the systematic checking upon factual compliance with the directives of the party and the government, in further improving the direction of the building of communism, and in struggling for an all around rise in the socialist economy." *Formy privlecheniya mass k upravleniyu sovetskim gosudarstvom (Means of Drawing the Masses into Administration of the Soviet State),* Sov. yus. No. 10, p. 1, at 2 (1963).

[93] Letters to the editor, purporting to be, but in fact not, spontaneous and unsolicited, are an effective means of demonstrating mass approval or instigation of investigative action. FINN, EXPERIENCES OF A SOVIET JOURNALIST 9-12 (Research Program for the U.S.S.R. Mimeo. Series No. 66, 1954); McCLOSKY & TURNER, *op. cit. supra* note 91, at 392, 548.

[94] See, for example, *Koren' zla—v raspylenii sredstv (The Root of All Evil Is in the Dissipation of Resources),* Pravda, July 13, 1963, p. 2, where lagging construction of an aluminum industrial complex is criticized. See also, *Oshibki nado ispravlyat' (Mistakes Must Be Corrected),* Izvestiya, July 6, 1963, p. 3, exposing the reason for losses in the operation of a state farm.

[95] See, for example, Pravda, July 13, 1963, p. 2.

[96] *Pod kontrol' mass! (Under the Control of the Masses!), id.,* March 22, 1963, p. 3.

[97] *Narodnyy kontrol' (People's Control),* Izvestiya, March 26, 1963, p. 3. See also the account of this new *Izvestiya* feature in *Narodnyy kontrol' (People's Control),* Pravda, March 26, 1963, p. 4.

> "Its tasks: to render assistance to the party and state in fulfilling the great program of communist construction, organizing a systematic check upon compliance with the directives of the party and government, further improving the management of the economy, [and] insuring observance of party and state discipline and socialist legality.
>
> . . .
>
> "The fire of criticism will be directed against bureaucrats, bamboozlers, and those who produce spoilage, squander the wealth of the state or impede our successful movement forward." [98]

Pravda noted that this new feature, to be published twice monthly, is intended as an "effective instrument in the struggle against deficiencies and for implementing the directives of the party and government." [99] It is to contain investigative reports of the committees of party and state control and the signals of the activists of these committees and of the readers of the press.[100]

In many cases, the investigative work of the press appears to be self-generated as part of regular press work [101] or connected with the work of committees of party-state control.[102] Where the investigation is prompted by a letter to the editor, it may take one of several forms. Cases of importance are personally investigated by a special correspondent of *Pravda* or *Izvestiya*.[103] In other cases, a newspaper in the locale of the incident which is the subject of the criticism or complaint may be given the responsibility for conducting an investigation and making a report on its findings.[104] At

[98] *Narodnyy kontrol', supra* note 97, at p. 3.

[99] *Pod kontrol' mass, supra* note 96, at p. 3.

[100] *Ibid.*

[101] *Koren' zla—v raspylenii sredstv, supra* note 94, and *Ratotat' nekogda . . . zasedayem (There Is No Time To Work—We Are in Conference)*, Pravda, Aug. 15, 1963, p. 2, criticizing local conference-mania. See also, *Razvitiye khimii—udarnyy front (The Development of the Chemical Industry Is the Shockworkers' Front), id.*, July 22, 1963, p. 3, reporting the results of a "raid" which investigated lagging development of the chemical industry in an economic region.

[102] *Sklady na kolecakh (Warehouses on Wheels), id.*, March 22, 1963, p. 4, criticizing improper transport management resulting in motorcycles being subjected to the elements while awaiting transport.

[103] See, for example, *Vneocherednye novoselya (Housing Accommodations Out of Turn), id.*, Oct. 28, 1963, p. 2, where a reporter of *Pravda* notes that he had personally verified the correctness of a letter complaining of improper local allocation of housing accommodations. See also, *Rech' idyot o detyakh (The Subject Is Children), id.*, Oct. 22, 1963, p. 4, where a *Pravda* reporter personally investigated a complaint concerning the inadequacy of premises occupied by 100 children.

[104] *Stroyka bez zabotlivogo khozyayna, (Construction Without a Careful Manager)*, Pravda, July 24, 1963, p. 2, wherein a signal received by *Pravda* concerning the slowness and poor quality of the construction of a sugar plant was sent to a local paper, *Yuzhnyy Kazakhstan (Southern Kazakhstan)*, for investigation and verification. See also, *Avtomashiny na prikole (Laid-up Vehicles), id.*, Sept. 22, 1963, p. 6, where the local press investigated for *Pravda* a complaint of improper management and use of a garage for public transportation.

times, the editors of *Pravda* refer "signals" to *rabsel'kor* personnel for verification and report.[105] *Rabsel'kor* personnel also participate in the press "raids" designed to investigate and correct shortcomings in the fulfillment of the economic plan.[106] A "raid" is described by a former Soviet journalist as follows:

> "Armed with press passes, the participants in the raid, so-called 'light cavalry-men,' gain free access to all sectors of production of the enterprise or collective farm. In effect, they replace the newspaper reporters and carry out the same investigations and control as the latter.
>
> "The editorial office put space at the disposal of the 'cavalry-men' and prints the materials brought in by the raiders." [107]

This journalist noted in 1954 that "in the late 1930's such raid became infrequent." [108] At the present time, however, "raids" are again a part of the Soviet scene. An indication of the scope of these operations can be gleaned from the report of more than 400 *rabsel'kory*, students at a *rabkor* university, and other press activists conducting a "raid" upon 370 stores investigating the shortages of clothing and other personal articles, the quality of available wares, and the poor treatment of customers.[109] In another recent "raid," 200 participants covered 17 cities in their investigation of delays and shortcomings in the timely distribution of the central newspapers to subscribers in outlying areas.[110] In still another, a party of 65 *rabsel'kory* and reporters investigated a report of the wastage of bread in Khar'kov and Alma Alta.[111] No matter what form it takes investigative work is an important part of the activities of a Soviet journalist.

> "Under Soviet conditions a newspaperman is considered not simply as the representative of a publication which is in no way connected with some field of production or supply. . . . A Soviet newspaperman is

[105] *Uchrezhdeniye i posetitel' (The Enterprise and the Visitor)*, Pravda, July 29, 1963, p. 2, containing *rabsel'kor* reports concerning the manner in which visitors are received and treated at enterprises and organizations.

[106] See, for example, report of a *rabkor* "raid" to check progress on activation of chemical plants in Uzbekistan, published in Pravda, Aug. 29, 1963, p. 2, under the heading *Vot tak i upuskayetsya vremya (This Is the Way That Time Is Also Lost)*. See follow-up corrective action resulting from the "raid" in *Mery prinyaty (Measures Taken)*, *id.*, Oct. 2, 1963, p. 4.

[107] Finn, *op. cit. supra* note 93, at 15.

[108] *Ibid.*

[109] *Na proverke—370 magazinov (Under Check: 370 Stores)*, Pravda, June 8, 1963, p. 3.

[110] *Kogda vy poluchayete gazetu? (When Do You Receive the Newspaper?)*, *id.*, Oct. 9, 1963, p. 4, condensed transl. in 15 C.D.S.P. No. 41, p. 25 (1963).

[111] *Polozhit' konets razbazarivaniyu khleba (End the Squandering of Bread)*, Pravda, Sept. 11, 1963, p. 2.

above all a representative of a higher Party organization which controls all production and civic activities within its purview.

. . .

"It is clear then, that the concept of the word correspondent and its meaning in the economic and public life of the country have been changed in the land of Soviets, where it has acquired an ugly police character."[112]

The effectiveness of the investigations conducted by Soviet journalists stems from general recognition of the special control function of the press.

"A correspondent of *Pravda* is admitted everywhere at all times. All economic, Party, trade-union and public organizations open their doors wide to a member of that newspaper's staff. People talk to him with deference and at length, putting aside the most urgent work, conferences and consultations. . . . A *Pravda* correspondent is a representative of the highest organ in the country—the Central Committee of the CPSU (b)."[113]

The investigative activities of the Soviet press are an integral part of its organizational role in the building of communism. Investigation complements the educational and control functions by uncovering conditions and situations which indicate the need for the exercise of the one or the other function.

IV. The Press as an Organ of Control and Supervision

The press is said to constitute a form of "control by the people" over "various spheres of government";[114] in fact, it is an organ of party control.[115] "Control" in the Soviet lexicon usually means "the systematic checking upon compliance with statutes, directives of the party, resolutions of the Government and decisions of higher organs."[116] The work of the press, however, extends beyond the mere uncovering of instances of lack of compliance. The press actively intervenes, when necessary, to effect the correction of deficiencies and insure punishment of those responsible for them.[117] The principal, formal technique for this aspect of Soviet press work is editorial criticism and editorial comment upon criticism and self-criticism, with corrective action demanded of appropriate agencies and officials. The failure of officials to react immediately to press comment and criticism

[112] Finn, *op. cit. supra* note 93, at 18.

[113] *Id.* at 17.

[114] Romashkin 126.

[115] Inkeles, Public Opinion in Soviet Russia 188-93, 203 (1950).

[116] 1 Yuridicheskiy slovar' (Juridical (Legal) Dictionary) 512 (2d ed. Moscow 1956).

[117] See McCloskey & Turner, *op. cit. supra* note 91, at 391.

becomes still another basis for critical comment. The press persists until corrective action is taken.[118] For example, in a recent case it was stated:

> "The Council of Ministers of the republic regional organizations has promised repeatedly to take effective measures but the situation doesn't change. Isn't it time to demand a reply from those whose fault yearly costs thousand of centners of livestock production?" [119]

In *Pravda*, reports of corrective measures taken are presented in a column entitled, "Pravde otvechayut: Mery prinyaty" (They Answer Pravda: Measures Have Been Taken), which, in effect, is a follow-up on the criticism previously printed. The corrective action ranges from arrest,[120] referral of the matter to the local procurator,[121] and criminal prosecution [122] of those guilty of criminal offenses to expulsion from membership [123] or candidature [124] in the party; disciplinary action against party members; [125] dismissal from position; [126] administrative fine; [127] personal pecuniary liability; [128] specific corrective action such as the ordering of the inclusion of newsreels and documentary films in motion picture programs,[129] the procurement of additional pumps and other fire fighting equipment,[130] the installation of electric filters on cement ovens to reduce air pollution,[131] or the rescission of unnecessary administrative reporting requirements; [132] and the promise of corrective action such as the installation of bath tubs by a stated time,[133] greater quality control in the production of radio sets,[134] or the completion of gravel roads and walks by a stated time.[135]

[118] See *Pochemu ne khvatayet uchebnikov dlya vuzov i tekhnikumov? (Why Are There Insufficient Textbooks for Institutions of Higher Education and Technical Schools?)*, Pravda, Sept. 30, 1963, p. 2, noting that a year had passed since *Pravda* criticized the Ministry of Higher and Secondary Specialized Education of the USSR and many leading publishing houses for improper planning of the output of books.

[119] *Oshibki priznayutsya . . . polozheniye ne menyayetsya, (Mistakes Are Acknowledged . . . The Situation Doesn't Change), id.*, July 26, 1963, p. 2.

[120] Pravda, Aug. 24, 1963, p. 4.

[121] *Id.*, Dec. 1, 1963, p. 2.

[122] *Id.*, Feb. 1, 1963, p. 2.

[123] *Id.*, June 9, 1963, p. 2.

[124] *Id.*, Oct. 5, 1963, p. 2.

[125] *Id.*, July 12, 1963, p. 2.

[126] *Id.*, Nov. 1, 1963, p. 4.

[127] *Ibid.*

[128] *Id.*, Sept. 30, 1963, p. 2.

[129] *Id.*, Aug. 12, 1963, p. 2.

[130] *Id.*, July 2, 1963, p. 4.

[131] *Id.*, Sept. 12, 1963, p. 2.

[132] *Id.*, Sept. 22, 1963, p. 6.

[133] *Id.*, July 9, 1963, p. 2.

[134] *Id.*, July 1, 1963, p. 4.

[135] *Id.*, July 4, 1963, p. 2.

The press has the capability of effectively intervening because it enjoys, as a party organ, the full support of the CPSU at all levels of administration.

> "Our party always supports the sharp criticism voiced by the Soviet press, demands that all executives regard the printed word respectfully and with Leninist attentiveness. Of course, there are still to be found persons who resist criticism." [136]
>
> "The province Party committee's bureau has charged province committee departments, province executive committees, city and district Party committees, agencies of Party-state control, the militia, the courts and the prosecutor's office with paying closer attention to the checking of complaints and statements from the working people, reacting promptly to statements in the press and striving for the elimination of shortcomings in work." [137]

This support of the party is further manifested in the continuing campaign against officials who ignore press criticism or take retaliatory measures or otherwise attempt to suppress criticism.

> "Last year at the meeting of workers' correspondents in the city of ———————— criticism was voiced concerning those managers who do not react to criticism in the press and persecute workers' correspondents. The Bureau *(Byuro)* of the regional committee of the CPSU strictly punishes those who suppress criticism." [138]

In a recent case, the failure of officials of a local enterprise to react properly to press criticism resulted in party disciplinary action against the offending officials and an obligation imposed by higher party officials upon the local party committee "to get a regular accounting of measures taken by the enterprise management in response to press comment." [139] In another, the refusal of the directors of an enterprise to reinstate a party member improperly dismissed because of his criticism of them was subjected to severe criticism as follows:

> "The good name of a communist remains besmirched. No one is calling to task that suppressor of criticism, Comrade ————————, and his

[136] Adzhubei, *The Party's Fighting Weapon,* Sov. phechat' No. 5, p. 1 (1963), transl. in 15 C.D.S.P. No. 25, p. 18 (1963).

[137] *Pravda Receives an Answer: STEPS TAKEN!,* 15 C.D.S.P. No. 47, p. 29, at 30 (1963), transl. from Pravda, Nov. 25, 1963, p. 2.

[138] *Iz odnogo kresla v drugoye (From One Armchair to Another)*, Pravda, Oct. 12, 1963, p. 2. The courts were recently criticized for not "always reacting properly to press comment." *(Za ukrepleniye svyazi sudov s organami partiyno-gosudarstvennogo kontrolya (For a Strengethening of the Ties of the Courts With the Organs of Party-State Control),* Sov. yus. No. 18, p. 1, at 3 (1963).

[139] *Mery prinyaty,* Pravda, July 16, 1963, p. 4.

henchmen. This must be done without fail. Those who attempt to mete out punishment for criticism must be made examples of." [140]

The control activities of the press have caused it to be regarded as the instance of appeal where resort to formal, institutional channels appear unproductive.[141] The central newspapers, in addition, are appealed to in cases where local press criticism has been ineffective and has not resulted in corrective action.[142] In its control activities the press cuts across institutional channels of administrative subordination in the sense that it calls for the correction of deficiencies wherever found.

The corrective action called for ranges from the construction at enterprises of shelters against the winter elements and devices for unloading flat cars,[143] to criminal prosecution of those considered by the press to be guilty of criminal conduct.[144] In many cases the call for action involves direct intervention in the work of specialized governmental organs [145] such as planning and administrative authorities and, more shockingly, the procuracy and the courts. For example, organs of the former type have been called upon to devote more resources to school construction,[146] provide adequate unloading

[140] *Zazhimishchikov kritiki—k strogomu otvetu (Suppressors of Criticism [Must Be Held] to Strict Account), id.*, July 22, 1963, p. 4. See also, *Neokonchennoye delo (Unfinished Business), id.*, Oct. 9, 1963, p. 2, to the effect that people who suppress criticism must be punished and those who have been persecuted for criticism must be rehabilitated.

[141] See, for example, *Negde kupit' knigi (There Is No Place To Buy Books), id.*, Sept. 4, 1963, p. 2, where, in complaining about the absence of a book store in a quarter-century old town, it is said: "The Komsomols of the village asked me to turn to *Pravda* for assistance as they have given up all hope of receiving sympathetic treatment by local authorities." See also, *Po signalu zheleznodorozhnikov (The Signal of the Railroad Workers)*, Pravda, Dec. 25, 1963, p. 2 (concerning the pile-up of rail shipments at the railhead) and *Oshibka ispravlena (The Mistake Is Corrected), id.*, July 18, 1963, p. 2 (concerning the rescission of a city architect's order which would have resulted in destruction of usable dwelling houses and orchards). In both cases, attempts to get corrective action from local authorities had failed prior to intervention by *Pravda.*

[142] *Den'gi vperyod (Money in Advance)*, Pravda, Aug. 19, 1963, p. 2, where a complaint of poor bus service to an oil refinery, attributed to the advance payment for service, was registered with *Pravda* after criticism in the city and regional newspapers had brought no results.

[143] *Oshibki povtoryayutsya (Mistakes Are Repeated), id.*, Aug. 12, 1963, p. 2.

[144] *Prestupnikov—k otvetu! (Criminals to Justice!), id.*, March 23, 1963, p. 2, calling for the attention of party organs and the procuracy of a republic to the case of an assault on a Komsomol member by a group whose involvement in the theft of milk had been exposed by that member. See also, *Operatsiya ryba (Operation Fish), id.*, Oct. 7, 1963, p. 2, calling for the criminal prosecution of individuals fishing with explosives.

[145] Lower party organs, as well; see *Koren' zla—v raspylenii sredstv (The Root of All Evil Is in the Dissipation of Resources), id.*, July 13, 1963, p. 2, calling, in effect, for action by the regional party committee to expedite the construction of aluminum industrial complexes in a named economic region.

[146] *Avralom delu ne pomozhezh' (The Matter Will Not Be Helped Even by an All-Out Effort), id.*, July 4, 1963, p. 2.

facilities for railroad rolling stock,[147] restore a good communist to the position from which he was improperly reduced,[148] and withhold apartment assignments and leave in the case of individuals who violate labor discipline.[149] Press intervention in the work of the procuracy and the courts involves a similar interference with the expertise, responsibility, and discretion of officials charged with state administration. In this area it undermines the stability of the administration of law and destroys the substance of the oft-repeated claim concerning the independence of the Soviet judiciary.[150] This is ignored in Soviet commentaries which only cite "instances of the press exposing shortcomings in the work of . . . [the] courts."[150a]

The Soviet press has itself provided examples of the distortions introduced into the administration of criminal justice by the intervention of the press. Recently, *Izvestiya* criticized a people's court which, influenced by the demand of the local press for strict punishment, convicted one not guilty of an offense. *Izvestiya* noted that local party officials, themselves involved in the offense, had caused the local press to influence the decision of the people's court. Asserting the claim that Soviet law protects the individual against injustices of this type, *Izvestiya* called for prompt correction of the situation.[151]

As indicated above, the press does not limit itself to exhortations that there be a general improvement in the work of judicial and procuratorial organs. The general nature of a recent comment suggests the low quality of the work of comrades' courts.[152] Rather, it intervenes in individual cases at all stages of the proceedings. For example, the detailed press report of wholesale bribe-taking by local officials at a named technical school was followed by the reporter's comment, "I trust the investigative agencies will be able to unravel the doings at the Chimkent Polytechnical School, and that the courts will mete out justice." [153] The clear intent was a call for "justice" as understood by the press. In another case, the press was instru-

[147] *Pochemu prostaivayut vagony (Why the Railroad Cars Are Idle), id.*, Sept. 9, 1963, p. 2.

[148] *Nel'zya svoyu vinu svalivat' na drugikh (One Must Not Dump His Own Guilt onto Others), id.*, Oct. 11, 1963, p. 2.

[149] *Obshchestvennye blaga tem, kto khorosho truditsya (Social Benefits for Those Who Work Well), id.*, Oct. 11, 1963, p. 2.

[150] Article 112 of the Soviet Constitution proclaims that "judges are independent and subject only to the law." (Transl. in DENISOV & KIRICHENKO, SOVIET STATE LAW app. 402 (Moscow 1960); see also, *id.* at 310, and ROMASHKIN 88, 449, 486.

[150a] SHEININ, PEOPLE'S COURTS IN THE U.S.S.R. 108-11 (Moscow 1957).

[151] *Kozly otpushcheniya (Scapegoats)*, Izvestiya, March 26, 1963, p. 4.

[152] *Pochemu v rayone zabyli o tovarishcheskikh sudakh? (Why Have They Forgotten About the Comrades' Courts in the Region?)*, Sov. yus. No. 16, p. 17 (1963).

[153] *How I Was Offered a Bribe*, 15 C.D.S.P. No. 39, p. 29 (1963).

mental in the punishment of regional procuratorial and police *(militsiya)* officials for not "demonstrating party principle" in the investigation of a named individual.[154] The intervention of the press in still another case resulted in a report from a regional procurator's office "that the resolution dropping criminal proceedings against . . . . has been cancelled. The . . . District Prosecutor's Office has been advised to go on with the investigation." [155] In addition, court decisions and proceedings are frequently criticized and attacked by the press.[156] In a recent case a judge of a people's court was criticized for having restored a criminal to the position from which he had been removed.[157] The aftermath of this criticism was reported as follows:

"The Deputy Chairman of the Supreme Court of the RSFSR notified the editors that a check of a letter published in *Pravda* on July 12, 1963, resulted in the setting aside of a decision of the people's court which restored the individual to the position from which he had allegedly been improperly removed. The Regional Court dismissed the complaint and the people's judge who heard the case was advised of the error in the proceedings." [158]

Other cases further indicate the extent to which press intervention in the judicial process has been institutionalized. A local newspaper intervened on behalf of a member of the Komsomol by requesting a regional (appellate) court to review the case and change the sentence to one committing the

[154] *Khapunam ne potvorstvovat'! (No Indulgence for Grabbers!)*, Pravda, July 22, 1963, p. 4. See also, *Mery prinyaty (Measures Taken)*, *id.*, Feb. 1, 1963, p. 2, where it is noted ominously that a named procurator had "demonstrated red tape in the initiation of a criminal prosecution" and that, as a consequence, "the question of party disciplinary measures against him will be considered separately."

[155] Follow-up on *Lumber*, 15 C.D.S.P. No. 29, p. 32 (1963), in *id.*, No. 43, at 30.

[156] See, for example, *Zashchitili progul'shchika (A Shirker Was Protected)*, Pravda, Aug. 24, 1963, p. 4, attacking the correctness of district and regional courts' decisions that the dismissal of an employee was not in accordance with law.

"The press also plays an important part in exercising control over the activities of the courts.

. . .

"In a number of cases Soviet newspapers and magazines have boldly opposed certain court findings that they considered either too mild or too severe. Court findings on civil cases are also criticized in the press whenever they are regarded as incorrect.

"In such cases the court findings are usually re-examined by a higher body acting in a supervisory capacity; a further investigation may be ordered and cases that are to be retried are always referred to a different court or are tried in the same court by different judges." SHEININ, *op. cit. supra* note 150a, at 108-09.

[157] *Vygorazhivayut zhulika (A Rogue Is Being Shielded)*, Pravda, July 12, 1963, p. 2.

[158] *Mery prinyaty (Measures Taken)*, *id.*, Aug. 28, 1963, p. 2.

convicted person to his workers' collective for rehabilitation. The regional court refused to change the sentence and rendered a separate opinion to the effect that members of the editorial board had acted improperly in attempting to intervene on behalf of the convicted person. The sentence was subsequently changed by the presidium of that regional court but the separate opinion remained in force. Based upon an account of this matter in *Pravda* on May 7, 1963, the supreme court of the republic reviewed the case with the following result:

> "The separate opinion rendered by the ——— regional court to the effect that the editorial staff had without legal basis defended ——— . . . was, on 23 May 1963, reversed by the Supreme Court . . . as incorrect and unfounded because the workers of the editorial board did not overstep their competence in so acting." [159]

This opinion, in effect, recognizes the competence and, thereby, the "party-in-interest" status of representatives of the press to prosecute an appeal in a criminal case.[160] Further, the December 1963 Plenum of the Supreme Court of the USSR issued an order to judicial organs to give careful consideration to criticism or indications of illegality which appear in the press.

> "The plenum bound the court to check carefully the communications of mass organizations and the press concerning violations of law, red tape and bureaucratism in the work of judicial organs and to inform the appropriate organizations and establishments of the measures taken." [161]

The press has also demanded that the procuracy and the courts give it an accounting of the handling of a case or a problem of judicial administration. For example, in protesting the improper exile of a woman under the parasite legislation, the editors of *Izvestiya* criticized all local police, procuratorial, and judicial organs and expressed the hope that "the personnel of the institutions where the above named persons work, the court agencies and the prosecutor's office will give the newspaper a comprehensive answer befitting the seriousness of the question." The editors commented further:

> "As is evident, the Moscow City Executive Committee's Administration for Safeguarding Public Order and the city prosecutor's office

[159] *Id.*, June 17, 1963, p. 2.

[160] Section 44 of the Basic Principles of Criminal Procedure of the USSR and the Constituent Republics (transl. in 7 HIGHLIGHTS OF CURRENT LEGISLATION AND ACTIVITIES IN MID-EUROPE 69, 83 (1959)), limits the right of appeal to the accused, his defense counsel or legal representative, the victim, the procurator, and the civil plaintiff and civil defendant (where a civil claim is heard as part of the criminal proceedings).

[161] *Vazhneyshaya obyazannost' sudebnykh organov (The Most Important Responsibility of Judicial Organs)*, Pravda, Dec. 27, 1963, p. 4.

> have not yet looked into this story and punished the persons guilty of arbitrary actions. Obviously the intervention of the republic prosecutor is required if justice is to triumph in the end." [162]

In the case of a complaint by the chairman of a comrades' court concerning the failure of a regional people's court to provide the assistance and advice requested of it, the editors of *Sovetskaya yustitsiya* commented as follows:

> "The reproach directed at the ———— regional people's court is very serious. The editors are awaiting a reply from the president of the court explaining why it has taken such an attitude towards the work and requests of the comrades' court of ———— and what measures have been taken to provide continuing assistance to comrades' courts." [163]

The effect of the open interference of the press in this area tends to institutionalize the subordination of the administration of law to party policy.

It would appear that intervention by the press in state administration is a quasi-institutionalized form of party control and supervision. With the complete backing of the entire party apparatus, the press wields an immense power capable of effecting the corrective action it deems indicated, including the punishment of those who persist in resisting suggestions from the press. "[O]rganizations, as well as Soviet citizens, see in a newspaper first of all the inspector having at his disposal all the potentialities and characteristics of control organizations." [164] Soviet officials are in the uncomfortable position of having a responsibility before and to the press. When called upon to reply to *Pravda (otvechayut pravde)* they, in effect, answer to it as well.

V. The Press and the System of Control (Kontrol')

State administration in the Soviet Union is basically a system of checks and additional checks.[165] At, and for, each level of administration there is an internal system of *proverka* or *kontrol'* (check-up) which functions along administrative lines of subordination.[166] There are two formal agencies with administrative control-like functions, the procuracy and the party-state control commissions, which operate across these lines of subordination.

The procuracy exercises general supervision over legality in administration by seeing to it "that the appropriate bodies, organizations and enterprises do not issue illegal decisions, orders or instructions, and that laws and

[162] *Admission Through Clenched Teeth*, 15 C.D.S.P. No. 39, p. 23, at 24 (1963), a follow-up to an earlier article, *A Sequence of Lies*, in 15 C.D.S.P. No. 35, p. 33 (1963).

[163] *Iz praktiki raboty tovarishcheskikh sudov (From the Practice of the Comrades' Courts)*, Sov. yus. No. 14, p. 21 (1963).

[164] Finn, Experiences of a Soviet Journalist 19 (1954).

[165] See generally, Romashkin 103-59.

[166] *Id.* at 115-23.

government decisions are not violated."[167] It does not verify the work of enterprises or state bodies in the sense of an audit or inspection except in connection with reported violations of the law.[168] The party-state control commissions, representing the merger of party and state control organs as a result of the resolution adopted at the November 1962 Plenum of the Central Committee of the CPSU,[169] are, on the other hand, agencies of verification and control. Their functions are:

> "to be of assistance to the Party and government in the execution of the CPSU Program, in the organization of systematic verification of the execution of Party and government directives, in further improvement of the management of Party and state discipline and socialist legality."[170]

In addition to these institutions of control, the party has its own informal system of control in that it is the express duty of each member

> "to develop criticism and self-criticism, boldly to lay bare shortcomings and strive for their removal; . . . firmly to rebuff all attempts at suppressing criticism; to resist all actions injurious to the Party and the state, and to give information about them to Party bodies, up to and including the Central Committee of the Communist Party of the Soviet Union."[171]

The party acts upon these reports behind the scenes through its control over the state administrative apparatus to insure that corrective action is taken. The press, another organ of party control, operates in much the same manner in that criticism and complaints are channeled to appropriate agencies and officials for corrective action.[172] These activities of the press, however, have become quasi-institutionalized in the sense that greater officiality is

[167] *Id.* at 123, 124.

[168] *Ibid.*, see also Chapter II of the Ordinance on the Supervisory Powers of the Procurator's Office in the U.S.S.R. (May 24, 1955), transl. in DENISOV & KIRICHENKO, *op. cit. supra* note 150, at 446-49.

[169] See *Economic Development of the USSR and Reorganization of Party Leadership of the National Economy*, 1 Soviet Law and Government No. 4, p. 3 (1963), containing the text of the Resolution of the CPSU Central Committee Plenum on the Report by Comrade N. S. Khrushchev, adopted Nov. 23, 1962, and printed in Pravda, Nov. 24, 1962.

[170] 1 Soviet Law and Government No. 4, p. 3 at 7 (1963).

[171] Rule 2(G) of the 1961 Rules of the CPSU, in SOVIET COMMUNISM: PROGRAM AND RULES 158-59 (Triska ed. 1962).

[172] INKELES, PUBLIC OPINION IN SOVIET RUSSIA 213 (1950). The value of the press in this area lies in its potential for making available to the Party, through letters to the editor, the reports of deficiencies and shortcomings from the masses rather than the this area lies in its potential for making available to the party, through letters to the party elite (see *id.* at 202-03) and the capability of representing its control and supervision activities as intervention by the masses. (ROMASHKIN 126).

being openly accorded them by the state apparatus.[173] Thus, the control and supervisory activities of the press lies somewhere between the formal (*i.e.*, party representation on party-state control commissions) and informal (the party network) control apparatus of the party.

VI. Conclusion

The Soviet press continues to function as agitator, propagandist and collective organizer with important educational, investigative, control and supervisory functions in support of the fulfillment of Party and governmental decisions and policies. The Soviet claim is that the work of the press is directed towards the achievement of the bright future that awaits all mankind under communism. "The Party and the Soviet people highly value the role of the press in our great march to communism." [174]

Competent Western commentators, on the other hand, have been inclined to view the activities of the press as either part and parcel of Soviet dictatorial control [175] or a necessary element in national planning.[176] Despite this difference in approach, however, both Soviet and Western commentators agree that complete environmental control is a necessary condition on the Soviet scene and that the press is, for this purpose, an important adjunct of formal state institutions of education, investigation, control and supervision.

In the Soviet view, state administration, "aimed at the practical fulfilment of the tasks of communist construction, . . . extends to all areas of economic, political, and cultural activities of society." [177] The breadth of the Soviet concept of state administration is the logical result of the two goals of communist construction *i.e.*, "the material and technical basis of communism" and "rearing of the new [Soviet] man." [178] A governmental system attempting to recast society, including the individual, in a new, more perfect mold must supplement its formal educational and control organs in order to achieve the complete environmental control necessary for the recasting process. The press as an institutionalized form of criticism and self-criticism is considered an important supplement in this process.[179] On

[173] For example, formal representation of the press on the party-state control commissions, judicial recognition of the competence of the press to intervene formally in the judicial process, and the ruling instruction of the December Plenum of the Supreme Court of the USSR.

[174] *Vsenarodnaya pechat (The Press of the Entire People)*, Pravda, Nov. 16, 1963, p. 2.

[175] McClosky & Turner, The Soviet Dictatorship 241 (1960).

[176] Inkeles, *op. cit. supra* note 172, at 195.

[177] Romashkin 103.

[178] Note 6 *supra*.

[179] See Pakhimbabayeva, *S dobrym slovom k lyudyam (With a Kind Word for the People)*, Pravda, May 5, 1963, p. 3.

the other hand, Western commentators, disposed to a more pragmatic approach to governmental processes in the Soviet Union, ascribe a less heroic or romantic role to the press:

> "Dictatorial control by the Party oligarchy is also maintained through a web of countervailing agencies which check each other on behalf of the ruling elite. The regime employs personnel commissions, control committees, auditing agencies, the economic enterprises, the police, the press, the trade unions and other mass organizations, etc., to watch and report on each other and thus to perform surveillance and control functions along with their regular duties. Information from all these agencies is sifted and eventually funneled into the Party center, furnishing the regime the intelligence it requires to detect weakness in the totalitarian structure and to preserve its own power." [180]

Further on, the specific role of the press is stated as follows:

> "[A] Soviet newspaper is conceived largely as a political instrument, an adjunct of the governing apparatus which links the regime with the people and mobilizes popular support. It functions as an agency for both indoctrination and surveillance." [181]

The Western commentator who cites the needs of national planning for the special "supervisory and critical activities" of the Soviet press notes the importance of environmental control in the following terms:

> "[National planning] rendered inadequate the common formal instruments of control such as a body of laws and the associated enforcement officers, court machinery, and legal sanctions. The scope of the plan was so great that the entire nation was transformed into one huge administrative hierarchy. Hence, the law, which on the whole specifies only those acts that are forbidden, had to be supplemented by administrative decisions specifying the behavior that was required. And when such administrative orders are issued, securing their fulfillment falls not to courts but to special supervisory bodies." [182]

The importance of the basic difference in Soviet and Western approaches to the goals of press work is negated by the fact that the impact of the means employed in such work can, at the current stage of social development in the Soviet Union, be related to each of the stated goals. For the individual who has to answer to *Pravda*, it matters little that his personal involvement is not for a greater cause than the maintenance of the current Soviet system of state administration.

[180] McCLOSKY & TURNER, *op. cit. supra* note 175, at 241.

[181] *Id.* at 545.

[182] INKELES, *op. cit. supra* note 172, at 195.

PLAN AND CONTRACT PERFORMANCE IN SOVIET LAW

The Impact of Planning Acts on the Performance of Delivery Contracts in the Post-War Practice of the USSR State Arbitrazh

BY DIETRICH A. LOEBER *

I. Introduction

IT IS DIFFICULT to conceive of any society which could function without the institution of contract.[1] It would require—as one legal scholar expressed it long before Marx—a "community of goods administered by the state as a public corporation in such a way that it [the state] allocates to everybody individually an amount of property rights in accordance with his needs." [2]

In the Soviet Union, in the early revolutionary years, an attempt was indeed undertaken to administer the economy without the instrument of contract. A decree of August 30, 1918 [3] ordered enterprises to place their production at the disposal of state agencies which distributed it. In turn enterprises applied to state agencies for materials needed. These transactions were settled exclusively "by bookkeeping entries without the use of monetary units." Centralized supply and distribution of materials, products, and food were carried out, as Venediktov, a distinguished Soviet legal scholar, observed, "almost exclusively in the form of administrative legal norms and acts and left almost no place for civil law transactions." [4]

* *DIETRICH A. LOEBER, J.D. 1949, University of Marburg; Diploma 1952, The Hague Academy of International Law; M.A. 1953, Columbia University; Staff member, Max Planck Institute for Foreign and International Private Law, Hamburg, Germany.*

The author is indebted to Professor Harold J. Berman of the Harvard Law School and Professor Peter B. Maggs of the University of Illinois College of Law who have read the manuscript and have been most helpful with their suggestions and criticisms.

[1] The term "contract" is used in this paper in the continental sense of the word including sales.

[2] MAREZOLL, LEHRBUCH DES MATURRECHTS (TEXTBOOK OF NATURAL LAW) § 178 (1819) quoted from VON HIPPEL, DAS PROBLEM DER RECHTSGESCHÄFTLICHEN PRIVATAUTONOMIE (THE PROBLEM OF THE INDIVIDUAL'S AUTONOMY IN LEGAL ACTS) 63 (Tübingen 1936). Marezoll (1794-1873) was a law professor at the University of Göttingen.

[3] [1918] Sob. uzak. R.S.F.S.R. No. 63, item 691.

[4] Venediktov, *Grazhdanskoye zakonodatel'stvo v period inostrannoy voennoy interventsiyi i grazhdenskoy voiny 1918-1920 (Civil Legislation in the Period of the Foreign Military Intervention and the Civil War* 1918-1920), in LGU, 201 UCHYONYYE ZAPISKI (SCHOLARLY NOTES) 70-119, at 96-97 and 117 (1955).

The experiment ended in failure, as Lenin admitted in 1921:

> "It was intended to exchange in a more or less socialist manner . . . the products of industry for the products of agriculture . . . But what happened? . . . the exchange of goods broke down: it broke down in the sense that it turned into purchase and sale. And we must now admit this if we do not want to hide our heads under our wings, if we do not want to be like those who do not realize when they are beaten. . . . Nothing came of the exchange of goods, the private market proved to be stronger than we and instead of an exchange of goods we ended up with ordinary purchase and sale, trade".[5]

As a result, contracts were reintroduced and contract law was codified in the then newly enacted Civil Codes. The codification by and large followed traditional patterns.

A new change was brought about with the introduction of large-scale and systematic planning, notably after approval of the first Five-Year-Plan (1928). Many contracts between socialist organizations became planned contracts. The law of planned contract, then created, has remained in force in its principal features up to the present time, despite constant changes in procedure and detail.

Planned contracts are characterized by the fact that an act of planning predetermines, in greater or lesser detail, essential conditions of the contract. The planning act is issued to concrete parties and has to be implemented in a concrete contract. It is thus the will of an administrative (planning) agency which substitutes, wholly or in part, for the will of the contract partners.

This feature distinguishes planned contracts from other types of contracts where the will of one or both parties is limited. Such limitations may be imposed by law (*e.g.*, shipowners are prohibited from waiving their liability in contracts with shippers), by regulations governing the use of public utilities, by the use of model contract forms, etc. In all these cases the will of the parties is restricted by abstract rules covering an unlimited number of cases. They apply to all potential contract partners. In a planned contract, on the other hand, the parties are not only bound by abstract rules, but in addition also by an administrative order addressed to them individually and which specifies concrete terms to be embodied in a given contract.

While the first (abstract or legislative) form for limiting the freedom of contract is a fairly well known phenomenon in all legal systems, the second (concrete and administrative) device is not commonly used outside the communist countries. Occasionally, however, it is practised in non-communist countries, too (*e.g.*, in times of shortages when a producer of agricultural products is ordered to deliver them to a specified buyer at a

[5] 33 LENIN, SOCHINENIYA (WORKS) 72 (4th ed. Moscow 1951); English translation in 9 LENIN, SELECTED WORKS 288-89 (12 vols. 1937).

specified time). In a period of growing government interference with economic relations everywhere, the Soviet experience is not only of theoretical interest.

In the Soviet Union itself planned contracts are of utmost economic and legal importance. To realize the quantitative scope involved some figures may be quoted. There are more than 200,000 industrial enterprises and 100,000 construction sites in the country.[6] The latter are administered by some 10,000 construction enterprises.[7] In addition, there are 587,000 retail enterprises,[8] and 8,000 organizations operate to regulate the supply and deliveries of these enterprises.[9] About 42,000 collective farms, 8,000 state farms and 3,000 intracollective-farm associations represent the agricultural branch of the economy.[10] Furthermore, there are transport and communication enterprises, municipal enterprises, and others. Although probably not all of them conclude economic contracts (some have no legal personality of their own),[11] the number of potential contract partners may come close to a half million.[12]

There are no statistics available as to how many contracts an average enterprise concludes every year. But A. Volin, the Deputy Chief Arbiter of the USSR State Arbitrazh, related in 1962 that "some factories and plants

[6] Figures from the Preamble of the Law of May 10, 1957, [1957] Ved. verkh. sov. S.S.S.R. No. 11, item 275; 1 Zakon. akty 27-32, 329-30; 4 DIREKTIVY KPSS I SOVETSKOGO PRAVITEL'STVA PO KHOZYAYSTVENNYM VOPROSAM. Sbornik dokumentov 1917-1957 gg. (DIRECTIVES OF THE CPSU AND THE SOVIET GOVERNMENT ON ECONOMIC QUESTIONS). Collection of Documents for the Years 1917-1957, at 732-38 (Compiled by Malin & Korobov in 4 vols. Moscow 1957-1958) [hereinafter cited as DIREKTIVY]; KHOZYAYSTVENNYYE DOGOVORY. SBORNIK NORMATIVNYKH AKTOV (ECONOMIC CONTRACTS. COLLECTION OF NORMATIVE ACTS) 33-36 (Yefimochkin ed. Moscow 1962) [hereinafter cited as KHOZ. DOGOVORY]; English excerpts in HAZARD & SHAPIRO, THE SOVIET LEGAL SYSTEM pt. 2, at 56-60 (1962) [hereinafter cited as HAZARD & SHAPIRO]; German: EUROPA-ARCHIV 10067 (1957). The same figures were quoted in Decree of Feb. 14, 1957, 4 DIREKTIVY 679-86, at 682; English: 8 C.D.S.P. No. 7, p. 27 (1957). The number of industrial enterprises in 1955 was 212,000. VLASOV & STUDENIKIN, SOVETSKOY ADMINISTRATIVNOY PRAVO (SOVIET ADMINISTRATIVE LAW) 319 (Moscow 1959).

[7] NARODNOYE KHOZYAYSTVO SSSR V 1961 g. STATISTICHESKIY YEZHEGODNIK (NATIONAL ECONOMY OF THE USSR FOR THE YEAR 1961. STATISTICAL YEARBOOK) 556-57 (Moscow 1962) [hereinafter cited as NARKHOZ].

[8] *Id.* at 655. The figure includes some 260,000 cooperative trade enterprises which account for about 30% of the retail turnover. VLASOV & STUDENIKIN, *op. cit. supra* note 6, at 385.

[9] SHEYN, MATERIAL'NO-TEKHNICHESKOYE SNABZHEIYE SOTSIALISTICHESKOGO PROMYSHLENNOGO PREDPRIYATIYA (THE MATERIAL-TECHNICAL SUPPLY OF A SOCIALIST INDUSTRIAL ENTERPRISE) 10, 41 (Moscow 1959) [hereinafter cited as SHEYNE]. Figures for 1957.

[10] NARKHOZ 291, 446, 448.

[11] Economically accountable shops are entitled to conclude contracts. This was ruled by RSFSR State Arbitrazh in 1962. Sov. yus. No. 11, p. 31 (1962).

[12] Birman mentions that there are 500,000 economic organizations in the USSR. BIRMAN, FINANSY PREDPRIYATIY I OTRASLEY NARODNOGO KHOZYAYSTVA (FINANCES OF ENTERPRISES AND BRANCHES OF THE NATIONAL ECONOMY) 12 (Moscow 1960).

conclude eight to ten thousand contracts per year. And there are not a few such enterprises."[13] If we take, merely for purposes of illustration, an average figure of, say 1,000 contracts per enterprise yearly, we arrive at a total of 250 million economic contracts concluded in the Soviet Union every year. These figures are, we repeat, only rough estimates based on insufficient numerical data; but they, nevertheless, reflect the purely factual magnitude of the issue.

This paper attempts to shed some light on the interrelation between plan and contract. It will analyze how and to what extent planning affects civil law contracts. Limits of space do not permit, however, an overall discussion of the subject. The study is focused, therefore, on one aspect only: the impact of planning on the performance (including the rescission) of contracts. The wide area of how planning affects the conclusion of contracts thus remains outside the scope of this paper. The mechanism of planning and the law of contracts are dealt with merely in the most cursory way to provide some background for evaluating the Arbitrazh cases summarized. The emphasis is on practice, not on theory.[14] For this purpose the study is based primarily on Soviet legislative material (as in effect in 1963)[14a] and on postwar Arbitrazh practice. Legal writings are used, as a rule, only insofar as they offer an insight into practice.[15]

II. Arbitrazh Practice as a Legal Source: A Note

The regular courts lack jurisdiction over disputes between socialist organizations.[16] Settling such disputes is the exclusive competence of Arbitrazh (or superior agencies of the litigants).[17] Arbitrazh is an admini-

[13] Volin, Novoye v grazhdanskom i grazhdansko-protsessual'nom zakonodatel'stve Soyuza SSR i Soyuznykh Respublik (New [Developments] in Civil and Civil-Procedural Legislation of the USSR and Union Republics) 170 (VIYuN, Moscow 1962).

[14] Some theoretical and comparative aspects of the subject will be dealt with in a forthcoming study by the author.

[14a] The new R.S.F.S.R. Civil Code of 1964 (Sov. yus. No. 13-14, pp. 4-57 (1964)) superceding its forerunner of 1922 on October 1, 1964, was enacted after the present study was set into type. Therefore, only a few references to the new code could be incorporated.

[15] Soviet works on the subject of plan and contract are listed in Sovetskoye grazhdanskoye pravo. Sovetskoye semeynoye pravo. Bibliografiya 1917-1960 (Soviet Civil Law. Soviet Family Law. Bibliography) 214-375 (Moscow 1962). It has a section entitled "Interrelation of Plan and Contract" (pp. 216-17) which, however, is not complete. Relevant titles are included also in other sections. See also the bibliography in Novitskiy & Lunts, Obshcheye ucheniye ob obyazatel'stve (General Doctrine Concerning Obligation) 266-69 and 12-13 (Moscow 1950).

[16] The term "socialist organizations" as used in this paper comprises both state and cooperative organizations.

[17] Only disputes of or with collective farms are excepted. They belong to the jurisdiction of regular courts.

strative agency, though it acts to a considerable extent in a judicial manner.[18] There are two categories of Arbitrazh agencies—state and departmental. Cases decided by Departmental Arbitrazh are not published, and of the many State Arbitrazh cases a small number settled by the highest organs, the State Arbitrazh on Union [19] and Republican [20] levels, is made available.

Departmental Arbitrazh have jurisdiction over disputes between organizations subordinated to the same agency of economic administration, and they operate within a given system of administrative organs (*e.g.*, within one Council of the National Economy, one Ministry, one State Committee, or within the cooperative system).[21] Almost all other disputes between socialist organizations are decided by State Arbitrazh organs,[22] and the majority of these are decided on the regional level while the more important disputes are handled in the organs of Arbitrazh attached to the Republican Councils of Ministers.

[18] On the legal nature of Arbitrazh and its procedure see, among others, Kleinman, *Pravovaya prioda arbitrazha v SSSR (The Legal Nature of Arbitrazh in the USSR)* in ARBITRAZH V SSSR (ARBITRAZH IN THE USSR) 39-49 (Moscow 1960); KALLISTRATOVA RAZRESHENIYE SPOROV V GOSUDARSTVENNOM ARBITRAZHE (THE SETTLEMENT OF DISPUTES IN GOVERNMENTAL ARBITRAZH) 12-20 (Moscow 1961), and the literature quoted there.

[19] Statute on State Arbitrazh attached to the Council of Ministers of the USSR, approved Aug. 17, 1960, [1960] Sob. post. S.S.S.R. No. 15, item 127; 15 Sbornik 3-9; Sov. yus. No. 12, p. 30 (1960); 1 Zakon. akty 745-50; English: 12 C.D.S.P. No. 42, p. 15 (1960); HAZARD & SHAPIRO pt. 2, at 113-16, excerpts. Sections 3 and 6 were amended by Decree of Oct. 29, 1962 [1962] Sob. post. S.S.S.R. No. 19, item 157; 22 Sbornik 6, section 13 by Decree of May 23, 1963, [1963] Sob. post. S.S.S.R. No. 10, item 105; 24 Sbornik 48. About rules of procedure, see note 93 *infra*.

[20] For the RSFSR, see Statute on State Arbitrazh attached to the Council of Ministers of the RSFSR and Statute on State Arbitrazh attached to . . . Regional Soviets . . . of the RSFSR, both approved Dec. 3, 1960, [1960] Sob. post. R.S.F.S.R. No. 42, item 206; English: HAZARD & SHAPIRO pt. 2 at 116-18, excerpts. These and statutes for the other 14 Republics are reprinted in 15 Sbornik 9-56; 16 *id.* at 3-42; 17 *id.* at 3-29.

[21] On the Arbitrazh of the Councils of National Economy see, among others, Yudel'son, in PRAVOVYYE VOPROSY ORGANIZATSIYI I DEYATEL'NOSTI SOVNARKHOZOV (LEGAL QUESTIONS OF THE ORGANIZATION AND ACTIVITIES OF THE SOVNARKHOZES) 255-338 (Moscow 1959), and *cf.* the Statute of the Council of National Economy of 1957, § 138, [1957] Sob. post. S.S.S.R., No. 12, item 121, amended *id.* No. 16, item 161; [1958] *id.* No. 20, item 155; [1960] *id.* No. 10, item 71; [1961] *id.* No. 1, item 3; 4 DIREKTIVY 784-805; 1 Zakon. akty 166-83, 361-65, 441; 1 KABALKIN 26-37; DOZORTSEV 131-44; English: HAZARD & SHAPIRO pt. 2, at 63-66, excerpts; German: HEINZIG, DIE SOWNARCHOSEN. Materialsammlung (THE SOVIET ECONOMIC COUNCILS. COLLECTION OF MATERIALS) 11-19 (Hamburg 1959); and the Statute of the All-Russian Council of National Economy of 1961 § 111, [1961] Sob. post. R.S.F.S.R., No. 14, item 52; KHOZ. DOGOVORY 54-58.

[22] The exceptions include disputes over taxes, certain bank operations, technical conditions, the establishment of prices, disputes involving less than 100 (new) rubles. To settle these disputes administrative procedures are provided. See the Statute on USSR State Arbitrazh § 15, [1960] Sob. post. S.S.S.R. No. 15, item 127; Edict of March 14, 1955, [1955] Ved. verkh. sov. S.S.S.R. No. 5, item 116; 1 Zakon. akty 753; Statute on the Conclusion of Contracts for Research and Design Works of 1961, § 15, KHOZ. DOGOVORY 135-50. R.S.F.S.R. Statute of Republican and Regional State Arbitrazh, [1960] Sob. post. R.S.F.S.R. No. 42, item 206. Banking operations, taxes and others are regulated by special rules.

The jurisdiction of the USSR State Arbitrazh extends to cases: (1) between organizations of different Republics; and (2) where one or both parties are subordinated directly to a Union organ and the amount in dispute exceeds one million (new) rubles in precontract cases and 10,000 (new) rubles in property cases. In addition, this body may examine cases decided by Republican State Arbitrazh and may stay the execution of their decisions if they contradict the interests of the USSR or the Republics. Republican State Arbitrazh has a corresponding right vis-a-vis Regional State Arbitrazh.[23]

Because current overall figures have not been published, the present volume of Arbitrazh cases can only be estimated.[24] There are 130 State Arbitrazh agencies operating in the USSR, consisting on the average of three arbiters each, and it can be estimated that they decide approximately 500,000 cases per year. Some 200 to 300 Departmental Arbitrazh organs may be at work in the Soviet Union, handling an estimated 400,000 or 500,000 cases. Thus it is likely that State and Departmental Arbitrazh together decide about one million cases yearly. If each case involves an average of 2000 (new) rubles, the amount in dispute every year would be two billion (new) rubles.

The present study will rely basically on the material published in the

[23] Statute on the USSR State Arbitrazh §§ 3, 18-20, [1960] Sob. post. S.S.S.R. No. 15, item 127; Statute on the RSFSR State Arbitrazh §§ 3, 18-20, [1960] Sob. post. R.S.F.S.R. No. 42, item 206. On the competence of State Arbitrazh, see also Decree of July 23, 1959, [1959] Sob. post. S.S.S.R. No. 15, item 105; 1 Zakon. akty 742-44; and Edict of July 27, 1959, [1959] Ved. verkh. sov. S.S.S.R. No. 30, item 163; 1 Zakon. akty 745. About the delegation of jurisdiction from USSR to Republican State Arbitrazh agencies, see Instructive Letter of May 24, 1961, 18 Sbornik 11, and from RSFSR State Arbitrazh to lower Arbitrazh agencies, see Sov. yus. No. 15, p. 32 (1961).

[24] Due to lack of space data on which the following estimate is based cannot be presented here in detail. The most important sources for estimating the number of State Arbitrazh cases are: Appendices to Instructive Letters of June 5, 1957 and Sept. 23, 1960, 5 Sbornik 28; 15 *id.* at 77; RSFSR Decree of Jan. 11, 1960, [1960] Sob. post. R.S.F.S.R. No. 5, item 13; KRASNOV, REAL'NOYE ISPOLNENIYE DOGOVORNYKH OBYAZATEL'STV MEZHDU SOTSIALISTICHESKIMI ORGANIZATSIYAMI (THE SPECIFIC PERFORMANCE OF CONTRACTUAL OBLIGATIONS BETWEEN SOCIALIST ORGANIZATIONS) 141 (Moscow 1959); as to the number of Department Arbitrazh cases see, among others, Yudel'son, *supra* note 21, at 261-62; Sov. gos. i pravo No. 11, p. 47 (1958); Appendices to Instructions of the USSR State Bank of Feb. 14, 1946, ARBITRAZH V SOVETSKOM KHOZYAYSTVE. SBORNIK (ARBITRAZH IN THE SOVIET ECONOMY. A COLLECTION) 300-01 (Compiled by Mozheyko & Shkundin, 4th ed. Moscow 1948), and of March 30, 1956, SBORNIK ZAKONODATEL'NYKH MATERIALOV I INSTRUKTIVNYKH UKAZANIY PO FINANSOVOY RABOTE V UGOL' NOY PROMYSHLENNOSTI (COLLECTION OF LEGISLATIVE MATERIALS AND INSTRUCTIVE LETTERS ON FINANCIAL WORK IN THE COAL INDUSTRY) 514 (Moscow 1958); SPRAVOCHNIK DLYA INSTRUKTOROV POTREBITEL'SKOY KOOPERATSIYI (HANDBOOK FOR INSTRUCTORS OF CONSUMERS' COOPERATIVES) 8 (Moscow 1961); BIRMAN, *op. cit. supra* note 12, at 35; Sots. zak. No. 11, p. 94 (1957); *id.* No. 11 p. 96 (1958). For pre-war figures, see, among others, ARBITRAZH V SOVETSKOM KHOZYAYST'VE *supra* (2d ed. 1938) at 14 and 184.

Arbitrazh Collections *(Sborniki)*.[25] The post-war Arbitrazh *Sbornik* [26] contains normative material (*e.g.*, Statutes on Deliveries, some Special Conditions), "Instructive Letters" and "Informative Letters," as well as summarized reports of cases decided by the USSR State Arbitrazh.[27] Instructive Letters are issued by the USSR State Arbitrazh and are directed to lower Arbitrazh agencies for guidance on questions of substantive law and procedure. Informative Letters are usually answers to inquiries from enterprises released for information. The number of individual cases reported in the collection so far reaches about 230.

Instructive Letters are of utmost practical importance. They are issued on "the practice of application of the Statutes on Deliveries of Production and other All-Union normative acts regulating economic relations," and are binding on both State and Departmental Arbitrazh.[28] This vast body of administrative rules, uniform throughout the country, governs the many millions of contracts concluded every year and the disputes arising out of these contracts.

III. Law of Economic Planning: Some Concepts of Planned Supply and Sales

There are many plans: All-Union plans, Republican plans, plans of Councils of National Economy, plans of enterprises, and each consists of numerous parts. But only a few of them are directly related to contracts. The plan of enterprises, that is of the contract partners, does not, for instance, specify to whom the production of the enterprise should be delivered, nor does it lay down who will supply the enterprise with the necessary materials. The enterprise's plan directs the work of the enterprise internally; it does not create relations with suppliers or buyers. The delivery and distribution plans of the superior agency of the enterprise

[25] Sbornik instruktivnykh ukazaniy Gosudarstvennogo arbitrazha pri Sovete Ministrov SSSR (Moscow), 1955 to date [Cited herein as Sbornik.] It appears at irregular intervals, usually every 3-6 months, in editions of 10,000 and more copies. Up to the winter of 1963-64, 24 issues with a total of about 2,500 pages were released. General editor (since issue 8) is A. Volin.

[26] Before the war Arbitrazh decisions and instructions used to appear in Arbitrazh (Moscow 1931-1940) and Byulleten' Gosarbitrazha pri Sovete Narodnykh Komissarov RSFSR (Bulletin of State Arbitrazh of the Council of Peoples' Commissars of the RSFSR) (Moscow 1932-1940).

[27] A number of Instructive Letters and decisions are also reported since 1957 in *Sots. zak.* It sometimes even carries material not published in the *Arbitrazh sbornik.* Instructions and decisions of Republican State Arbitrazh agencies are not included in the *Sbornik*, but selected materials of the RSFSR and Ukrainian State Arbitrazh may be found in *Sov. yus.* (since 1957) and *Radians'ke pravo (Soviet Law)* (since 1958) respectively. Arbitrazh materials of other Republican State Arbitrazh agencies are not available. About Statutes of Deliveries, see note 39 *infra;* about Special Conditions, note 43 *infra.*

[28] Statute on the USSR State Arbitrazh § 5, [1960] Sob. post. S.S.S.R. No. 15, item 127.

(*e.g.*, a Council of National Economy) have the most immediate impact on contracts. But even these plans are not self-executing. They mostly consist of mere figures. Delivery and distribution plans of a superior agency contain, for example, output targets and supply needs in numerical form broken down by individual types of products. To fill these plans with life, figures must be transformed into specific planned tasks addressed to individual enterprises; consumer-enterprises must be "attached" (prikrepleniye) to supplier-enterprises. Only after such individualization of plans is a basis created for establishing inter-enterprise relations and hence contracts. "Transmitting" (dovedeniye) delivery and distribution plans to enterprises is, therefore, an important step in the planning process. It is here that plan and contract meet.[29]

The task of transforming general plans into individual planning acts is accomplished in several stages.

A. First Stage

The first stage has a preparatory character. After approval of the All-Union plan the superior agency of the enterprise (*e.g.*, a Council of National Economy) receives its "plan of material-technical supply." It shows the types and quantities of products allocated to it for the given planning year. The superior agency administers this allocation as the "main *fond*-holder" (holder of allocated material) and distributes it, usually through its sales organizations, among the enterprises under its direction. The distribution should take place within 15 days and "in strict accordance" with the production plans of the enterprises.[30] In practice, however, allocations often correspond neither to the applications received from enterprises in the draft-

[29] Soviet literature on planning is mostly economic and there are relatively few publications on the legal aspects of planning. *Cf.* notes 40, 112 *infra*. For a bibliography on the theory and organization of economic planning in the USSR and the Peoples' Democracies covering 1917-1960, see Norakidze, in SOROKIN, PLANIROVANIYE NARODNOGO KHOZYAYSTVA SSSR (PLANNING OF THE NATIONAL ECONOMY OF THE USSR) 420-57 (Moscow 1961). An informative source in English on the economic aspects of supply planning is Levine, *The Centralized Planning of Supply in Soviet Industry*, in JOINT ECONOMIC COMM., 86TH CONG., 1ST SESS., COMPARISONS OF THE UNITED STATES AND SOVIET ECONOMIES pt. 1, at 151-76 (Joint Comm. Print. 1959).

[30] Decree of June 30, 1962 on the Further Improvement of the Procedure for Concluding Contracts for the Delivery of Products for the Material-Technical Supply of Enterprises § 2, [1962] Sob. post. S.S.S.R. No. 12, item 94; SPRAVOCHNIK PO MATERIAL'NO-TEKHNICHESKOMU SNABZHENIYU I SBYTU (HANDBOOK ON MATERIAL-TECHNICAL SUPPLY AND SALE) 176-80 (Moscow 1963). An amendment of a number of statutes in connection with this Decree was ordered by Decree of Oct. 29, 1962, [1962] Sob. post. S.S.S.R. No. 19, item 157; 22 Sbornik 4. A corresponding Decree on the Further Improvement of the Procedure for Concluding Contracts for the Delivery of Goods for Popular Consumption was enacted August 22, 1963, [1963] Sob. post. S.S.S.R. No. 17, item 176 (quoted in Sov. yus. No. 9 p. 14 (1964)). Inter-republican deliveries are planned and directed by central agencies. *Cf.* at note 57 *infra*.

ing stage of the plan [31] nor to the planned needs. Under-allocations result in applications for additional materials, over-allocations lead to refusals.

The form for allocating products is a "*fond*-notification," issued for individual materials by the *fond*-holder to its subordinate enterprises.[32] It lists types and quantities of the *fond*, *i.e.* of the materials allocated to the enterprise for a given period,[33] usually the planning year.[34] The total of individual *fondy* of an enterprise represents the volume of its planned supply for this period. But the *fond*-notification gives the consumer enterprise no enforceable right to claim the allocated *fondy*, neither from the *fond*-holder, nor from the prospective supplier (the latter is generally assigned only at a later stage). The right of the consumer-enterprise to demand the allocated *fondy* arises only after: (1) the *fond*-holder has issued a delivery or distribution order to the supplier; and (2) supplier and consumer have concluded a contract on the basis of such order.[35]

The function of the *fond*-notification is to serve as a basis for the enterprise to specify its needs within the allotted *fond*. This is necessary since the *fondy* usually read only in general terms. If one enterprise, for example, is allotted *x*-tons of rolled steel, it must specify quantities and qualities of individual items within the *fond*: types, profile, and size of the steel needed.[36] Specifications are worked out at the beginning of the planning year, but also at monthly and quarterly intervals. They are submitted to the superior

[31] Nikitina, *Planirovaniye postavok produktsiyi gosudarstvennymi predpriyatiyami (The Planning of Deliveries of Production by State Enterprises)*, in VYuZI, 8 UCHYONYYE ZAPISKI (SCHOLARLY NOTES) 186-210, at 196 (1960); *cf.* Tanchuk, *Pravovyye voprosy material'no-tekhnicheskogo snabzheniya v sisteme sovnarkhozov (Legal Questions of Material-technical Supply in the System of Sovnarkhozes)*, in VOPROSY PRAVOVOGO REGULIROVANIYA NARODNOGO KHOZYAYSTVA (QUESTIONS OF THE LEGAL REGULATION OF THE NATIONAL ECONOMY) 107-41, at 136 (Moscow 1962).

[32] Samples: Yakobi, in EKONOMIKA MATERIAL'NO-TEKHNICHESKOGO SNABZHENIYA (ECONOMICS OF MATERIAL-TECHNICAL SUPPLY) 346 (Moscow 1960) [hereinafter cited as EKONOMIKA]; SAVITSKIY, *et al.*, PLANIROVANYIE I ORGANIZATSIYA MATERIAL'NO SNABZHENIYA PREDPRIYATIY I STROYEK (THE PLANNING AND ORGANIZATION OF THE MATERIAL-TECHNICAL SUPPLY OF ENTERPRISES AND CONSTRUCTION PROJECTS) 50 (Moscow 1962). The term *fondy* is used for the planned supply of individual consumer enterprises as well as of the main *fond*-holder (*e.g.*, a Council of National Economy). See also note 35 *infra*.

[33] About *fondy*, see SHKUNDIN, OBYAZATEL'STVO POSTAVKI TOVAROV V SOVETSKOM PRAVE (THE OBLIGATION FOR THE DELIVERY OF GOODS IN SOVIET LAW) 144, 157-58 (Moscow 1948); Nikitina, *supra* note 31, at 198-99; Yakobi, *supra* note 32, at 343-46; Syrneva, in PRAVOVYYE VOPROSY ORGANIZATSIYI I DEYATEL'NOSTI SOVNARKHOZOV (LEGAL QUESTIONS OF THE ORGANIZATION AND ACTIVITY OF SOVNARKHOZES) 219-20 (Moscow 1959).

[34] Decree of Aug. 29, 1946, § 5, 3, DIREKTIVY 89-91; 1 Zakon. akty 367, 427, excerpts; *cf.* notes 99, 100 *infra*.

[35] The language used in practice does not always conform to this legal distinction. Sometimes the word *fond* is used as a short form for "distribution of *fondy* through distribution orders."

[36] Lokshin, and Yakobi, in EKONOMIKA 62, 346-51. The specification must be based on the input norms of material. The procedure for working out these norms is laid down in a Decree of Oct. 13, 1961 §§ 16-17, [1961] Sob. post. S.S.S.R. No. 16, item 127; KHOZ. DOGOVORY 60-69, excerpts.

agency (*e.g.*, to the supply department of a Council of National Economy). This agency, after proper examination, arranges the specifications received from its subordinate enterprises by groups of materials (usually in aggregate form) [37] and by consumer-enterprises and then forwards this vast body of documentation to the sales department (*e.g.*, of the same Council of National Economy) which is competent to place production orders and to issue delivery orders.[38]

B. Second Stage

Issuing of production and delivery orders is a second and, legally, the decisive stage in transforming a program (the plan) into legally binding administrative orders. They are issued by administratively superior agencies and create rights and obligations under administrative law.

Production orders (zakazy) and delivery orders (naryady) are frequently combined into one document: naryad-zakaz. In addition distribution orders (raznaryadki) are used. As a basis for the delivery of consumer goods, "distribution plans" (instead of delivery orders) are also issued.[39] The word "planning act" (planovyy akt) is used as a generic term comprising these and other administrative orders issued by superior (planning) agencies.[40]

[37] Samples: EKONOMIKA 350; Syrneva, *supra* note 33, at 225; Smirnov, in SMIRNOV & TARASYANTS, ORGANIZATSIYA I PLANIROVANIYE SBYTA PROMYSHLENNOY PRODUKTSIYI V SSSR (THE ORGANIZATION AND PLANNING OF THE SALE OF INDUSTRIAL PRODUCTION IN THE USSR) 126 (Moscow 1960); FASOLYAK, MATERIAL'NO-TEKHNICHESKOYE SNABZHENIYE V EKONOMICHESKOM ADMINISTRATIVNOM RAYONE (MATERIAL-TECHNICAL SUPPLY IN AN ECONOMIC-ADMINISTRATIVE DISTRICT) 145 (Moscow 1961).

[38] Decree of June 30, 1962 § 2, [1962] Sob. post. S.S.S.R. No. 12, item 94; EKONOMIKA 349-51; Tanchuk, *supra* note 31, at 135; Syrneva, *supra* note 33, at 221-25; Gus'kova, *Pravovyye formy regulirovaniya metallosnabzheniya (Legal Forms of the Regulation of Metal Supply)*, in VIYuN, 9 UCHYONYYE ZAPISKI (SCHOLARLY NOTES) 205-37, at 223 (1959).

[39] Statute on Deliveries of Products §§ 7-8, and Statute on Deliveries of Goods §§ 8-9, both approved May 22, 1959, [1959] Sob. post. S.S.S.R. No. 11, item 68 [hereinafter all citations of these statutes are to this source]; 10 Sbornik 9-27, and 27-46; 1 Zakon. akty 443-59, and 467-84; 3 KABALKIN 105-27, and 138-62; DOZORTSEV 450-80; KHOZ. DOGOVORY 123-38, 168-74, 185-94, 210-14, 281-85. The Statute on Deliveries of Products was amended by Decree of Oct. 29, 1962, [1962] Sob. post. S.S.S.R. No. 19, item 157; 22 Sbornik 4-6, and the Statute on Deliveries of Goods by Decree of May 23, 1963, [1963] Sob. post. S.S.S.R. No. 10, item 105; 24 Sbornik 48 [hereinafter all citations of the amended statutes are to these sources.] KHALFINA, ZNACHENIYE I SUSHNOST' DOGOVORA (IMPORTANCE AND NATURE OF CONTRACT) 124-44 (Moscow 1954) (German translation: Berlin 1958). For references to samples see notes 49-50 *infra*.

[40] Little attention has been paid to delivery orders and other planning acts in Soviet literature on administrative law; but some aspects of planning acts are discussed in the context of works on civil law, primarily in two books published in 1948: VENEDIKTOV, GOSUDARSTVENNAYA SOTSIALISTICHESKAYA SOBSTVENNOST' (GOVERNMENT SOCIALIST PROPERTY) 489, 627, 747, 752-54, 764 (Moscow, Leningrad 1948), and SHKUNDIN, *op. cit. supra* note 33, at 157-59. As to more recent publications, see Syrneva, *supra* note 33, at 221-26, and Nikitina, *supra* note 31, at 194, 199. No monographic studies on the legal aspects of planning acts seem to have appeared; *cf.* notes 29 *supra* and 112 *infra*. The recent civil law codifications failed to contribute to a consistent terminology.

The term is sometimes used interchangeably with "planned task" (planovoye zadaniye), although the latter has a less clear legal connotation.

There is no overall and systematic codification of the law governing production, delivery, and distribution orders, the competence and procedure for issuing them, or their legal effect. Some relevant provisions can be found in recent decrees on the subject of material supply,[41] in the 1959 Statutes on Deliveries,[42] in special conditions for the delivery of individual types of production,[43] and mainly in instructions of agencies issuing the orders.[44]

The practice of delivery and distribution orders shows some variety. The terminology, moreover, is not used consistently and often depends on the custom of the agency issuing them as well as on the kind of production in question.

The complexity is further increased by the fact that different types of delivery and distribution orders are used in practice. Proceeding from their role in establishing contract relations, two types of delivery orders (naryady) and two types of distribution orders (raznaryadki) can be distinguished. Each one serves as a basis for establishing contract relations when the others do not:

(1) The delivery order names the supplier and buyer individually and directly. Such an order obliges the parties named to conclude a contract.

(2) The delivery order names the supplier, but leaves the name of the buyer blank and lists the *fond*-holder as recipient (*e.g.*, a Council of

The terms "act of planning" (akt planirovaniya), "planning act" (planovyy akt), and "planned task" (planovoye zadaniye) are used without a clear legal differentiation in the 1961 Principles (*e.g.*, in arts. 4, 34, 44) and in the RSFSR Civil Code of 1964 (in the corresponding arts. 4, 166, 258).

[41] Decree of April 17, 1958 §§ 5 and 8, [1958] Sob. post. S.S.S.R. No. 8, item 68; 1 Zakon. akty 337-39, 416-19; 3 KABALKIN 102-04; DOZORTSEV 155-58, excerpts; KHOZ. DOGOVORY 69-71; German: BORCHERS, DIE REFORM DER SOWJETISCHEN WIRTSCHAFTSVERWALTUNG (THE REFORM OF SOVIET ECONOMIC ADMINISTRATION) 81-86 (Hamburg 1960); Decree of Jan. 22, 1959, § 5, 1 Zakon. akty 336-37, 419-20; 2 SPRAVOCHNIK PARTIYNOGO RABOTNIKA (HANDBOOK OF THE PARTY WORKER) 374-76 (1959); DOZORTSEV 433-35, excerpts; Decree of Oct. 7, 1961, § 11, KHOZ. DOGOVORY 364-77; Decree of Oct. 13, 1961, § 11, [1961] Sob. post. S.S.S.R. No. 16, item 127; Decree of June 30, 1962 §§ 2-3, [1962] Sob. post. S.S.S.R. No. 12, item 94.

[42] Statute on Deliveries of Products §§ 7-8, as amended, and of Goods §§ 8-9.

[43] *E.g.*, in the Special Conditions for Delivery of Metal and Metal Products, §§ 6-11, approved Feb. 24, 1962, 21 Sbornik 25-38. Special conditions approved between 1959 and 1961 are collected in POLOZHENIYA O POSTAVKAKH, INSTRUKTSIYI O PORYADKE PRIYOMKI PO KOLICHESTVU I KACHESTVU, OSOBYYE USLOVIYA POSTAVKI. Sbornik normativnykh aktov (STATUTES ON DELIVERIES, INSTRUCTIONS ON THE PROCEDURE FOR ACCEPTING [GOODS] ACCORDING TO QUANTITY AND QUALITY, SPECIAL CONDITIONS OF DELIVERY. COLLECTION OF NORMATIVE ACTS) (Moscow 2d ed. 1963), quoted in KHOZ. DOGOVORY 123, n.1). Some Special Conditions can also be found in 3 KABALKIN 176-96; DOZORTSEV 481-84; 21 Sbornik 3-24; 23 *id.* at 14-30; 24 *id.* at 57-66.

[44] SHAPKINA, OFORMLENIYE POSTAVOK DOGOVORAMI I RAZRESHENIYE PREDDOGOVORNYKH SPOROV (THE FORMALIZING OF DELIVERIES BY CONTRACTS AND THE RESOLUTION OF PRE-CONTRACTUAL DISPUTES) 27 (Moscow 1961).

National Economy). Here the delivery order does not have the function of establishing contract relations. The production listed in the delivery order has to be distributed by the *fond*-holder within 15 days among its subordinate organizations by issuing distribution orders.[45]

(3) The distribution order of a *fond*-holder, as just described, serves as a basis for contracts of the supplier with the buyer named therein.[46]

(4) The unloading order of a buyer to his contract partner, the supplier, is also called a distribution order and is used to have products delivered to third parties. It is based on an already existing contract between supplier and buyer and does not, therefore, establish contract relations between them.[47]

The delivery and distribution orders listed under (1) through (3) are planning acts, but the unloading order has a civil law character. To avoid confusion the latter will be called hereinafter "distribution (unloading) order."

The delivery order listed under (1) is addressed to the supplier-enterprise. Copies of it are sent to the consumer-enterprise which is allotted the production in question, its superior agency (the main *fond*-holder, *e.g.*, the supply department of a Council of National Economy), and to others.[48] The decisive standard formula in the delivery order is: "Do produce and deliver . . . ." [49] If the assortment of products to be delivered is not complicated, the issuing agency (usually a sales department or sales organization) may confirm the specification submitted by the consumer-enterprise at an earlier stage and combine it with the *naryad-zakaz* into a single document, the *zakaz*-specification.[50] Delivery orders are issued for a year, half a year, or a quarter.[51] They are effective until performed or annulled, but not longer than the given planning year.[52]

A delivery order as under (1) can be defined as the order of a sales organization of a planning agency addressed to an economic organization

[45] Decree of June 30, 1962, §§ 2-3, [1962] Sob. post. S.S.S.R. No. 12, item 94; Statute on Deliveries of Products §§ 7 and 70, as amended.

[46] Instruction of Dec. 18, 1962, § 1, 22 Sbornik 12-15; *cf.* EKONOMIKA note 32 at 354-55; SHEYN 192.

[47] Statutes on Deliveries of Products § 28 (and § 73) and of Goods § 15 (and § 76); Instruction of Dec. 18, 1962 § 8, 22 Sbornik 12-15.

[48] Syrneva, *supra* note 33, at 222.

[49] Sample: FASOLYAK, *op. cit. supra* note 37, at 147. For delivery orders in the field of construction, see 2 Zakon. akty 226, and KHOZ. DOGOVORY 426, and in the field of export, ORGANIZATSIYA I TEKHNIKA VNESHNEY TORGOVLI SSSR I DRUGIKH SOTSIALISTICHESKIKH STRAN (THE ORGANIZATION AND TECHNIQUES OF FOREIGN TRADE OF THE USSR AND OTHER SOCIALIST COUNTRIES) 50-55 and appendix (Moscow 1963).

[50] Sample: Yakobi, *supra* note 32, at 350; FASOLYAK, *op. cit. supra* note 37, at 145, 147; see also Syrneva, *supra* note 33, at 225.

[51] Statute on Deliveries of Products § 7, as amended.

[52] Syrneva, *supra* note 33, at 223, quoting an unpublished Arbitrazh decision.

on the operative level to unload or issue specified products at a given time to a named recipient.[53] From the consumer's point of view the delivery order has the function of a procurement permit.[54]

The process of issuing planning acts starts at the beginning of the planning year and is repeated, depending on the material involved, at monthly and quarterly intervals. In case of disruptions of the plan or in other cases of need, delivery and distribution orders are also issued on an *ad hoc* basis and for individual deliveries. Thus it can be said that the transformation of the plan into individual planning acts is a continuous process.

The delivery (distribution) order binds its recipients, but only administratively, *i.e.*, through administrative channels of subordination. There is general agreement among Soviet jurists that the delivery (distribution) order as such does not create "civil law" obligations for delivery or acceptance and payment. Such obligations arise only in connection with and on the basis of a contract. Planning acts do not replace civil law contracts.[55] But the question is whether the delivery (distribution) order creates a legal obligation for supplier and consumer to conclude a civil law contract (a so-called "pre-contract obligation"). Soviet jurists answer in the affirmative. The obligation to enter into a contract is said to be twofold and to consist, as a rule, of: (1) an administrative legal obligation vis-a-vis the state, represented by the superior agency of each partner; and (2) a civil law obligation between supplier and consumer.

The issue of delivery and distribution orders and the assignment of consumer-enterprises to suppliers requires "an enormous flow of documentation."[56] This "labor-intensive" process is connected in practice with some degree of tension. Such friction is partly due to deficiencies of planning

[53] A similar definition was used in an Instructive Letter of March 3, 1950, repealed 1961, 3 Sbornik 88; 18 *id.* at 39. The 1950 definition was based on the system of "general contracts" (concluded between ministries and other central organizations), now replaced by the system of "direct contracts."

[54] Berman translates *naryad* as "procurement permit." Berman, Justice in the USSR 107, 118, 137, 139 (2d ed. 1963). This term suggests that it is up to the discretion of the consumer-enterprise to make use of the "permit." In fact, however, the *naryad* is addressed to the supplier-enterprise and contains an order to deliver. Both parties, the supplier as well as the consumer, are under a legal obligation to enter into a contract. This obligation is stated, among others, in a Decree of April 21, 1949, [1949] Sob. post. S.S.S.R. No. 9, item 68; 3 Direktivy 368-71; 1 Kabalkin 176-78; German: Pfuhl, Der Wirtschaftsvertrag im sowjetischen Recht (Economic Contract in Soviet Law) 54-57 (mimeo. Berlin 1958). *Cf.* at note 55 *infra.*

[55] But there is no unanimity among Soviet writers about the relative weight of plan and contract in creating civil law obligations to perform. The majority holds that the obligation arises out of a combination of planning act and contract, whereas others claim it is based on contract only; the view that the obligation rests merely on the planning act has been rejected. *Cf.* at notes 62, 93, 212 *infra.*

[56] Tanchuk, *supra* note 31, at 135, quotes as an example that sales and supply offices in the Donyets Council of National Economy have to issue 2,000 to 5,000 distributions orders a year each.

and may partly be explained by shortages of material resources. I to maintain the opportunity of manipulation, superior agencies and supply organizations (*fond*-holders) have shown a tendency to withhold, delay, or redistribute allocations and to cut the *fondy* of enterprises.[57] "Therefore enterprises are occupied the whole year with questions of supply; they struggle for . . . [being named as recipients in] delivery orders for each quarter, month, and sometimes even for each individual delivery." [58]

IV. Law of Economic Contracts: A Short Summary

Planning, as just described, cannot but influence contract law. Soviet contract law is codified in the 1961 Principles of Civil Legislation,[59] in the Civil Codes of the individual Republics,[60] presently in a stage of reform,[60a] in the Statutes on Deliveries, and in some special Union and Republic laws and regulations.[61]

Civil rights and obligations arise—according to the 1961 Principles—not only from transactions, but also "from administrative acts, . . . and from planning acts." [62] This probably is the first statutory formulation of the

[57] Preamble of Decree of June 30, 1962 [1962] Sob. post. S.S.S.R. No. 12, item 94; Laptev, Sov. gos. i pravo No. 3, p. 95, at 104 (1963); Shapkina, *id.* No. 5, p. 140, at 140-42; Khalfina, Pravovoye regulirovaniye postavki produktsiyi v narodnom khozaistve (Legal Regulation of Delivery of Production in the National Economy) 95-96, 102, 132, 180-81 (Moscow 1962); Shapkina, *op. cit. supra* note 44, at 56; Tanchuk, *supra* note 31, at 135; *cf.* at note 30 *supra.*

[58] Khalfina, *op. cit. supra* note 57, at 95.

[59] These 1961 Principles of Civil Legislation of the Union of the SSR and the Union Republic [hereinafter cited in both text and footnotes as 1961 Principles] may be found in [1961] Ved. verkh. sov. S.S.S.R. No. 50, item 525; and have also been published as a 96 page book in Moscow in 1962; in English, 14 C.D.S.P. No. 4, p. 3 (1962); 7 Law in Eastern Europe 263-98 (1963); 3 Soviet Review No. 5, p. 22; *id.* No. 6 p. 50 (1962) (to be continued); Soviet Civil Legislation and Procedure 55-114 (Moscow 1963[?]); French: Notes et Etudes Documentaires (Notes and Documentary Studies No. 2942, p. 13 (1962); German: 11 Staat und Recht (State and Law) 357-68, 528-54; Berichte des Osteuropa-Instituts der Freien Universitat Berlin (Reports of the East European Institute of the Free University of Berlin) No. 53, pp. 7-76 (1962).

[60] There are presently 15 Republics forming the U.S.S.R., but only 10 of them had their own Civil Codes in 1961; 5 Republics used the Civil Codes of their neighbor Republics. The Russian texts of the Codes as of 1957 are collected in Grazhdanskoye zakonodatel'stvo SSSR i soyuznykh respublik (Civil Legislation of the USSR and Union Republics) (Moscow 1957). Only the R.S.F.S.R. Civil Code of 1922 is translated into English, in 2 Gsovski, Soviet Civil Law 2-235 (1949).

[60a] After the enactment of the 1961 Principles new Civil Codes were adopted in 1964 in the RSFSR (see note 14a *supra*) and in 1963 in the Uzbek, Ukrainian, Latvian, Tadzhik, Kazakh and Turkmen Republics.

[61] The oldest ones date back to 1931 and earlier; the most recent one is a Decree of June 30, 1962, [1962] Sob. post. S.S.S.R. No. 12, item 94.

[62] 1961 Principles art. 4. Article 33, which regulates the grounds on which obligations arise, contains a reference to this provision. R.S.F.S.R. Civil Code of 1964 arts. 4 and 158. *Cf.* at notes 55 *supra,* and 93, 212 *infra.*

principle[63] in legal history.[64] No other legal system seems to have embodied such a principle in its Civil Code, though many of them have come to recognize the existence of civil obligations arising out of administrative acts. The classical civil codes know only of civil obligations based on contract or law (*e.g.*, torts and unjust enrichment).

The 1961 Principles, after having stated this general rule of economic contract law, provide further that the "content of a contract concluded on the basis of a planned task must conform to this task" (art. 34). Differences arising during the conclusion of a contract between socialist organizations are resolved by Arbitrazh (art. 34), in the so-called "pre-contract dispute" procedure. Once concluded, the obligation must be carried out "in accordance with the instructions of the law, planning act or contract" (art. 33). If one party fails to do so, it is liable to compensate the creditor, but "an agreement between socialist organizations concerning limitations of their liability is not permitted" (art. 36). The law provides for the payment of fixed fines, penalties and forfeits for late or improper fulfillment of delivery obligations. The fines, penalties, and forfeitures cannot be waived by the parties and "do not release the debtor from fulfillment of the obligation in kind" (art. 36). Even compensation for damages does not release the debtor from his obligation of specific performance (art. 36).[64a]

But the law provides for exceptions from the obligation to contract imposed by a planning act. In some cases deliveries are allowed without contract (*e.g.*, deliveries during the first two months after the plans of supply are approved,[65] deliveries for export[66] or for the State Reserves).[67] In other

[63] It is based on the theoretical work done by Professor Mikhail Agarkov (1890-1947), one of the most able Soviet civil law scholars. He laid the foundation for the now generally accepted doctrine of the impact of plan on contracts in a study: *Obyazatel'stvo po sovetskomu grazhdanskomu prava (Obligation in Soviet Civil Law)*, in VIYuN, 3 UCHYONYYE TRUDY (SCHOLARLY WORKS) (Moscow 1940). It appeared in only 400 copies and is now a bibliographical rarity.

[64] A similar provision is envisaged in Poland in the 1960 Draft of a Civil Code art. 1, quoted in English by Wagner, 11 AM. J. COMP. L. 348, 358 (1962). The law of economic contracts in other European Peoples' Democracies does not contain an analogous rule, but usually stipulates that planning agencies are empowered to impose a duty to contract. The formulations vary.

[64a] Corresponding rules are provided in the R.S.F.S.R. CIVIL CODE OF 1964. See arts. 159, 166, 168, 186-191, 258-266.

[65] Statute on Deliveries of Products § 11 and of Goods § 11. The same rule is laid down in Decree of April 21, 1949, § 2, [1949] Sob. post. S.S.S.R. No. 9, item 68. See also 3 Sbornik 207, 218; 7 *id.* at 43; 9 *id.* at 3, 7, and Instruction No. 2 of the USSR State Bank of 1960, § 48, KHOZ. DOGOVORY 308-63, excerpts.

[66] Statute on Deliveries of Products § 4 n.2, as amended and of Goods § 3 n.1; Decree of Oct. 3, 1940, on Conditions of Delivery of Goods for Export, [1940] Sob. post. S.S.S.R. No. 27, item 636; Mozheyko & Shkundin, *op. cit. supra* note 24, at 458-64; 2 KABALKIN 26-27, excerpts; German: PFUHL, *op. cit. supra* note 54, at 45-51.

[67] Resolution of the 18th Congress of the CPSU of March 20, 1939, 2 DIREKTIVY 557-86, at 563; Decree of Aug. 29, 1946, § 4, 3 DIREKTIVY 89-91; see also Decree of May 4, 1958, § 7, [1958] Sob. post. S.S.S.R. No. 9, item 76; 1 Zakon. akty 330-33; 3 KABALKIN

cases contracts may be concluded freely, *i.e.* without a planning act imposing an obligation to contract. Such free contracts are used to procure products not included in plans of deliveries and distribution, mainly material produced locally or available in sufficient supply.[68]

Planned contracts are concluded only between socialist organizations. The main forms are delivery contracts (1961 Principles, arts. 44-50), contracts for the purchase of farm products (arts. 51-52), contracts for capital construction (arts. 67-71), shipment contracts (arts. 72-77), certain clearing and credit relations (arts. 83-85). This paper deals primarily with delivery contracts, probably the most widely used contract form within the planned economy.

Contracts are concluded, as a rule, for one year or for the period necessary to produce and deliver the product.[69] They must be entered into within 60 days after the plan of material-technical supply has been approved.[70] "In practice, however, during a number of years, the majority of contracts has been concluded . . . with a gross violation of the periods fixed . . . ." [71]

Normally the supplier, after receiving the delivery (distribution) order, drafts a contract and sends it to the buyer, indicated in the order.[72] If the buyer agrees with the draft he returns it with his signature and the contract is concluded. But if the buyer wishes to have some contract clauses changed, or if he refuses to contract altogether, he draws up a "Protocol of Disagree-

99-102; DOZORTSEV 378-80, excerpts; KHOZ. DOGOVORY 72-74, excerpts; Law of Oct. 30, 1959, §§ 13-14, [1959] Ved. verkh. sov. No. 44, item 221; 1 Zakon. akty 20-27; Lokshin, in EKONOMIKA, *supra* note 32, at 59, 306.

[68] A decree of Oct. 13, 1961, note 36, § 5, [1961] Sob. post. S.S.S.R. No. 16, item 127, ordered that the list *(nomenklatura)* of products distributed by Gosplan of the U.S.S.R. should be expanded. In 1959 the list contained about 1,000 types of production, whereas the *nomenklatura* of Union Republics and Councils of National Economy included more than 5,000 items. Syrneva, *supra* note 33, at 216. For the 1958 list of food and industrial goods distributed by the RSFSR Ministry of Trade, see [1958] Sob. post. R.S.F.S.R. No. 7, item 62, partly amended in 1960, [1960] Sob. post. R.S.F.S.R. No. 42, item 207. See also Decree of Aug. 9, 1955, § 23, 4 DIREKTIVY 451-57; 1 Zakon. akty 185-90; English: HAZARD & SHAPIRO pt. 2, at 89-92; Decree of May 4, 1955, No. 861, § 76, 4 DIREKTIVY 400-17; 1 Zakon. akty 35-39, 355-59, 437-38; SHKUNDIN, *op. cit. supra* note 33, at 151-53; SHEYN 175; EKONOMIKA 65-73. Birman, Ekonomicheskaya gazeta, March 30, 1963, p. 7. The law governing contracts concluded "at the discretion" of the partners (free, unplanned contracts) differs in some respects, see, *e.g.*, 1961 Principles arts. 34, 44; R.S.F.S.R. CIVIL CODE OF 1964 arts. 166, 258; Sots. zak. No. 2, p. 92 (1958); *id.* No. 5, p. 95 (1959). It is not considered here.

[69] Decree of June 30, 1962, § 5, [1962] Sob. post. S.S.S.R. No. 12, item 94; Statute on Deliveries of Products § 9, as amended, and of Goods § 11.

[70] See note 65 *supra*.

[71] Shapkina, Sov. gos. i pravo No. 5, p. 140 (1963); see also Liberman, Sots zak. No. 10, p. 23, at 24 (1962). Shapkina is Deputy Head of the Section for Issuing Instructions, and Liberman is Head of the Codification Group, both of the USSR State Arbitrazh in Moscow.

[72] Statute on Deliveries of Products § 12 and of Goods § 12; *cf.* Sov. yus. No. 6, p. 89 (1963); Sots. zak. No. 2, p. 92, (1958).

ment" [73] and forwards it to the supplier. It is now up to the supplier to agree or else to file the protocol with Arbitrazh.[74] If he fails to do so within 10 days he is considered to have agreed with the contract version of the buyer as laid down in his Protocol of Disagreement.[75]

A simplified procedure for concluding contracts is envisaged in cases of lesser importance (*e.g.*, for products with a value of less than 7500 (new) rubles or for a single delivery,[76] or in cases where no agreement on assortment is needed). Here the buyer, after having received a copy of the delivery (distribution) order, sends an order (zakaz) to the seller within 60 days after approval of the supply plan. The order is considered to be accepted by the supplier if he does not refuse within 10 days.[77] If the supplier refuses to accept the order, the dispute can be brought before Arbitrazh.[78]

The third and simplest way of concluding contracts is used if the delivery (distribution) order contains all necessary data, such as quantity, assortment, quality, time, etc. In such case it suffices if both parties "accept" the order. Acceptance need not find an outward expression, like sending or confirming an order. Acceptance is presumed if none of the "parties" to the delivery order refuses within 10 days. After this "negative acceptance"—as it is called in Soviet legal writings—the delivery order "acquires the force of a contract" [79] and contract rules begin to regulate the relations of the

[73] Samples in SBORNIK GRAZHDANSKO-PRAVOVYKH I PROTSESSUAL'NYKH DOKUMENTOV (COLLECTION OF CIVIL LAW AND PROCEDURAL DOCUMENTS) 65 (Moscow 1961).

[74] Samples of pre-contract suits brought before Arbitrazh: *Id.* 65-67, 257-65; VYuZI, SBORNIK TEKSTOV I FORM GRAZHDANSKO-PRAVOVYKH DOKUMENTOV (COLLECTION OF TEXTS AND FORMS OF CIVIL-LEGAL DOCUMENTS) 111-16 (Moscow 1959); SBORNIK FORM DOKUMENTOV PO PRAVOVYM VOPROSAM DLYA SISTEMY POTREBITEL'SKOY KOOPERATSIYI (COLLECTION OF FORMS OF DOCUMENTS ON LEGAL QUESTIONS FOR THE SYSTEM OF CONSUMERS' COOPERATIVES) 30-32 (Moscow 1960).

[75] Statute on Deliveries of Products § 16 and of Goods § 12; see also 3 Sbornik 80, 93, 126, 249.

[76] Sample: SBORNIK GRAZHDANSKO-PRAVOVYKH I PROTSESSUAL'NYKH DOKUMENTOV (COLLECTION OF CIVIL LAW AND PROCEDURAL DOCUMENTS) 55, 57.

[77] Statute on Deliveries of Products §§ 10-11, as amended 1962, and of Goods §§ 6, 11; see also 11 Sbornik 23; 12 *id.* at 24, 35; 21 *id.* at 96; Sots. zak. No. 10, p. 87 (1960); Sov. yus. No. 10 p. 92 (1959).

[78] Instructive Letter of Dec. 30, 1959, 12 Sbornik 19 with further details; Sov. yus. No. 10, p. 29 (1959).

[79] Decree of June 30, 1962, § 4, [1962] Sob. post. S.S.S.R. No. 12, item 94; Statute on Deliveries of Products § 10, as amended 1962; Instruction of Dec. 18, 1962, §§ 5, 10, 22 Sbornik 12-15; Instructive Letter of Oct. 6, 1962, 21 *id.* at 96; *cf.* Letter of Sept. 7, 1959, 11 *id.* at 24. There is an exception to the automatic effect of accepted delivery orders. Certain categories of delivery contracts are valid only if the buyer submits a document showing the availability of appropriations to pay for the delivery. If he fails to submit such document, contract relations are considered not to have been established. Statute on Deliveries of Products § 13. Decree of June 30, 1962, § 9; Instruction of Dec. 18, 1962, § 9, 21 Sbornik 98; *cf.* case cited in note 151 *infra,* and Sov. yus. No. 12, p. 89 (1959); *id.* No. 17, p. 30 (1963).

parties.[80] This peculiar contract form amounts to a statutory fiction that mere inaction of the parties with respect to an administrative act is equal to agreeing with a civil-law contract.[81] A party which refuses to accept the delivery order has to apply to the issuing agency and inform the other party within the 10-day period. "Contract relations are not formalized" until the issuing agency has decided upon the objections raised. If the objections are held unfounded, contract relations are established "in accordance with general rules," *i.e.* by agreement or, if it cannot be achieved, on the basis of an Arbitrazh decision.[82]

If one or both parties feels it has grounds for not concluding a contract as ordered in the delivery (distribution) order, two procedures are open to them for settlement: an administrative procedure and the procedure before Arbitrazh.

The administrative procedure is limited to relations within the given channel of subordination and, therefore, is closed to a partner of the dispute outside this channel. It is to be followed, for example, if the buyer believes he is allocated excess and unneeded products. In this case he is entitled to "refuse" to conclude a contract by informing within 10 days the supplier, the *fond*-holder and the agency which issued the delivery order. The latter has to assign a new buyer to the supplier within another 10 days,[83] unless it considers the buyer's refusal to be unfounded.[84] The "refusal" of the

[80] The enterprise director (or a person authorized by him) is instructed to note on the delivery order that it "has acquired the force of a contract." (Instruction of Dec. 18, 1962, § 6, 22 Sbornik 12-15. *Cf.* Krylova, *Spory pri oformlenii dogovorov (Disputes over Formalizing Contracts)*, Sov. yus. No. 9, pp. 14-15 (1964).

[81] To speak of a "contract" concluded by negative acceptance has been called a strained interpretation and was criticized as artificial and farfetched by Shkundin, a distinguished worker of Arbitrazh. His remarks, written in 1948, referred to a similar procedure provided between 1938 and 1949 for the delivery of ferrous metals, SHKUNDIN, *op. cit. supra* note 33 , at 89; *cf.* Ovsiyenko, *Nekotoryye voprosy obyazatel'nykh otnosheniy po postavke metalloproduktsiy*, in KHAR'KOVKSIY YURICHICHESKIY INSTITUT (KHAR'KOV JURIDICAL INSTITUTE), 8 UCHYONYYE ZAPISKI (SCHOLARLY NOTES) 53-74, at 61 (1957).

[82] Instruction of Dec. 18, 1962, § 4, 22 Sbornik 12-15.

[83] Decree of June 30, 1962, § 8, [1962] Sob. post. S.S.S.R. No. 12, item 94; Statute on Deliveries of Products § 14, as amended 1962, and of Goods § 13. The Statute on Deliveries of Goods (§ 13) does not provide for a similar right of "refusal." An organization allocated unwanted consumer goods is only permitted to "raise the question" of cancelling the allocation.

[84] If the agency which issued the delivery (distribution) order refuses to re-assign the products, Arbitrazh may decide the dispute on its merits. Instruction of Dec. 18, 1962, § 4, 22 Sbornik 12-15. But this procedure is envisaged, so far, only for contracts concluded by "negative acceptance" and only for products to be used in production. See at note 79 *supra.* In other cases the decision of the issuing agency prevails and Arbitrazh has merely the right to suggest the annulling of the delivery order in question: 3 Sbornik 101 (1951); *id.* at 108 (1952); *id.* at 112 (1953); *id.* at 117 (1953); *id.* at 121 (1953); 4 *id.* at 4 (1955); 12 *id.* at 7 (1959). *Cf.* Shapkina, Sov. gos. i pravo No. 5, p. 140, at 145-46 (1963). Instructive Letter of Oct. 6, 1962, 21 Sbornik 98; Letter of Feb. 16, 1963, 23 *id.* at 61; Sots. zak. No. 4, p. 81 (1964); and at notes 87, 116, 140 *infra.*

buyer is, therefore, not the negative answer to a contract offer made in the course of contract negotiations, but the remonstration of an administratively subordinate organization against orders of its superior agency.

The Arbitrazh procedure is used to force a reluctant partner to conclude a contract, and also as a means to settle disputes over the terms of a draft contract. Both types of disputes are called "pre-contract disputes" and are decided by Arbitrazh.[85] Its decision replaces the will of the reluctant partner.[86] Disputes before Arbitrazh are not necessarily legal in character; they may also involve questions of economic expediency, such as the refusal to buy unwanted products.[87] Arbitrazh decisions have often an operative rather than a judicial character: they are part of day-to-day economic administration.[88]

The delivery (distribution) order may be more or less detailed. Accordingly many or few of the contract terms are left for agreement by the parties. Particulars which most often are open to free bargaining of the parties are assortment, time of delivery (within a fixed period, *e.g.*, a quarter of the year), technicalities of payment, packing, etc.

This leads to the question of the legal effect of those contract terms which are predetermined by the planning act and thus exempted from free bargaining of the parties. Do they create new legal obligations or are they merely a declaratory repetition of preexisting planned tasks? A way to find the answer is to examine the effect of: (1) contracts failing to reproduce terms predetermined by planning acts; and (2) contract terms violating planning acts.

Cases of the first group are governed by the rule that a "contract is considered concluded when agreement on all its essential points has been reached." Essential are those points "which are . . . necessary for contracts of the given type." [89] The question is whether the repetition of all or parts

[85] 1961 Principles art. 34; R.S.F.S.R. CIVIL CODE OF 1964 art. 166; Statute on Deliveries of Products §§ 12 and 16 and of Goods § 13.

[86] *Cf.* Instructive Letter of Jan. 5, 1951, 3 Sbornik 93.

[87] This follows from the task of Arbitrazh to help to fulfill delivery plans and to eliminate deficiencies in the work of enterprises. *Cf.* Statute on the USSR State Arbitrazh, § 2, [1960] Sob. post. S.S.S.R. No. 15, item 127. Some Arbitrazh decisions were (in part) expressly based on expediency, *e.g.*, two 1958 cases, in 8 Sbornik 48 and 9 *id.* at 47.

[88] This is illustrated by a technical detail: the period for keeping the files of an average Arbitrazh dispute is one year (List in 21 Sbornik 54-73, at 64, point 37). They lose their significance, as a rule, with the end of the given planning year.

[89] 1961 Principles art. 34; R.S.F.S.R. CIVIL CODE OF 1964, art. 160. The corresponding rule in the R.S.F.S.R. CIVIL CODE OF 1922 art. 130 did not qualify its definition of "essential points" by a reference to the given type of contract. *Cf.* note 91 *infra* and an unpublished Arbitrazh decision reported by Gribanov, *Otvetstvennost' storon za nedopostavku po dogovoru postavki (Responsibility of the Parties After Failure of Delivery According to Delivery Contract)*, in MGU YURIDICHESKIY FAKUL'TET, VOPROSY SOVETSKOGO GRAZHDANSKOGO PRAVA V PRAKTIKE SUDA I ARBITRAZHA (MOSCOW STATE UNIVERSITY LAW FACULTY, QUESTIONS OF SOVIET CIVIL LAW IN COURT AND ARBITRAZH PRACTICE) 331,

of the planned task is "essential" for a planned contract. Arbitrazh agencies hold it is not. They consider planned contracts concluded even if the parties failed to reproduce this or that "essential" point predetermined by the planning act.[90] A different situation exists if the planning act leaves "essential points" to the agreement of the parties.[91]

Contract terms violating the law of planning act are invalid.[92] But the nullity of some clauses do not invalidate the rest of the contract.[93] The contract continues to be in effect, even if "essential points" of it are void, provided these points are covered by the planning act.

The answer to the above question is, therefore, that contract terms merely duplicating the contents of a planning act are declaratory in character. The constitutive element is the planned task. This conclusion, however, does not reduce the contract to a mere formality. The conclusion has validity only for one part of the contract, *i.e.*, for the obligations as defined in the delivery (distribution) order. It does not extend to those parts of the contract which stipulate corresponding rights, such as the right to demand delivery or payment, and also not to contract terms freely negotiated between the parties. The explanation for this split between obligations and rights is that planning acts contain only administrative orders to subordinate organizations; they do not grant civil law rights to their partners. Such rights

at 371 (Moscow 1959). In the case the parties did not stipulate the time of delivery and Arbitrazh denied the suit of the buyer against the supplier for assessing sanctions for nondelivery.

[90] This is reported by Zamengov, *Sochetaniye gosudarstvennogo planovogo rukovodstva i khozyaystvennoy samostoyatel'nosti v dogovornykh otnosheniyakh (The Combination of State Planning Guidance and Economic Autonomy in Contractual Relations)*, Sov. gos. i pravo No. 2, p. 33, at 38-39 (1963). He substantiates it by referring to Arbitrazh practice with respect to contract terms violating planning acts. See note 93 *infra*. Legal science is divided, see *e.g.*, the authors quoted by Zamengov, *supra* at 36 and 38 nn.6 and 16.

[91] See Instructive Letter of Dec. 25, 1953, 3 Sbornik 116; Instructive Letter of April 29, 1957, 5 *id.* at 14; Sov. yus. No. 4, p. 80 (1957); Letter of July 22, 1960, 15 Sbornik 59, correcting a summary published in Sots. zak. No. 6, p. 91 (1960); 1958 case in 8 Sbornik 62; 1957 case in 5 *id.* at 46; Yazev, *O primeneniyi st. 130 GK RSFSR k dogovoram, zaklyuchayemym mezhdu khozyaystvennymi organami (Concerning the Application of Article 130 of the Civil Code of the RSFSR to Contracts Concluded Between Economic Organs)*, Pravovedeniye No. 3, p. 121 (1960).

[92] 1961 Principles art. 34; Statute on Deliveries of Products § 18 and of Goods § 17; R.S.F.S.R. Civil Code of 1964, arts. 48, 159 (Code of 1922, arts. 30, 147).

[93] R.S.F.S.R. Civil Code of 1964, art. 60 (Code of 1922 art. 37); Instructive Letter of April 18, 3 Sbornik 291; *cf.* Rules for Deciding Property Disputes by Arbitrazh Agencies of Aug. 10, 1934, § 2, Arbitrazh v sovetskom khozyaystve. Sbornik (Arbitration in the Soviet Economy. A Collection) 199-211 (Compiled by Mozheyko & Shkundin, 4th ed. Moscow 1948), now superseded by Rules for Deciding Economic Disputes by Arbitrazh of July 1, 1963. 24 Sbornik 3-23. One pertinent Arbitrazh case is briefly summarized by Zamengov, *supra* note 90, at 39 n.18, but "one could quote," Zamengov writes, "a great number of Arbitrazh decisions." With regard to contract terms violating price regulations, see a 1958 and a 1959 case in 10 Sbornik 102 and 103; a 1960 case in 15 *id.* at 112; and a 1961 case in 18 *id.* at 55.

may be acquired only by way of concluding a contract with the organization to which the planning act is addressed.

V. Impact of Plan on Performance of Contracts

The impact of planning on the performance of contracts manifests itself mainly in four situations: (1) in cases of improper performance; (2) when a change of contract terms is sought; (3) in cases where the planning act, having served as a basis for the contract, appears to have been issued in violation of existing regulations (and is, therefore, voidable or void); and (4) when after the contract is concluded new planning acts are issued which affect the performance of the contract.

A. Improper Performance

Improper performance may have been the fault of the debtor or may have resulted from events beyond his control. Both groups of cases will be discussed here only insofar as they are related or connected with actions (or inaction) of planning organs, *i.e.*, again only in the area where contract and plan meet. Thus the wide range of problems usually connected with contract performance—such as late or bad quality deliveries, liability, etc. —will not be the subject of this review.

The question of whether the failure of planning agencies to allocate sufficient *fondy* is a valid defense for nonperformance was decided in a 1959 case:

> The buyer, a Stalingrad [now Volgograd] office of the RSFSR Ferrous Metal Sales and Supply Administration, sued for a forfeit for incomplete delivery of cast iron. The producer, a metallurgy factory in the Ukrainian Republic, asked to be released from liability since its Council of National Economy did not allocate it enough *fondy*, although it had raised the question of insufficient *fondy* in time. Incomplete delivery was therefore, producer claims, not its fault. *Held:* Producer is liable, since it is the producer's concern to see that it is supplied with material *fondy*.[94]

It seems harsh to hold a producer liable for nonperformance if his requests for necessary materials were not acted upon by planning agencies. But to decide otherwise would allow producers to use shortcomings of planning authorities as a welcome excuse for their own failures, to relax their efforts in procuring planned material, and to rely passively on the mechanism of planning. Arbitrazh, however, did release producers from liability for nonperformance under exceptional circumstances. The Bobrov-Insulation-Fac-

[94] Stalingrad Office v. Alchevsk Metallurgical Plant, 1959, 10 Sbornik 110. See also two unpublished Arbitrazh cases reported by Gribanov, *supra* note 89, at 337, 339. *Cf.* note 116 *infra.*

tory case, decided in 1960, is an example.[95] But the Arbiter was careful in pointing to the special features of the case.

A different rule applies if the producer is prevented from performing because he did not receive a distribution (unloading) order in time. This is not an exception to the rule just discussed that inaction of planning agencies in the allocation of planned products may not serve as a valid defense. Distribution (unloading) orders are not planning acts, but instructions of the buyer based on a contract.[96] A case involving a late issue of distribution (unloading) orders was decided in 1959:

> The supplier, a Moscow warehouse of a RSFSR Trade Administration (Rostekstil'torg) was obliged under a contract to have its producer-factories deliver cloth to the buyer, a warehouse of the Ukrainian Trade Administration. The buyer had to submit, by December 15, 1958, a distribution (unloading) order showing to which trade organizations the goods should be delivered. Instead of this order the supplier received in the first week of January 1959 a "distribution plan" from the Ukrainian Trade Administration, *i.e.*, the superior agency of the buyer. The buyer claimed a forfeit for incomplete delivery of specified items during the first three months of 1959. *Held:* Suit dismissed. If buyer submits the distribution (unloading) order late the supplier is not able to perform properly. Supplier is not liable for a violation of assortment if it took place under circumstances beyond his control.[97]

Failure of a sub-supplier to fulfill his plan was the defense of a supplier in a 1958 case:

> Plaintiff, an All-Union Trade Administration, brought suits for fines against defendant, a Meat Combine in Frunze (Kirgiz SSR) which failed to deliver the required amount of meat products for an All-Union pool. Defendant claimed that his own supplier did not fulfill his plan of delivering cattle. *Held:* For plaintiff. Defendant is liable to pay fines since he had "sufficient" resources for a priority delivery to the All-Union consumer. He preferred, however, to deliver for Republican and local needs.[98]

The obligation to perform continues even if no new *fondy* are allocated. This was the ruling in an Instructive Letter of 1958:

[95] Bobrov Insulation Factory v. Khar'kov Factory "Elektrotyazhmash," 1960, Sots. zak. No. 10, p. 87 (1960), and correction in *id.* No. 12, at 77; the correction is translated in HAZARD & SHAPIRO pt. 2, at 127-28. The case is summarized and commented on by Berman, in his JUSTICE IN THE USSR, at 137-38 (2d ed. 1963).

[96] See at notes 47 *supra* and 120-121 *infra*.

[97] Khmel'nitskaya Trade Warehouse v. Moscow Warehouse, 1959, 12 Sbornik 42. See also Instructive Letter of Nov. 19, 1957, 6 *id.* 10; Sov. yus. No. 3 p. 78 (1958); *id.* No. 9, p. 92 (1958); Sots. zak. No. 1, p. 92 (1958).

[98] Kirgiz Office of the Chief Meat and Fish Trade Administration v. Frunze Meat Combine, 1958, 8 Sbornik 40. See also three unpublished Arbitrazh cases summarized by Gribanov, *supra* note 89, at 340.

A producer who fails to deliver goods for mass consumption in time is obliged (in accordance with the Special Conditions applicable here) to make up for the shortage within two months of the next quarter. This obligation is ruled by Arbitrazh to exist also if producer is not allocated *fondy* for this quarter.[99]

Planned tasks, on the other hand, may protect an obligor in default from bearing responsibility in kind, as this 1957 Instructive Letter shows:

A contractor used material furnished to him by a customer (out of the latter's planned *fondy* for the last year) for purposes other than agreed in the contract. The contractor is liable to pay a fine and to refund the value of the materials improperly used, but he is not obliged to return them in kind out of *fondy* he received for fulfilling planned tasks in the current year.[100]

If the supplier delivers late and the buyer refuses acceptance because of the delay, the supplier has to ask his superior agency to assign him a new buyer.[101]

Summing up, it appears that planned contracts have to be performed regardless of whether planning agencies have allocated enough *fondy* and regardless of whether sub-suppliers have fulfilled their own plans or not. It follows that the system of planned supplies does not change the general rule known also in non-socialist civil law, that failure of the supplier to procure the materials necessary for performing his contract obligations does not relieve him from liability.

B. Change of Contract Terms

The parties may agree on a change of their contract terms "if this does not contradict the confirmed plan." [102] A relevant Instructive Letter was issued by State Arbitrazh in 1959:

A wholesale warehouse had directed its contract partner, the producer, to deliver goods to a retail trade organization. The assortment of goods delivered was not in accordance with the contract, but corresponded to the orders of the receiver (the retail organization). Arbitrazh decreed that no sanctions should be applied against the producer if the "buyer" agreed with a change of the assortment against the contract terms. But sanctions should be assessed if the producer delivered less than originally agreed.[103]

[99] Letter of Jan. 25, 1958, 6 Sbornik 36. See also Sots. zak. No. 5, p. 94 (1958).

[100] Instructive Letter of April 29, 1957, 5 *id.* at 12; Sov. yus. No. 4 p. 80 (1957). *Cf.* at notes 33 *supra* and 154 *infra.*

[101] Statute on Deliveries of Goods § 72; Sots. zak. No. 11, p. 91 (1962; *cf.* cases at notes 135-36 *infra.*

[102] Statute on Deliveries of Products § 17 and of Goods § 16.

[103] Letter of July 22, 1959, 11 Sbornik 17.

A similar rule is expressed in a 1958 Instructive Letter:

> A buyer personally selecting goods in the warehouse of the supplier, refused the assortment of goods which corresponded to the previously agreed upon specification, and accepted goods in another assortment. In this case the buyer has no right to claim sanctions against the supplier.[104]

Parties to a contract may not mutually waive each other's obligations to pay sanctions, after improper performance, although there is "sometimes a tendency" toward a set-off of sanctions.[105] Agreements to decrease or not to apply sanctions are legal only if they do not violate the Special Conditions or the terms of the original contract.[106] Nor are Arbitrazh agencies allowed to free the debtor from payment of sanctions; they are granted discretion to do so only "in extra-ordinary cases if there are legal reasons" for waiving sanctions.[107] It remains open what the "legal reasons" are.

In one case the producer did not deliver within the time fixed in the contract. After the due date the parties agreed on a new time for delivery. This agreement, State Arbitrazh ruled, does not relieve the producer at fault from sanctions for nondelivery at the time agreed originally.[108] But in certain cases an enterprise director is granted the right to change production plans if the buyer agrees.[109]

In general, it may be concluded, the freedom to change the terms of a planned contract is rather limited. This follows from the principle of specific performance [110] and corresponds to the limited freedom in concluding contracts.

[104] Letter of Jan. 16, 1958, 6 *id.* at 35.

[105] Novitskiy, Rol' sovetskogo grazhdanskogo prava v osushchestvleniyi khozraschyota i rezhima ekonomiyi (The Role of Soviet Civil Law in the Implementation of Cost Accounting and a Regime of Economizing) 95 (Moscow 1955). For other citations see notes 190-91 *infra*. *Cf*. an unpublished Arbitrazh case reported by Gribanov, *supra* note 89, at 360.

[106] 1961 Principles art. 36; R.S.F.S.R. Civil Code of 1964, art. 220; Statute on Deliveries of Products § 81 and of Goods § 82. See also 3 Sbornik 154, 158 and 189; 5 *id.* at 36; (amended 18 *id.* at 34) 9 *id.* at 54; and *cf*. Sov. yus. No. 22, p. 32 (1963).

[107] Instructive Letter of July 22, 1950, 3 *id.* at 183.

[108] Letter of Aug. 29, 1957, 6 *id.* at 31. See also Sots. zak. No. 12, p. 82 (1957); *id.* No. 12, p. 78 (1958); *id.* No. 9, p. 92 (1963).

[109] Decree of May 4, 1955, No. 861, 4 Direktivy 400-17; 1 Zakon. akty 35-49, 355-59, 437-38; Khoz. dogovory 84-89, excerpts; Dozortsev 103-08, excerpts); Decree of Aug. 9, 1955, § 2, 4 Direktivy 451-57; 1 Zakon. akty 185-90; Khoz. dogovory 94-97, excerpts; Dozortsev 78-81, excerpts; Instructive Letter of Dec. 9, 1955, 4 Sbornik 7; *cf*. Statute on the Council of National Economy, §§ 49, 51, [1957] Sob. post. S.S.S.R. No. 13, item 121.

[110] 1961 Principles art. 36; R.S.F.S.R. Civil Code of 1964, arts. 191, 221; see at note 64 *supra* and *cf*. at notes 147, 213 *infra*.

C. Planning Acts in Violation of the Law

Planning acts are, as shown above, administrative acts issued to individual addressees ordering a concrete action or satisfying a concrete demand. The possibility, indeed, the likelihood that here and there a planning act does not accord with existing regulations or requirements of the plan is apparent. Being administrative acts, the consequences of such faulty acts are to be judged by the rules of administrative law. Disregarding the exceptional case of "non-acts" (*e.g.*, issued by a completely incompetent agency), administrative law distinguishes between void acts and voidable acts. The latter category is subdivided by the time nullity is ruled to take effect: from the moment the act was issued (*ex tunc*) or from the moment it was declared to be void *(ex nunc)*.[111] There is no systematic codification of rules relating to void and voidable planning acts.[112] If such acts are issued they are rectified through the usual administrative channels and procedures. The initiative for this may come from the higher agency or the obligee or Arbitrazh deciding a case arising out of such acts.

Delivery orders must correspond to the production plan of the producer-enterprise. This rule is expressly stated in a recent Decree of 1962,[113] and is stressed in legal writings. Laptev, a Soviet expert on economic law, demands that all plan indicators should correspond to each other and observes that "most often disharmony arises between the plans of production and . . . . supply." [114] State Arbitrazh has issued a few relevant Instructions. It ruled in a 1962 Instructive Letter that Arbitrazh agencies should not force parties to enter a contract if the delivery order does not correspond to the production plan of the supplier-enterprise. However, if it appears that not the delivery order but the production plan was issued in a manner violating the established procedure and contradicts plans of higher agencies, Arbitrazh may rule that the contract should be concluded on the basis of the delivery order.[115] In case a delivery order demands delivery of products outside the plan and for which raw materials are not provided, Arbitrazh agencies are

[111] Karadzhe-Iskrov, *Nedeystvitel'nyy administrativnyy akt i predely ego obyazatel'nosti dlya suda (An Inoperative Administrative Act and the Limits of Its Legal Force for a Court)*, Lecture summarized in Sov. gos. i pravo Nos. 5-6, p. 73, at 74 (1946).

[112] The problems connected herewith are somewhat neglected in Soviet legal science. *Cf.* notes 29, 40 *supra*.

[113] Decree of June 30, 1962, § 2, [1962] Sob. post. S.S.S.R. No. 12, item 94. This rule renders obsolete a previous Arbitrazh Instruction, Sots. zak. No. 10, p. 93 (1959), permitting delivery orders "beyond plans" issued on special orders of the government. See also 21 Sbornik 97 and *cf.* Gribanov, *supra* note 89, at 337, 343, 357.

[114] Laptev, Sov. gos. i pravo No. 3, p. 95, at 103 (1963).

[115] Instructive Letter of Oct. 6, 1962, 21 Sbornik 97.

instructed to raise the question of eliminating planning mistakes that had been made.[116]

In a 1961 case the new planning act was declared not to deserve consideration:

> The buyer, a Meat Combine in the Kazakh SSR, refused to accept livestock from the supplier, an office of "Livestock-Import" (an All-Union Foreign Trade Combine). The refusal was based on an order of the superior agency of the buyer, the Semipalatinsk Council of National Economy (Kazakh SSR) to accept cattle henceforth only from organizations in the Kazakh SSR and to refuse cattle from Altai (a province in the RSFSR) and "Livestock-Import". Supplier, relying on his contract with the buyer, demanded a penalty for non-acceptance. *Held:* Claim granted. The order of the Semipalatinsk Council of National Economy was a manifestation of localism. Therefore buyer could not be freed from the penalty.[117]

An allocation may be unrealistic, *e.g.*, if the producer who is to deliver the allocated goods will begin production only in the following year. In the given case (1960) the Republican Gosplan—on the proposal of State Arbitrazh—freed the factory from its obligation to deliver and allotted the consumer materials from another producer.[118] A case of 1957 shows some practical implications:

> The producer received a delivery order *(zakaz-naryad)* from his superior agency (Glavmetallosbyt) which exceeded his production program. He informed the consumer, a supply office, and its superior agency as required in internal regulations. The consumer, nevertheless, demanded a fine for nondelivery. *Held:* Suit dismissed, since producer did not accept the delivery order and informed the consumer as required. The consumer should have asked his superior agency to allocate him another supplier.[119]

Distribution (unloading) orders, although not planning acts, may be held void, too. In a 1958 case:

> The producer-factory was obliged under a contract to deliver dishes to a number of recipients listed in distribution (unloading) orders of the buyer, a warehouse. The producer fulfilled his production plan by 107 per cent and delivered dishes with a value of 48 million (old) rubles.

[116] Instructive Letter of Dec. 23, 1961, 19-20 Sbornik 8; Instructive Letter of Sept. 23, 1960, 15 *id.* at 79; 12 *id.* at 7; this case arose before a contract had been concluded and has to be distinguished from case at note 94 *supra. Cf.* at notes 84, 87, 124, 140 *supra.*

[117] Semipalatinsk Office of "Skotoimport" v. Semipalatinsk Meat Combine, 1961, 21 Sbornik 101; *cf.* 7 *id.* at 14; Sov. yus. No. 9, p. 93 (1958).

[118] Instructive Letter of Sept. 23, 1960, 15 *id.* at 83. Unrealistic plans and delivery orders as well as other planning deficiencies were criticized at a 1962 Conference of Chief Arbiters, 22 *id.* at 42, 59-61, 64-65.

[119] Libknekht Plant v. Kuz'min Plant, 1957, 6 *id.* at 40.

> The total value of dishes listed in the distribution (unloading) orders of the buyer amounted, however, to 55 million (old) rubles. Buyer sued for sanctions for incomplete delivery. *Held:* Suit dismissed. Producer is not liable for incomplete delivery since he fulfilled his plan and since the distribution (unloading) orders of the buyer exceeded the obligations of the producer.[120]

Another case where a distribution (unloading) order was erroneous is reported by Liberman.[121] A case, decided in 1959, deals with a planning act contradicting existing price regulations:

> Plaintiff, a wood Sales and Supply organization of the Armenian SSR in Yerevan, received 9700 cubic meters of wood materials from defendant, an office of the Gorki Council of National Economy. Plaintiff paid transportation costs from Astrakhan to Yerevan and asked defendant for a refund. He based his claim on the delivery order of the Gorki Economic Council which ordered delivery in cars at the destination station. Defendant refused payment, relying upon the price list which assigned transportation costs to the consumer. State Arbitrazh asked Gosplan of the USSR for guidance. Gosplan ruled that transportation costs are to be paid in accordance with the delivery order. Arbitrazh therefore satisfied the claim of the plaintiff.[122]

Thus in this case it was decided that price regulations could be overruled by a delivery order. Similarly ministerial directives claiming a deposit for packing materials may be held to be without effect:

> A factory used to receive—in accordance with directives of its superior (meanwhile abolished) Ministries—a deposit sum of 100 (old) rubles for each box (for the delivery of yarn) in addition to the value of the boxes. State Arbitrazh ruled that the factory had no right to do so since the Special Conditions for delivery of yarn do not provide for a deposit, but only for a fine of 5 per cent of the box-value per day of delayed return (but not more than 200 per cent).[123]

The general picture emerging from the materials quoted is that planning acts in violation of the law are usually corrected in informal administrative procedures before a contract is concluded, often on the suggestion of Arbitrazh.

[120] Moscow Wholesale Warehouse v. Dulevskiy Porcelain Plant, 1958, 9 *id.* at 54; *cf.* at notes 47 and 97 *supra.*

[121] LIBERMAN, VOPROSY RASCHYOTOV ZA PRODUKTSIYU I USLUGI V PRAKTIKE GOSARBITRAZHA (QUESTIONS OF PAYMENTS FOR PRODUCTION AND SERVICES IN GOSARBITRAZH PRACTICE) 51 (Moscow 1959).

[122] Armenian Timber-Paper Supply and Sales Administration v. Timber Administration of the Gor'ki Council of National Economy, 1959, 13 Sbornik 31.

[123] Letter of Feb. 29, 1960, 13 *id.* at 19; *cf.* 1961 Principles art. 35.

D. New Planning Acts

The changing of planning acts seem to be a widespread practice. Though highly unwelcome in theory, it is sometimes unavoidable in practice. *Pravda* reports, for example, that orders for almost 6 million (new) rubles were annulled by planning agencies for four chemical machine-building enterprises in the Tambov region for the first half of 1963.[124] Frequent changes "fever" *(likhoradiyat)* enterprises.[125]

Planning acts issued after contracts have been concluded may either affect their terms or their actual performance, usually both. New planning acts affecting the terms of existing contracts must be incorporated into the original agreement. This has to be formalized through an additional contract or by way of an exchange of letters, telegrams or simply by attaching the notification of the change to the original contract.[126] If the parties fail to do so, sanctions may be assessed against them.[127] The important question of whether in such cases of failure relations between the parties are governed by the new planning act or by the old contract is decided by Arbitrazh in favor of the first alternative. This interpretation is supported by Ioffe, a law professor in Leningrad,[128] Krasnov,[129] and Zamengov[130] but is criticized by Khalfina, an authority on contract law in Moscow.[131]

The principle of the overriding effect of new planning acts is expressed in a 1955 Instructive Letter:

> In case the amount of products allocated to a buyer *(fond)* is reduced in a procedure established for it, the question of assessing sanctions

[124] Belyak, *Plan i proizvodstvo (Plan and Production)*, Pravda, Oct. 21, 1963, p. 2.

[125] Laptev, *Voprosy pravovogo polozheniya promyshlennykh predpriyatiy (Questions of the Legal Status of Industrial Enterprises)* Sov. gos. i pravo No. 3, p. 95, at 103 (1963); cf. Frid, *Kakim dolzhen byt' Zakon o sotsialisticheskom predpriyatiyi (What Sort of Statute There Should Be in Regard to a Socialist Enterprise)*, Sov. gos. i pravo No. 4, p. 104 (1963).

[126] Statute on Deliveries of Products § 20, as amended 1962, and of Goods § 16; Rules on Construction Contracts of 1955, § 11, 2 Zakon. akty 263-72; KHOZ. DOGOVORY 406-16; 24 Sbornik 48; Rules on Contracts for Architectural Works of 1959, §§ 15-16, 2 Zakon. akty 216-28; KHOZ. DOGOVORY 416; 11 Sbornik 8; *cf.* case at note 160 *infra.*

[127] Statute on Deliveries of Products § 71 and of Goods § 80; *cf.* Instructive Letter of July 10, 1956, partly repealed 1961, 4 Sbornik 42; 18 *id.* at 32.

[128] IOFFE, OTVETSTVENNOST' PO SOVETSKOMU GRAZHDANSKOMU PRAVU (RESPONSIBILITY IN SOVIET CIVIL LAW), 107-08 (Leningrad 1955).

[129] KRASNOV, REAL'NOYE ISPOLNENIYE DOGOVORNYKH OBYAZATEL'STV MEZHDU SVTSIALISTICHESKIMI ORGANIZATSIYAMI (THE SPECIFIC PERFORMANCE OF CONTRACTUAL OBLIGATIONS BETWEEN ORGANIZATIONS) 179 (Moscow 1959).

[130] Zamengov, *supra* note 90, at 40-41 and the literature quoted there in note 22. Zamengov points out, however, that the new planning act is not sufficient if it needs concretization by the parties.

[131] KHALFINA, PRAVOVOYE REGULIROVANIYE POSTAVKI PRODUKTSIYI V NARODNOM KHOZAISTYE (LEGAL REGULATION OF DELIVERY OF PRODUCTION IN THE NATIONAL ECONOMY) 187-90 (Moscow 1962).

> against the supplier for nondelivery should be judged on the basis of the new *fond* [distribution order] and not of the old one, since the latter "after its reduction ceased to be effective." [132]

This ruling, if applied, relieves a supplier from sanctions even when he violated times of delivery (or other contract terms) *before* the change of the planning act became effective.[133]

A leading case confirming the principle was decided in 1960:

> The supplier, a wholesale warehouse in Penza (RSFSR), was under a contract obligation to deliver to the buyer, a wholesale warehouse in the Latvian SSR, 4000 ladies' wrist watches in gold cases and 6000 watches in steel cases. After the specifications were agreed upon the All-Union Chief Trade Administration changed the delivery plan. The supplier was ordered to deliver 7600 gold watches and only 1000 steel watches. The parties failed to incorporate the change into their contract. The buyer, proceeding from the original contract, demanded sanctions from the supplier for nondelivery. *Held:* Claim denied. Insofar as supplier performed in accordance with the corrected plan he is not guilty of nondelivery.[134]

In this case the change of the planning act was ordered by an agency having power over both contract partners. The change was binding, therefore, on both partners. A different situation exists with regard to plan changes ordered by an authority to which only one of the contract partners is subordinate. The following 1959 case is in point:

> Plaintiff, a Moscow warehouse of the RSFSR Trade Administration *(Roskul'ttorg)*, offered to defendant, the Odessa warehouse of a Ukrainian trade organization, to deliver—in accordance with the distribution plan—7400 cameras. Defendant signed the contract with a Protocol of Disagreement. It refused to accept more than 4400 cameras, explaining that its superior organ (the Ukrainian trade organization) had reduced its sales plan by 3000 cameras. *Held:* Defendant is ordered to accept the contract as drafted by plaintiff, *i.e.*, obliged to buy 7400 cameras. The Ukrainian trade organization was obliged to assign to plaintiff another buyer for 3000 cameras, which it failed to do.[135]

[132] Instructive Letter of July 6, 1955, 3 Sbornik 194; see also two unpublished Arbitrazh cases reported by Gribanov, *supra* note 89, at 345, 357; *cf.* at note 162, *infra.*

[133] The ruling is criticized by KRASNOV, *op. cit. supra* note 129, at 165-66, who summarized three unpublished Arbitrazh decisions showing an opposite practice and one case supporting the ruling of the 1955 Instructive Letter. *Id.* at 161-62. *Cf.* also the case in Sov. yus. No. 19, p. 32 (1961).

[134] Warehouse in the Latvian SSR v. Penza Warehouse, 1960, 14 Sbornik 58. See also three unpublished Arbitrazh cases reported by Gribanov, *supra* note 89, at 354-56; *cf.* at note 160 *infra.*

[135] Moscow Warehouse v. Odessa Warehouse, 1959, 11 Sbornik 37. Two further relevant cases are summarized by KRASNOV, *op. cit. supra* note 129, at 169.

Thus the buyer was held responsible for the action (rather, inaction) of his superior agency. An Arbitrazh Instruction of 1959 is also relevant:

> The supplier, a canning factory, delivered its goods to wholesale warehouses of the RSFSR Trade Administration of Groceries *(Rosbakaleya)*, but *Rosbakaleya* unilaterally—at the request of its warehouses—changed the quantity of goods to be delivered. In this case, Arbitrazh decreed, *Rosbakaleya* was obliged to indicate to the supplier other buyers willing to take over the balance.[136]

The rule following from these cases is that a one-sided planning act (which binds only one of the contract partners) does not affect the contract rights of the other partner.

This principle needs a qualification if the superior agency of one party ordering the change of a planning act seeks and reaches agreement with the superior agency of the other contract party. As a result the plan change becomes binding on both partners. In such a case the rule laid down for a planning change ordered by an agency superior to both contract partners can and should be applied, therefore:

> The supplier, according to a contract, was supposed to deliver three sets of a certain type of equipment to the buyer. The superior agency of the buyer, a Ministry, increased the delivery obligation by two more sets to be unloaded in the second half of 1957. The buyer was informed by the supplier about this change in the first quarter of 1957. In June 1957, *i.e.*, before the agreed time of delivery, the buyer, refused to accept the two additional sets. The supplier demanded refund of his costs so far incurred. *Held:* Buyer is obliged to refund these to supplier, since he refused only after supplier had begun work.[137]

The parties, obviously, had not incorporated the additional planned task into their contract, but the change was apparently agreed upon by the superior agencies of both contract partners (this can be inferred from the fact that it was the supplier who informed the buyer about the change ordered by the superior agency of the buyer). Therefore Arbitrazh found the new planned task to be binding on both parties (and not only in relation between the supplier and his superior agency).

In the case of contracts concluded by mere acceptance of a delivery order, the plan change is considered to be "accepted" by the parties if none of them raises objections or demands an additional agreement within ten

[136] Letter of Feb. 18, 1959, 9 Sbornik 19. The duty to assign a new buyer in case of changes is stressed in Instructive Letter of Dec. 10, 1960, 16 *id.* at 48. *Cf.* Sots. zak. No. 2, p. 93 (1958) and at note 101 *supra.*

[137] Novo-Kramatorskiy Machine-Building Plant v. Izhorskiy Plant, 1957, 6 Sbornik 38. Another pertinent case is quoted by Krasnov, *op. cit. supra* note 129, at 170.

days. This rule corresponds to the procedure for accepting the original delivery order.[138]

New planning acts may also affect bypassing (transit) contracts, *e.g.*, if a planning agency replaces the recipient of products. In such a case the buyer has to change the distribution (unloading) order and the supplier is obliged to deliver in accordance with the changed distribution (unloading) order. Although the supplier is normally entitled to claim sanctions from the buyer envisaged for a delayed issue of distribution (unloading) orders, he has no such right if the delay was due to a new planning act.[139]

A few Instructions and cases relating to post-contract changes of contract terms by planning acts will exemplify the principle.

The change of a delivery time by a new planning act was the subject of a 1959 case:

> The All-Union Meat and Fish Trade Organization ordered its Azerbaydzhan Office to have the Kishinev (Moldavian SSR) Meat-Combine deliver, ahead of time (in the third quarter instead of the fourth quarter of 1959), 407 tons of pork to the Baku (Azerbaydzhan SSR) Meat Combine. The premature delivery resulted in damages to the Baku Combine since it had no cold storage facilities ready to receive the shipment. The Baku Combine brought suit against the Azerbaydzhan Office (and three co-defendants) for the damages sustained. State Arbitrazh *held:* The Azerbaydzahn Office is liable for damages. The office did not raise the question of revoking the order of the All-Union agency in time and did not seek the agreement of the buyer for premature delivery, as required by law.[140]

Provisions on price changes also affect current contracts. The new price applies, as a rule, to those products which have not yet been delivered at the time the new price takes effect. This principle can be inferred from three Arbitrazh decisions (of 1948, 1949 and 1953) reported by Insarova.[141]

As to transport, Arbitrazh issued the following ruling in 1957:

> If the number of railroad freight cars allotted to the supplier is reduced with the result that he is unable to deliver wholly or in part, he shall not be liable (this follows by implication). But the supplier should

[138] Instruction of Dec. 18, 1962, § 11, 22 Sbornik 12-15; see at note 79 *supra.*

[139] Letter of Dec. 31, 1960, 17 Sbornik 38. *Cf.* Statute on Deliveries of Products § 73 and of Goods § 76.

[140] Baku Meat Combine v. Azerbaydzhan Office of Meat and Fish Trade Administration, 1959, 13 Sbornik 38. See also an unpublished Arbitrazh case reported by Gribanov, *supra* note 89, at 337. *Cf.* at note 116 *supra.*

[141] Insarova, *Nekotoryye voprosy vliyaniya aktov planirovaniya na izmeneniye i prekrashcheniye dogovora postavki (Some Questions of the Impact of Planning Acts on Alteration and Cessation of a Contract of Delivery)* in VYuZI, VOPROSY SOVETSKOGO GRAZHDANSKOGO PRAVA (QUESTIONS OF SOVIET CIVIL LAW) 43-63, at 51-53 (Moscow 1955).

not be freed from liability for non-delivery, if the buyer had agreed to provide transport himself.[142]

The general rule following from the materials presented is that new planning acts take precedence over existing contracts.

VI. Impact of Plan on Dissolution of Contracts

A. Rescission of Contracts by Agreement

"Rescission of a contract can take place by agreement of the parties which concluded the contract if this does not contradict the confirmed plan." [143] It follows that contracts based on delivery orders cannot be rescinded at the free will of the parties. This rule effects the traditional freedom of contract partners to rescind their relations by mutual consent.

Another problem connected with the rescission of contracts by agreement is whether the parties are entitled to include a clause in their contract permitting them to rescind the contract unilaterally under certain specified conditions. Arbitrazh agencies have not worked out clear rules. This is related by Zamengov,[144] who believes such clauses should be permitted. Reasonable as this view is, it nevertheless may be in conflict with article 33 of the 1961 Principles, forbidding a "unilateral refusal to fulfill an obligation . . . except in cases provided by law." Zamengov did not cite any law permitting such unilateral refusal.

B. Ending a Contract Against Payment of Indemnity

This possibility is excluded in Soviet contract law. The 1961 Principles stipulate in article 36: "The payment of a forfeit . . . and compensation for damages caused by improper fulfillment do not release the debtor from fulfillment of the obligation in kind, except in instances where a planned

[142] Letter of Aug. 12, 1957, 6 Sbornik 30; see also an unpublished Arbitrazh case reported by Gribanov, *Otvetstvennost' storon za nedopostavku po dogovoru postavki (Responsibility of the Parties After Failure of Delivery According to Delivery Contract)*, in MGU Yuridicheskiy Fakul'tet, Voprosy sovetskogo grazhdanskogo prava v praktike suda i arbitrazha (Moscow State University Law Faculty, Questions of Soviet Civil Law in Court and Arbitration Practice) 351 (Moscow 1959).

[143] Statutes on Deliveries of Products § 17 and of Goods § 16; R.S.F.S.R. Civil Code of 1964, art. 233; Instruction of Dec. 18, 1962, § 12, 22 Sbornik 12-15. But a dissolution of contract by agreement is permitted under certain conditions by Rules on Construction Contracts of 1955, §§ 10, 11, 16, 2 Zakon. akty 263-72; Statute for the Dissemination . . . of Periodicals of 1961, § 10, 21 Sbornik 45-53. The rescission of an obligation by agreement was allowed without qualification in the field of traditional contract law by article 129 of the R.S.F.S.R. Civil Code of 1922, art. 129; *cf.* also Decree of Dec. 19, 1933, § 22, [1933] Sob. zak. S.S.S.R. No. 73, item 445; Mozheyko & Shkundin, *op. cit. supra* note 93, at 379-83, excerpts; English: Hazard & Shapiro pt. 2 at 103-07, excerpts; repealed by Decree of May 25, 1963, § 1, [1963] Sob. post. S.S.S.R. No. 10, item 105; 24 Sbornik 48.

[144] Zamengov, *Rastorzheniye i izmeneiye dogovorov v praktike Gosarbitrazha (Dissolution and Alteration of Contracts in Gosarbitrazh Practice)*, Sots. zak. No. 1, p. 84 (1963).

task on which an obligation between socialist organizations is based has lost its force." This rule is laid down also in the 1959 Statutes on Deliveries [145] and found reflection in a 1951 Instructive Letter.[146]

The principle of specific performance—as it is called in Soviet legal science—is hailed by some as one of the main characteristics of Soviet contract law distinguishing it from bourgeois law.[147]

C. Unilateral Refusal To Perform

A unilateral refusal to fulfill an obligation, except in cases provided by law, is not permitted. This rule of the 1961 Principles (Art. 33)[147a] is in harmony with established contract rules throughout the world. But the question is to what extent improper performance of the other side or other circumstances beyond the control of the obligor may serve as grounds for rescinding a contract concluded under orders of planning authorities.

Arbitrazh is prepared, under certain conditions, to recognize such reasons for dissolving planned contracts. Judging from a 1958 case, one of the conditions for rescinding a contract not properly performed by the other side is that the obligee has forewarned the partner at default.

> Plaintiff was ordered by a sales office to deliver pipes to defendant by February 1958. Plaintiff was not able to fulfill the order in time. In March 1958 the defendant asked plaintiff not to deliver since, in view of the delay, he had managed without the pipes. Despite this, plaintiff delivered in May 1958. The parties did not conclude a contract. *Held:* Defendant was entitled to refuse acceptance of products the delivery of which was delayed. The decision was based on the Decree of December 19, 1933.[148]

In two other cases the obligee failed to forewarn the partner at default:

> Late delivery of canned products served as a reason for the buyer to refuse payment, and apparently also for demanding that the seller take the goods back. The products were supposed to be unloaded by April 1958 when no fresh vegetables were available, but they were delivered only in May 1958 (railway transport was not available earlier). *Held:* Buyer is ordered to pay, but is granted the right to defer payment for three months. A return of the cans to the seller is economically un-

[145] Statute on Deliveries of Products § 80 and of Goods § 81.

[146] Instructive Letter of April 20, 1951, § 19, 3 Sbornik 189, based on Decree of Dec. 19, 1933, § 19, [1933] Sob. zak. S.S.S.R. No. 73, item 445, repealed 1963 (see note 143 *supra*).

[147] MOZHEYKO, KHOZAISTVENNYY DOGOVOR V SSSR (THE ECONOMIC CONTRACT IN THE USSR) 162 (Moscow 1962); *cf.* at notes 110 *supra* and 213 *infra*.

[147a] Repeated in the R.S.F.S.R. CIVIL CODE OF 1964, in art. 169.

[148] Moscow Office v. Power Institute, 1958, 8 Sbornik 47. About the Decree of Dec. 19, 1933, see note 143 *supra*.

justified (but after the decision was rendered the buyer returned part of the products on his own initiative to the seller, it is reported).[149]

The defendant, a book-trade organization, refused, in August 1957, to accept for sale from the State Construction Publishing House (plaintiff) the rest of an edition of the *Architecture of Leningrad.* This book was prepared for the occasion of the 250th anniversary of Leningrad celebrated in June 1957. But according to the plan of the Publishing House, to which the contract of the parties referred, delivery was due only in the fourth quarter of 1957. *Held:* Plaintiff was entitled to rely on the contract. Defendant did not forewarn that he would refuse to accept the publication after the anniversary celebration.[150]

In a 1959 case lack of assets was the reason for a request to rescind a contract:

The contract of a customer and a contractor provided that the work of the contractor will be financed through a State Bank credit of the customer. After the contract was concluded, the State Bank denied the request of the customer for a credit. The customer, thereupon, wished to rescind the contract, but the contractor (relying on a pertinent contract clause) insisted on payment for the work already performed. *Held:* Claim of contractor granted. Customer was advised that payment could be effected with current funds and need not be made from a [bank credit] account of capital investment.[151]

Other economic considerations of the buyer are equally considered by Arbitrazh not to justify a dissolution of planned contracts:

The buyer asked the supplier not to deliver as agreed in the contract since he was no longer in need of the products in question. The supplier, however, delivered and brought suit for payment. State Arbitrazh ordered buyer to pay since his refusal to accept and pay was unilateral.[152]

An analogous decision was rendered in a 1960 case:

The buyer refused payment on the grounds that the goods delivered were not in demand by the public. State Arbitrazh deciding for the supplier, informed the buyer that he should have stated his objections before concluding the contract in a Protocol of Disagreement.[153]

In one case refusal was based on a contract condition not materialized:

A contractor agreed to produce oxide for a customer, but it was stipulated that the customer would hand over *fondy* for the necessary

[149] Izmailovskiy Canned Food Combine v. Ivanovskaya Office, 1958, 8 Sbornik 48.

[150] Leningrad Book Trade Administration v. Leningrad Branch of Gosstroiizdat, 1959, 10 Sbornik 84.

[151] Novocherkasskiy Polytechnical Institute v. Plant No. 6 in Sverdlovsk, 1959, 12 Sbornik 44. *Cf.* at note 79 *supra* and also the case in Sov. yus. No. 22, p. 32 (1961).

[152] Plant "Prozhektornyye ugli" v. Kiev Plant, 1958, 8 Sbornik 49.

[153] Kostroma Warehouse v. Dnepropetrovsk Warehouse, 1960, 13 Sbornik 41.

raw material (so-called order from own materials furnished by customer). Customer did not succeed in procuring *fondy*. Contractor nevertheless delivered oxide half a year later and demanded payment. *Held:* Suit denied. Contract was based on a condition (handing over of *fondy*) and the condition did not materialize.[154]

Generally the obligee has a strong interest in specific performance by the obligor, particularly if the products to be delivered are in short supply. To assure timely delivery the creditor may in some cases send a representative (a so-called *tolkach*) to the producer-enterprise.[155]

D. Dissolution of Contracts Called for by New Planning Acts

A new planning act may call for a dissolution of existing contracts. This will be the case if the new task takes priority over previous tasks and the production capacity of the producer is limited so as to exclude performance of both the old and new tasks at the same time. The less important (old) planned task will then be withdrawn and the contract based on it will be rescinded. If one partner to that contract does not agree with such dissolution he may be ordered by Arbitrazh to do so. Such disputes correspond to pre-contract disputes. There the agreement to conclude a contract is replaced by a decision of Arbitrazh; here an order of Arbitrazh is substituted for an agreement to dissolve the contract.

No express legal rules govern disputes over the dissolution of contracts. Neither the 1961 Principles, the 1959 Statutes on Deliveries, nor the 1960 Arbitrazh Statutes regulate or even mention them. But such disputes come up in practice and are decided by Arbitrazh. It is generally agreed that contracts based on planning acts may, and in some cases ought, to be dissolved if affected by a new planning act. The reasons advanced vary. Some hold the new planning act leads automatically to a termination of the contract, others consider the planning act to be a basis for an agreement to rescind the contract, while according to a third view the new planning act renders performance impossible.[156] Arbitrazh proceeds from the first alternative: new planning acts affect contracts automatically. Zamengov cites

[154] Dulevskiy Plant v. Chernovitskiy Plant "Emal'posuda," 1958, 9 Sbornik 52. About *fondy* see at notes 33, 57, 99, 100 *supra*, and 216 *infra*.

[155] KHALFINA, *op. cit. supra* note 131, at 95; FASOLYAK, MATERIAL'NO-TEKHNICHESKOYE SNABZHENIYE V EKONOMICHESKOM ADMINISTRATIVOM RAYONE (MATERIAL-TECHNICAL SUPPLY IN AN ECONOMIC-ADMINISTRATION DISTRICT) 158 (Moscow 1961); *cf.* Rules of July 15, 1958, § 2, 1 Zakon. akty 120-22; Instruction No. 2 of the USSR State Bank of 1960, § 389, KHOZ. DOGOVORY 308-63, excerpts.

[156] See the literature quoted by Zamengov, *Sochetaniye gosudarstvennogo planovogo rukovodstva in khozyaystvennoy samostoyatel'nosti v dogovornykh otnosheniyakh (The Combination of State Planning Guidance and Economic Autonomy in Contractual Relations)*, Sov. gos. i pravo No. 2, pp. 36 and 41 nn.6 and 22; KRASNOV, *op. cit. supra* note 129, at 163.

two unpublished cases confirming this practice,[157] and quotes statutory provisions to support it.[158] An agreement of the parties to rescind the original contract is, therefore, not more than a declaratory statement that the contract has come to an end due to a change of the planning act. No relevant cases are reported in the collection of the USSR State Arbitrazh.

Practically, the dispute will frequently amount to the question of whether the partner urging the dissolution of a contract is liable to pay a sanction to his contract partner for nonperformance.[159] In a 1962 case it was decided that a change in plan frees the customer from responsibilities for sanctions. The work provided for in a construction plan for 1961 was excluded from it on order of the RSFSR Council of Ministers.[160] This case, again, shows that planning acts override current contracts.[161] According to Zamengov no firm Arbitrazh practice has as yet developed with regard to sanctions in case of plan changes, but the tendency is—it seems—to require the debtor to pay sanctions if the new planning act originates in or relates to his "sphere" of economic activities.[162]

If nonperformance resulted in damages for the other contract partner which are not covered by the amount of the sanction, the enterprise which was the "object" of the change in plan may be ordered by Arbitrazh to compensate these damages also. This, at least, was the practice of State Arbitrazh before 1930 and after 1933. A few pertinent cases are reported by Insarova.[163] The only post-war case she relates was decided by State Arbitrazh in 1948:

> Plaintiff, a factory in Chelyabinsk, delivered in March 1948 (at the time the contract was concluded) parts of an item to defendant, a factory subordinate to the Ministry of Transport-Machine Building, on its orders. Defendant refused payment, arguing that, as from January 1948 he became subordinate to another Ministry which changed its industrial profile, he therefore no longer needed the products ordered, and that in February 1948 he had asked his own (previous) Ministry not to effect delivery. *Held:* Defendant is obliged to pay for delivery

[157] Zamengov, *supra* note 156, at 41-42 nn.23-24; see also Zamengov, *supra* note 144, at 84. Shapkina, Oformleniye postavok dogovorami i razresheniye preddogovornykh sporov (The Registration of Deliveries by Contracts and the Resolution of Pre-Contractual Disputes) 48 n.1 (Moscow 1961).

[158] Statute on Deliveries of Products § 20; Rules on Contracts for Architectural Works of 1959, § 15, 2 Zakon. akty 216-28; Zamengov, *supra* note 156, at 42-43. A new relevant provision is now contained in R.S.F.S.R. Civil Code of 1964, art. 234.

[159] 1961 Principles art. 36; R.S.F.S.R. Civil Code of 1964, arts. 186, 187, 189, 219; Statute on Deliveries of Products §§ 59, 80, and of Goods §§ 57, 81.

[160] Sots. zak. No. 11, p. 92 (1962); *cf.* at notes 126, 143, 158 *supra.*

[161] See case at note 134 *supra.*

[162] Zamengov *supra* note 144 at 86; *cf.* at notes 131, 132 *supra.*

[163] Insarova, *supra* note 141, at 58-61.

since the change of subordination cannot serve as a reason for refusing products produced for him.[164]

Thus both in the question of sanction as well as damages the enterprise which was the "object" of the change in plan is held liable without fault. This is a deviation from the general principle that a "person who has not fulfilled his obligation . . . bears property liability (Art. 36 of these Principles) only given the existence of fault (intention or carelessness), except in cases provided by law or contract." [165]

VII. Economic Contracts in the Crucible of Practice: Some Conclusions

Reviewing the law of economic contracts, many questions may be asked. What actually creates the legal obligation to deliver, to construct, to pay? Is it the planning act or the contract, or both? Insofar as the contract is predetermined by a planning act, is it really the will of a "third" person which is substituted for the will of the contract partner? Are not planning agencies and contract partners ultimately one and the same person, all being agencies of the state? How far is the nature of "civil law contracts" affected by the administrative subordination of the contract partners, by the limitation of their legal capacity, by the binding force of planned tasks and plan changes? These questions lead into theory. Since this study is restricted to practice, no attempt will be made to answer them here.

But, from the practical point of view as well, the Soviet experience with economic contracts poses questions. If many of the contracts are predetermined by law and planning acts, why conclude contracts at all? Are they not a mere formality? What role do they play in the realities of economic practice? What are the weaknesses and strengths of economic contracts? What developments in the law of economic contracts may we expect in the future? Will the area of "free" contracts increase as the national economy grows, the need for rigid distribution of scarce materials decreases, and relative abundance is achieved?

An attempt will be made to answer some of these questions in the light of Arbitrazh materials. Much emphasis, indeed, pressure, has been used by the Soviet leadership to enforce the use of contracts. Since 1933 yearly "contracts campaigns" have been conducted, heavy sanctions have been provided for evasion of the obligation to conclude contracts, enterprise managers have been urged time and again to live up to contract discipline, Arbitrazh agencies have been constantly instructed to enforce it, and the demand has been repeated in a stream of publications throughout the years.[166]

[164] *Id.* at 61; *cf.* Sots. zak. No. 9, p. 93 (1957); Sov. yus. No. 8, p. 93 (1958).

[165] 1961 Principles art. 37; R.S.F.S.R. Civil Code of 1964, art. 221.

[166] During the war and early postwar years, however, it was considered expedient to rely more directly on planning acts, although the laws requiring the conclusion of contracts remained in effect. *Cf.* the case in Sots. zak. No. 10, p. 94 (1958).

The most obvious explanation of these efforts is that a planned economy does not offer enough spontaneous stimuli for concluding contracts between socialist organizations. Therefore such stimuli have to be created artificially, by way of directives from above and financial sanctions imposed against reluctant managers. This consideration, however, still does not explain sufficiently why it is precisely the instrument of contract which is deemed so desirable. Its main advantages over any other device may be sought on two levels: administrative and economic.

No planning can be so perfect as to foresee the last detail. A certain area will always be left for a decision at the operative level, *i.e.*, by the supplier and recipient of goods exchanged or services rendered. In this sense, contract is a "means for concretization of planned tasks and for improving economic leadership." [167] Some writers believe that one of the functions of contract is also to expose shortcomings of planning.[168] This, however, seems unconvincing since defective planning acts have to be corrected before a contract is concluded, not after. The contract itself has to correspond to the planning act. It is, therefore, not the contract, but the planning act which brings planning mistakes to light.

While the concretization of planning may be seen as the main administrative effect of contracts, their economic significance stems from their "civil law" character. Contracts—and only contracts—create those reciprocal and equivalent relations which characterize money-commodity exchanges between equal economic partners. This element of reciprocity so essential to any economic activity and initiative is missing in the sphere of planning based on subordination and administrative orders. To inject spontaneity into the working of a planned economy, contracts, the natural companion of a market economy, were introduced by government order. They are considered to be the optimum means for linking the principles of planning with the principles of economic rationality. This was expressed by Molotov as early as 1931 when he described the system of contract relations as "the best means to coordinate the economic plan and the principles of economic accountability." [169] This characterization was hailed as "classic" by Venediktov [170] and was quoted in many Soviet works on economic contracts up to 1957, when Molotov was ousted.

The advantages which civil law contracts offer (and which no administrative device, however ingenious, can replace) are: (1) they provide an adequate form for mutual obligations *(vozmezdnost')* and for realizing

[167] Instructive Letter of Oct. 6, 1962, 21 Sbornik 94.

[168] KHALFINA, *op. cit. supra* note 131, at 30-35, and Zamengov *supra* note 156, at 37 nn.10-11 and the literature quoted there.

[169] MOLOTOV, V BOR'BE ZA SOTSIALIZM. RECHI I STAT'I (IN THE STRUGGLE FOR SOCIALISM. SPEECHES AND ARTICLES) 258 (2d ed. Moscow 1935).

[170] VENEDIKTOV, GOSUDARSTVENNAYA SOTSIALISTICHESKAYA SOBSTVENNOST' (STATE SOCIALIST PROPERTY) 488 (Moscow, Leningrad 1948).

the elements of monetary value, *i.e.* for "compensative relations" between socialist organizations which otherwise would not exist; (2) they impose mutually applicable sanctions for nonfulfillment or improper performance of obligations.

None of these functions can be achieved so effectively by administrative means or by disciplinary measures and criminal law. The instruments at the disposal of an administrative agency for performing operative tasks is limited to issuing orders (administrative acts). If the subordinate agency defies the order its responsible officers can be fired, or the organization may even be liquidated, but all such measures do not necessarily ensure performance in kind. They affect the subordinate enterprise as an administrative organization, not as an economic unit. To achieve economic results, economic means are most effective. They can be strengthened, but not replaced by administrative means. This is true in an even more striking manner with regard to disciplinary and criminal sanctions. They are exclusively aimed at individuals, but not at the debtor, the enterprise itself.

The insistence on contracts has, therefore, its good reasons. Another question, however, is how effectively this postulate is transformed into practice. The requirement to conclude contracts has been viewed by many a factory manager as a bureaucratic burden, at least in the early thirties when the yearly contract campaigns were initiated.[171] But with the years Arbitrazh practice and administrative pressure have achieved a marked improvement of contract work. World War II caused a setback, but it was overcome—the year 1949 marks the change—and development toward strengthening contract principles continued, though deficiencies still exist. The main weaknesses are, first, evasion of the obligation to conclude contracts, or, if they are concluded, leaving them vague; and, second, failure to apply sanctions for improper performance as provided in the contract.

The following quotations from Arbitrazh and other directives may serve as an illustration:

> *1949.* "Despite the great importance of contracts in securing the fulfillment of . . . plans and in the matter of supplying the national economy with production . . . many economic organs, contrary to law, do not conclude contracts. A portion of the contracts that are concluded have a formal character [and] do not provide for concrete obligations of the parties." [172]
>
> *1950.* "In practice one still encounters deliveries effected without con-

[171] Yel'yevich, *K voprosu o dogovornykh kampaniyakh i kachestve dogovorov (On the Question of Contract Campaigns and the Quality of Contracts)*, in SOTSIALISTICHESKAYA PROMYSHLENNOST' I KHOZYAYSTVENNOYE PRAVO (SOCIALIST INDUSTRIAL AND ECONOMIC LAW) 131-56 (Leningrad 1935).

[172] Decree of April 21, 1949, Preamble, [1949] Sob. post. S.S.S.R. No. 9, item 68.

cluding contracts and the consequences of such deliveries—the forwarding of unnecessary products not ordered by the receiver." [173]

1951. "An examination . . . of the practice of deciding disputes connected with refusals of buyers-payers to pay for products unloaded has revealed numerous cases of deliveries of products without concluding contracts . . . merely on the basis of delivery orders . . . ." [174]

1952. "In the practice of concluding local and direct contracts in 1952 essential deficiencies occurred. The most serious of these deficiencies were: . . . vagueness of the contracts concluded, for example, fixing the quantity of products to be delivered in approximate terms and not in definite quantities . . . [and] references to delivery orders . . . instead of fixing a concrete assortment." [175]

1955. "The practice of concluding economic contracts for 1954 showed that the main deficiencies in the work of economic agencies in concluding contracts and of State Arbitrazh in deciding precontract disputes, recorded in Instructive Letters . . . in earlier years, continued to take place in 1954. These deficiencies include, in particular: delay in concluding contracts against the periods set; vagueness of the contracts concluded . . . ." [176]

1957. "Arbitrazh agencies are obliged to wage a struggle against violations of the periods for concluding economic contracts and against the practice of evading . . . . [the obligation] to conclude contracts." [177]

1959. "In deciding cases it is necessary . . . to wage a struggle against the practice of evasion by suppliers and buyers [of the obligation] to conclude contracts." [178]

1959. The Ministry of Trade of the RSFSR noted "that in the system of trade insufficient attention is attached to the contract of delivery. Frequently contracts are concluded formally, [and] do not reflect the actual mutual relations of the parties . . . , the contracts concluded are in their content often . . . not concrete." [179]

1960. "In 1959-1960 State Arbitrazh agencies improved their work in deciding precontract disputes . . . . At the same time the work connected with the conclusion of contracts and deciding precontract disputes suffers from serious deficiencies . . . . There are facts of considerable delay in the conclusion of contracts and unjustified evasion of concluding them; often the necessary essential terms are missing in the contracts." [180]

173 Instructive Letter of Nov. 3, 1950, repealed 1961, 3 Sbornik 91; 18 *id.* at 39.

174 Instructive Letter of Jan. 5, 1951, 3 *id.* at 92, 217.

175 Instructive Letter of Nov. 18, 1952, 3 *id.* at 105-06.

176 Instructive Letter of Jan. 12, 1955, repealed 1961, 3 *id.* at 127; 18 *id.* at 40.

177 Instructive Letter of Dec. 31, 1957, amended 1961, 6 *id.* at 13; 18 *id.* at 35.

178 Instructive Letter of Dec. 30, 1959, 12 *id.* at 19.

179 Order of the RSFSR Ministry of Trade of Dec. 24, 1959. Summary in PRAVILA RABOTY TORGOVYKH PREDPRIYATIY . . . SBORNIK (WORK RULES OF TRADE ENTERPRISES . . . A COLLECTION) at 54 (Moscow 1961).

180 Instructive Letter of Dec. 10, 1960, 16 Sbornik 44.

1962. "The conclusion of contracts . . . is inadmissably delayed; the contracts, in a number of cases, do not contain concrete obligations of the parties . . . ." [181]

The State Arbitrazh of the USSR gives the following directives: "To wage a decisive struggle against the practice of delivery of products without contracts, having in mind that this disorganizes supply and inflicts damage on the national economy." [182]

The formal character of some contracts is also criticized in legal writings. For example:

Khalfina, 1957: "In a number of industrial branches the conclusion and performance of contracts had a formal character, since each delivery was planned at the center." [183]

Shor, 1957: "In case of deliveries of products planned and allocated at the center, the conclusion of contracts of delivery has an utterly formal character." [184]

Ovsiyenko, 1957: "The conclusion of contracts for the realization of metal output is hampered by the extremely rigid centralization of the sale of metal. This, probably, is the main reason why the obligation-relations between producer-factories and offices of the Chief Administration of Metal-Sale *(Glavmetallosbyt)* continued to remain on a non-contract basis." [185]

Baranov, 1958: "Contracts had in many cases a formal character insofar as contract links were divorced from real economic relations." [186]

Gus'kova, 1959: "[T]he majority of contracts in the field of supply of metals . . . were without effect since all questions of delivery were fixed in other acts: delivery orders, . . . in General Conditions." [187]

Volin, 1962: "[M]any enterprises and organizations according to present requirements are obliged to conclude each year numerous contracts for the delivery of products . . . . The result is that the process of concluding contracts becomes a formal campaign, which stretches

[181] Decree of June 30, 1962, Preamble, [1962] Sob. post. S.S.S.R. No. 12, item 94.

[182] Instructive Letter of Oct. 6, 1962, 21 Sbornik 95. For additional quotations see, among others, 3 *id.* at 86, 113, 116, 117, 121, 152, 157, 261; 4 *id.* at 5, 5 *id.* at 35; 9 *id.* at 7; 15 *id.* at 62; Sots. zak. No. 3, p. 95 (1962).

[183] Khalfina, *Perestroyka upravleniya promyshlennost'yu i dogovornyye svyazi sotsialisticheskikh organizatsiy (Reorganization of Administration by Industry and the Contractual Ties of Socialist Organizations)*, Sov. gos. i pravo No. 5, p. 34, at 35 (1957).

[184] Shor, *O pravovom polozheniyi promyshlennykh predpriyatiy (Concerning the Legal Position of Industrial Enterprises)*, Sov. gos. i pravo No. 5, p. 51 (1957).

[185] Ovsiyenko, *Nekotoryye voprosy obyazatel'nykh otnosheniy po postavke metalloproduktsiy*, in KHAR'KOVKSIY YURIDICHESKIY INSTITUT (KHAR'KOV JURIDICAL INSTITUTE), 8 UCHYONYYE ZAPISKI (SCHOLARLY NOTES) 63 (1957).

[186] Baranov, *Voprosy ukrepleniya dogovornoy distsipliny (Questions of Strengthening Contractual Discipline)*, Sov. gos. i pravo No. 2, p. 32 (1958).

[187] Gus'kova, *Pravovyye formy regulirovaniya metallosnabzheniya (Legal Forms of the Regulation of Metal Supply)* in VIYuN, 9 UCHYONYYE ZAPISKI (SCHOLARLY NOTES) 220 (1959).

out for a long time, and the contracts themselves often become standardized, empty and do not fulfill the role which they are supposed to play."[188]

Gibanov, 1963: "Practice shows that contracts concluded by enterprises at the present time have in a number of cases a formal character."[189]

In the field of contract performance the tendency to "mutual amnesty" seems to be widespread. By this term Arbitrazh agencies mean the failure to claim sanctions for improper performance of contracts. This is not only the individual affair of the contract partners concerned, but is also of overall economic importance since it endangers achieving one of the very purposes which contracts are supposed to serve. Here are excerpts from relevant Arbitrazh Instructions:

1950. "The . . . agreement of the parties to waive . . . property liability conceals in a number of cases . . . mutual amnesty of the parties. . . . A reference of the debtor to the excessiveness of the forfeit in relation to the actual damages of the creditor . . . cannot be accepted without considering the overall damage inflicted to the national economy by not fulfilling the plan. . . . Arbitrazh agencies . . . must wage a decisive struggle against the practice of freeing economic organizations . . . from economic liability for not performing or not properly performing contract obligations."[190]

1962. "Many Arbitrazh agencies in deciding disputes do not assess on their own initiative a fine from suppliers prescribed for delivery of products and goods of improper quality, which in essence amounts to an amnesty of the enterprises violating legislation on the quality of production. Arbitrazh agencies in a number of cases did not apply sanctions against suppliers for delivery of products of improper quality . . . rely on the readiness of the supplier to replace it. . . . Assessing fines from the supplier . . . is not only a right of the consumer, but also a duty to the State."[191]

The reluctance to collect sanctions may perhaps be explained by the following reasons:

[188] Volin, NOVOYE V GRAZHDANSKOM I GRAZHDANSKO-PROTSESSUAL'NOM ZAKONDATEL'STVE SOYUZA SSR I SOYUZNYKH RESPUBLIK (NEW [DEVELOPMENTS] IN CIVIL AND CIVIL-PROCEDURAL LEGISLATION OF THE USSR AND UNION REPUBLICS) 170 (VIYuN, Moscow 1962).

[189] Gribanov, *Dal'neysheye razvitiye yuridicheskoy lichnosti gosudarstvennogo predpriyatiya (Further Development of the Juridical Personality of a State Enterprise)*, Vestnik Moskovskogo Universiteta, Seriya Prava (Moscow University Herald, Legal Series) No. 2, p. 3, at 12 (1963); English: 2 Soviet Law and Government No. 2, p. 35 (Fall 1963).

[190] Instructive Letter of July 22, 1950, 3 Sbornik 184. Three relevant cases are related in Instructive Letter of April 5, 1951, 3 *id.* at 261. *Cf.* at note 105 *supra.*

[191] Instructive Letter of March 29, 1962, 19-20 *id.* at 12-13 and 15. See also the case reported at 48 and Sots. zak. No. 3, p. 95 (1962).

(1) Collected sanctions do not always add to the Enterprise Fund, i.e. to those means earmarked for the needs of the enterprise and for premiums to individual employees, including the enterprise management. The difference of sanctions collected over those paid may be included into the Enterprise Fund only to the extent it represents a "planned profit" (technically, if it appears in the financial plan of the enterprise). Sanctions amounting to "beyond-plan profits" are not considered for fixing the size of the Fund. Fines, penalties and forfeits received do not depend, as the Statute on the Enterprise Fund requires, "on the productive activity of the [creditor's] enterprise." [192]

(2) Unsuccesful attempts to assess sanctions have a negative influence on the balance sheet of the creditor. A sanction, once claimed,[193] cannot be simply waived. It is on the balance sheet [194] and can be disposed of only by collecting it or by "writing it off" as a "loss." [195] The latter presupposes an expiration of the period of limitation (six months) [196] or an adverse Arbitrazh decision.[197] The higher agency has to be informed of any writing off of claims.[198]

(3) The "principle of specific performance" may sometimes operate as a factor contributing to an "abstain-from-claiming" attitude. This applies at least to those cases where the creditor is entitled to claim specific performance plus sanctions as well as damages not covered by the fine.[199]

[192] Statute on the Enterprise's Fund of 1961 § 9, [1961] Sob. post. S.S.S.R. No. 2, item 11; 2 Zakon, akty 572-75, excerpts; KHOZ. DOGOVORY 97-100; Instruction of the USSR Ministry of Finance of 1961 on the Application of the Statute §§ 9, 12, in BUKHGALTERSKIY UCHYOT I KONTROL'NO-REVIZIONNAYA RABOTA NA RECHNOM TRANSPORTE. SBORNIK RUKOVODYASCHIKH DOKUMENTOV (ACCOUNTING AND INSPECTION-CONTROL WORK IN RIVER TRANSPORT. COLLECTION OF LEADING DOCUMENTS) 404-10, excerpts (Moscow 1962).

[193] The procedure for claiming sanctions in case of incomplete deliveries and deliveries of improper quality is regulated in four Instructions of May 27, 1959, 10 Sbornik 47-67; 1 Zakon. akty 459-67, 484-94; KHOZ. DOGOVORY 175-83, 190-99.

[194] Statute on Accounting Reports and Statements of Sept. 12, 1951, § 47 as amended, 1 Zakon. akty 671-86.

[195] *Id.* § 53.

[196] 1961 Principles art. 16; R.S.F.S.R. CIVIL CODE OF 1964, art. 79; Decrees of Sept. 3, 1934, and Oct. 7, 1934, [1934] Sob. zak. S.S.S.R. No. 44, item 347, and *id.* No. 52, item 404; 1 Zakon. akty 753-54, excerpts; about the effect of sanctions paid, see note 201 *infra*.

[197] The Arbitrazh of the Sverdlovsk Council of National Economy satisfied between 50 and 78% of claims for sanctions in 1958. YUDEL'SON, PRAVOVYYE VOPROSY ORGANIZATSIYI I DEYATEL'NOSTI SOVNARKHOZOV (LEGAL QUESTIONS OF THE ORGANIZATION AND ACTIVITIES OF THE SOVNARKHOZES) 264-65 (Moscow 1959). About the practice of filing unfounded claims for purposes of writing-off, see KOPNYAYEV, ANALIZ FINANSOVO-KHOZYAYSTVENNOY DEYATEL-NOSTI PREDPRIYATIY (AN ANALYSIS OF THE FINANCIAL ECONOMIC ACTIVITY OF ENTERPRISES) 124 (Moscow 1962).

[198] Statute on Accounting Reports and Statements of Sept. 12, 1951, § 53, 1 Zakon. akty 671-86.

[199] 1961 Principles art. 36; Statute on Deliveries of Products § 80 and of Goods § 81.

The creditor, after receiving proper performance in kind, may retain the amount paid as sanction, even if it exceeds his damages sustained from the original failure to perform. To this extent the creditor is enriched, but the debtor penalized.[200] A consumer-creditor which depends on the output and future deliveries of the supplier-debtor may be reluctant to act as a collector of such penalizing sanctions imposed by law. He might be willing to sacrifice his formal right to a sanction for the goodwill of his partner. Demands for sanctions may, indeed, destroy goodwill since fines, penalties, etc., pair are losses of the debtor[201] and indicate deficiencies in his work to superior agencies.

But the system in effect provides, on the other hand, for devices intended to serve as incentives for claiming sanctions. At least three stand out:

(1) Collected fines, penalties, etc., add to the financial resources of the creditor. Such increase is highly welcome in most cases. But the advantage is strictly limited by the financial plan of the enterprise and does not extend beyond the given planning year. Sanctions received from debtor-enterprises can be used for payments against expenses envisaged in the financial plan. They may not be spent freely, *i.e.*, for purposes other than those provided in the plan. This applies not only if the enterprise works at a loss, but also if it makes a profit and the sanctions add to the profit. The financial plan provides that the bulk of the enterprise's profit (including collected sanctions) is paid into the state budget.[202] The use of *beyond-plan* profits (including collected sanctions) is also regulated. Such profits are not available for free disposal by the enterprise. But they add to the liquidity of the creditor's enterprise, increasing the active balance in its State Bank account.

For some groups of enterprises[203] a special procedure for distributing

[200] A refund of fines to the debtor is envisaged (only) for sanctions paid for late performance of individual construction phases provided the final overall day of performance is kept. Rules on Construction Contracts of 1955, 2 Zakon. akty 263-72.

[201] They affect adversely the cost-reduction plan of the enterprise and, thus also the amount of premiums for employees. *Cf.* Gribanov, *supra* note 189, at 15.

[202] Statute of Sept. 3, 1931, on the Deduction of Profits of State Enterprises into the State Treasury, [1931] Sob. zak. S.S.S.R. No. 57, item 367; 2 SPRAVOCHNIK PO ZAKONODATEL'STVU DLYA ISPOLNITEL'NYKH KOMITETOV . . . (HANDBOOK ON LEGISLATION FOR EXECUTIVE COMMITTEES . . .) 40-41 (Moscow 1947); Instruction of the USSR Ministry of Finance of Aug. 26, 1958, SBORNIK POSTANOVLENIY . . . PO FINANSORVO-KHOZYAYSTVENNYM VOPROSAM (COLLECTION OF DECISIONS . . . ON FINANCIAL-ECONOMIC QUESTIONS) No. 2, p. 2 (1959); SBORNIK PO OSNOVNYKH NORMATIVNYKH AKTOV PO SOVETSKOMU FINANSOVOMU PRAVU (COLLECTION OF BASIC NORMATIVE ACTS ON SOVIET FINANCIAL LAW) 74-78, excerpts (Moscow 1961); summarized in AZARKH, SPRAVOCHNIK PO GOSUDARSTVENNYM DOKHODAM (HANDBOOK ON GOVERNMENTAL REVENUES) 116-19 and 168-70 (2d ed. Moscow 1959).

[203] They include sales organizations of All-Union Ministries and Departments, wholesale offices of Union Republics, electric power stations, railway administrations, shipping enterprises and ports. AZARKH, *op. cit. supra* note 202, at 161.

collected fines (including penalties and forfeits) is established.[204] They pay collected fines only into the state budget. Seventy-five to 95 per cent of the differences of fines collected over those paid are transferred after collection and the rest at the end of the plan year. This special procedure thus operates independently of whether the enterprise fulfilled its profit plan or not.[205]

Summarizing, it appears that sanctions collected do not increase the working capital of the enterprise beyond the plan and beyond a given planning year, but they help to pay debts envisaged in the financial plan. Even if the enterprise has achieved beyond-plan profits, the amount of sanctions collected (over those paid) is not earmarked at the end of the year for the needs of the creditor.

(2) Personal responsibility of enterprise managers for claiming sanctions is another incentive. Officials guilty of allowing periods of limitation to run out and of illegal writing off of claims are to be held responsible under disciplinary law and, in appropriate cases, also under criminal law. The chief accountant is obliged to ensure that claims for incomplete or improper deliveries are presented to suppliers and that these claims are collected in time.[206]

(3) Living up to these obligations is controlled by financial agencies [207] and by Arbitrazh.[208]

The latter is entitled to initiate *ex officio* claims for fines against the debtor.

The incentives discussed thus seem to counterbalance to a considerable extent the factors suggesting passiveness, but apparently they are not sufficiently effective in all cases.

It would be a mistake to infer from the Instructions, statements, and cases quoted that all economic contracts in the Soviet Union are a mere fiction, that their conclusion is regarded as formality, and that their performance is evaded. Such a conclusion would underestimate the various systems of control and checks. The administratively superior agencies and the State Bank are effective machineries for enforcing contract dis-

[204] Instruction of the USSR Ministry of Finance of March 16, 1954, SPRAVOCHNIK PO BUKHGALTERSKOMU UCHYOTU V TORGOVLE (HANDBOOK ON ACCOUNTING IN TRADE) 385-86 (Moscow 1958); Instructions of Dec. 30, 1956, Feb. 21, 1957, and Dec. 30, 1957, summarized in AZARKH, *op. cit. supra* note 202, at 161-62. See also Instruction of the RSFSR Ministry of River Transport of 1958, amended 1961, BUKHGALTERSKIY UCHYOT, *op. cit. supra* note 192, at 393-95.

[205] See PAYEVSKIY & MARGULIS, OTCHISLENIYA OT PRIBYLI V BYUDZHET (DEDUCTIONS FROM PROFITS IN THE BUDGET) 25-26, 34-35, 48-49, 91-92 (Moscow 1956); SPRAVOCHNIK PO BUKHGALTERSKOMU UCHYOTU (HANDBOOK ON ACCOUNTING), 456 (Compiled by Goloshchapov, 3d ed. Moscow 1961); KOPNYAYEV, *op. cit. supra* note 197, at 134.

[206] Statute of Sept. 17, 1947 on Chief Accountants, § 8, 1 Zakon. akty 691-99; Statute on Accounting Reports and Statements of Sept. 12, 1951, § 46, *id.* 671-86; Rules on Money Deductions [from the Salary] by the Committee of Party-State Control of April 20, 1963, § 1, [1963] Sob. post. S.S.S.R. No. 7, item 81; 24 Sbornik 26.

[207] 1 SPVAVOCHNIK RAYONNOGO FINANSOVOGO RABOTNIKA (HANDBOOK FOR THE RAYON FINANCIAL WORKER) 482, 506 (Moscow 1952); and 2 *id.* at 527, 530 (1953).

[208] *Cf.* at notes 190-91 *supra.*

cipline. An important role, without question, is also played by Arbitrazh agencies. It may even be said that within the body of the law of a planned economy—this new branch of law, distinguishing Soviet law from other legal systems—Arbitrazh is one of the most remarkable and ingenious institutions.[209]

Any discussion of whether economic contracts are genuine contracts or only contracts by name, "sham contracts," [210] is meaningful only, of course, if there is agreement on what the essential characteristics of a contract are. In considering Soviet contracts it is proper to proceed from the definition given by Soviet law. It provides that a contract is concluded "when agreement on all its essential points has been reached between the parties." [211] Applying this definition to economic contracts as practiced in the Soviet Union, it is necessary to distinguish between those contracts (or parts of contracts) the substance of which is predetermined by a planning act, on the one hand, and unplanned contracts (or parts thereof), on the other. The character of a contract in the sense of a meeting of minds seems apparent in unplanned contracts as well as in the "free" parts of planned contracts.

The problem begins with the plan-determined parts of planned contracts. Here no room is left for agreement and still it is the contract and only the contract which creates rights and obligations between the partners. The duty to perform is fixed in the planning act, but it exists only vertically, *i.e.*, between the addressee of the planning act and his superior agency which issued the planning act. No legal relations as yet bind supplier and buyer. The planning act does not give the buyer a right to demand delivery from the supplier. Neither does the planning act serve as a legal basis for the supplier to demand that the buyer accept the products delivered to him and that he pay for them. To create this horizontal link the form of contract is used. Both parties grant each other a legal basis for mutual claims which otherwise would not exist. Each concedes to his partner that he should have a right to demand performance and, in case of improper performance, a right to claim sanctions. In doing so, the parties go beyond the planning act. They do not merely repeate an existing act

[209] Scamell suggested reception of Soviet-type Arbitrazh for hearing disputes of nationalized enterprises in Great Britain. Scamell, *Nationalization in Legal Perspective*, 5 CURRENT LEGAL PROBLEMS 30, 52-53 (1952).

[210] 1 GSOVSKI, SOVIET CIVIL LAW 393, 437-38 (1949); see also 2 GOVERNMENT, LAW AND COURTS IN THE SOVIET UNION AND EASTERN EUROPE 1137-39 and 1146-51 (Gsovski & Grzybowski ed. London 1959); GUINS, SOVIET LAW AND SOVIET SOCIETY 120 (The Hague 1954). Langrod characterizes planned contracts as a technical instrument sui generis of cooperation between administrative units, Langrod, *Administrative Contracts*, 4 AM. J. COMP. L. 325, 361 (1955); FRIEDMANN, LAW AND SOCIAL CHANGE IN CONTEMPORARY BRITAIN 65-67 (London 1951), and his article, *Modern Trends in Soviet Law*, 10 U. TORONTO L.J. 87 (1953); GRZYBOWSKI, SOVIET LEGAL INSTITUTIONS 85-97 (1962).

[211] 1961 Principles art. 34.

but set forth a new act of legal relevance. This act is not necessarily an agreement in the contractual sense. The parties grant each other rights because they are required to do so by law. If they do not live up to this requirement, an Arbitrazh decision may be substituted for the will of the reluctant partner.

In other words, the essential element of those parts of contracts which are predetermined by planning acts is not agreement. It is rather a form required by positive law for granting each partner civil law remedies as a means for ensuring mutual performance in accordance with the planned task. Conceived in such functional, rather than conceptual, terms, plan-determined contracts are more than a mere fiction. The rationale in using them is to create an additional channel for control of performance, this time on a horizontal level.

The function of planned contracts as a device to ensure performance of planned tasks by providing civil law remedies irrespective of agreement is evident in cases where the parties have failed to incorporate the planned task (wholly or in part) into their contract. Even if "essential points" are missing the contract nevertheless has full legal effect. The subservient role of contracts also manifests itself in the statutory fiction that under certain circumstances mere "acceptance" of a delivery order is equal to agreeing with a contract. The overriding effect of planning acts over contracts is further illustrated in case of changes in the plan.

A new planning act changing the object of performance or abolishing a planned task directly affects civil law responsibilities by changing or waiving them. The new planning act must, it is true, be incorporated into the contract by agreement of the partners, but it governs contract relations regardless of whether the parties lived up to this obligation or not.[212] It also seems unnecessary to formally rescind a contract which has lost its planning basis.

In addition to the functions mentioned, an extra-legal aspect of contracts in a planned economy should not be overlooked. The power granted to enterprise managers to make contracts conveys, even within the given limits, a feeling of some independence and autonomy. It introduces an element of initiative which helps to counterweigh to some extent the rigidities of a planning bureaurcracy.

The planned and free elements of contract taken together may be characterized as an attempt to harmonize the principles of direction and initiative and to embody a balance between them in a workable legal instrument.

[212] See Warehouse in the Latvian SSR v. Penza Warehouse, 1960, 14 Sbornik 58, and *cf.* at notes 55, 62, 80, 90, 134 *supra.*

It is a matter of speculation to predict whether the role and function of economic contracts will change as the material-technical basis of the economy widens and Soviet society eventually enters a stage called "communism." Bratus' believes that the need to enforce specific performance will decrease as abundance is achieved. The creditor will be able to content himself with "money compensation" from the debtor in default "if he can purchase the production necessary to him at a warehouse or a trade *baza*." [213] Mozheyko contends that "one of the reasons calling for the need to distribute this or that type of products is that they as yet are produced in insufficient quantities, not fully satisfying existing demands." But he is confident that the number of scarce materials will be limited,[214] and Kaminskaya, too, writes that the area of free materials will widen.[215] Similarly Alekseyev foresees that "to the extent that the number of scarce products decreases, it will be possible to deliver without delivery orders and *fondy*." [216]

Although an elimination of the planning of distribution does not necessarily imply the concurrent abolishment of planning production and investment, it will not be easy to dispense with the distribution system now in operation. It would not only require that shortages and bottlenecks be overcome, but also that some form of market mechanism be introduced, which in turn would pose the central problem of price-formation. Such a reform, moreover, would call for a revision of some ideological tenets, since communist society is said to be based on distribution according to needs and not on money-commodity relations. According to the Program of the CPSU of 1961:

> "An abundance of material and cultural benefits for the whole population will be attained in the course of the second decade [1971-1980], and material prerequisites will be created for the transition in the

[213] Bratus', in VIYuN, TRUDY NAUCHNOY SESSIYI . . . 1957 g (WORKS OF THE SCIENTIFIC SESSION . . .) 30-61, at 54 (Moscow 1958), reprinted (abridged) in Sov. gos. i pravo No. 11, p. 86, at 98 (1957).

[214] MOZHEYKO, KHOZAISTVENNYY DOGOVOR V SSSR (THE ECONOMIC CONTRACT IN THE USSR) 121 (Moscow 1962).

[215] Kaminskaya, in MGU, 1 SOVETSKOYE GRAZHDANSKOYE PRAVO (SOVIET CIVIL LAW) 405 (Moscow 1959).

[216] ALEKSEYEV, GRAZHDANSKOYE PRAVO V PERIOD RAZVYORNUTOGO STROITEL'STVA KOMMUNIZMA (CIVIL LAW IN THE PERIOD OF THE FULL-SCALE BUILDING OF COMMUNISM) 121 (Moscow 1962). Far-reaching suggestions for a reform of the present planning system have been made by Soviet economists. Academician Nemchinov recently advocated abolishing distribution "through the infinitely complicated system of physical *fondy*," Pravda, Nov. 21, 1963, p. 2. See, *e.g.*, Birman, Ekonomicheskaya gazeta, March 30, 1963, p. 7.

period to follow, according to the communist principle of distribution according to need. . . . With the transition . . . the communist system of distribution, commodity-money relations will become economically outdated and will wither away. . . ." [217]

If this vision is transformed into practice no room would be left for traditional contracts or for economic contracts as presently used in the Soviet Union. But before this stage is achieved, if ever, the role of contracts is likely to increase. This is suggested by the present efforts of Soviet economists to make increased use of the stimuli a market economy provides.

The Soviet experience in the field of contracts allows at least two general conclusions. First, it illustrates tellingly that contract cannot be introduced into a planned economy merely by an order of the law. In addition, continuous and effective administrative measures are needed in order to ensure their use and proper application. Secondly, contracts as practiced between socialist organizations show a predominance of administrative elements. They are concluded between State (and cooperative) organs with limited administrative and financial autonomy, their substance is predetermined to a varying degree by planning acts, their conclusion, performance and dissolution is controlled by administrative organs, and they serve to fulfill State tasks. These features, however, do not eliminate or exclude civil law elements of contracts, expressed in such principles as mutuality and property liability.

Pashukanis [218] was the first Soviet writer to have spelled out this distinction between "links . . . expressed in the form of the value of . . . goods, and consequently, in the legal form of transactions" on the one hand, and relations subject to "direct, that is to say, technically fertile directives in the form of programs, production and distribution plans, and so on" on the other hand. "Without doubt," Pashukanis asserted, "direct, that is to say, the administrative-technical direction in the form of subordination to a general economic plan . . . will increase." [219]

Proceeding from his commodity-exchange concept of law, Pashukanis believed that the juridical form (civil law in the first place) will ultimately

[217] Programme of the CPSU 63, 61 (London 1961). The abolition of money was also envisaged in the (preceding) Program of 1919. Materials for the Study of the Soviet System 100-21, at 118 (Meisel & Kozera ed. 2d ed. 1953).

[218] Yevgeniy B. Pashukanis (1891-1937) was Director of the Institute of Soviet Construction and Law of the Communist Academy in Moscow.

[219] Pashukanis, Obshchaya teoriya prava i marksizm (A General Legal Theory and Marxism) 80 (4th ed. Moscow 1928). For an English translation of the third edition of this work, see Soviet Legal Philosophy 178 (Hazard ed. 1951); a German translation appeared in 1929, Allgemeine Rechtslehre und Marxismus (Wien, Berlin 1929). *Cf.* Pashukanis, in Sov. gos. i pravo Nos. 11-12, p. 43 (1930).

be replaced by technical directives (pure administration without compulsion) and that the juridicial element in the relations of men will gradually disappear altogether.[220] This revolutionary vision, which probably caused his downfall in 1937, is not shared by contemporary Soviet doctrine. The Program of the CPSU of 1961 limits itself to predict that

> "the organs of planning and economic management, . . . now government bodies, will lose their political character and will become organs of public self-government. . . . Generally recognized uniform rules of communist community life will be established, the observance of which will become an organic need and habit with everyone. Historical development inevitably leads to the withering away of the state." [221]

But the divergence over the future does not diminish the importance of Pashukanis' work for understanding the present. In an article published in 1929, at the time when the first Five-Year Plan had just been enacted, Pashukanis formulated concretely some characteristic effects of planning on law.[222] It seems appropriate to quote from this article for two reasons. First, actual developments confirmed to a surprisingly close degree Pashukanis' observations. This becomes apparent when Pashukanis' article is compared with writings some thirty years later, although—and this is the second reason—no credit is given to Pashukanis for his prophetic insights. His 1929 article (together with other works of the author) was the target of wild attacks after his arrest and disappearance in 1937.[223] It took 20 years before Pashukanis was rehabilitated politically (in 1957),[224] but the time has apparently not yet come to restore his name as a great scholar.

[220] Pashukanis, *op. cit. supra* note 219, at 23, 36-38, 54-55, 80-81.

[221] PROGRAMME OF THE CPSU 73 (London 1961).

[222] Pashukanis, *Ekonomika i pravovoye regulirovaniye (Economics and Legal Regulation)*, Revolyutsiya prava (Revolution of Law) No. 4, p. 12, and No. 5, p. 20 (1929). Chapter 4 of this article is devoted to the legal regulation of the Soviet economy, *id.* No. 5, at 33.

[223] Bratus', *O sostoyaniyi teoreticheskoy raboty po sovetskomu grazhdanskomu pravu (On the Condition of Theoretical Work in Soviet Civil Law)*, Sov. gos. i pravo Nos. 1-2, p. 49 (1937); Vyshinskiy, *Osnovnyye zadachi nauki sovetskogo sotsialisticheskogo prava (Basic Tasks of the Science of Soviet Socialist Law)* 46 (Moscow 1938); English translation in SOVIET LEGAL PHILISOPHY, *op. cit. supra* note 219.

[224] Hazard, *Pashukanis Is No Traitor*, 51 AM. J. INT'L L. 385 (1957).

This is what Pashukanis wrote in 1929 and what contemporary Soviet writers observed in 1961:

Pashukanis, 1929 [225]

"What changes in the area of law follow from the fact of regulating the national economy?

"The first and most important is the fusion of legislation with administration. . . . This principle penetrates especially deeply into practice when we pass over to a regulating and planning activity. It is sufficient to quote such examples as the approval of industrial-financial plans in individual branches of production, approval of . . . plans of capital construction—in all these cases creation of a general norm is inseparably fused with individual concrete acts of administration. . . ."

Yampol'skaya, 1961 [226]

"Three main groups of decrees of Councils of the National Economy are to be found in practice. . . . [To the second group belong] decrees in the text of which norms of law are mixed with individual orders of a one-time character. Such acts one can find in great numbers in any Council of National Economy. . . . [T]hese are mixed decrees. . . . [T]hey are precisely the most widely used form of acts of [these] Councils. . . . These acts are, as a rule, operative-organizational plans of measures in this or that area."

[Secondly] at the same time "State regulation is characterized by a predominance of technical-organizational elements over formal elements. Legislative and administrative acts are transformed into operative tasks, they retain only a very thin admixture of juridical, *i.e.*, formal, elements. . . ."

Golunskiy, 1961 [227]

"[A]t the present time, organizational measures . . . on the part of the State . . . are acquiring an ever-greater significance (in particular for norms in which a given task is set). . . . This explains one of the characteristic features of legislative acts on questions of economic and cultural construction promulgated in recent times: all of them contain a whole series of assignments to various State agencies to carry out given measures."

[225] Pashukanis, *supra* note 222, at No. 5, pp. 33-34.

[226] Yampol'skaya, in YAMPOL'SKAYA, LUZHIN & PRIBLUDA, PRAVOVYYE VOPROSY ORGANIZATSIYI I DEYATEL'NOSTI SOVNARKHOZOV (LEGAL QUESTIONS OF THE ORGANIZATION AND ACTIVITY OF SOVNARKHOZES) 115-16 (Moscow 1961).

[227] Golunskiy, *K voprosu o ponyatiyi pravovykh norm v teoriyi sotsialisticheskogo prava (On the Question of the Concept of Legal Norms in the Theory of Socialist Law)*, Sov. gos. i pravo No. 4, p. 21, at 29 (1961).

The legal phenomena which Pashukanis observed with remarkable ingenuity in their initial stage of development have become permanent and inherent institutions now. They constitute in essence some of the characteristic legal features of a planned economy, as practised in contemporary times in the Soviet Union. Stressing the new, Pashukanis at the same time did not lose sight of the civil-law aspects of planning. "Between the spheres of commodity-turnover and pure planning there is naturally no blank wall," Pashukanis observed in 1929. "These relations penetrate each other. A borderline area is created." As examples, he quoted general contracts and purchase-sale contracts within enterprises of the same "sindikat." "As long as administration as a certain formal function and economy, *i.e.*, the carrying out of purely productive tasks, are not fully fused," Pashukanis continued, "there remains the necessity for a systematization of these formal elements, let us say, the limits of competence of individual organizations, their subordination to each other, *et cetera.* Consequently, there remains a certain legal system which one could call . . . a system of administrative-economic law." [228]

Present-day Soviet legal science rejects the idea of an administrative-economic law and distinguishes sharply between administrative and civil legal aspects of economic planning.[229] Economic contracts are believed to fall in the area of civil law. The lawmakers have endorsed this view in the 1961 Principles. The problem thus seems to be solved by legislative action. But the impression persists that this decision, however authoritative and lasting it may be, is somewhat artificial, just as it would be artificial to relegate economic contracts unqualifiedly to the body of administrative law. The question is bound to come up again before long.[230] There is not and cannot be a clear-cut barrier between administrative and civil law in the field of economic planning. It is just the combination of the principles and techniques of both which characterize the particular features of economic contracts. The institution of Arbitrazh and its practice is a living demonstration of this truth.

[228] Pashukanis, *supra* note 222, at No. 5, pp. 35-36.

[229] 1961 Principles arts. 2 and 6 (and Principles on Civil Procedure of the USSR and Union Republics of 1961 arts. 1 and 4). The discussion on the "subject" of civil, economic, and administrative law and their delineation has been lead for more than 30 years. More than 100 relevant titles are listed in the bibliography, SOVETSKOYE GRAZHDANSKOYE PRAVO. SOVETSKOYE SEMEYNOYE PRAVO 1917-1960 (SOVIET CIVIL LAW. SOVIET FAMILY. Bibliography) 21-34 (Moscow 1962).

[230] Recently the creation of an "administrative-economic code" was suggested in Sov. gos. i pravo No. 7, p. 102 (1963); and "economic law" was quoted as an example for a discipline bordering various sciences. Il'yichev, at a Session of the Presidium of the USSR Academy of Sciences, reported in Kommunist No. 16, p. 59, at 60 (1963).

SOVIET TORT LAW: THE NEW PRINCIPLES ANNOTATED

BY WHITMORE GRAY *

INTRODUCTION

"AT 2:20 A.M. ON MAY 1, 1962, while riding his bicycle along the Simferopol' Highway in the company of Baturin, Pronin fell and injured his shoulder. Leaving his bicycle with Pronin, Baturin went on foot to a nearby village to summon medical aid. Pronin waited for him for awhile, and then decided to go back to the village of Volosovo in a passing car. Seeing the Tula-Moscow bus coming, he ran onto the road and waved. The driver, Markelov, seeing Pronin run onto the road 50 feet ahead of the bus, swerved to the left, went into the left lane, and struck a Volga automobile driven by Tabulin coming in the opposite direction.

"Auto experts established that the bus driver, Markelov, had violated Article 2 of the Traffic Rules for Streets and Roads of the USSR. His violation was caused by improper acts of the pedestrian, Pronin, who created the dangerous situation.

"Autobase No. 12 of the Autopark Administration, the owner of the Volga, sued Tabulin for 576 rubles, asserting that he had rented the car and damaged it.

"The People's Court of Krasnopresnensk Region gave judgment for 576 rubles in favor of Autobase No. 12 against Tabulin for the damage inflicted.

"Tabulin sued the owner of the bus, Motor Transport Unit 21 of the Tula Auto Trust, and Pronin, for reimbursement in this amount.

"The Tula District Court gave judgment in favor of Tabulin against Unit 21 for 576 rubles. [The Court does not mention any judgment against Pronin.]

"The Court College for Civil Matters of the Supreme Court of the RSFSR, in its decision of March 28, 1963, left the decision unchanged and rejected the appeal of Unit 21.

"In its decision, the Court pointed out the following.

"According to Article 90 of the Fundamental Principles of Civil Legislation of the USSR and the Union Republics, organizations and citizens whose activity is connected with a source of increased danger for those in the vicinity are obligated to compensate for injury caused by such source, unless they can show that the injury was caused by irresistible force or the intent of the injured party.

"The owner of the bus was Unit 21. Therefore, it is obligated to compensate for the injury caused by this source of increased danger.

"The fact that the collision occurred as a result of the creation of a dangerous situation by Pronin does not free Unit 21 from the obliga-

* *WHITMORE GRAY. A.B. 1954, Principia College; J.D. 1957, University of Michigan; Associate Professor of Law, University of Michigan.*

tion to compensate for the injury, since such an obligation also arises under Article 90 of the above-mentioned Principles in those instances in which the culpable conduct of a third party has contributed to the causing of an injury."[1]

This recent Soviet case is a typical example of the role that contemporary tort law plays in the Soviet Union. Contrary to the expectations of the early Marxists, familiar concepts of civil liability continue to be used to work out compensation patterns for traffic accidents, industrial injuries and governmental torts, not to mention stones thrown by children through neighbors' windows.

We might expect, as the early Marxists did, that in a state which proclaims its intention to care for all its citizens in all ways, the various risks and duties reflected in our private law of tort would have been swallowed up in one grand scheme of state compensation from public funds, coupled, perhaps, with criminal or financial sanctions against those who cause harm by deviations from the established norms of conduct. Whatever the theoretical desirability of such a system might be, it has never been introduced in the Soviet Union. During the early years of the regime, the means to do so were lacking, and indications in recent years are that there is no desire to alter radically the more traditional system which has evolved.[2]

Certain broad social programs have had an influence on the scope of tort recovery.[3] Medical care is provided free of charge for the whole population, though some fringe medical services are paid for by the individual. Broad pension programs and benefits for unemployment caused by sickness or injury are provided for most people with regular employment, but not for housewives, children, or some self-employed persons and farmers.[4] Even those who are covered receive in benefits only a part of wages lost in the case of permanent injury, and must resort to a normal tort recovery to obtain full compensation.[5] Property insurance is apparently common only in

[1] [1963] Byul. verkh. suda R.S.F.S.R. No. 7, p. 1 (Civ. Coll. R.S.F.S.R. Sup. Ct.).

[2] The new Principles are based on concepts of liability common to most modern legal systems. *E.g.*, articles 88 and 91 reemphasize the paramount role of civil fault, and article 89 significantly extends the area of application of tort law as a basis for redress against harm inflicted by official governmental acts. Regarding the role of strict liability, see under article 90 *infra*.

[3] The impact of these programs on the personal injury recovery is set forth at length in 2 IOFFE, SOVETSKOYE GRAZHDANSKOYE PRAVO (SOVIET CIVIL LAW) 500 (Leningrad 1961) [hereinafter cited as IOFFE]. See also Hazard, *Personal Injury and Soviet Socialism*, 65 HARV. L. REV. 545 (1952).

[4] Similar benefits are provided on many collective farms from special funds set up by the farm itself. 2 SOVETSKOYE GRAZHDANSKOYE PRAVO (SOVIET CIVIL LAW) 390 (Orlovskiy ed. 1961) [hereinafter cited as ORLOVSKIY].

[5] For example, in a recent case a man who was injured in an industrial accident lost 80% of his capacity to perform his former work. He was awarded a pension of 150 rubles a month, while his former average salary had been 867 rubles a month. He sued for a supplementary recovery in tort and was successful. Valov, [1963] Byul. verkh. suda S.S.S.R. No. 1, p. 17 (Plenum U.S.S.R. Sup. Ct. 1962).

certain limited areas, and liability insurance is not available.[5a] In most cases of personal or property injury, therefore, full compensation is available only if applicable tort law will support a direct recovery from the person who caused the damage.

Over the past 40 years Soviet courts and legal writers have created a body of tort law, based, as is the rest of Soviet private law, on the civil codes adopted in the Twenties.[6] The unsatisfactory nature of the tort provisions in those codes, caused by a combination of revolutionary zeal and poor draftsmanship, quickly led to a situation where a major portion of tort law was in the court rulings[7] and the textbooks.[8] Recodification was delayed for over 30 years, and the court decisions show that it was almost as difficult for the Soviet courts as for the outsider to spell out with accuracy even the general principles being applied.[9]

In 1961, the federal legislature, the USSR Supreme Soviet, finally adopted a skeleton code of fundamental principles of civil law.[10] This recodification, which incorporates 40 years of case law and doctrinal development as well as some major innovations, will be the basis for individual civil codes to be adopted in each of the 15 union republics. While there may be some slight modifications, and certainly some variety in the degree of additional detail included in the individual codes by each republic,[11] these Principles present already a fairly comprehensive picture of the shape of the future law. They are about as detailed as the tort provisions in other modern civil codes, and cover the grounds of liability, the defenses which are to be recognized, and the scope of compensable injury. In addition, they include

[5a] See note 86 *infra*.

[6] Citations to pre-Principles law will be given from the most important of these republic codes, the R.S.F.S.R. CIVIL CODE of 1922 (Kodeks grazhdanskogo prava R.S.F.S.R.) [hereinafter cited as CIVIL CODE].

[7] Soviet court rulings include case decisions like the one translated above, and also general directives to lower courts. As the case translated at note 1 *supra* shows, ordinary case decisions are disappointingly short on factual detail and careful analysis. More helpful as guides to future decisions, since they are more likely to be referred to by lawyers and cited by the courts, are the general rulings, which may treat a specific point such as procedure for cases under a new statute (note 102 *infra*), or a whole field of law such as tort (see, *e.g.*, the 1943 ruling, note 8 *infra*).

[8] Basic fault liability, comparative negligence, and *respondeat superior* doctrines were all worked out by the courts during the Twenties. The USSR Supreme Court in effect codified experience to date in a 1943 ruling, reprinted along with other basic tort material in DOZORTSEV, ISTOCHNIKI SOVETSKOGO GRAZHDANSKOGO PRAVA (SOURCES OF SOVIET CIVIL LAW) 806 (1961) [hereinafter cited as DOZORTSEV].

[9] *E.g.*, the confusion which arose over the standard for liability of organizations for injuries to their employees, discussed at length in note 98 *infra*.

[10] PRINCIPLES OF CIVIL LEGISLATION, Ved. verkh. sov. S.S.R. No. 50(1085) p. 1273 (1961). An English translation appeared in 14 C.D.S.P. No. 4, p. 1 (1962).

[11] See, *e.g.*, the description of the tort provisions of the new R.S.F.S.R. Civil Code in Boldyrev, *O proyekte grazhdanskogo kodeksa R.S.F.S.R. (On the Project of the Civil Code of the R.S.F.S.R.)*, Sov. gos. i pravo No. 8, pp. 15, 23 (1962).

provisions relating to workmen's compensation claims, wrongful death actions, and rules governing governmental tort liability.

This article is an attempt to restate in the form of an annotation to these Principles the broad outlines of the contemporary Soviet law of tort.

"PRINCIPLES OF CIVIL LEGISLATION OF THE USSR AND THE UNION REPUBLICS

"PART III. LAW OF OBLIGATIONS

"CHAPTER XII. OBLIGATIONS ARISING FROM THE INFLICTION OF INJURY

"ARTICLE 88. GENERAL GROUNDS OF LIABILITY FOR THE INFLICTION OF INJURY

"Injury caused to the person or property of a citizen, as well as injury caused to an organization, is to be compensated for in full by the person who has caused the injury.

"The person who has caused the injury may free himself from having to compensate for it if he shows that the injury was not caused through his fault."

This article, together with article 90 which imposes a strict liability for damage caused by a source of increased danger, provides the general basis for tort liability in Soviet law.[12] It is the basis upon which liability is predicated in damage cases ranging from trespassing cows [13] to failure to come to the rescue of endangered persons or property.[14]

Soviet writers say that the provision of the Principles to the effect that a person is liable for damage caused by his act, unless he shows it did not occur by his fault, states a general principle of liability based on fault.[15] While we might feel that the burden of proof of lack of fault imposed by the section could lead to causation-based liability in practice, the experience under prior law tends to support the Soviets' position.

Article 403 of the RSFSR Civil Code of 1922 provides: "One who injures the person or property of another is liable for the injury caused. He

[12] Articles 91 and 92 can also be read as establishing the general basis for tort recovery for death or personal injury, but they simply incorporate by reference the standards of articles 88 and 90. There was a doctrinal controversy on this point under the old law which may continue, however. 2 ORLOVSKIY 387. See the general discussion under arts. 91 and 92 *infra.*

[13] The development of Soviet tort law after the revolution, from the first cases involving injury to crops by straying cattle down to the adoption of the Principles, is described in the excellent introduction to the chapter on tort law in HAZARD & SHAPIRO, THE SOVIET LEGAL SYSTEM pt. 3, at 72 (1962) [hereinafter cited as HAZARD & SHAPIRO]. While none of the translated cases in that chapter involved direct application of the 1961 Principles, they illustrate for the most part fundamental principles or problems which continue to be of significance under the new Principles. Since they constitute the most readily available source of Soviet materials in English translation, citations will be given to them in the material which follows wherever possible.

[14] 2 ORLOVSKIY 397. See discussion at note 130, *infra.*

[15] *E.g.,* Maleyin, *Pravovoye regulirovaniye obyazatel'stv po vozmeshchenii vreda (The Legal Regulation of Compulsory Compensations for Damage),* Sov. gos. i pravo No. 10, p. 68 (1962).

is not liable if he proves that he could not prevent the injury." The absence of any "fault" requirement was a departure from the French and German models which were followed by the Soviet drafters in many other respects.[16] It is likely that they meant to lay down a different principle, for some early Marxists advocated liability based on causation.[17] In any case, whatever revolutionary element may have existed was lost in the court practice which developed under the section. By 1926, the RSFSR Supreme Court held that liability should be based on a finding of fault, and pointed out that "Section 403 is by no means peculiar to soviet law, as the courts have often indicated in their decisions, but has been borrowed from the civil law of capitalist codes (*e.g.*, the French Code)." [18]

In other words, whatever the original intent of the drafters of section 403 was, the Supreme Court, and subsequently the writers, read into the phrase "could not prevent the injury" a general "fault" basis for liability, thus bringing Soviet law into line with other modern systems.[19] The use of the word "fault" in the Principles, therefore, simply continues prior practice.

The interesting thing is that the drafters of the new Principles continued the burden-of-proof pattern of the prior law, under which the defendant must prove that he was not at fault in causing the injury.[20] The repetition of the old formula with simply the addition of the word "fault" in the generally conservative draft was understandable, but its retention in the final form adopted is surprising, for there was very free and detailed criticism of the draft for an extended period. The most forceful suggestion made on this point was that the section should read, "unless an absence of fault on his part is established," [21] thereby avoiding the imposition of any specific burden of proof, but even this compromise was not adopted.

[16] For a short description of the French and German provisions, see RYAN, INTRODUCTION TO THE CIVIL LAW 111 (1962).

[17] The views of the drafters are discussed in 1 GSOVSKI, SOVIET CIVIL LAW 496 (1948) [hereinafter cited as GSOVSKI]. Gsovski points out that the formulation of the general principle in Tsarist law, also different from the continental models, was similar to the one adopted by the Soviets in that it did not specifically mention "fault," and this may have influenced their choice of language. *Id.* at 494-95. Both provisions were interpreted by the courts, however, to imply a fault basis of liability.

[18] Quoted in 1 GSOVSKI 485.

[19] Of course this refers only to the general basis of liability. Through devices such as *res ipsa loquitur* shifts can be made in this basic pattern, and modern systems commonly have special areas in which liability without fault is imposed. See the description of French and German law in RYAN, *op. cit. supra* note 16, at 120. The Soviet provisions are discussed under art. 90 *infra.*

[20] The burden of proving that the defendant "caused" the injury is clearly on the plaintiff.

[21] Ioffe, *et al., O proyekte osnov grazhdanskogo zakonodatel'stva Soyuza SSR i Soyuznykh Respublik (Concerning the Draft for the Foundations of Civil Legislation of the Soviet Union and Union Republics),* Sov. gos. i pravo No. 2, pp. 93, 100 (1961).

Perhaps familiarity with the practice under the old rule made it clear to those concerned that the change was not of real importance.[22] The general civilian principle of very free evaluation of the evidence by the trial judges which is followed, coupled with the duty imposed on the Soviet judge to pursue an active role in ascertaining all the facts of the matter before him, creates an atmosphere in which technical burden-of-proof formulations do not have the importance which we might attach to them.

The application of the present rule in practice is described in the standard civil law textbook as follows:

> "Under this article, the victim is not required to prove that the injury arose through the fault of the inflictor. The inflictor, provided he wants to be relieved of liability, must himself prove that he was not at fault in inflicting the injury. Thus, a person who has inflicted injury is presumed to have been at fault until he rebuts this presumption. The position of the victim in the civil trial is thereby made easier. The presumption of fault on the part of the inflictor may not correspond to reality, yet he may not be in a position to rebut it. In such a case, the court itself must take steps to clarify the actual nature of the interrelationships of the parties(Article 5 of the Code of Civil Procedure). Because of this, the distribution of the burden of proof provided for in Article 403 is of only relative importance." [23]

In view of the fact that the provision mentioned above imposing on the trial judge a duty to investigate all aspects of the case is continued in article 16 of the new Principles of Civil Procedure,[24] the position seems to remain basically the same as under prior law.

The ordinary basis of tort liability in Soviet law seems to be, therefore, (1) an injury to a person or property, coupled with (2) a finding of the cause in fact thereof,[25] and (3) a finding of "fault" on the part of the person

[22] It is also possible that real pressure for reformulation on this was felt to constitute unnecessary criticism of the draft, and that it was best to concentrate on changes where basic principles were involved, *e.g.*, art. 89.

[23] 2 Orlovskiy 375. The author would like to acknowledge the able assistance of Raymond Stults, M.A. in Russian Studies, Harvard, a second year student at the University of Michigan Law School, in the preparation of first drafts of the translation of this and some other text materials quoted in this article, as well as for assistance in final checking of the manuscript before publication. W.G.

[24] Ved. verkh. sov. SSR No. 50 (1085), pp. 1307, 1310 (1961). *Cf.* also the special instruction to courts examining cases of damage done by workers to investigate thoroughly the circumstances of the case. Para. 1, USSR Supreme Court Plenum Ruling of Dec. 18, 1961, [1962] Byul. verkh. suda S.S.S.R. No. 1, pp. 12, 13.

[25] Soviet cases tend to treat causation as a simple matter of fact, rather than to use it as an additional test for defining the scope of liability. Perhaps the development of useful causation theories has been inordinately hindered by the close connection with political and economic Marxian dialectic. It has at least made the Soviets extremely sensitive to any suggestion that their use of theories which look like cause in fact or adequate cause tests have any similarity to Western concepts. See in this regard the excellent discussion of the Soviet theory and practice in 2 Ioffe 447.

who caused the injury. The "fault" may consist in a violation of a criminal prohibition or in unjustified noncriminal intentional infliction of injury, or in failure to conform to a standard of reasonable care.[26]

What is the nature and extent of the normal tort recovery? The Principles simply state in this general section that "injury . . . is subject to compensation in full," and no details are given concerning the intended scope of recovery or the nature of the obligation.[27] It is likely, therefore, that the new republic codes will reflect the practice under prior law.

The standard civil law textbook says that under pre-Principles law, "compensation for injury takes the form of restoration to the former condition. . . . The law gives a favored position to compensation for injury in the form of restoration to the former condition." [28] This is based on article 410 of the RSFSR Civil Code, which provides that "reparation of injury shall consist in the restoration of the condition existing before the injury and, to the extent to which such restoration is impossible, in compensation for the damage caused." In other words, the Code establishes a primary obligation to repair or replace damaged or destroyed goods, etc., and a secondary obligation to pay damages.

This is probably not, however, in line with the actual practice which has developed. The other leading civil law treatise says that specific replacement or repair is very seldom applied in practice.[29] In the case of personal injury it is not possible, and, in the case of property injury, because of the increase in the supply of goods for the people, "it is usually more convenient [for the plaintiff] to receive monetary compensation."[30] Implying that a choice is sometimes open to the parties, the text says that the defendant sometimes chooses compensation in kind where the law imposes a rate for monetary compensation higher than the value of the article, but that plaintiffs seldom ask for specific relief.[31] Sometimes the choice has been made by

[26] Conduct which results in liability is generally also characterized as "illegal" or "unlawful." In practice this usually amounts to finding of "fault" or a basis for strict liability, and does not constitute an independent criterion. The standard text says that "in those cases in which the appropriate rules of conduct are not established by law, the norms of liability for the infliction of injury are themselves the rules of proper conduct." 2 ORLOVSKIY 369. In other words, whether or not liability is found is the test of "illegality," and not vice versa. See the discussion under art. 88, para. 3 *infra.*

[27] The special rules given in articles 91 and 92 in connection with recovery for personal injury are discussed below and under those articles.

[28] 2 ORLOVSKIY 389.

[29] 2 IOFFE 492.

[30] *Ibid.* The result in practice under the German provision, BGB § 249, which also provides for specific relief, is usually also a money recovery. 1 MOLITOR, SCHULDRECHT (LAW OF OBLIGATIONS) 43 (1959).

[31] 2 IOFFE 492.

the court, as in the case of a recent ruling regarding damage to crops of a kolkhoz,[32] and sometimes the law has limited the plaintiff to money damages.[33]

It seems clear that the secondary form of relief in article 410, money damages, "has acquired fundamental significance in Soviet court practice." [34] In view of this, it is unlikely that the new codes will continue the old formulation. It is more difficult to say what will be substituted for it. One commentary states simply that "the choice of one form or the other (specific replacement or repair or damages) depends on the particular characteristics of the case in question, and it is therefore inexpedient for such a choice to be made ahead of time by the law." [35] The problem has not been discussed in articles dealing with the new draft civil codes, so this may be a question which will be left to case law and doctrinal development.

The amount of money damages in the case of injury to property generally is described in the standard text as being equal to the actual decrease in value or the replacement value in case of destruction.[36] While the text recognizes that there also may be lost profits from loss of the use of the thing, it takes the view [37] that under recent USSR Supreme Court rulings, these may not be included in the recovery.[38]

In the case of personal injury,[39] recovery always takes the form of money damages, and includes all expenses of caring for the injured party not provided directly under the public health program,[40] as well as lost

[32] USSR Supreme Court Plenum Ruling of March 26, 1960, [1960] Byul. verkh. suda S.S.S.R. No. 3, p. 11.

[33] 2 IOFFE 492.

[34] *Ibid.*

[35] IOFFE & TOLSTOY, OSNOVY SOVETSKOGO GRAZHDANSKOGO ZAKONODATEL'STVA (PRINCIPLES OF SOVIET CIVIL LEGISLATION) 164 (Leningrad 1962) [hereinafter cited as IOFFE & TOLSTOY].

[36] 2 ORLOVSKIY 381.

[37] *Ibid.*

[38] The Ioffe-Tolstoy commentary says, "The tortfeasor is required to compensate for all expenditures, losses or damage to property, as well as for all income not received by the victim because of the infraction" (IOFFE & TOLSTOY 164), leaving an ambiguity on this point. There are a few exceptional cases of liability for more than the actual amount of harm inflicted as an increased deterrent for certain kinds of conduct. 2 IOFFE 493. There is also an important restriction on the amount of recovery by an employer against his employee to one-third of the employee's salary, unless his acts constituted a crime. LABOR CODE art. 83. The broader provisions for equitable reduction of the amount of recovery by the court available in all cases are discussed in 2 IOFFE 493 with respect to prior law, and under article 93 of the Principles *infra.*

[39] For general background, see the comprehensive article by Hazard, *Personal Injury and Soviet Socialism,* 65 HARV. L. REV. 545 (1952).

earnings attributable to the injury.[41] Recovery for pain and suffering is not allowed.[42]

The recovery of lost wages may be either for the loss during a temporary disability, which can be quite accurately computed in most cases, or may also include the more speculative item of impairment of future earning capacity. This latter portion of the recovery must be awarded in the form of a monthly payment.[43] Periodic re-examinations of the victim re-establish his right to continued receipt of such payment,[44] and either party has in addition a right to petition the court for a change in the amount of compensation in case of a subsequent change in the party's ability to work.[45]

Two kinds of capacity are generally recognized—general capacity to work, *i.e.*, to do manual labor, and ability to do the work for which a person has been specially trained, *i.e.*, his professional capacity.[46] If an injured party is found to have lost 30 per cent of his professional capacity, then his monthly damage payments will be a proportionate sum of his prior average wage. If he has lost all of his professional capacity, then his recovery will be the full amount of his former average wage, less whatever his probable earning power will be from whatever general capacity he has retained.[47]

[40] See, *e.g.*, Zolotukhina, [1962] Byul. verkh. suda R.S.F.S.R. (Civ. Coll. R.S.F.S.R. Sup. Ct.).

[41] 2 Ioffe 501.

[42] This is theoretically justified on the ground that there should only be recovery for "property" losses, or loss of income which can be equated thereto. For the extent of this "property" orientation, see the introduction to the whole law of obligations in 1 Ioffe 368. Perhaps the fact that Tsarist law also refused recovery for other than property damage influenced the formation of the Soviet position. 1 Gsovski 539.

[43] 2 Orlovskiy 392. Though this is a long-established principle, some courts still feel the desirability of a lump-sum recovery. See, *e.g.*, Kurbatova v. Pogodaev, [1961] Byul. verkh. suda R.S.F.S.R. No. 5, p. 15 (Presid. Yakut A.S.S.R. Sup. Ct.), Hazard & Shapiro pt. 3, at 97.

[44] Orlovskiy 392, *E.g.*, Krylov, [1962] Byul. verkh. suda R.S.F.S.R. No. 4, p. 2 (Civ. Coll. R.S.F.S.R. Sup. Ct.).

[45] 2 Orlovskiy 392. *E.g.*, a judgment in the amount of "539 rubles monthly until [the plaintiff] recovered." Bekhtin v. Factory, [1960] Sov. yus. No. 4, p. 83, Case No. 3 (Presid. R.S.F.S.R. Sup. Ct.), Hazard & Shapiro pt. 3, at 98.

[46] The ramifications of the formulae used for computing the monthly recovery have been one of the most troublesome points in Soviet tort practice and are beyond the scope of this article. The basic problems are summarized in a clear exposition of recent practice in 2 Ioffe 502-12.

[47] A good recent example of how this works out in practice is Valov, [1963] Byul. verkh. suda S.S.S.R. No. 1, p. 17 (Plenum U.S.S.R. Sup. Ct. 1962). The formula applied there is the formalized estimate of future earning power through the use of the percent of capacity lost and the prior average wage. The court goes on to say, however, at 18, that if the guess is wrong, *i.e.*, if it turns out that he is able to earn more than the amount predicted, there will be applied to his total income, *i.e.*, salary plus pension plus this recovery, a *de facto* limitation to his average prior wage, and that this limitation can be invoked by the defendant in the light of subsequent evidence at the time of execution. This unfortunately seems to overlook the possibility of inflation, effect of increased skill, *etc.*, which could justify higher total income.

Articles 91 and 92 contain a special provision which makes it clear that assistance and pensions actually being received by the plaintiff because of the injury sued upon are to be deducted from any recovery against the person with tort liability, but that benefits from other sources, *e.g.*, veterans' benefits, are to be disregarded. In the past there had been some difference of opinion on this point, based on the idea that a person's full income expectation from labor should be the upper limit of his recovery. It is interesting that the Principles have reaffirmed the more favorable position for the individual, *i.e.*, that he may have his full work income, and in addition any other benefits to which he is entitled.[48]

Some Soviet writers seem to favor a more comprehensive personal injury recovery. There has been criticism, for example, of the rule that loss of general capacity to work is not compensated under existing law if a part of professional capacity is retained.[49] The suggestion has been made that actual income loss is not the only economic injury sustained, and that the loss of ability to do housework or care for relatives, as well as loss of mobility, etc., should be compensated in the future.[50]

It is still too early to say whether the theoretical limitation to recovery of "economic" losses, or the practical consideration of avoiding large recoveries which might unduly burden the production units, will keep the scope of recovery within the more narrow limits of present rules. If the scope of recovery is expanded, however, it will mean that even claims for temporary disability would not be fully covered by the social insurance salary payments, and so would require a tort claim to secure full compensation.

"An organization must compensate for injury caused through the fault of its employees in the performance of their duties."

[48] *E.g.*, applying article 91 of the Principles, Klopyzhnikov, [1962] Byul. verkh. suda R.S.F.S.R. No. 10, p. 10 (Civ. Coll. R.S.F.S.R. Sup. Ct.). The same rule had been applied under the prior provisions, *e.g.*, Likhachev, [1960] Byul. verkh. suda R.S.F.S.R. No. 1, p. 15 (Plenum U.S.S.R. Sup. Ct. 1959). A holding also resulting in a favorable recovery in the case of suit by dependents declared it improper to deduct income tax from the amount of the breadwinner's income before fixing the amount of dependents' recovery based thereon. Veselova, [1962] Byul. verkh. suda R.S.F.S.R. No. 6, pp. 35, 36 (Plenum U.S.S.R. Sup. Ct.). However, the tendency to restrict the amount of recovery is evidenced by other recent decisions refusing to allow the inclusion of other than regular salary income in computing prior average earnings. Shulkina, [1962] Byul. verkh. suda R.S.F.S.R. No. 2, p. 2 (Civ. Coll. R.S.F.S.R. Sup. Ct. 1961); Korostyleva, [1962] Byul. verkh, suda R.S.F.S.R. No. 11, p. 14 (Presid. Dagestan A.S.S.R. Sup. Ct.). See 2 ORLOVSKIY 394 to the same effect *re* exclusion of a collective farmer's income from working of his private plot.

[49] As applied, *e.g.*, in the *Likhachev* case, *supra* note 48.

[50] Maleyin, *Pravovoye regulirovaniye obyazatel'stv po vozmeshchenii vreda, (The Legal Regulation of Obligations for Compensation of Injury)* Sov. gos. i. pravo No. 10, pp. 68, 74 (1962).

This provision resolves a problem which has been a source of controversy in Soviet law. A clear provision on the point was lacking in the 1922 Code,[51] and several views were advanced as to the liability of juridical persons for the acts of their employees.

Some authors rejected the possibility of *respondeat* liability for the acts of employees, and said that liability could be found only on the basis of independent fault of the organization, *e.g.*, an improper selection or supervision of the employee.[52] Most writers and many decisions, however, took the view that fault should be attributed.[53] Some courts even held the organization liable when the acts in question were outside the scope of the person's employment.[54]

The Principles clearly establish liability on the part of the juridical person for injury caused by the fault of its employees, and at the same time place a scope of employment limitation on such liability.

Nothing is said as to the right of the organization to reimbursement from the employee who caused the injury, but such a right will certainly be recognized as it was under prior law,[55] subject to the general limitation of article 83 of the Labor Code limiting recovery against a worker for harm inflicted by him on his employer to one-third of his salary,[56] unless his acts constituted a crime. It would also be available only in cases of "fault" liability, and not in cases where the worker by his act incurs strict liability only for the organization.[57]

[51] The only explicit provision in the 1922 R.S.F.S.R. CIVIL CODE (art. 407) stated that government institutions were liable for harm caused by improper acts of their officials in cases specially provided for by law. *Re* this specific question under the Principles, see under article 89 *infra*.

[52] *E.g.*, the standard civil law text rejects the idea that fault of the worker is to be attributed to the organization. 2 ORLOVSKIY 384. Compare the German provision in BGB § 831 which allows the organization to relieve itself of liability by showing proper care in the selection and supervision of its personnel.

[53] 2 IOFFE 474. See also FLEYSHITS, OBYAZATEL'STVA IZ PRICHINENIYA VREDA (OBLIGATIONS [ARISING] OUT OF THE CAUSING OF INJURY) 110 (1951), and the review of authorities in Savitskaya, *Otvetstvennost' gosudarstvennykh uchrezhdeniy za vred, prichinennyy deystviyami ikh dolzhnostnykh lits (The Responsibility of Government Institutions for Damage Caused by Actions of Their Officials)*, Sov. gos. i pravo No. 8, pp. 48, 52 n.8 (1962).

[54] IOFFE & TOLSTOY 161.

[55] 2 IOFFE 474-75. See, *e.g.*, Timoshkin, [1961] Byul. verkh. suda R.S.F.S.R. No. 2, p. 15 (Presid. Sverdlovsk Oblast Ct.).

[56] The limitation was not available under prior law in the case of government officials sued for reimbursement in connection with governmental liability under CIVIL CODE art. 407. There is an additional limiting aspect of this recovery scheme against employees, viz. that the employer may be subjected to long term monthly payment obligations, whereas recovery from the employee has to be in a lump sum. See *Timoshkin*, *supra* note 55. The possibility of a limitation on recovery even where the acts constituted a crime is discussed at note 119 *infra*.

[57] Some of the strict liability cases have contributed to the confusion over whose liability is used as a basis for recovery. *E.g.*, in a case where a drunken employee not

"*Injury caused through lawful acts is to be compensated for only in cases provided for by law.*"

This provision might seem to create an additional basic test of "illegality" for the imposition of liability. One of the leading Soviet writers says in a commentary on the Principles that this clause means just that, *i.e.*, that "liability for injury arises only when that injury is brought about by unlawful conduct." [58] If "unlawful" is taken to describe any conduct which results in liability under the circumstances, then this is obviously true.[59] His statement is misleading, however, if it implies that there is liability only in cases where the conduct constitutes a crime or contravenes some general regulation.[60]

What is intended in this section is expressed perhaps more clearly in the old RSFSR Civil Code provision, "The person who inflicts the injury frees himself from liability if he shows . . . that he was legally entitled to inflict the injury." [61] This is designed, in other words, to take care of the situation

employed as a driver took a company car and had an accident, the court held that the company had strict liability as owner. It went on to show, however, how the company had been at fault (by an employee's fault attributed to it) in leaving the keys in the ignition of the vehicle and in letting him get out of the yard with it. Lomov, [1962] Byul. verkh. suda R.S.F.S.R. No. 3, p. 1 (Civ. Coll. R.S.F.S.R. Sup. Ct. 1961). It would be easy for a court in a subsequent case to interpret the holding as requiring a finding of independent fault on the part of the company, or as attributing fault on the part of the other employees to the company as a basis for liability, even though the court must have actually decided the case only on strict liability grounds, *i.e.*, liability without fault, since only that code section was cited. For a discussion of the rule the court may have been laying down, as well as of the precise question as to what interrupts "possession" for purposes of the imposition of strict liability, see note 91 *infra*.

[58] Ioffe & Tolstoy 160. The question of whether there is a separate test of "unlawfulness" for the imposition of liability is discussed in note 26 *supra*.

[59] The mere infliction of injury by an extra-hazardous source is described as "unlawful." 2 Orlovskiy 369. One leading Soviet writer has objected to this. "It is impossible to characterize as illegal the activities of Soviet industrial enterprises, railroads and construction organization carried out in conformity with all the requirements of the law." Fleyshits, *Obshchiye nachala otvetstvennosti po osnovan grazhdanskogo zakonodatel'stva Soyuza SSR i Soyuznykh Respublik, (The General Principles of Responsibility on the Bases of Civil Legislation of the Soviet Union and Union Republics)*, Sov. gos. i pravo No. 3, p. 34, at 39 (1962). He goes on to say, however, that the new Principles, in order to promote maximum safety precautions, make the mere infliction of injury by an extra-hazardous source "unlawful." *Ibid.*

[60] There is no need to show a violation of any criminal statute or other regulation. 2 Orlovskiy 373. The civil court is bound, however, by the criminal court's verdict where criminal proceedings are brought on the same grounds. *Id.* 374. See, *e.g.*, Daychenko v. Ostashkov, [1961] Sov. yus. No. 12, p. 27, Case No. 2, (Civ. Coll. R.S.F.S.R. Sup. Ct. 1960), translated in Hazard & Shapiro pt. 3, at 81, where the court even felt bound to refuse to find civil liability after criminal charges had merely been dismissed for lack of evidence. *Cf.* Rubstov, [1962] Byul. verkh. suda R.S.F.S.R. No. 5, p. 13 (Civ. Coll. R.S.F.S.R. Sup. Ct.), where the court cited in support of its holding in a civil case the decision of a prosecutor not to bring criminal charges against the defendant.

[61] Civil Code art. 403.

where cattle infected with a contagious disease are destroyed by order of the appropriate authority, or where firemen inflict damage in the course of their work." [62] In discussing this provision of the Principles, one Soviet author used the two examples of injury inflicted in self-defense and destruction by an individual of property in cases of extreme necessity.[63]

The section suggests a related question which, while it has not received much attention in Soviet literature, has become an important facet of tort law in other civil law jurisdictions.[64] Even in a case where a defendant can show that he had a "right" to do the act which inflicted injury, can he be said to have abused that right, misused it, in such a way that he may be held liable for the injury? For example, is there a limitation through some more basic norm on the property "right" of a home owner to build a spite fence, or does the above clause allow him to inflict injury in that way without incurring liability?

The Soviets will certainly reject any such protection of absolute private rights under this provision, and it is likely that either the right itself will be said to be relative, or a general clause of the Principles will be brought into play. Article 5 provides:

> "Civil rights are protected by law, except in cases where they are exercised in a manner which contradicts the purpose of these rights in a socialist society in the period of the building of communism.
>
> "In exercising their rights and fulfilling their obligations, citizens and organizations must comply with the law, and respect the rules of socialistic communal life and the moral principles of a society which is building communism."

This is a continuation and broadening of article 1 of the RSFSR Civil Code, which was inserted to provide a safety valve if attempts were made to misuse the technical provisions of the Code during the limited return to capitalism in the early Twenties. After a period of disuse, there has been some revival of interest in it on the part of the courts in recent years.[65]

[62] 2 ORLOVSKIY 372. In Makagon v. Ministry of Agriculture, [1960] Sov. yus. No. 5, p. 85, Case No. 2 (Civ. Coll. R.S.F.S.R. Sup. Ct. 1959), HAZARD & SHAPIRO pt. 3, at 82, bees were destroyed as a result of spraying of crops. Held, no liability since proper methods were used by the Ministry of Agriculture and Civil Air Fleet, and all regulations were complied with by the collective farm for which the spraying was done.

[63] The same two examples are cited in a common law treatise as cases in which "on supervening grounds of public policy a special privilege is recognized." FLEMING, TORTS 6 (1961).

[64] For a concise discussion of the development and application of the doctrine of abuse of rights in French and German law, see RYAN, INTRODUCTION TO CIVIL LAW 128 (1962).

[65] 1 IOFFE 20-22. There have also been indications of concern about possible misuse of rights in discussions of the new Principles. *E.g.*, Fleyshits & Makovskiy, *Teoreticheskiye voprosy kodifikatsiyi respublikanskogo grazhdanskogo zakonodatel'stva (Theoretical Questions of the Codification of Republic Civil Legislation)*, Sov. gos. i pravo No. 1, p. 79, at 90 (1963).

Whether or not this doctrine will be used generally under the new law to work out a balance between public and private interests remains to be seen.

"ARTICLE 89. LIABILITY OF GOVERNMENT INSTITUTIONS FOR INJURY CAUSED BY ACTS OF THEIR OFFICIALS

"Government institutions are liable for injury caused to citizens by improper official acts of their officials in the area of administration in accordance with the general grounds of liability (Article 88 of these Principles), unless otherwise specially provided for by law. For injury caused to organizations by such acts of officials, government institutions are liable in the manner established by law.

"For injury caused by improper official acts of officials of the organs of inquest and preliminary investigation, the procuracy, and the courts, the government institutions in question are financially liable in those cases and within the limits specially provided for by law."

General tort liability on the part of the government was recognized under prior Soviet law for injuries caused in performing economic and technical functions.[66] Injuries from hospital negligence or from being run over by a car of the police administration were compensated for on general tort grounds.[67] These claims were treated in the same way as those against production units "owned" by the government, where questions of liability to citizens for defective products, workmen's compensation claims, and tort claims for accidents involving delivery trucks, were all considered to be free of any claim of sovereign immunity.

A concept like sovereign immunity was only brought into play in connection with official "governmental" acts.[68] Article 407 of the RSFSR Civil Code provided for liability in such instances only in cases specially provided for by law.[69] While some special provisions were later enacted,[70] these few isolated cases remained an insignificant exception to what became a well-established principle of immunity for injury inflicted by governmental acts.

Soon after the de-Stalinization go-ahead given by the Twentieth Party Congress, a leading Soviet criminologist, Strogovich, said that the time had come "to decide by legislative action the question of compensating the

[66] Ruling of the USSR Supreme Court Plenum of June 10, 1943, para. 4, reprinted in DOZORTSEV. For a text discussion, see 2 ORLOVSKIY 384.

[67] 2 IOFFE 483.

[68] There has been considerable controversy, however, over what acts should be considered economic and technical, and what considered "official" or "acts of authority." See, *e.g.*, the discussion *re* hospitals in Savitskaya, *supra* note 53, at 53.

[69] The original draft contained a provision for general liability in such cases, but it was modified prior to adoption. Savitskaya, *supra* note 53, at 49.

[70] The four principal exceptions provide for liability in connection with illegal confiscation of property, certain injuries to collective farms, harm inflicted by the fault of government harbor pilots, and liability of organs of the legal system for property deposited with them. See the list with commentary in 2 IOFFE 484-85.

rehabilitated citizen for damages suffered through illegal subjection to criminal proceedings, arrest, or conviction."[71] At the February 1957 meeting of the USSR Supreme Soviet, a delegate from the Ukraine criticized the old provision of Civil Code article 407 as being inconsistent with ideas of "socialist legality":

> "In connection with the preparation of the civil codes of the union republics, consideration should be given to the question of the property liability of governmental organizations for damage caused by their workers. The current system has established limited liability. This liability exists only in cases prescribed by law. Essentially, no one bears liability in practice under Article 407 of the Civil Code of the Ukrainian SSR. Such a situation contradicts the principle of strengthening socialist legality and makes it a real necessity to broaden the property liability of governmental organizations for damage caused by their workers. The broadening of property liability will promote full protection of the rights of working people and improvement in the work of the governmental apparatus."[72]

There was no immediate broad response to these trial balloons, and some writers said that the question should be left to individual republic formulation, despite the obvious general significance of the issue.[73]

Debate behind the scenes on the desirability of including a clause introducing general governmental liability continued, and the author was told by legal specialists at the Academy of Sciences in Kiev in late 1959 that the decision to include such a provision in the new Ukrainian Civil Code had already been made. A similar decision seems to have been reached at a conference held at the same time in Moscow at the RSFSR Ministry of Justice. According to a summary of the proceedings published later, "It was proposed that a rule be included in the draft of the Civil Code according to which governmental institutions would bear material liability according to general principles for injury caused by improper acts of officials."[74] While

[71] Strogovich, *Teoreticheskiye voprosy sovetskoy zakonnosti (Theoretical Questions of Soviet Legality)*, Sov. gos. i pravo No. 4, p. 15, at 25 (1956). A full review of the history summarized below of the adoption of the present form of article 89 is given in the excellent as-yet-unpublished dissertation by BERRY, GOVERNMENTAL TORT LIABILITY IN THE SOVIET UNION ch. VII (Syracuse 1963).

[72] Zasedaniya verkhovnogo soveta SSSR, (Session of the Supreme Soviet USSR), 4th meeting, 6th Sess., Feb. 5-12, 1957. From the Stenographic Record 500 (Moscow 1957).

[73] See *e.g., Orlovskiy, K razrabotke osnov grazhdanskogo zakonodatel'stva Soyuza SSR (Toward the Working Out of the Civil Legislation of the USSR.)*, Sov. gos. i pravo No. 7, p. 81, at 86 (1957).

[74] Shabanov, "*Soveshchaniye po voprosam kodifikatsiyi grazhdanskogo, grazhdansko-protssessual'nogo i trudovogo zakonodatel'stva Soyuza SSR i Soyuznkh Respublik, (Conference on Questions of the Codification of Civil, Civil Procedure and Labor Legislation of the Soviet Union and Union Republics)* Pravovedeniye No. 4, p. 33, at 44 (1960).

the report does not indicate the degree of support, Tolstoy, one of the leading civil law writers, said in 1960 that there was "unanimous" support among scientific and practical workers for the introduction of liability for injury caused by administrative acts, and cited in support of this the response of the participants at the 1959 conference.[75]

Conservative lawyers in the Ministry of Justice, perhaps armed with direct political instructions from policy sources, still seemed unconvinced by the reaction at the meeting, for when the draft was published for public discussion in 1960, the provision had not been included. The draft stated: "The conditions and limits of liability of state institutions for injury caused by the improper official acts of their officials in the sphere of administration and judicial activity are to be established by USSR and Union-Republic legislation." [76]

The advocates of a clear statement of governmental liability in the general principles were not daunted, however, even by what might have seemed like a political rebuff to the group sentiment expressed at the 1959 meeting. The provision was criticized from almost every side by eminent legal writers, and the drafters were taken to task: "The compilers of the draft of the Principles should listen to the voice of the wide scientific public and of authoritative practicing jurists and radically change their approach to the liability of governmental institutions for injury caused by administrative acts." [77] A group article by distinguished civil law writers suggested the following formulation: "Governmental institutions are liable on the basis of the general [tort] principles for injury caused by the improper official acts of their officials in the area of administration and judicial activity, except in cases provided for by USSR legislation." [78]

When the final version was adopted as article 89 of the Principles in December 1961, the battle was shown to have been won only in part. While

[75] Tolstoy, *O proyekte osnov grazhdanskogo zakonodatel'stva Soyuza SSR i Soyuznykh Respublik (Concerning the Draft of the Principles of the Civil Legislation of the Soviet Union and Union Republics)*, Pravovedeniye No. 4, p. 33, at 44 (1960).

[76] Draft: *Principles of Civil Legislation of the USSR and the Union Republics*, art. 75, Sov. gos. i pravo No. 7, p. 3, at 17 (1960). An English translation of the draft appeared in 12 C.D.S.P. No. 34, pp. 3-10 (1960).

[77] Tolstoy, *supra* note 75.

[78] Ioffe, *et al.*, *O proyekte osnov grazhdanskogo zakonodatel'stva, (Concerning the Draft of the Principles of Civil Legislation . . .)*, Sov. gos. i pravo No. 2, pp. 93, 101 (1961). Note particularly their suggestion that any exceptions to the general principle could only be made by federal legislation. This additional safeguard was not included in the final draft, although in some other articles, *e.g.*, article 91, federal control of exceptions was provided for. In an article commenting on the final version, Savitskaya reiterates the need for federal legislation on the question of liability of legal organs, where the article reads only "provided by law." The planned inclusion of provision for liability in such cases in the RSFSR Civil Code would indicate that federal legislation will not be forthcoming (*infra* note 80), although writers continue to stress the need for uniformity (*infra* note 134).

the essential principle was recognized, it was severely limited. First, only citizens were given a right to compensation.[79] Second, the provision excepted the activities of organs of the legal system—ironically, the very source of original pressure for increased liability.[80]

A balance sheet is hard to establish at the present time. Certainly there is a potential basis for increased protection of individual rights, but the Soviet jurists have been silent as to just what interpretation will be given to crucial terms in the provision. What are "official" acts, what acts are "improper," as well as what administrative remedies will have to be pursued before judicial action is appropriate,[81] all remain to be elaborated. So far, the author has discovered no cases interpreting the provision, and an authoritative book-length commentary on the Principles simply restates the wording of the provision, without interpretation of any kind.[82]

While the Principles make no specific provision for a right of recovery by the government institution held liable against the official who caused the injury, this was provided for even under old law and will undoubtedly be continued.[83]

"ARTICLE 90. LIABILITY FOR INJURY CAUSED BY A SOURCE OF INCREASED DANGER

"Organizations and citizens whose activity involves increased danger to those in the vicinity (transport organizations, production enterprises, builders, possessors of automobiles, and the like) are required to compen-

[79] Savitskaya, *supra* note 53, at 50, interprets the provision to mean that organizations also got the same "right," but that the statute requires a special procedure to be set up for asserting such claims.

[80] Provisions on liability of the organs of the legal system are likely to appear in the republic codes. The RSFSR draft code is reported to contain a provision providing for liability for certain acts of legal organs if they are found to have been committed intentionally or by gross negligence. Boldyrev, *O proyekte grazhdanskogo kodeksa RSFSR (Concerning the Draft of the Civil Code of the RSFSR)*, Sov. gos. i pravo No. 8, pp. 15, 23 (1962). The suggestion that this liability should be provided for in a federal statute to insure uniformity continues to be advanced. See note 134 *infra.*

[81] Under some of the old exceptions, cited note 70 *supra*, redress was by administrative action. One Soviet writer has assumed that under the new Principles, claims may in all cases be taken directly to the courts. Savitskaya, *supra* note 53, at 50. Recent trends in adjudication of labor disputes and workers' injury claims, discussed at note 102 *infra*, give reason to expect, however, provision for some kind of preliminary administrative decision and/or review, and a requirement that these remedies be first exhausted.

[82] IOFFE & TOLSTOY 163. The article by Savitskaya, *supra* note 53, is much more detailed, but still stops short of elaborating just what would constitute typical situations in which to invoke the new liability.

[83] The liability for full reimbursement provided under the old act may be continued, even though an ordinary worker in such case would have the benefit of a limitation to one-third of his salary, unless his acts constituted a crime. A suggestion to this effect is made by Savitskaya, *supra* note 53, at 52. See the general discussion on reimbursement under art. 88, para. 2, *supra.*

sate for injury caused by the source of increased danger, unless they show that the injury arose as a result of irresistible force or the intent of the injured party."

The parallel provision of the present RSFSR Civil Code reads:

"Individuals and enterprises whose activities involve increased danger for those in the vicinity, such as railways, tramways, industrial establishments, dealers in inflammable materials, keepers of wild animals, persons erecting buildings and other structures, etc., shall be liable for the injury caused by the source of increased danger, unless they prove that the injury was caused by irresistible force or the intent or gross negligence of the injured party." [84]

The Principles thus continued without substantial change the institution of strict liability for those whose activity involves increased danger to others.[85] The criteria are now, however, oriented towards the activities of the persons, rather than the specific things employed. While it would appear that the defense of contributory negligence has been dropped, it has merely been shifted to the omnibus provision in article 93.

The fact that the institution of strict liability has been carried over in this basic reformulation of general principles of liability presents one of the paradoxes of Soviet tort law. In a society where public responsibility for the individual's welfare is a dominant theme, it would seem natural to place at least the unavoidable risks of modern mechanized society on society as a whole, rather than on a blameless individual or production unit. Accidental injury from the hazardous operations of railroads, construction machinery, automobiles, etc., might well be compensated through tax-supported programs. Even compulsory liability insurance programs for the owners of such sources would convert the onus of absolute liability into an obligation to pay premiums. To the author's knowledge, however, there is no liability insurance available in the Soviet Union to spread the burden imposed on the individual auto owner [86] or the transport or production organization.[86a]

While it can be said that this constitutes an ordinary business cost, and is spread by being passed on to the consumer through the price of the

[84] CIVIL CODE art. 404.

[85] The new wording makes it clear that governmental institutions as well as individual citizens and enterprises are to be subject to strict liability, though this had already been held to be true through broad interpretation of the old provision. 2 ORLOVSKIY 383.

[86] Recent tourists entering the Soviet Union in their own cars have been offered liability insurance by the State Insurance Agency, but this does not seem to be available to Soviets.

[86a] There are limitations on the burden itself, principally through the defenses of contributory conduct on the part of the injured party, irresistible force, and the exemption from any strict liability for employers whose extra-hazardous sources inflict injury on their employees. See discussion under arts. 91 and 93, *infra*.

product or service, this is an effective argument only where the liability is imposed on an institution aimed at end profits. It is not a satisfactory rationale for liability from municipal snow-clearing activities, or from the cautious operation of the private automobile. In the case translated at the beginning of this article, the full burden of compensation was imposed on the public transportation unit, with only the possibility of reimbursement from a bicycle-owning peasant, and then only if fault on his part could be shown.

The rationale often advanced, that this increased liability is justified as a stimulation for persons who control such sources of increased danger to observe the rules of operation of such equipment and to take all possible measures to improve the safety of the operation,[87] ignores the fact that this purpose would be accomplished by a rule which allowed a person to show that he had used the utmost caution in employing his source of increased danger, *i.e.*, a rule which would exclude liability for mere accident.

In article 404 of the RSFSR Civil Code, the sources of increased danger listed were held by the courts to constitute examples rather than an exhaustive list, and the courts added such important sources as automobiles.[88] While the new list in article 90 is built on types of activity, *e.g.*, transport, certain traditional specific sources which have been omitted, such as wild animals and inflammable materials, are still within the meaning of the new provision according to the Soviet writers.[89]

It is important to note that these sources or categories of activity will not always be considered extrahazardous. It is possible that injury may be caused by a car when it is not engaged in its hazardous activity of moving at high speeds. If someone shuts his hand in the door of the car, this does not come within article 90. "An empty truck is a source of increased danger only if it is moving, while a steam engine presents a danger if it is under steam, even though not moving." [90]

Who is the "possessor" of the dangerous source for purposes of liability? While there has been some doctrinal controversy, the generally accepted view now is that "possessors" should be held to include persons using sources of increased danger as owners or on the basis of some other civil-law relationship, *e.g.*, a property rental contract.[91] Employees using such sources

[87] See, *e.g.*, Fleyshits, *supra* note 53.

[88] 2 Orlovskiy 377. While giving every auto accident victim a recovery without proof of fault may seem drastic to us, a similar solution (though with some limitations not yet recognized in Soviet practice) has been adopted by statute or worked out by the courts in many civil law jurisdictions. For a description of the French and German schemes, see Ryan, Introduction to the Civil Law 122, 127 (1962).

[89] Ioffe & Tolstoy 162. In an earlier article Ioffe and others had said these should be specifically included. Ioffe, *et al.*, *supra* note 78.

[90] 2 Orlovskiy 377.

[91] *Ibid.* This includes an owner using it through his servant, and also seems to include use through someone who misappropriates the source (though perhaps only if the owner is at fault in allowing the misappropriation). See the *Lomov* case, *supra* note 57. Case law development is reviewed in a passage translated from an article by

are not included, however, so that a hired taxi driver who collides with another car incurs liability for his employer and not for himself under article 90.[92]

The possessor may relieve himself of liability only by showing that the injury has been brought about by an irresistible force,[93] or as the result of the intent or gross negligence of the injured party, discussed under article 93 *infra*.[94]

This is an area in which there is likely to be a good deal of development in the coming years.[95] The liability imposed is a heavy one, and unless liability insurance intervenes to equalize the burden, it would not be surprising to see either a limitation imposed on the basic principle or a modification of the recovery pattern.[96]

Dobrovol'skiy, *Novoye v sudebnoy praktike po delam o vozmeshchenii vreda (New [Developments] in Court Practice in Cases of Compensation of Damage)*, Sots. zak. No. 8, p. 59 (1960), HAZARD & SHAPIRO pt. 3, at 86. For the resolution in practice of the complicated problem between organizations using each other's equipment, see 2 IOFFE 481.

[92] The bus driver in the translated lead case of the article incurred no strict liability for himself. 2 ORLOVSKIY 378 points out that he probably incurred no direct liability at all, even if at fault, for even where there seems to be a clear element of fault on the part of the employee, the strict liability of the employer has been held to be the exclusive ground available for recovery. *E.g.*, Collective Farm v. Okuneva, [1959] Sov. yus. No. 3, p. 83, Case No. 4, (Presid. R.S.F.S.R. Sup. Ct. 1958), HAZARD & SHAPIRO pt. 3, at 85. As to his liability to reimburse his employer if he was at fault, see discussion under art. 88, para. 2, *supra*. There is no limitation to use within the scope of the servant's employment. Lomov, *supra* note 57, and Ministry of Foreign Affairs Motor Pool v. Collective Farm, [1960] Sov. yus. No. 12, p. 26, Case No. 2, (Civ. Coll. R.S.F.S.R. Supt. Ct.), HAZARD & SHAPIRO pt. 3, at 86.

[93] See generally the excellent article by Matveyev, *O ponyatii nepreodolimoy sily v sovetskom grazhdanskom prave, (On the Concept of Irresistible Force in Soviet Civil Law)*, Sov. gos. i pravo No. 8, p. 95 (1963). Ioffe states that this defense is rarely encountered in practice. 2 IOFFE 480. In the lead case, *supra* note 1, and in the *Lomov* case, *supra* note 57, the court held in effect that intervening wrongdoing by a third party was not such a force.

[94] As to whether a defendant can relieve himself of liability by showing that there is no specific regulation prohibiting what he did, the answer is clearly "No". His fault is not at issue, and there is no "lawful activity" clause as under article 88 from which the argument could be developed. The general conclusion of "unlawfulness" of the conduct follows from the fact of liability. See notes 26 and 59 *supra*.

[95] Some variations in the pattern of liability have been made in special statutes. Article 101 of the new USSR Air Code continues the provision of article 78 of the old Air Code imposing even the risk of *force majeure* upon the airline. The only defense is the intent or gross negligence of the injured party. There is a translation in HAZARD & SHAPIRO pt. 3, at 87. A limitation on liability is provided in the provisions of articles 157 and 158 of the Ocean Navigation Code. While ships would normally be counted as sources of increased danger, liability in the case of collision of ocean ships is made to depend on fault. There is an English translation in 4 LAW IN EASTERN EUROPE 23, 56 (1960).

[96] It is possible for the courts to give relief in specific cases of hardship under the general equitable power to reduce tort recoveries after consideration of the means of the defendant, discussed below under article 93, though this is hardly a satisfactory substitute for insurance protection from either party's point of view.

"ARTICLE 91. LIABILITY FOR INJURING OR CAUSING THE DEATH OF A CITIZEN FOR WHOM THE PERSON WHO CAUSED THE INJURY IS REQUIRED TO PROVIDE INSURANCE COVERAGE

"If a worker is disabled or otherwise injured in the course of his work through the fault of the organization or citizen required to make state social insurance payments in his behalf, such organization or citizen must compensate the injured party for the injury insofar as it exceeds the amount of assistance payments received by him or any pension awarded to and actually received by him after the injury to his health. Exceptions to this rule may be established by USSR legislation."

This article purports to establish a separate pattern of tort liability for the insuring employer, *i.e.*, for the party who provided insurance coverage for an injured claimant.[97] In effect, however, it seems merely to limit his liability to cases where there is fault on his part, and the same result could have been obtained by including under article 90 a clause to the effect that an employer has no strict liability toward his employees when they are injured by an extrahazardous source under his control.

As the article states, an enterprise or an individual citizen (who may employ a maid, chauffeur, secretary, etc.) whose employee is injured in connection with the performance of his work is liable only if the employer was at "fault," just as under the ordinary principles of liability of article 88. This continues in effect article 413 of the RSFSR Civil Code, which provided for liability in cases where "the injury is caused by a *criminal act or omission* on the part of the person making the payments." (Emphasis added.) While the substitution of "fault" for "criminal act or omission" may seem to be a major increase in the scope of employers' liability, court practice had already reduced this requirement to one of simple "fault." [98]

[97] To the effect that the corresponding provision of prior law should be viewed as setting up independent bases for recovery, see 2 ORLOVSKIY 387. In most writing, a separate section is devoted to personal injury claims with these special provisions as the basis for discussion. In fact, some courts took the position that since the tort recovery "supplements" the pension payments, no tort recovery should be allowed where no right to a pension was recognized, while other supreme courts took the contrary view. See Anan'yeva & Laasik, *Ob obyazatel'stvakh voznikayushchikh vsledstviye prichineniya vreda (Concerning the Obligations Arising in Consequence of the Causing of Damage)*, Sov. gos. i pravo No. 3, p. 101, at 103 (1961). Perhaps this separate treatment of employers' liability was what led to the apparent claim in some cases that the employment relationship alone furnished a basis for recovery in tort. See, *e.g.*, Barmotin, [1963] Byul. verkh. suda S.S.S.R. No. 5, p. 7 (Plenum U.S.S.R. Sup. Ct.), where the lower court had imposed liability on that basis without any finding of fault in a case where a worker was injured on his way home from work. An apparently similar lack of causal relation and fault was present in the suit brought in Neff, [1963] Byul. verkh. suda R.S.F.S.R. No. 6, p. 4 (Civ. Coll. R.S.F.S.R. Sup. Ct.). The claims were finally rejected, but the fact that they were brought at all and had to go through so many levels of courts testifies to the confusion which exists.

[98] The Ioffe-Tolstoy commentary takes the position, at 167, that this new language is a significant expansion of liability. The standard text states clearly, however, that even

Far from expanding the employer's liability, the Principles are perpetuating the exemption of the employer from strict liability toward his employees, a position which has been vigorously attacked by Soviet writers.[99] Absent a showing of fault, the employee must content himself with his social insurance recovery, which is usually less, and sometimes nowhere close to, full compensation.[100] A nonemployee injured by the same source has a right to *full* compensation without any showing of fault.

The rationale given is that industries do not employ people to work with ultradangerous sources who are not competently trained, so that there is no need for the strict liability.[101] A more satisfactory rationale might be the fact that this is some compensation to employers for the burden imposed on them to pay for comprehensive social insurance benefits for workers—insurance which covers the strict liability situations, but which in addition provides benefits even for sickness or injury which has no relation to their work.

Since January 1, 1962, the supplemental portion of a worker's recovery —that part based on the fault of the enterprise, has been subjected to preliminary determination by the plant administration and review by the local trade union committee.[102] Only in the event that either party is dissatisfied with the disposition of the claim by these bodies is it to be brought to the people's court. This procedure, which also applies to claims by dependents,[103] should not be confused with a workmen's compensation board award. This

under pre-Principles law "civil fault in the infliction of the injury on the part of the person providing insurance is sufficient for liability to be imposed on him under article 413 of the Civil Code." 2 Orlovskiy 287. See to the same effect Dobrovol'skiy, *supra* note 91. Court practice in recent years does in fact appear uncertain as to the standard. For example, the old "criminal" standard was repeated by the USSR Supreme Court Plenum even in 1962. Azarov, [1962] Byul. verkh. suda S.S.S.R. No. 4, pp. 28, 29 (Plenum U.S.S.R. Sup. Ct.). In 1961 the same test was applied by the RSFSR Supreme Court Presidium in a case where no liability was found, Guba, [1961] Byul. verkh. suda R.S.F.S.R. No. 4, pp. 2, 3 (Presid. R.S.F.S.R. Sup. Ct.), but in a more recent case the Civil College of the same court held there was liability in a case where a worker was placed in dangerous work while in poor health, apparently a case of simple civil "fault." Krylov, [1962] Byul. verkh. suda R.S.F.S.R. No. 4, p. 2 (Civ. Coll. R.S.F.S.R. Sup. Ct.).

[99] Ioffe, *et al., supra* note 78. Evidence of continued pressure for change even after the rebuff through readoption of the old rule in the Principles is found in the letter to the editor by Khvostov answered by Maleyin in Sov. gos. i pravo No. 4, p. 138 (1963).

[100] See the example cited in note 5 *supra.* Note that provision is made for exceptions to this pattern by USSR legislation, continuing past practice. Ioffe & Tolstoy 167.

[101] 2 Orlovskiy 387.

[102] Decree on Procedure for Settling Disputes Concerning Payment of Damages by Enterprises . . ., [1961] Ved. verkh. sov. S.S.S.R. No. 41(1076), item 420. There is an English translation in Hazard & Shapiro pt. 3, at 95. The ruling of Dec. 14, 1961, of the USSR Supreme Court Plenum implementing this decree is in [1962] Byul. verkh. suda S.S.S.R. No. 1, p. 8.

[103] *Infra* under para. 2 of this article.

is merely an introduction of mandatory direct negotiation between the parties, followed by an appeal to a trade union committee, before the possibility of "judicial" determination of the same "tort" claim.[104] The basis of liability, the fault of the employer, remains the same, as does the scope of recovery.

The effect of the scheme of compensation for work injuries is, then, that the worker does get the benefit of workmen's-compensation-type quick recovery for part of his claim through social insurance. He is then allowed to get full recovery if he can prove a formal tort claim based on fault. This part of his claim, however, is subjected to an administrative decision and to the possibility of trade union committee review as outlined above before it gets into the regular courts.

From our point of view, the lack of discussion of the possibility of making the workmen's-compensation-type recovery a substitute for ordinary tort liability is perhaps the most significant feature of the compensation picture. Most of the Soviet literature has taken the opposite tack; it has criticized the continuation of the strict liability exemption, and would establish a triple possibility of recovery for industrial injuries: social insurance, fault liability, and strict liability for injury caused by an extrahazardous source.

> "*In the event of the death of an injured party, there is a right to compensation on the part of persons unable to work who were dependent for support on the deceased, or who had at the time of his death the right to receive support from him, and also on the part of children of the deceased born after his death.*"

This last part of article 91 of the Principles gives an independent right of recovery for wrongful death to two groups of persons: first, those who are unable to work and who were, in fact, dependent on the deceased at the time of his death, *i.e.*, those whom he chose to support; and second, those who at the time of his death were entitled to be supported by him, even though they were not in fact receiving support, including children of the deceased born after his death. These people have an independent right of recovery based on the amount of support they were in fact receiving or the amount of support to which they were entitled.

The provision of the old Code was more limited: "Art. 409. In the event that death is caused by an injury, the right to compensation belongs to the persons who had been supported by the deceased and who have no other means of support." By judicial practice, however, a right to compensation

[104] For example, in a case where the administration declined to grant a recovery, the worker took his case to the factory trade union committee and was also unsuccessful. He then brought his tort suit in the people's court as he would have done before the new system. After hearings in the rayon court, the civil college of the oblast' court, the presidium of the oblast' court, the Civil College of the Supreme Court of the RSFSR, and finally the Presidium of the Supreme Court of the RSFSR, he got his recovery. Lebedev, [1963] Byul. verkh. suda S.S.S.R. No. 5, p. 46 (Presid. R.S.F.S.R. Sup. Ct.).

was recognized in persons who, although not in fact dependent upon the deceased, had by operation of law a right to receive means of subsistence from him, *i.e.*, minor children, and disabled and indigent parents.[105]

It is significant that under the new provisions, persons have a right to support without regard to their means. This carries out the general idea of the article that tort recoveries should not be limited to cases of actual need. As pointed out above in relation to the basic right of the employee, the difference-money tort recovery in industrial accidents is subject to being reduced only by the amount of pensions being received because of this accident, and is independent of the general income of the injured party.[106]

In all of these cases the amount of compensation is determined according to the portion of the deceased's wages which in fact went for the maintenance of the dependent or to which an entitled person would have had a right.[107] As in the case of recovery by the deceased, the amounts of any social insurance pensions which these persons receive in connection with the death of the deceased are to be deducted from any recovery against the tortfeasor. Children retain the right to compensation until they reach 16, or if they are still in school, until they reach 18.[108]

"ARTICLE 92. LIABILITY FOR INJURING OR CAUSING THE DEATH OF A CITIZEN FOR WHOM THE PERSON WHO CAUSED THE INJURY IS NOT OBLIGATED TO PROVIDE INSURANCE COVERAGE

"If a person is disabled or otherwise injured by an organization or citizen not obligated to make state social insurance payments in his behalf, such organization or citizen must compensate the injured party for the injury according to the rules of Articles 88 and 90 of these Principles, insofar as it exceeds the amount of assistance payments received by him or any pension awarded to and actually received by him after the injury to his health.

"In the event of the death of the injured party, there is a right to compensation on the part of those persons mentioned in the second paragraph of Article 91 of these Principles."

This article taken together with article 91 may be read as providing the basis for all tort recoveries for causing the injury or death of a citizen. As pointed out above, however, article 91 simply limits the employer's liability

[105] 2 ORLOVSKIY 393.

[106] Text accompanying note 48 *supra.* It is only with regard to the means of the *defendant* that the recovery can be reduced. See discussion under art. 93, para. 2 *infra.*

[107] In a recent case under the Principles it was held that all who are entitled to support are in effect necessary parties, and that even though they have not joined in the original action, they must be brought in and their shares determined in order to allocate the recovery property. Uvarova, [1962] Byul. verkh. suda R.S.F.S.R. No. 12, p. 2 (Civ. Coll. R.S.F.S.R. Sup. Ct.).

[108] 2 ORLOVSKIY 393. *E.g.*, Veselova, [1962] Byul. verkh. suda S.S.S.R. No. 6, p. 35 (Plenum U.S.S.R. Sup. Ct.). No. 6, 35 (1962).

to cases where normal fault can be shown, and the present article says that where the person who causes the injury is not one who pays insurance premiums, then the general rules apply, *i.e.*, articles 88 and 90.[109]

The only real significance of the article is the inclusion of what amounts to a wrongful death provision parallel to the one in article 91. Taken together, they provide for an independent right of recovery for persons within the protected group in all cases where the deceased would have had a recovery had he lived.

"Article 93. Account To Be Taken of the Fault of the Injured Party and the Means of the Person Who Caused the Injury

"*If gross negligence of the injured party contributed to or increased the extent of the injury, then the amount of compensation for such injury is to be reduced or denied entirely, taking into consideration the degree of fault of the injured party (and where there is fault on the part of the person who caused the injury, the degree of his fault as well).*"

This is in effect a reformulation of the court practice under existing law. The RSFSR Civil Code provided in article 403 that a person who caused injury was "absolved from liability if he proved . . . that the injury arose as a result of the intent or gross negligence of the person injured."

It quickly became apparent that the clause either applied only where the injury was wholly caused by the injured party, in which case there would be no liability anyway, or relieved the tort-feasor of all liability if the requisite fault or intent of the victim contributed to the injury, the effect we give to contributory negligence. The court chose to introduce a scheme of comparative negligence rather than to apply the provision literally.[110] The rules to be applied in cases where careless conduct of the injured party partially caused or aggravated the injury were restated in the basic ruling on tort law of the USSR Supreme Court of June 10, 1943:

"Para. 12. Where it is established by the facts of the case that the injury occurred not only as a result of improper acts of the person who caused the injury, but also as a result of the gross negligence or gross carelessness of the injured party himself, the court may, applying the

[109] Some important problems regarding the employer's liability are not mentioned in this section or under the general provisions. Under prior law, it was held that an employer could not exculpate himself through a clause in the labor contract putting his responsibility for careful observation of proper work standards on the employee. Feoktistov v. Lumber Combine, [1960] Sov. yus. No. 7, p. 27, Case No. 3 (Civ. Coll. R.S.F.S.R. Sup. Ct.). Hazard & Shapiro pt. 3, at 93. The independent contractor status is recognized, however, and if such a relationship is found to exist it is proper to include an appropriate exculpatory clause. Mokshin, [1962] Byul. verkh. suda R.S.F.S.R. No. 4, p. 3 (Civ. Coll. R.S.F.S.R. Sup. Ct.).

[110] Gsovski points out that the Tsarist courts faced a similar problem and arrived at the same conclusion. 1 Gsovski 518.

principle of mixed liability, impose upon the person who caused the injury the duty of partial compensation for the injury in accordance with the degree of fault of each party." [111]

In practice, however, it seems that the courts have not usually undertaken the kind of sophisticated comparison of fault called for by the Supreme Court's ruling, as well as by the similar language in the Principles.[112] In most cases the court has simply made a finding of "mixed fault" and then proceeded to assess 50 per cent of the damages found against the defendant.[113] This is particularly inappropriate in view of the fact that the Soviet law did not and still does not under the new Principles recognize simple fault as a basis for deduction.[114] Since it is only gross negligence which will reduce the recovery, in any case where only simple negligence on the defendant's part is proved and mixed liability is applied, it would seem appropriate to assess less than 50 per cent of the proved damages against the defendant. Practice to date is probably a good indication, however, of the difficulty of weighing simple negligence against gross negligence, or strict liability against gross negligence, and no amount of additional guidance in the republic codes will help to solve the problem.[115]

"The court may reduce the amount of compensation for injury caused by a citizen after taking into consideration his means."

The RSFSR Civil Code contained a provision to the effect that "in determining the amount of compensation to be awarded for an injury, a court in all instances must take into consideration the property status of the party injured and that of the party causing the injury." [116] Under the Principles there is now to be no such comparison, and it is the property position of the tort-feasor alone (along with the fault or intent of the injured party) which may be considered by the court as grounds for reducing the recovery.

[111] Reprinted in DOZORTSEV 804, 807.

[112] For example, in Zernov v. Factory, [1960] Sov. yus. No. 6, p. 84 (Civ. Coll. R.S.F.S.R. Sup. Ct.), HAZARD & SHAPIRO pt. 3, at 82, the court simply states that both parties were "negligent," and indicates no attempt to determine the *degree* of fault of either party.

[113] 2 IOFFE 500. *E.g.*, Takhtambetov, [1961] Byul. verkh. suda S.S.S.R. No. 5, p. 21 (Plenum U.S.S.R. Sup. Ct.).

[114] See cases cited in 2 IOFFE 499.

[115] For example, in Kosartsev v. Auto Transport Office, [1960] Sots. zak. No. 11, p. 86 (Presid. Kustanay Prov. Ct.). HAZARD & SHAPIRO pt. 3, at 83, the court rejected the application of the idea of mixed liability entirely. The driver of the truck in which the plaintiff was riding was speeding (and intoxicated) at the time of the accident, and the court said that the lower court could not consider as grounds for a possible reduction the fact that the plaintiff was negligent in riding in the back of the truck instead of in the cab with the driver.

[116] CIVIL CODE art. 411. Practice under this provision is discussed in 2 ORLOVSKIY 39[?]

A practice not too different from the new provision had already developed in prior law, for the courts had long held that the means of an organization should not be considered under the provision quoted above.[117] This meant that in many cases it was only the means of the citizen tort-feasor which were to be considered. A statutory provision based on the same idea was written into Labor Code article 83, limiting recovery against an employee who damaged his employer to one-third of his salary,[118] except where his acts constituted a crime. Even this full liability where the acts constituted a crime was made subject to the means test by a 1954 ruling of the USSR Supreme Court Plenum,[119] so that in effect the rules now embodied in the Principles in article 93, that the size of the recovery should be determined with regard to the comparative degree of fault and the means of the tort-feasor, had already been widely applied.[120]

It is still too early to say whether this provision might lead to a pattern in Soviet tort cases of frequently awarding less than full compensation. It seems unlikely that it will have so broad an application, for the basic provisions in the Principles are inspired generally by the desirability of imposing liability for fault in order to encourage careful conduct. It might be invoked, however, to relieve the heavy burden of strict liability in extreme cases.

"ARTICLE 94. REIMBURSEMENT CLAIMS

"*Organizations or citizens who are liable for injury caused by them are required to reimburse on demand the organs of social insurance or social security for assistance payments or pensions paid by them to persons mentioned in Articles 91 and 92 of these Principles.*

"*In the event of a reduction in the size of compensation for injury (Article 93 of these Principles), the size of the reimbursement is reduced accordingly.*"

[117] Ruling of the USSR Supreme Court Plenum of June 10, 1943, reprinted in DOZORTSEV 804, 807.

[118] The ease of the recovery provides some compensation for the limitation, for the employer is allowed to deduct the amount directly from the employee's pay without suit. *E.g.*, Kuvaltsov, [1962] Byul. verkh. suda R.S.F.S.R. No. 12, p. 2 (Civ. Coll. R.S.F.S.R. Sup. Ct.). For the procedure if the employee objects to the amount withheld, see para. 2, Ruling of the USSR Sup. Ct. Plenum of Dec. 18, 1961, [1962] Byul. verkh. suda S.S.S.R. No. 1, pp. 12, 13.

[119] Ruling of May 28, 1954, reprinted in DOZORTSEV 810, 811. See, *e.g.*, Pochuyev and Ogorodnikov, [1961] Byul. verkh. suda R.S.F.S.R. No. 1, p. 12 (Presid. R.S.F.S.R. Sup. Ct. 1960). The Plenum reminds the lower courts once again (as it has in the 1943 ruling) that of course article 411 is to be applied in all other cases.

[120] In a 1960 ruling, the Plenum reemphasized the application of the general principle in cases of injury to kolkhoz property by individual members. [1960] Byul. verkh. suda S.S.S.R. No. 3, p. 11. (These claims are not considered to be employer-employee disputes, but ordinary tort actions which must be brought in the ordinary courts. Nikiforov, [1962] Byul. verkh. suda R.S.F.S.R. No. 12, p. 1 (Civ. Coll. R.S.F.S.R. Sup. Ct. 1961). In Korostyleva, [1962] Byul. verkh. suda R.S.F.S.R. No. 11, p. 14 (Civ. Coll. R.S.F.S.R. Sup. Ct. 1961), the appellate court chided the lower court for not looking into the question of the defendant's means on its own initiative.

This article gives to an insurance agency a right to reimbursement from the tort-feasor to the extent that the agency has made payments to the injured party or his dependents. The formulation is not a particularly happy one. The first paragraph seems to say that if the person who caused the injury is liable at all, then there is a right to full reimbursement on the part of the insurance agency, *i.e.*, that no reduction for mixed liability or limited means is to be made, as would be done in the tort recovery. This was in fact what some courts allowed under the similar provision of the old law,[121] so the second paragraph has been tacked on to make it clear that this was not the result intended. It might have been better simply to say that an agency which has made a payment because of an injury caused by *X* is subrogated to the extent of its payments to whatever claim the injured party may be found to have against X. This would make it clear that all of the possibilities for reduction under article 93 were to be applied in the reimbursement action.

Such a formulation would also help to clarify the ambiguity created by articles 91 and 92, and by the language of this section, as to the nature and scope of the injured party's claim. On the one hand, under the language of article 91, it would seem that there is a certain preemption of the ordinary liability provided for under article 88, *i.e.*, that there is no claim against the tort-feasor on the part of the injured party up to the amount of his insurance recovery. He has a right to the insurance payments without regard to the source of his injury, and then a limited tort right to recover the difference between this amount and his full damages.[122] In other words, he has no "claim" for the amount of the insurance to which the insurance agency could be subrogated, and it is therefore necessary in article 94 to reintroduce a quasi-tort liability plus all the normal defenses in order to define properly the scope of the "reimbursement" recovery.[123] On the other hand, articles 91 and 92 seem to assume a full claim on the part of the worker which is reduced by subsequent insurance payments if and when received. Since the insurance agency's right is only for reimbursement of sums actually paid, subrogation would then seem to be the appropriate way to describe this right to reimbursement. Article 94 might better have provided simply for the transfer to the insurance agency, at the time a payment is made, of any claim the injured party might have up to the amount of the payment.

It should not be overlooked that the recovery pattern laid down by this

[121] IOFFE & TOLSTOY 169.

[122] In effect this interpretation supports the theoretical position of some writers, mentioned in note 97 *supra*, that this is an independent scheme of liability.

[123] The recovery pattern is in fact complicated by the practice of deciding reimbursement suits against organizations in Gozarbitrazh, *i.e.*, the arbitration tribunals for disputes among governmental and production units, instead of in the ordinary courts. See Order of the Presidium of the USSR Supreme Court of July 27, 1959, in [1959] Ved. verkh. sov. S.S.S.R. No. 30, p. 163.

article eliminates any liability "insurance" effect of the social insurance program so far as the industrial enterprise is concerned. It bears full liability for all injuries caused by its fault, and simply pays part of the damages direct to the employee and part to the social insurance agency.[124] The "insurance" payments are in effect a tax on the employer to provide benefits for sickness and accidental injury for which the employer would not be liable. They are not used to provide the kind of workmen's compensation recovery which relieves the employer of ordinary tort liability.[125]

Conclusion

The tort provisions of the Principles show that familiar problems will, for the most part, be solved in familiar ways in the new Soviet tort law about to take shape in the civil code of each republic. Fault liability has been retained, and a significant expansion in the area of application of tort law may result from the provisions for broad governmental liability under article 89.

Some of the "changes" in the 1922 Code provisions made by the new Principles constitute merely a recodification of the extensive changes introduced by the courts as conditions and legal thinking changed over the years.[126] Others resolve doctrinal controversies or clarify provisions which had given rise to varying interpretations in practice.[127]

Some of the questions left unanswered by the Principles will be covered in the more detailed provisions of the republic codes, while others will only be worked out in practice after the codes are adopted. For example, there are no provisions in either the tort chapter or the general sections of the Principles relating to the liability of infants and others with limited capacity. Provisions in some detail on this topic are contained, however, in the as-yet-unpublished draft of the new RSFSR Civil Code,[128] including a pro-

[124] Employers receive some relief through being exempted from strict liability toward their workers (see discussion under art. 90, *supra.*).

[125] See the discussion on this point following note 104 *supra.*

[126] Other examples of this type of "change" would be the wrongful death recovery of persons having a right to support under articles 91 and 92, and the addition of the automobile as an extrahazardous source under article 90.

[127] *E.g.*, the *respondeat* provisions of article 88, paragraph 2, the substitution of "organizations" for "enterprise" in article 91, and the reimbursement provisions of article 94, paragraph 2.

[128] Boldyrev, *O proyekte grazhdanskogo kodeksa RSFSR (Concerning the Draft Civil Code of the RSFSR)*, Sov. gos. i pravo No. 8, p. 15, at 23 (1962). Under existing law, liability of those with limited capacity is divided into two categories. *Incompetents*, including infants under 14 and adults who have been declared incompetent, are not liable for their torts, though the persons responsible for their supervision (parents, guardians, director of an insane asylum) may be liable if they can be shown to be at fault in failing to exercise proper supervision. 2 Ioffe 487. Minors from 14 to 18 are liable for their torts. Civil Code art. 9. There is, in addition, a joint liability with the latter on the part of their guardians, although Ioffe cites a case where a court thought it might be appropriate to relieve parents of this joint liability. 2 Ioffe 490. According to Boldyrev, RSFSR Minister of Justice, the RSFSR draft provides that "schools and

vision relieving a person under the influence of alcohol or drugs of liability unless he was responsible for getting himself into that condition.[129]

One interesting question which will probably not be covered in the republic codes but will have to be worked out in practice is that of the duty to rescue life or property. While article 131 of the 1936 USSR Constitution establishes a universal duty to protect and strengthen common socialist property, and article 130 summons all citizens to render assistance in those situations in which common socialist property and the life, health, or property of another is endangered, no general provision for civil liability for a breach of this duty has ever been enacted or applied in court practice.[130] The Principles contain no provision for such liability, but they do provide for an obligation to reimburse a person who does in fact rescue socialist property, and even broader compensation provisions covering saving of life as well as property have been included in some republic code drafts.[131] There is no indication that the codes will go so far as to provide explicitly for liability for failure to rescue, however, and the courts will probably have to work out in practice the scope of the duty and the recovery for its breach.[132]

The area of governmental tort liability will undoubtedly continue to receive a good deal of attention in the near future. The additional provisions of the RSFSR Civil Code draft providing for liability of organs of the legal system, an important area sidestepped by the Principles, have already been discussed above, and it is possible that additional statutory regulation may be forthcoming. The major question will be, however, the patterns of recovery that the courts work out under the general liability provisions. This area of contact between the courts and the "official" acts of government is bound to be a sensitive one, and the actual recoveries allowed will be watched with

medical institutions are liable for harm done by infants under their control, unless they show it did not occur through any fault on their part. The liability of parents and guardians for harm done by minors without sufficient means of their own to make compensation ends when the minor reaches majority or when he acquires sufficient means." Boldyrev, *supra* at 23. While this only hints at the content of the general provisions, it at least indicates that the subject of tort liability of incompetents and minors will be covered in some detail in the forthcoming code, and will contain some modifications of present practice.

[129] Boldyrev, *supra* note 128, at 23.

[130] While the standard text recognizes the basis for liability under the general tort provisions, it is quick to add that "under Soviet conditions suits of this nature are singular occurrences." 2 ORLOVSKIY 397. They are so singular that no case or authority is cited for the statement advocating liability.

[131] Fleyshits & Makovskiy, *Teoreticheskiye voprosy kodifikatsiyi respublikanskogo grazhdanskogo zakonodatel'stva, (Theoretical Questions of the Codification of Republic Civil Legislation)*, Sov. gos. i pravo No. 1, pp. 79, 91 (1963).

[132] For an excellent discussion of this problem in Soviet law, see Hazard, *Soviet Socialism and the Duty To Rescue*, in XXTH CENTURY COMPARATIVE AND CONFLICTS LAW: LEGAL ESSAYS IN HONOR OF HESSEL E. YNTEMA 160-71 (Nadelmann ed. 1961).

great interest by all countries interested in developing "legal" sanctions for harm inflicted by governmental acts.

Some expansion in the scope of the personal injury recovery, probably through court practice, seems to be likely, and it is possible that there will be some satisfaction of the pressure for something like strict liability for injuries to employees caused by extrahazardous sources. This may come about through modification of the tort rule, or may be effected simply by increasing the level of social insurance benefits for job-connected injuries generally to the point where they approximate full compensation.

The whole question of strict liability is likely to be re-examined to some extent. Either some restriction will be imposed on the liability or the scope of recovery in line with European patterns, as mentioned above, or liability insurance will be introduced to spread the heavy risks of accidental injury now imposed on the individual citizen or the governmental or production unit.

These and the problems to be worked out in other areas of Soviet law call for serious discussion by legal writers, and the most important question of the immediate future will be whether the climate of relatively free discussion in which the Principles were adopted will be maintained. As was pointed out above, there has been some tendency on the part of Soviet writers to return to a passive role now that the Principles have been adopted,[133] and the temptation will be even greater once the republic codes are enacted.[134] It is probably too much to expect real criticism from Soviet legal

[133] Ioffe, one of the leading civil law writers, for example, authored with others a very incisive critical article during the discussion of the draft. The article made among others five specific suggestions in the tort area—federal control over exceptions to the principle of governmental tort liability, inclusion of liability of organs of the legal system, inclusion of certain items in the list of extrahazardous sources, removal of the strict liability exemption from the employer, and the inclusion of federal principles governing liability of incompetents and minors—which were described as "necessary," "extremely desirable," or "shown to be necessary by prior practice." Ioffe *et al.*, *O proyekte osnov grazhdanskogo zakonodatel'stva Soyuza SSR i Soyuznykh Respublik (Concerning the Draft of the Principles of Civil Legislation of the Soviet Union and Union Republics)*, Sov. gos. i pravo No. 2, p. 93, at 100 (1961). All of these suggestions were rejected in the final version of the Principles. In Ioffe's authoritative commentary on the tort provisions of the Principles (Ioffe & Tolstoy 159) there is no mention of the fact that there had ever been any controversy over these provisions. While this may seem at least less than scholarly to a Western jurist, it is typical of much of Soviet writing over the past 40 years, and is an example of how much favorable light has been shed on the quality and quantity of critical thinking in Soviet legal circles by the discussion of the Principles.

[134] One of the most vigorous post-Principles debates has centered on the many problems of federalism raised in connection with the enactment of republic codes and related federal and republic legislation. The picture of interlocking USSR and republic legislation presented by the Principles' constant references to laws and procedures to be established at one or the other level (or both, *e.g.*, "limited legal capacity of minors is to be established by federal and union republic legislation." Art. 8) is far from specific or complete. In the process of drafting the codes and implementing legislation, the wisdom of some of these provisions themselves seems to have been questioned as it was

writers of some of the basic policy decisions discussed above, but we may at least hope that the fact that prominent writers took strong positions opposing some of the provisions of the Principles which were subsequently enacted in spite of this opposition [135] will be taken as an indication of the possibility of honest academic discussion, and not of the futility of reasonable criticism. There is some evidence that they have not been entirely discouraged, for serious discussion has continued over the provisions of the republic codes, and there has even been some continued criticism of certain of the provisions of the Principles.[136]

Practice has not yet been significantly affected by the Principles, for it will not be until the republic codes go into effect that real interpretation by the courts will be possible. The crucial test of whether the recodification process will result in improvement in the law as applied, or will merely change the statutes, is still to come. While the Principles constitute a good beginning, much will depend on the solution of other problems which affect the application of the rules in practice,[137] and the kind of people who will be attracted into the legal system in the years to come.

in the pre-Principles discussions. See the emphasis on the desirability of more uniformity than required by the Principles in connection with the capacity provisions (discussed in note 128 *supra*) in Fleyshits & Makovskiy, *supra* note 131, at 83. They also stress the need for uniformity in provisions for tort liability of the organs of the legal system. *Ibid.* To the same effect, see Savitskaya, *Otvetstvennost' gosudarstvennykh uchrezhdeniy za vred, prichinennyy deystviyami ikh dolzhnostnykh lits (The Responsibility of Government Institutions for Damage Caused by the Actions of Their Officials)*, Sov. gos. i pravo No. 8, pp. 48, 52 n.8 (1962).

[135] See note 133 *supra.*

[136] See notes 99 and 134 *supra.*

[137] The most crucial of these is the continued uncertainty injected into the judicial process by the possibility of "review" and reversal *ad infinitum* of what appear to be final decisions. Protests by a prosecutor or the head of a superior court regarding a decision often result in a given case being heard six or eight times, as illustrated in the labor case cited note 104 *supra.* From the point of view of the parties involved, not to mention the legal writers commenting on the decisions, the certainty of the new statutory provisions is outweighed by the hazards of the judicial process. Perhaps the eventual elimination of the political insecurity which probably provided the justification for this elaborate control mechanism in early practice, coupled with an increasing supply of higher quality personnel with better training for the legal system, will lead to a decision in the not too distant future in favor of increased security of decision.

LAW AND THE DISTRIBUTION OF CONSUMER GOODS IN THE SOVIET UNION

BY ZIGURDS L. ZILE *

I. Introduction

TO CONCEDE THAT in the Soviet Union production for further production continues to take precedence over production for consumption is not to say that the consumption aspect of the Soviet economy is insignificant. Recent reports from the Soviet Union are virtually unanimous in asserting that the Soviet consumer is better off today than at any time since the revolution.

General amelioration of conditions began almost immediately upon the little-lamented passing of Stalin on March 5, 1953. Already in the second quarter of that year the volume of retail trade increased by 23 per cent. The turn was so sudden as to suggest, at first, that stocks of consumer goods were released purely for political ends—presumably to preserve popular stability in the short run.[1] But even after the struggle for power and leadership had subsided, trade in consumer goods continued to expand, albeit at a somewhat lower rate. A pattern of progressive improvement has remained. Instead of being held to fixed low consumption norms, the Soviet consumer is now given a chance to participate in a relatively constant share of a growing national product.[2] In 1962 the retail turnover in state and cooperative trade amounted to 86,300,000,000 rubles or 6 per cent over the previous year. The total was slightly more than 50 per cent of the national income, which also had added a 6 per cent increment over the same period.[3] Furthermore, the people have an opportunity to spend their incomes on consumer goods of an ever-increasing variety.

The current Soviet policies of resource allocation still give an edge to heavy industry, and recently the consumption of several basic necessities (especially foodstuffs) has been curtailed. Still, there is no evidence that the relative position of consumers is being deliberately subverted. Khrushchev has promised "to achieve in the coming 20 years a living standard

* *ZIGURDS L. ZILE. A.B. 1956, LL.B. 1958, LL.M. 1959, University of Wisconsin; Fellow, Russian Research Center of Harvard University, 1959-61; Associate Professor of Law, University of Wisconsin.*

[1] Goldman, *The Soviet Standard of Living, and Ours*, 38 Foreign Affairs 625, 626 (1960).

[2] Hearings Together With Compilation of Studies Prepared for the Joint Economic Comm., 87th Cong., 2d Sess., Dimensions of Soviet Economic Power 351-52 (Comm. Print 1962).

[3] Pravda, Jan. 26, 1963, p. 2.

higher than that of any capitalist country and to create the necessary conditions for achieving an abundance of material and cultural values." [4] And although at times it seems that in the Soviet Union the magnitude of future promises is directly proportional to the depth of present failures,[5] one can nonetheless discern a strong ideological commitment to raising the people's standard of living. There are also weighty practical reasons that militate against indifference toward the levels and patterns of consumption. Ever since the early "left-wing" notion of uniform rewards for all participants in the economic process was scrapped as unfeasible, the Soviet economy has functioned with the help of a system of incentives based on sharp disparity between the distributed shares of the social product. Nothing indicates that a system of this kind has ceased to be indispensable under Soviet-type socialism. In fact, instead of talking of its abandonment, the Soviet leaders extol its virtues and advocate its further expansion in those areas of economy where performance has been poorest, notably in agriculture. Of course, incentive pay without opportunities for converting the hard-earned rubles into desired goods and services would be mere ostentation. Finally, quite aside from any doctrinal tenets or pressure of economic realities, it is not inconceivable that the present Soviet leaders wish to be not only feared but also liked and accepted as beneficent rulers. Perhaps they too feel an occasional urge to bestow on their people gifts that can be enjoyed today and are not mere assurances of a good life generations from now.

When consumption was confined to the barest necessities and transactions between distributors and buyers were conducted on a simple cash-and-carry basis, there was little room for the development of a law of consumer trade. The Civil Code,[6] to be sure, contained numerous articles brooding over the intricacies of offer and acceptance, passage of title, incidence of fortuitous losses, and many other problems, but they intrigued neither the sellers nor those who were queuing up before the stores. How-

[4] Khrushchev, *Report on the Program of the Communist Party of the Soviet Union*, published as 2 DOCUMENTS OF THE 22ND CONGRESS OF THE CPSU 83 (1961).

[5] Erro, *And What of the Consumer?*, 12 Problems of Communism No. 6, p. 34 (1963).

[6] The USSR is a union (federation) of 15 union republics (states). The republics have their own codes of civil and criminal law and procedure. Since the codes vary little from republic to republic, it is customary to cite the codes of the RSFSR as representative "Soviet" codes. In this article, unless otherwise indicated, all references to codes are to the codes of the RSFSR: Civil Code (1922), Code of Civil Procedure (1923), Criminal Code (1960). The high degree of uniformity is achieved through federally enacted guiding "Principles" of law. This article cites the Principles of Civil Law of the USSR and the Union Republics (1961). At present, the civil codes of the 1920's are being rewritten to conform to the 1961 Principles.

As this issue was going to the printer, the RSFSR adopted its new Civil Code and the Code of Civil Procedure, which will go into effect on October 1, 1964. A quick examination of some of the provisions relating to trade in consumer goods did not reveal any striking innovations.

ever, the recent changes in the economic climate and the greater emphasis on the consumption aspect have shown a need for new institutions and procedures. As a result, a body of consumer trade law has been in the making over the past decade. A good part of it concerns the organization and internal functioning of an expanding network of planning, distribution, and service agencies and is thus, to use a Western category, essentially "public law." At the same time, several revitalized or newly introduced devices of "private law" [7] have accompanied the coming of durable consumer goods—guarantees of quality, sales on installment credit, and rentals of automobiles, to name a few. Judging by what has happened so far under the new policies, any further advances in the direction of consumer prosperity should necessitate a still greater reliance on legal regulation of the relationships between agencies which distribute and service the goods and the people who acquire and use them, as well as the relationships between the consumers themselves. A simple increase in the numbers of available items, for instance, should be expected to lead to more disputes over quality; a greater volume of credit sales should entail more defaults; sales and rentals of progressively more complex mechanical and electrical gadgets should lay the groundwork for something along the lines of products liability.

The Soviets disagree. As a rule, they vehemently deny any inability on the part of their system to reduce drastically (if not to eliminate completely) the relative share of defective goods. Consequently, they do not envision a greater role for "private law" on account of mushrooming contract and tort liability traceable to defects in design and manufacture or failures properly to warn and instruct. Furthermore, they challenge the proposition that the defaults on credit sales would probably remain at least at the present rate and that, therefore, they would be more numerous in absolute terms. They insist that dishonesty and irresponsibility in meeting just obligations are alien to the Soviet people, and that the infrequent manifestations of such conduct are being effectively eradicated from the Soviet scene as "pernicious vestiges of the past."

Occasionally the same ultimate conclusion is reached by a different course of reasoning, as the Soviet legal theoretician, Alekseyev, has done in a recently published monograph.[8] It is a pity that this otherwise fascinating piece of work too is an exposition of faith rather than a product of

[7] The use of these terms in Soviet context can be misleading. Soviet legal doctrine denies the dichotomy of public and private law. In the civil law sense, private law governs relations between private persons *inter sese*. Such relations in the Soviet Union are relatively insignificant. I have expanded the concept of private law to include all relations in which at least one of the parties directly involved is an individual.

[8] ALEKSEYEV, GRAZHDANSKOYE PRAVO V PERIOD RAZVERNUTOGO STROITEL'STVA KOMMUNIZMA (CIVIL LAW IN THE PERIOD OF ALL-OUT CONSTRUCTION OF COMMUNISM) (1962).

responsible research into social and economic facts. According to Alekseyev, law, as a means of controlling consumer relations, will not rise in stature. Indeed, it is bound to lose much of its present limited function. He reiterates the promise of affluence but stresses that it will not be enjoyed through personally owned property. The growth of personal property will be kept "within reasonable bounds," lest it become an end in itself. Eventually, declares Alekseyev, individuals will own, besides some provisions and wearing apparel, only a handful of attributes of the good communist life, such as, books, barbells, and balalaikas.[9] Of course, during the current phase of "all-out construction of communism" material incentives will remain intact, and consumer goods will be supplied in ever greater quantities. He predicts, however, that simultaneously vast segments of civil law relationships will fall into disuse, as various needs are met through central allocation. In one way or another, things capable of producing income and thus not fitting comfortably within the category of personal property,[10] will be removed from personal ownership. Alekseyev intimates that the very extensive "private law" relations which surround personally owned housing will perhaps be the first to fall victim to massive socialization. As more and more public housing is provided, the various transactions relative to construction, leasing, and transfer of personal houses will wither away. Moreover, when the new apartments are equipped with such innovations as built-in closets,[11] kitchen appliances and other conveniences, including furniture, purchases of these items (as well as arrangements for moving and servicing them) by individual citizens will drop. The enjoyment of most other major consumer items will likewise be based on principles of rental rather than ownership. By implication, the bulk of civil law relations involving individuals will take the form of sundry leases with the state.

For these reasons, one who sets out to examine the legal machinery of Soviet consumer trade is confronted with an ambiguity. The increased activity of Soviet lawyers in dealing with problems concomitant to the increased flow and wider use of consumer durables is presented by doctrinal diatribes as a mere prelude to an inevitable atrophy of law. However, the available evidence does not support a conclusion that speculations about life under communism are actually backed by conscious deeds.

[9] Alekseyev includes "books, musical instruments and personal sporting equipment" among "articles of importance for individuals." *Id.* at 193.

[10] "Citizens may personally own property intended for the satisfaction of their material and cultural needs. . . . Property that is personally owned by citizens may not be used for the derivation of unearned income." PRINCIPLES OF CIVIL LAW art. 25. The Principles are translated in 7 LAW IN EASTERN EUROPE 263 (Szirmai ed. 1963).

[11] It is not clear whether the decision to have built-in closets was made before or after discovering that the old bulky wardrobes could not be lugged into the new tight apartments.

Soviet consumers continue buying things and calling them their own. Undoubtedly they expect to go on doing the same indefinitely. Alekseyev himself warns that

> "[T]he question of personal property cannot be resolved in isolation from the actual economic conditions. A premature banning of personal property may hamper the efforts at satisfying the citizens' needs and undermine the principle of material incentive. Inasmuch as over the next twenty years compensation in accordance with [quantity and quality of] work will remain the principal means for raising the level of citizens' well-being, there should be no experimentation with unjustified constraints in the area of personal property law." [12]

This paper presents a description and analysis of the organizational structure of Soviet trade in consumer goods, transmission of consumer demand to producers, devices for shaping consumer demand, protection of buyers' interests, in particular with respect to the quality of service and merchandise, and the extent and function of illicit private trade.

II. The Organizational Structure of Soviet Trade in Consumer Goods

The main branches of Soviet economy, including trade, are hierarchically organized, with the government and the party constantly endeavoring to strike a politically and economically acceptable balance between direction from the top and initiative at the lower levels. The individual hierarchies, of course, do not exist as isolated organisms, but function in coordination with other hierarchies to the tune of a single national economic plan. Description of these hierarchies and their interrelationships is an especially ungrateful task for at least two reasons. The component agencies possess both governmental and nongovernmental powers and responsibilities, so that any attempt to discuss their economic operations thoroughly is destined to be overwhelmed by details regarding state bureaucracy and party machinery. Secondly, the organizational structure is overhauled so often that it is almost impossible to come to comprehend the impact of a series of previous changes before new variations are announced.

Partly out of timidity to face the difficult task squarely and partly because of a preconceived analytical framework, I have decided to present the material on the organizational structure in two segments. This section provides only a rather formal view of trading by the state and tells something about the status and peculiarities of cooperative and private trade. A further look at the socialist (*i.e.*, state and cooperative) sector in action

[12] ALEKSEYEV, *op. cit. supra* note 8, at 199-200.

is postponed to the section on "Transmission of Consumer Demand to Producers." [13]

After a series of recent reorganizations, the State Committee of Trade of the Council of Ministers of the USSR is, at the moment, the top agency in the area of consumer commodity circulation.[14] It coordinates the work of all other agencies engaged in the distribution of consumer goods: ministries of trade of the 15 union republics, other ministries and departments conducting trade,[15] and the Central Union of Consumer Cooperatives *(Tsentrosoyuz)*. The Committee investigates consumer demand, makes suggestions concerning output of needed goods and discontinuation of lines for which there is no demand, studies modern merchandising techniques and promotes their adoption, and proposes legislation on matters of domestic trade. Through its Chief Administration of Interrepublic Deliveries, the Committee plans and supervises shipments of selected important goods across republic boundaries, in accordance with the national economic plan, to satisfy certain countrywide needs.

Distribution of goods produced within a republic and not destined to points outside its territory, as well as goods received by a republic from the outside, is, as a rule, the responsibility of the ministry of trade of the republic.

A. State Trade

Most of the trade network is state-owned and operated.[16] In 1962 state trade accounted for 66.8 per cent of the total volume of retail trade.[17]

Typically, a republic organizes [18] its trade network into trading systems *(torgovyye sistemy)*, each specializing in related lines of products. A system, in turn, is made up of wholesale trading organizations *(optovyye torgovyye organizatsiyi)* and retail trading organizations *(roznichnyye torgovyye organizatsiyi* or *torgy)*. Wholesale trading organizations, sometimes called offices *(kontory)* or administrations *(upravleniya)* of whole-

[13] See text pp. 230-40 *infra*.

[14] Edict of Dec. 7, 1962 (U.S.S.R.), [1962] Ved. verkh. sov. S.S.S.R. text 520, approved by Law of Dec. 13, 1962 (U.S.S.R.), *id.* text 529, art. 1. Struyev was appointed to head the Committee. Edict of Dec. 26, 1962 (U.S.S.R.), [1963] Ved. verkh. sov. S.S.S.R. text 5.

[15] Pharmacies and medical supply stores are run by the Ministry of Health; bookstores, by the Ministry of Culture; and newsstands, by the Ministry of Communications. There are also workers' stores (*orsy*) attached to some industrial plants and the "red PX system" of the Ministry of Defense.

[16] Including both wholesale and retail facilities.

[17] PAVLOV, SOVETSKAYA TORGOVLYA V SOVREMENNYKH USLOVIYAKH (SOVIET TRADE UNDER CONTEMPORARY CONDITIONS) 37 (1962).

[18] The description of Soviet state trade network is taken mainly from PAVLOV, *op. cit. supra* note 17, at 66-68 and EKONOMIKA SOVETSKOY TORGOVLI (ECONOMICS OF SOVIET TRADE) 55-59 (1962).

sale trade, are in the main directly subordinate to the ministry of trade of the republic; some are under the wings of various ministries or committees of procurement and the councils of national economy *(sovnarkhozy)*.[19] They operate shipping *(vykhodnyye)* and purchasing warehouses *(torgovo-zakupochnyye bazy)* located in the proximity of centers of production, and sales warehouses *(torgovyye bazy)* located in districts of consumption. In addition to channelling goods to retail outlets within their geographical areas and trading systems, the republic offices of wholesale trade engage in exchange of goods between regions and republics, make goods available for export, allocate imported goods, etc. Unlike the wholesale trading organizations, only relatively few retail organizations are directly subordinate to the republic ministry of trade.[20] The soviets of territories, regions, districts, and cities have set up administrations or sections of trade within their executive committees. Most retail trading organizations are adjuncts of these lower echelon administrative units.[21] Ordinarily a retail trading organization embraces several outlets, or stores, which actually conduct business with customers. Organizations whose outlets engage in public catering are known as dining-room trusts *(tresty stolovykh)* or restaurant trusts *(tresty restoranov)*. Both stores and catering establishments go under the generic name of "trading enterprises" *(torgovyye predpriyatiya)*.

Each state trading organization has a charter defining the scope of its activities (*e.g.*, trade in foodstuffs, manufactured goods; wholesale, retail) and endowing it with a juristic personality.[22] As a juristic person it is entitled to possess separate property, acquire rights and assume obligations and sue and be sued.[23] An organization so constituted must operate in accordance with the principle of economic accountability *(khozraschyot)*. Having been originally allocated certain fixed and working capital, the organization is expected subsequently to work so as to make its income exceed the outgo. It answers for its obligations with its own resources. The state is not responsible for the obligations of state organizations which are juristic persons and, conversely, the organizations cannot be held for the obligations

[19] *Sovnarkhozy* are responsible for the operation of workers' stores at industrial plants. *Cf.* note 122 *infra.*

[20] Thus the Ministry of Trade of the RSFSR has Chief Administrations for trade in resorts *(Glavkurorttorg)*, railway restaurants *(Glavdorrestoran)*, and mail order sales *(Posyltorg)*. Two wholesale outfits conduct retail trade as well—*Roslesstroytorg*, in forest products and building materials, and *Rosyuvelirtorg*, in jewelry.

[21] *E.g.*, R.S.F.S.R. Const. arts. 92, 96, 99; Uzbek S.S.R. Const. arts. 90, 93, 96. "The chief officials of the trade organizations serve as the commercial representatives in the regular governmental body at each administrative level. The city trade organization is represented by its director on the municipal council or city soviet." Goldman, Soviet Marketing: Distribution in a Controlled Economy 28 (1963).

[22] State trade organizations are still formally regulated by Decree of Aug. 17, 1927 (U.S.S.R.), [1927] Sob. zak. i raspor. S.S.S.R. text 502.

[23] Principles of Civil Law art. 11.

of the state.[24] One should be cautious, though, not to carry the private enterprise analogy too far. Whereas the principle of economic accountability encourages businesslike management of an organization, the opening of a new establishment is not necessarily prompted by business considerations. A local soviet is not to be likened to a group of potential investors scanning the economic horizons for an opportunity to make a killing. Their decision to open a store, a restaurant, or a repair shop will not be an economic one. They may do it because they are genuinely conscientious, or because they simply execute a mandate of the party or the government, or because they wish to impress their superiors.[25]

While the legal status of trading organizations is, on the whole, uniform, the same cannot be said about trading enterprises.[26] Some of them are fully on economic accountability and enjoy juristic personality, others use only a system of internal cost accounting and are not juristically independent participants in the economic process. The enterprises which are not juristic persons do not, for instance, conclude contracts in their own name. Such contracts, when needed, are made by the juristic person which comprises them.[27]

A trading organization or enterprise is headed by a single person—a director, who combines the functions of a representative of a juristic person with those of a state official. By transactions within the charter powers of the organization or enterprise its director creates and extinguishes various rights and duties on behalf of the entity. On the other hand, his managerial activities must conform with directives of the superior governmental units as well as all general laws and regulations in force. As a state official, an "organization man, filling a slot in an industrial bureaucracy,"[28] the director is personally responsible for the administration of the sector of the economy entrusted to him through the device of economic accountability,[29] and may incur civil, administrative, or even criminal liability for any acts of mismanagement.[30]

[24] *Id.* art. 13.

[25] *Cf.* BUDARAGIN, EKONOMICHESKIYE SVYAZI TORGOVLI S PROMYSHLENNOST'YU (ECONOMIC TIES BETWEEN TRADE AND INDUSTRY) 130 (1963).

[26] Genkin, *Aktual'nye voprosy pravovogo requlirovaniya sovetskoy qosudarstvennoy torgovli (Current Problems of Legal Regulation of Soviet State Trade)*, Sov. gos. i pravo No. 8, p. 39, 40-41 (1961).

[27] PRAV. REG. GOS. TORG. SSSR (LEGAL REGULATION OF STATE TRADE IN THE USSR) 34-36 (1957).

[28] GRANICK, THE RED EXECUTIVE 318 (1960).

[29] "In the modern Soviet system, the establishment is indeed a separate unit and feels itself to be such, even though it has very few powers of independent decision. This is largely because, although deprived of such freedoms, it has had responsibility squarely thrust upon it." WILES, THE POLITICAL ECONOMY OF COMMUNISM 34 (1962).

[30] PRAV. REG. GOS. TORG. SSSR 40-41.

B. Cooperative Trade

The statistics for 1962 show that cooperative trade accounted for a substantial portion—28.8 per cent—of the total volume of retail trade.[31] But the figure is really quite meaningless. As a result of a series of restrictive enactments,[32] the consumer cooperative system has been reduced virtually to the status of the rural branch of the state network of retail trade. In urban centers, the outlets of consumer cooperatives are used mainly to sell farm produce received from peasant households (both collectivized and noncollectivized) or collective farms *(kolkhozy)*, on a commission basis.[33]

Since January 1, 1958, when collective farm families and most other people living on farmland in rural areas were freed from compulsory deliveries of specified quantities of farm products to the state, the volume of produce available for commission sale has been limited only by the producers' own needs or their desire to use alternative avenues of disposal. The commission contract *(dogovor komissiyi)* is governed by provisions of the Civil Code, [34] insofar as they have not been superseded by special laws or regulations.[35] From a common law point of view, it resembles a contract creating a bailment (consignment) relationship between a principal and agent, the latter being known as a factor or commission merchant. The Conditions of Commission Sales require cooperatives to accept all products "of good quality" offered to them by growers.[36] A written contract is made describing the products and specifying a time for delivery, an approximate term for realization, sale price, and the manner of settling accounts.[37] If the sale is to take place within the local administrative district, the grower gets his money within three days following the sale. For produce accepted in inter-district trade, the cooperative advances 50 per cent[38] of the stipulated sale price within two days after the receipt of either the products themselves or shipping documents, and settles the balance within three days after the realization of the products.[39] The cooperatives are inclined to calculate the expected price as the mean figure between the lower retail

[31] PAVLOV, *op. cit. supra* note 17, at 41.

[32] Especially Decree of Sept. 29, 1935 (U.S.S.R.), discussed in BLANK, OSNOVY TEORIYI I ISTORIYI POTREBITEL'SKOY KOOPERATSIYI (FUNDAMENTALS OF THE THEORY AND HISTORY OF CONSUMER COOPERATIVES) 151-52 (1963).

[33] Commission sales were inaugurated by Decree of Oct. 12, 1953, (U.S.S.R.) art. 43, ISTOCH. SOV. GRAZH. PRAV. 647 (1961).

[34] Arts. 275 a-y.

[35] Such as the Conditions of Commission Sales approved by the Ministry of Trade of the USSR, May 22, 1954, ISTOCH. SOV. GRAZH. PRAV. 648.

[36] Art. 2.

[37] Art. 4; CIVIL CODE art. 275b. A form contract has been used by the *Tsentrosoyuz* since 1955. 2 SOVETSKOYE GRAZHDANSKOYE PRAVO (SOVIET CIVIL LAW) 221 (1961).

[38] *Compare* GOLDMAN, *op. cit. supra* note 21, at 43 (75%).

[39] Conditions of Commission Sales art. 11.

price fixed by the government and the higher price prevailing on the vestigial free market—the so-called collective farm market, which I shall discuss next. Barring administrative modification, government prices are stable. Consequently, the prices inserted in commission contracts vary solely because of fluctuating "market conditions"; a strange extension of the interplay of market forces in a socialist economy.[40] If by reason of a downswing in market or danger of spoilage the cooperative agent is unable to obtain the stipulated amount, the products may be sold at a reduced price, without the cooperative becoming liable for the difference, provided, however, that necessity is proved in the manner prescribed by law.[41] The grower is obligated to pay the cooperative a commission pursuant to a schedule established by the *Tsentrosoyuz*,[42] and to assume all expense of moving the produce to the place of realization.[43] Although the goods after their delivery to the cooperative remain the grower's property, the cooperative is liable for their loss or damage to them, unless it proves that the loss or damage resulted from circumstances which it could not prevent by the exercise of due diligence.[44] The requirement that the agent exonerate himself contrasts with the American rule, which shifts the burden of proving fault to the principal after the agent has shown that the goods indeed perished in the alleged manner. But the difference is not due to a peculiarly Soviet appraisal of the inherent merits of the parties. In fact, the Soviet text very closely parallels the German Commercial Code.[45] And, of course, today it would be impossible to apply a class point of view to a transaction between two cooperatives (i.e., a consumer cooperative and a collective farm) or a cooperative and a small individual producer.

Formally, most rural householders hold one share each in the cooperative system, and each one is entitled to rebates, the total amount of which must not exceed 20 per cent of total profits. However, as I pointed out earlier, the consumer cooperatives enjoy only a very incomplete autonomy. The *Tsentrosoyuz*, the highest organ of the cooperative system, works under the supervision of the State Committee of Trade; the trade plans of cooperatives are ultimately determined by the planning authorities of the state, their managers appointed in the same manner as directors of state trading organizations and enterprises, and their employees included in all statistics with state-employed persons.[46] The cooperatives must place the require-

[40] Goldman, *Commission Trade and the Kolkhoz Market*, 10 SOVIET STUDIES 136, 137-38 (1958). A more recent Soviet work states that the prices are set at 10 to 15% below the market. 2 SOVETSKOYE GRAZHDANSKOYE PRAVO (SOVIET CIVIL LAW) 224 (1961).

[41] Conditions of Commission Sales art. 6; CIVIL CODE art. 275-1.

[42] *Tsentrosoyuz* Regulations of Oct. 29, 1956, ISTOCH. SOV. GRAZH. PRAV. 650.

[43] Conditions of Commission Sales art. 9; CIVIL CODE arts. 275-g, 275-r.

[44] CIVIL CODE art. 275-i.

[45] Arts. 383-406.

[46] NOVE, THE SOVIET ECONOMY 41 (1961).

ments of the entire state and trade program above the immediate advantages of their membership. Whereas consumer cooperatives in Western countries strive to provide lower prices for their members, in the Soviet Union the prices charged at their rural outlets are some seven per cent above the comparable prices charged in cities. Since year-end rebates are an exception, the rural residents derive from their practically compulsory membership (there being no other stores around) little besides an increased tax burden.[47]

Cooperative trade has lost the stature it had in the early post-revolutionary period. At that time it constituted the almost exclusive machinery for the distribution of consumer goods. From the very beginning, though, the movement was mistrusted by the Communist Party. It was regarded as an embodiment of rival economic ideas and as a rallying point of elements hostile to the Soviet regime.[48] Only a lack of practicable alternatives compelled retention of the cooperative system in trade. Today, of course, trade through state establishments is an obvious alternative; still cooperatives have not disappeared, certainly not in name. Having been put under tight state control, they do not represent any kind of threat. They can be likened to a confidence scheme which, notwithstanding its transparency, has some exploitable potentialities.[49] For whatever it might be worth, the draft of the 1961 Party Program was amended to include the following sentence: "Consumers' cooperatives will be developed and used to improve trade in the countryside and to organize the sale of agricultural products." [50]

According to doctrine, the fact that cooperative ownership of property and cooperative economic efforts are considered socialist institutions,[51] will not save them at the arrival of full communism. At that point in history, they and state-owned property and state economic efforts are to merge into communist property and give rise to communist economic relations.[52]

C. Legitimate Private Trade

As a general proposition, trade by private persons has been a crime in

[47] Goldman, *op. cit. supra* note 21, at 37. There were about 42,000,000 members in 1962. Pavlov, *op. cit. supra* note 17, at 40.

[48] See the verbatim record of the debate at the 10th Party Congress, March 15, 1921, 1 Zile, Readings on the Soviet Legal Process Va: 1 (mimeo. 1962).

[49] "A greater role will be played by *co-operatives* . . . as a form of drawing the masses into communist construction, as media of communist education and schools of public self-government." 1961 Program of the Communist Party of the Soviet Union pt. 2, § III (2), translated in Soviet Communism: Programs and Rules 23 (Triska ed. 1962).

[50] *Id.* pt. 2, § 11(a).

[51] U.S.S.R. Const. arts. 5, 7.

[52] For an elaborate discussion of this thesis, see Sdobnov, Dve formy sotsialisticheskoy sobstvennosti i puti ikh sblizheniya (Two Forms of Socialist Property and Their Convergence) (1961).

the Soviet Union since 1932.[53] But the wrath of the law is directed against the private merchant—the middleman, whose activity is regarded as socially useless and therefore parasitic. By contrast, the small-scale private producer —the lone "nonexploiting" craftsman or the peasant working a small holding, either within or without the collective farm system[54]—may sell his wares, insofar as his operation is sanctioned by licensing or agricultural laws. As a possible safeguard against covert trade, some operations are licensed only on the condition that the customer provide the raw materials.[55] Not unlike the cooperative network, private trade was heavily relied on by the Soviets during the period of the New Economic Policy (NEP), 1921-1928, in an effort to restore the country's economy through the participation of private enterprise. Indeed, it was into trade that the rehabilitated entrepreneurs and their resources tended to gravitate. Notwithstanding the efforts of the Soviet government to channel private capital into industry and nonindustrial long-term investments, such as large apartment houses, the majority of investors found the high rate of capital turnover and the quick profits of trade more attractive.[56] This natural but, from the Soviet point of view, noncooperative, or even defiantly hostile, attitude of the business groups only seemed to confirm the dim view that the communists had taken of free enterprise.

Today the bulk of legitimate private trade is conducted by the rural population. The same 1932 decree which enjoined "the opening of stores and stalls by private traders" and urged the "use of every means for the eradication of second-hand dealers and speculators, who are striving to make profits at the expense of workers and peasants," declared that "trade by collective farms, collective farmers and individual toiling peasants is to be conducted at prevailing market prices." [57] The clear implication was that direct retailing of farm output by individual peasant households was permissible. With the food shortage in cities acting as a catalyst, these early marketing arrangements developed into the collective farm market system. Collective farm markets are maintained by the local authorities of trade in almost all densely populated places. As of December 1961, there were over 9,000 such

[53] See Decree of Nov. 10, 1932 (R.S.F.S.R.), [1932] Sob. ukaz. i raspor. R.S.F.S.R. text 385, amending art. 107 of the R.S.F.S.R. CRIMINAL CODE (1926). See text pp. 272-76 *infra*. There have been some strange exceptions to this law. *E.g.*, at least at one time bootblacks could buy and resell at a profit accessories to footwear. 1 GSOVSKI, SOVIET CIVIL LAW 351 (1948).

[54] The outer limits of permissive private enterprise are defined in U.S.S.R. CONST. arts. 7, 9, 10.

[55] For an interesting discussion of the licensing laws, see HAZARD, LAW AND SOCIAL CHANGE IN THE U.S.S.R. 9-12 (1953).

[56] MOROZOV, RESHAYUSHCHIY ETAP BOR'BY S NEPMANSKOY BURZHUAZIEY, 1926-1929 gg (THE DECISIVE STAGE IN THE STRUGGLE AGAINST NEPMEN BOURGEOISIE) 10-11 (1960).

[57] Decree of May 20, 1932 (U.S.S.R.) arts. 9, 10, ISTOCH. SOV. GRAZH. PRAV. 421.

markets throughout the Soviet Union.[58] A few years ago, Moscow, for example, had at least 30 such markets.[59] A director appointed by the local trade authorities administers the market, enforces compliance with the regulations of the market place, including pricing and sanitary standards, and imposes administrative fines for their violation. Farm products may be sold by their producers at prices prevailing on the market. This, in practice, means prices set by them in the light of supply and demand. The sellers are only required to display price lists and, in addition, put price tags on their merchandise.[60] Of course, the interplay of truly free market forces is prevented by the existence of state outlets, sometimes on the same market place,[61] selling the same goods at administered prices which have little or no relevance to supply and demand. Generally, however, the "freely set" prices are above those charged in the state stores and stands. Two reasons have been assigned for this reversal of the common Western experience of farmers' market prices being lower. First, the state prices are too low for many scarce products. Second, the products supplied by individual growers are able to command a higher price because their quality is usually better.[62]

Apart from the farm folk who constitute the majority of sellers, the law makes the collective farm markets accessible also to urban inhabitants who do some farming on the side and to craftsmen licensed to market their output. They too are allowed to sell at "free" prices.[63]

Considering the primitiveness of the collective farm markets, the volume of trade[64] on them is quite large. In 1962, 4.4 per cent of the entire retail trade[65] and a considerably larger percentage of the trade in foodstuffs passed through the collective farm markets.[66] While the collective farm markets' relative share of the total retail trade has been steadily falling, its volume, in absolute terms, however, has declined less markedly.[67] The

[58] GOLDMAN, *op. cit. supra* note 21, at 47.

[59] Goldman, *Retailing in the Soviet Union*, Journal of Marketing, April 1960, pp. 9, 12.

[60] Decree of Feb. 4, 1936 (U.S.S.R.), 2 ZAK. AKTY NAR. KHOZ. SSSR 530 (1961); Model Rules of Trade on Collective Farm Markets of March 4, 1939 (U.S.S.R.), ISTOCH. SOV. GRAZH. PRAV. 422.

[61] Model Rules art. 3(a).

[62] Goldman, *supra* note 59, at 12. Frequently state stores cannot compete simply because they do not have enough produce to sell. See Ekonomicheskaya gazeta, July 6, 1963, p. 40.

[63] Model Rules arts. 3(c) & (d), 14.

[64] I assume that Soviet statistics do not include state and cooperative trade conducted on "collective farm market places" as "collective farm market trade."

[65] PAVLOV, *op. cit. supra* note 17, at 65.

[66] In 1961, 7.5% of all retail trade in foodstuffs went through the collective farm markets. NARODNOYE KHOZYAYSTVO SSSR V 1961 GODU: STATISTICHESKIY YEZHEGODNIK (THE NATIONAL ECONOMY OF THE USSR IN 1961: STATISTICAL YEARBOOK) 632 (1962).

[67] *Ibid.*

dwindling of the importance of the collective farm markets is attributable to several factors, among which the overall improvement and expansion of the network of state trade are perhaps the most significant. To the same effect are higher prices paid to agricultural producers by the state and the lifting of the one-time ban on the use of commission contracts by consumer cooperatives.[68] As a matter of fact, a decision to limit personal trading by collective farmers led to the Decree of October 12, 1953.[69] The act was to stem the diversion of farm labor force for tending small market stalls, often in faraway towns. Calculations showed that about 500,000 collective farmers were engaged in selling on the collective farm markets.[70] Expert opinion holds that, although the decree caused a further shrinkage in the "free" market, it had not been intended as a covert assault on the institution as such. It merely sought economies through a more rational division of labor and a somewhat more effective control over the doings on the collective farm markets.[71] For instance, a 1956 decree of the Council of Ministers of the USSR urges the councils of ministers of the union republics to encourage "the bringing of . . . [meat and milk products and eggs] to urban collective farm markets."[72] Similarly, the 1961 Party Program does not prognosticate the elimination of collective farm markets. Quite on the contrary, it asserts, in a sentence added to the draft version, that "collective farm markets will preserve their significance."[73] As long as the constitutionally recognized collective farm-garden plot economy is retained (and there is every indication that it will be around for some time to come), a machinery will be needed for channelling the output of many small producers to consumers. It would seem that individual collective farmers and noncollectivized growers will resort to the new scheme of division of labor only if their losses occasioned by lower returns from commission sales are outweighed by gains they can realize, during the time saved, from alternative income-producing pursuits. For an individual collective farmer, participation in the collective work of the farm (as contrasted to work on his garden plot) is the normal alternative. Ordinarily he will make up his mind in the light of the promise that the farm's incentive system holds out for him. If in his estimation the system is unsatisfactory, he will hesitate to give up those immediate advantages which can be secured by direct marketing.

Shortly before the 1932 law making private trade a crime, another law urged the use of "every means for the eradication of second-hand dealers

[68] The Model Rules art. 5 specifically outlawed commission sales by state and cooperative trading establishments.

[69] See note 33 *supra*.

[70] SCHWARTZ, RUSSIA'S SOVIET ECONOMY 435-36 (2d ed. 1954).

[71] Goldman, *supra* note 40, at 144.

[72] Decree of Oct. 25, 1956 (U.S.S.R.) art. 6, 2 ZAK. AKTY NAR. KHOZ. SSSR 535.

[73] 1961 Program of the Communist Party of the Soviet Union pt. 2 § II(a).

and speculators, who are striving to make profits at the expense of workers and peasants." [73a]

It is perfectly clear that this slogan-like provision was not intended to prevent Soviet citizens from reselling articles of consumption for which they no longer had any use. The phrase had in mind the business of private middlemen and not direct sales by consumers. To facilitate much needed redistribution of personally owned things, second-hand sales have been to some extent institutionalized. Article 3 of the Model Rules of Trade on Collective Farm Markets of 1939 [74] permits "the working people to sell their household articles on [collective farm] markets, at places specially designated for this purpose." However, the number and the monetary value of transactions of this kind are probably negligible. Resale of surplus property, when need arises, is far more conveniently accomplished through any of the state-owned commission stores put into operation in the mid-1930's.[75] Fundamentally, the legal framework of this form of trade resembles that of the subsequently introduced commission trade in agricultural products by consumer cooperatives.[76] The pricing provisions, however, deserve a special mention. Whereas the cooperatives are free to sell the agricultural products consigned to them at prices above the state retail prices and often approaching the "free market" prices, the prices of second-hand manufactured goods must be kept below the state retail prices charged by local stores for comparable articles when new.[77] Thus higher prices are tolerated when they encourage production, but not when they merely bring a windfall to a nonproducer. Evidently, the Soviets are disposed to forego the advantages obtainable through redistribution of some consumer goods, if in so doing they can keep down the number of opportunities for making "unearned income." This policy is also evidenced by the rule which permits registered craftsmen to sell their manufactures on collective farm markets at "free" prices.[78]

It seems that a considerable volume of consumer goods is redistributed through private second-hand sales outside the institutionalized channels. These transactions, in general, are governed solely by the pertinent provisions of the Civil Code and the new Principles of Civil Law. The law expressly states that "a sale by citizens of their property is carried out on the basis of prices established by agreement of the parties." [79] A commentary

[73a] Decree of May 20, 1932 (U.S.S.R.) arts. 9, 10, ISTOCH SOV. GRAZH. PRAV. 421.

[74] See note 60 *supra.*

[75] Decree of July 29, 1935 (U.S.S.R.), 2 ZAK. AKTY NAR. KHOZ. SSSR 533.

[76] Apparently the most recent Rules of Commission Trade through state commission stores are those of June 4, 1959 (R.S.F.S.R.), ISTOCH. SOV. GRAZH. PRAV. 645.

[77] Decree of July 29, 1935 art. 4; Model Rules art. 15; Rules of Commission Trade art. 6.

[78] Model Rules art. 14(b).

adds that "Soviet law severely punishes those who engage in speculation." [80] One may doubt, however, whether truly free agreement as to price operates even with regard to those transactions which lack the elements of speculation. While surely countless sales of scarce items have brought the private sellers high prices relative to the administered prices, most of these bargains have been performed voluntarily. In spite of article 36 of the Principles of Civil Law and article 117 of the Civil Code,[81] it cannot be said with certainty that Soviet courts would permit a seller to recover from a defaulting buyer an inflated price. The Soviet court might reason that the state retail price of comparable items represents the "true value" of the product and might view any attempt to recover an amount over and above the state price as a quest of surplus value. Such behavior, the court might say, is characteristic of life under capitalism but violates the rules of conduct in a socialist society. By analogy, taking (by individuals) of compensation for temporary use of furnishings or utensils, charging interest on money loans, and rendering personal services for pay are treated as departures from these socialist rules.[82]

Reports in the Soviet press indicate that profiteering through sales of personal property is widespread and, as long as the parties do not publicly discuss their dealings, virtually undetectable. Comprehensive state control over such transactions is unfeasible, but as the regulation of private sales of motor vehicles demonstrates, the state will intervene where high demand drives up the prices that individuals are willing to pay and the articles can be identified and traced.

In 1959, the Ministry of Trade of the RSFSR assured the readers of *Izvestiya* that "an automobile, like any other item, is the personal property of the owner, who is free to dispose of it at his discretion. He can sell, exchange or give away his automobile to whomever he wishes." To be sure, there were commission stores dealing in used cars, but nothing precluded an owner from selling his vehicle directly.[83] Within two years, however,

[79] PRINCIPLES OF CIVIL LAW art. 40.

[80] NAUCHNO-PRAKTICHESKIY KOMMENTARIY K OSNOVAM GRAZHDANSKOGO ZAKONODATEL'STVA SOYUZA SSR I SOYUZNYKH RESPUBLIK (SCHOLARLY AND PRACTICAL COMMENTARY ON THE PRINCIPLES OF CIVIL LAW OF THE USSR AND THE UNION REPUBLICS) [hereinafter cited as KOMMENTARIY] 194 (1962). See text pp. 272, 274 *infra* for definition of speculation.

[81] Art. 36 of the Principles of Civil Law: ". . . By damages is meant the expenditures made by the obligee, loss or damage to his property, and also income not received by the obligee which he would have received if the obligation had been fulfilled by the obligor. . . ."

Art. 117 of the Civil Code: ". . . Damage shall be deemed not only the positive loss to property but also loss of such profit as would occur under normal conditions of trade."

[82] ALEKSEYEV, GRAZHDANSKOYE PRAVO V PERIOD RAZVERNUTOVO STROITEL'STVA KOMMUNIZMA (CIVIL LAW IN THE PERIOD OF ALL-OUT CONSTRUCTION OF COMMUNISM) 215 (1962).

[83] Izvestiya, Nov. 27, 1959, p. 6.

the system was reappraised and revised. Since 1961, resale of automobiles by individuals must be conducted exclusively through state or cooperative stores, by means of commission contracts. The State Automobile Inspectorate will not register automobiles sold in any other way.[84] Immediately, the Soviet citizens reacted by displaying a commendable aptitude for evasion of the newly imposed restraints. By far the simplest device is to give an automobile away, as a gift, simultaneously receiving cash on the side. If deferred payments are intended, a written instrument is prepared showing the receipt of a money loan by the donee and containing a promise by the latter to repay it in stated installments.[85] Because a contract of donation *(dogovor dareniya)* for an amount in excess of one hundred rubles must be notarized,[86] there is an opportunity for official scrutiny of the transactions. In practice, however, this does not seem to amount to very much. The *mala fides* of the parties does not appear on the face of the instrument. The notaries, who are public officials, are urged to withhold certification until all surrounding circumstances have been investigated.[87] But perhaps in many cases they have neither any understanding of the problem nor the qualifications for making an effective inquiry. Some owners, instead of purporting to give away their automobiles, empower their secret buyers to use them over long periods of time, sometimes for as long as 10 years,[88] which should pretty well wear out an average "Moskvich." The transfer is accomplished by a notarially certified civil law *procuratio* [89] *(doverennost')*. Evasion of law by this device has been facilitated by carelessness of the notaries. According to article 268 of the Civil Code, the duration of a *procuratio* must not exceed three years. Consequently, an instrument providing for a longer term is void and certainly should not be certified.[90] This particular error occurs probably because article 268 appears in a little used part of the Code.

In case the parties resort to trickery in the extralegal phase of their transaction, and a dispute flares out into the open,[91] they both stand to lose

[84] ALEKSEYEV, *op. cit. supra* note 82, at 220. See also Decree of April 25, 1961 (Lith. S.S.R.) arts. 2, 5, 6, Sots. zak. No. 7, p. 85 (1961).

[85] Stepanova, *Udostovereniye sdelok s avtomashinami, prinadlezhashchimi k grazhdanam (Certification of Transactions Involving Automobiles Owned by Citizens)*, Sov. yus. No. 14, pp. 24-25 (1962). See also Kaznin, *Organy notariata na strazhe sotsialisticheskoyi zakonnosti (The Organs of the Notariat Guarding Socialist Legality)*, Sots. zak. No. 5, pp. 18, 19-20 (1963).

[86] CIVIL CODE art. 138. It is possible to conclude a gratuitous contract in Soviet law.

[87] See note 85 *supra.*

[88] *Ibid.*

[89] Express power to act conferred on an agent; when in writing, similar to our power of attorney.

[90] Laxity is not universal among Soviet notaries; some are so cautious that it is almost impossible to get them to certify a legitimate transaction. See note 85 *supra.*

[91] As where a party refuses to pay over the purchase money, once outside the notary's office.

a great deal. A private agreement made for the purpose of circumventing the laws against private sales of automobiles would probably be regarded by the courts as a transaction "concluded deliberately against the interests of the socialist state and society" [92] or "directed to the obvious detriment of the state." [93] If so, all the property affected thereby, that is, both the automobile and the purchase money, would inure to the state.[94] But "honesty in personal dealings, as distinct from cheating the law, is conspicuous in Russia." [95]

In the summer of 1963 the regulations governing the sales of automobiles were extended to heavy motorcycles (over 500 cc) with sidecars.[96] The classification probably was made because the income-producing capacity of the heavier machines caused demand for them far to exceed the available supply. The state stepped in to preclude profiteering through private sales.

Purchase-sale of consumer goods ordinarily takes the form of simultaneous performances, but fully or partly executory contracts also occur, both between individuals and between individuals and state and cooperative enterprises. Until May 1, 1962, the buyer of an individually described thing acquired ownership rights at the time of making the contract.[97] Neither nonpayment of the purchase price nor leaving the thing in the possession of the seller had any effect on the buyer's title. If the seller retained it after the time set for delivery had passed, the buyer could sue to recover it. The buyer seemed to have two kinds of civil actions available to him; he could sue either to vindicate his property rights [98] or to demand actual performance (specific performance) of the contract of purchase-sale.[99] The argument was made, however, that in Soviet law the same legal relationship could not be regulated in different ways. Accordingly, where the violation of property rights stemmed from nonperformance of a contractual obligation, the vindicative action was unavailable.[100] It is impossible to say whether there was more to this than a love of symmetry in legal doctrine. At any rate, the question has now been rendered moot by the new Principles, which

[92] PRINCIPLES OF CIVIL LAW art. 14.

[93] CIVIL CODE art. 30.

[94] PRINCIPLES OF CIVIL LAW art. 14; CIVIL CODE art. 147.

[95] Brain, *On the Road in Russia,* Harper's Magazine, May 1961, pp. 147, 150. "The regime tries to focus shame on nonperformance and on failures . . . to observe formal bureaucratic rules . . . . [T]he Russian is little shamed by these kinds of performance failures and is more likely to feel shame for moral failures." BAUER, INKELES & KLUCKHOHN, HOW THE SOVIET SYSTEM WORKS 165 (1960).

[96] Sov. yus. No. 16, p. 30 (1963).

[97] CIVIL CODE art. 66.

[98] CIVIL CODE art. 59.

[99] CIVIL CODE arts. 107, 189.

[100] YURCHENKO, OKHRANA IMUSHCHESTVENNYKH PRAV SOVETSKIKH GRAZHDAN (PROTECTION OF THE PROPERTY RIGHTS OF SOVIET CITIZENS) 16-18 (1962).

provide for passage of title as of the moment of delivery, unless otherwise specified by law or contract.[101] The rule regarding individually described things was thus brought in line with that which had governed the ownership rights in generically described things.[102] The change was hailed as a beneficial one in that it removed a point of contention (individually described thing vs. thing described by generic characteristics) and afforded greater protection to the consumer with respect to accidental loss or damage.[103] The Principles left intact the rule placing the risk of accidental loss or damage of property on its owner, in the absence of an agreement to the contrary. But in the event of default (either by nondelivery or nonacceptance), the risk is on the defaulting party.[104]

As we saw before, the owner has the right to recover his property from another person's illegal possession in a property action.[105] Here Soviet law makes an exception in favor of the bona fide purchaser for value. As against a bona fide purchaser, the owner or another person entitled to immediate possession of the property has a superior right only if the property has been lost by the claimant, stolen from him, or removed from his possession by means other than his volition. By contrast, state property and property of collective farms and other cooperative and public organizations, unlawfully alienated by whatever method, can be recovered by the organization concerned from any possessor.[106]

A quick survey of the available decisional material failed to disclose any consumer litigation involving the problems just discussed. As between private individuals *inter sese* and individuals and socialist organizations, these problems may well be academic.

III. Transmission of Consumer Demand to Producers

Stalin's decision to combine central planning with money and monetary incentives has left a lasting mark on the Soviety economy. In addition to making possible decentralized initiative in managing the country's economy through the principle of economic accountability, money gives considerable freedom to the consumer. He can either save it or spend it. If he decides to spend, he has a choice among several objects. However, consumer sovereignty, in the sense of the pattern of production being determined by consumer choices, does not exist in the Soviet economy. For example, long waiting lists for the purchase of automobiles one year do not assure that more automobiles will be produced the next year. The decision of how

[101] Principles of Civil Law art. 30.
[102] Civil Code art. 66.
[103] Kommentariy 149.
[104] Civil Code art. 186.
[105] Principles of Civil Law art. 28; Civil Code art. 59.
[106] Principles of Civil Law arts. 28, 29; Civil Code arts. 59, 60, 183.

many, if any, automobiles should enter the consumer sector is influenced far less by potential consumer demand than by considerations of an entirely different order, some tainted by ideology, but most of them dictated by economics. It is conceivable, for instance, that automobile sales to individuals are held down because of a fear that their ownership will adversely affect the attitudes and ways of the people. One can detect a strong concern about the persistence of "private proprietary tendencies" in the Soviet Union and about the fact that many citizens, especially the younger generation, seek to live comfortable, joy-centered lives. But the continued low output of automobiles is explainable also in terms of priorities in resource allocation between producer and consumer goods or the reluctance to create new urban problems before a host of others have been solved.[107]

On the other hand, when a line of goods is produced, there is no guarantee that it will be favorably received by consumers. While Soviet trade in consumer goods still has features of a seller's market, many prime necessities of the population have been fairly well satisfied, so that the consumer does not invariably rush to buy whatever is put on the counter. It is in this limited area that the Soviet consumer exercises a modicum of sovereignty. As Professor Wiles has aptly put it, "the consumer [can] react but not influence." [108] But his mere reaction can, of course, force a manufacturer to either improve its product or adapt its equipment to something different. In the contrary event, unsaleable goods will begin to clutter up warehouses.

In this section we are concerned with the devices for transmitting consumer preferences ascertained at the retail level. If a retail trading organization, through the experience of its outlets or by independent survey, observes that men have ceased buying wide, flapping trousers, that housewives pass over salted herring and demand marinated, and that young couples search for light compact furniture and reject bulky unfashionable items, two problems arise. Does the organization have any incentive for changing the composition of its stock of merchandise? Assuming such incentive, how can it secure the flow of new, desirable products?

A. The Function of Money

There are several reasons why the management of a retail trading organization wants its stores to "move the goods." Because the organization is governed by the principle of economic accountability, it must produce income to cover costs, many of which are fixed, in the sense that they do not vary with the volume of sales. Operating revenue is derived from percentage rebates *(skidki)* set by the state for each category of goods. The

[107] Zile, *Programs and Problems of City Planning in the Soviet Union*, 1963 WASH. U.L.Q. 19, 43-44.

[108] WILES, THE POLITICAL ECONOMY OF COMMUNISM 35 (1962).

mechanical side is handled by the local branch of the State Bank *(Gosbank)* which, having accepted the organization's receipts for deposit, transfers an appropriate portion to a separate operating account.[109] The percentage rebate thus is not the same as profit. True profit appears only when the organization has not exhausted its operating account to finance the expense of distribution, including payments into an asset amortization account. Therefore, a trading organization must attain a certain volume of sales just to stay out of the red. But there is more to it. The financial plan of an organization usually calls for a definite amount by way of true profits. A major portion of these profits is to be eventually drawn upon to finance capital expenditures over and above those chargeable against the amortization account and to expand working capital. However, another portion of the profits goes into the so-called enterprise fund *(fond predpriyatiya)*. The money paid into the enterprise fund is used principally to improve the working and living conditions of the employees (including housing and passes to resorts) and to pay occasional cash bonuses to outstanding workers. If an organization shows a profit in excess of the planned sum, the law permits the use of a larger portion of this surplus to replenish the enterprise fund.[110] However, the benefits which the employees, as individuals, derive from the enterprise fund are ordinarily very modest. Consequently, they provide a weak incentive for keeping the profit margin high.

It would seem that a much stronger material incentive to increase sales arises from another success indicator—the volume of sales expressed in thousands of rubles. As a general rule, each employee of a trading organization works on a base pay which varies with the type and location of the organization, and the qualifications and duties of the employee. All employees who have a reasonably direct connection with the actual distributive process get pay increments when their organization (or store, department, section) exceeds the volume of sales planned for the period. The increments rise progressively with the magnitude of the plan fulfillment. Top managers get bigger benefits than minor managers or common salespeople.[111] There is little doubt that, just as in the case of industrial executives,[112] the bonuses constitute a substantial part of retail managers' income. Their weight may be substantial even in the case of rank-and-file personnel. For example, in a Leningrad department store "the employees receive 120 per cent of their salary if the store plan is fulfilled by 105.1—110.0 per cent, and 130 per cent of their salary if the plan is overfulfilled by 110.1 to 115.0 per cent. This

[109] GOLDMAN, SOVIET MARKETING: DISTRIBUTION IN A CONTROLLED ECONOMY 108-09, 120 (1963). Retail price equals wholesale price plus turnover tax plus rebate (which varies not only from product to product but also from region to region).

[110] KONDRASHEV, TSENA I KHOZYAYSTVENNYY RASCHYOT (PRICE AND ECONOMIC ACCOUNTABILITY) 90-92 (1961).

[111] EKONOMIKA SOVETSKOY TORGOVLI (ECONOMICS OF SOVIET TRADE) 375-80 (1962).

[112] GRANICK, THE RED EXECUTIVE 130-32 (1960).

increase continues until salaries reach 170 per cent of the base amount." [113] The gross sales criterion naturally leads to pushing of goods which are best for the index. *Izvestiya* carried a story about a waitress who was observed to express her disappointment with two young coffee-drinking patrons. First she coaxed them into ordering 300 grams of wine as a supplement; but once the wall of resistance had been broken, she came through with a full bottle. "[I]t may happen," the reporter concluded, "that the waitress who got the two fellows drunk will have her name displayed on the honor roll." [114]

Since a Soviet retail organization and its management and staff have an interest in raising or at least maintaining a fairly high volume of sales, and since we saw that merchandise could not normally be forced on disinclined customers, it follows that the organization has a further interest in carrying goods that sell. From the point of view of the organization and its personnel, consumer reaction is determinant of their own success. A clothing store would not receive with equanimity a suggestion from its superiors or suppliers that it fulfill its plan for the month of May through sales of men's overcoats—wool, navy blue, size 40.

B. The Planning Process

Economic planning in all its ramifications—industrial and agricultural output, the level of new investment, allocations for the armed forces and the space effort, and the volume of sales to households—is a complicated multistage undertaking. A plan for retail trade cannot be prepared without regard to plans for the development of agriculture, light industry, and transportation. The output of consumer goods and the plan for their distribution must be coordinated with the purchasing power in the hands of the people during the term covered by the plan. Intersector relations are coordinated by specialized agencies, among which the State Planning Committee *(Gosplan)* of the USSR [115] is the ranking one.

Procurement and distribution of several important classes of consumer goods rest with the Council of Ministers of the USSR and the *Gosplan* of the USSR. The present list of "centrally planned" commodities consists of meat and meat products, milk and milk products, flour, groats, macaroni products, sugar, confections, vegetable oil, margarine, fish, herring, canned fish, cotton, wool, linen and silk fabrics, clothing (including knitwear), leather, rubber and felt footwear, furniture and automobiles.[116] For purposes

[113] GOLDMAN, *op. cit. supra* note 109, at 144.

[114] Izvestiya, April 3, 1962, p. 3.

[115] As a result of the latest reorganization, the *Gosplan* was made into a union-republic agency subordinate to the Supreme Council of National Economy. Edict of March 13, 1963 (U.S.S.R.), [1963] Ved. verkh. sov. S.S.S.R. text 133.

[116] PAVLOV, SOVETSKAYA TORGOVLYA V SOVREMENNYKH USLOVIYAKH (SOVIET TRADE UNDER CONTEMPORARY CONDITIONS) 51 (1962).

of distribution of these commodities, all republics are divided into two groups, in essence, the "haves" and the "have nots." Each republic is told what and how much it will have to ship to other republics and what and how much it will receive from the others. It is the responsibility of the government of each republic to implement these all-union plans of procurement and allocation. By contrast, before 1957 the Council of Ministers of the USSR did not stop merely at distributing the key commodities among the republics, but went on to prescribe, at the proposal of the *Gosplan* of the USSR and the former union-republic Ministry of Trade, their detailed allocation throughout the trading systems of each republic. In keeping with the spirit of decentralization, the republic authorities are, in turn, supposed to make only the most important decisions regarding the distribution of these and other goods, leaving the rest to their administrative subdivisions. Thus it was reported in 1963 that the Ministry of Trade of the RSFSR reserved the right of approval of the allocation plans for only 12 foodstuffs and 42 different industrial products.[117] In some republics, however, the ministries are reluctant to relinquish their power of approval and attempt to impose their schemes on the local agencies. One reason for this may be the republic governments' fear of unfounded requests from the local units; unfounded in the sense that consumer income in the locality does not justify the quantity of consumer goods requested.[118] By retaining the power to review the retail trade plans practically down to the level of the ultimate buyers, a republic government is in a position to determine whether a request represents a bona fide projection of demand or a bid for "reserve" stocks by officials who have succumbed to "localist tendencies."

The planning of retail trade is not an entirely arbitrary process. It is a two-way street on which the top decision-makers' broad goal formulations are met and influenced by the requests received from below. The latter reflect the estimates of consumer demand made by the trading organizations and enterprises. Within the total mass of consumer goods, broad product groups are calculated on the basis of "physiological norms" for foodstuffs and "rational norms" for manufactured goods.[119] The product mix to be allocated to the retail outlets depends to some degree on the accuracy of the various estimates.

C. The Law of Contract

The separation of the law of contract from the planning process, even

[117] BUDARAGIN, EKONOMICHESKIYE SVYAZI TORGOVLI S PROMYSHLENNOST'YU (ECONOMIC TIES BETWEEN TRADE AND INDUSTRY) 129 (1963).

[118] Sapel'nikov, *Rol' mestnykh organizatsiy v planirovaniyi tovarooborota (The Role of Local Organizations in Planning Circulation of Commodities)*, Sov. torg. No. 6, pp. 16, 17 (1960).

[119] Hanson, *The Assortment Problem in Soviet Retail Trade*, 14 SOVIET STUDIES 347, 351 (1963).

if only for the convenience of discussion, may be cogently objected to, because the contract device here discussed is actually but a facet of planning. Perhaps more has been written in Soviet legal literature about contract than any other phase of economic law, but to my knowledge, its use in the consumer sector of the Soviet economy has never been satisfactorily analyzed and elucidated. The writers are apt to paraphrase the pertinent laws, which are legion,[120] without frankly explaining their administration in practice. The reader is supplied with stock phrases but little insight. Plans are described as rough-hewn documents, since the planners are not asked to plan everything down to grade, style, size, shape, and color. These details, as well as exact delivery schedules, are hammered out in negotiations between producers and distributors and eventually put into documents outwardly resembling written agreements or contracts. "A contract makes the plan assignment concrete and reinforces the administrative planning discipline by means of civil law sanctions." [121]

During the early months of the year preceding the year for which the plan is being prepared, the retail trading organizations are required to submit requests or orders *(zakazy)* for consumer goods they will need. In those instances in which they have been permitted to deal directly with designated industrial enterprises, their orders must reach the producers by May 15. If they are required to deal with wholesalers, their orders must reach the latter by April 15. The wholesale trading organizations combine the requests and, with possible additions of their own, forward the totals to the appropriate producers, also by May 15. At this point differences are bound to arise regarding the ability of a producer to turn out the requested goods. Factory managers are inclined to schedule production so as to achieve the best possible showing under their success indices (usually gross output expressed in either physical quantity or monetary value). They frequently refuse to produce what trading organizations desire. After all, a factory manager is responsible only for making the industry look successful; the problems of trade are not his problems.[122] Ultimately an agreement is reached. The supplier undertakes to deliver goods of given quality, in specified assortment, at stated times; the buyer agrees to receive and pay for them in a manner agreed upon. Other provisions may refer to transportation arrangements, handling of packing materials, etc.

[120] *E.g.*, Decree of May 22, 1959 (U.S.S.R.), ISTOCH. SOV. GRAZH. PRAV. 465; Decree of Aug. 8, 1960 (U.S.S.R.), *id.* at 435; Decree of Jan. 26, 1961 (R.S.F.S.R.), KHOZYAYSTVENNYYE DOGOVORY: SBORNIK NORMATIVNYKH AKTOV (ECONOMIC CONTRACTS: A COLLECTION OF NORMATIVE ACTS) 151 (1962).

[121] Genkin, *Aktual'nyye voprosy pravovogo regulirovaniya sovetskoy gosudarstvennoy torgovli (Current Problems of Legal Regulation of Soviet Trade)*, Sov. gos. i pravo No. 8, p. 41 (1961).

[122] PAVLOV, *op. cit. supra* note 116, at 74-75. "The fact that sovnarkhozy are not responsible for retail trade but are responsible for the output of the bulk of the goods supplied to it is a source of friction . . . ." Hanson, *supra* note 119, at 352.

Direct ties between local retail distributors and local industry are quite useful, because they are close. The retailers' wishes can be more vividly presented to the industrial enterprises and more accurately incorporated into contractual arrangements.[123] Moreover, intimate personal relationships between managers of industry and trade and local planning officials facilitate settlement of differences. The close contacts between the heads of the various economic units developed by reason of their membership in the same lower level (*e.g.*, city or district) party organization can be of considerable working importance.

The apparently satisfactory experience with direct ties with local industry has been eyed as a possible solution for the difficulties that arise when distant manufacturers are involved. Some larger stores deal directly and successfully with industrial suppliers; economists and lawyers urge the extension of the method. This by-passing of wholesale trading organizations can yield positive results only up to a point. As Goldman admonishes, there are situations where the wholesaling function is indispensable. If a squeeze-out is attempted, "the wholesaling activity inevitably bulges up somewhere else, causing a serious disruption of services and increasing costs." [124] Certainly a store of the size of Moscow's GUM can deal effectively with manufacturers; it has storage facilities and can purchase by whole lots. Consider now a provincial retailing outfit approaching a major factory. Will the factory break lots to assemble an order? Will the retailer be in a position to bargain advantageously with the manufacturer and influence the product mix?

Notwithstanding the agitation in favor of direct contracts between retailers and producers, most contracts for delivery of consumer goods are concluded between wholesale organizations and producers and thereafter between the wholesale organizations and retail trading organizations. Sometimes, when both purchasing and sales warehouses are involved, there is a chain of three contractual relationships.[125]

Quite apart from the accuracy with which consumer demand is investigated at the retail level and transmitted to wholesalers, the selection of goods that find their way to retailers' shelves and counters depends also on the determination with which the consumers' case is presented to producers. One of the major criticisms against wholesalers is that, despite their virtual monopoly power in negotiating the output of consumer goods with light industry, they do their job poorly.[126] Nove remarks that the interven-

[123] BUDARAGIN, *op. cit. supra* note 117, at 131-33.

[124] Goldman, *Marketing—a Lesson for Marx*, Harv. Bus. Rev., Jan.-Feb. 1960, pp. 79, 81.

[125] KHALFINA, PRAVOVOYE REGULIROVANIYE POSTAVKI PRODUKTSIYI V NARODNOM KHOZYAYSTVE (LEGAL REGULATION OF DELIVERY OF PRODUCTS IN THE NATIONAL ECONOMY) 138 (1963).

[126] Kolenko, *Rasshirit' pryamyye svyazi s promyshlennost'yu (Direct Ties With Industry Should Be Expanded)*, Sov. torg. No. 7, pp. 18, 20 (1961).

tion by a wholesale organization "depersonalizes the product." [127] Wholesale organizations which go out of their way to accommodate self-centered producers find themselves overburdened with unpopular merchandise. In some cases such goods are then practically forced on retailers by methods that smack of tie-in sales or by administrative pressure, the state agencies controlling the wholesalers being superior to the state agencies controlling the retailers. Purchase orders are accepted and contracts are made, but according to the principle "take what is given to you." [128] Sometimes no duress is evident and yet a retailer would sign a contract giving the supplier practically a free hand. For example, a contract might say merely that the wholesale warehouse will supply "fish, herring and canned goods" in a certain monetary amount, without requiring any definite assortment.[129] Frequently commodities move in apparent disregard of contractual ties or in their absence. A distress call came from Kazaen': "Halt shipments of pressed tea. We have reserves for five years." [130] A newspaper correspondent who found piles of tables, chairs, sofas, and wardrobes stacked in front of a furniture store in Riga reported his conversation with the store's director:

> " 'Why did you order so much?'
>
> " 'We did not; they simply brought it,' sighed the director. 'For example, we ordered 50 chairs from the furniture factory "Association"; they brought 100. The manufacturer's employees told us bluntly: "We carry only full truckloads. If you don't take this shipment, you won't get anything." ' " [131]

Soviet laws emphatically state that unordered shipments of goods must be rejected. Similarly, the trade organizations must refuse to accept goods the quality and assortment of which deviate from the specifications. Perhaps of late the organizations of trade are learning to regard their legal obligations more seriously. Smirnov, the head of the Chief Administration of Trade, reported recently, by way of an example, that at the beginning of the planning year 1962 many trade organizations balked, refusing to accept any more ready-made clothing from 16 enterprises in the RSFSR and 14 in the Ukrainian SSR.[132] Furthermore, mindful of the impossibility of making accurate demand forecasts a year or more in advance, the law provides

[127] NOVE, THE SOVIET ECONOMY 175 (1961), quoting a Soviet critic, Kulyov, in Kommunist No. 9, p. 27 (1959).

[128] Ivanov, *Ustranit' nedostatki dogovornoy praktiki (Incorrect Contract Practices Should Be Eliminated)*, Sov. torg. No. 2, pp. 7, 8 (1960); Cina, Dec. 2, 1961, p. 2.

[129] Fialkov, *Khozyaystvennym dogovoram—neoslabnoye vnimaniye (Economic Contracts [Deserve] Unremitting Attention)*, Sov. torg. No. 2, p. 3 (1960).

[130] Izvestiya, July 25, 1962, p. 3.

[131] Cina, July 31, 1963, p. 2.

[132] Pravda, June 12, 1962, p. 2.

for renegotiation of contracts in the face of changed circumstances. If the revision affects plan assignments, it must be approved by the planning authorities. Manufacturers as a rule will oppose any suggestion that plans be revised in mid-term. Their production has been scheduled for the entire year and is in full swing when the petition for modification reaches the authorities. Numerous suppliers are delivering raw materials and parts to them, pursuant to other plans and contracts. Any rescheduling of output would raise havoc with the plant's incentive system, especially when gross output is its principal indicator of success. If the manufacturers prevail, unneeded goods will be produced until the end of the planning year. It was reported in the Soviet press that there were 300,000 unsold sewing machines in storage in the warehouses of the RSFSR trade organizations in the fall of 1962, with the manufacturing plants expected to accumulate an equal number of finished machines by the end of the year.[133] Soviet reaction to problems of this sort seems to be one of mild bewilderment; the phenomenon of over-production is new to their economy. As product differentiation progresses and the products involved are not necessities for which demand is relatively inelastic, the Soviet consumer begins ever more often to search and wait for a favorite product, letting Brand X lie on the shelves. The planners who have been reared in a seller's market will have to learn a more sophisticated approach to consumer resistance. Smirnov reported in June of 1962 that while sales volume increased in the USSR in 1958-1961 by 24 per cent, the inventories in retail trade went up by 70 per cent. The value of merchandise accumulated above the norms reached almost two billion rubles in 1961. In some republics the figure was set at more than a quarter of the total value of goods in the trade network.[134] A few months later *Pravda* complained that

> "in many organizations the demands for a number of products are not satisfied, while at the same time inventories have grown. Clothing and shoes accumulate in especially large amounts. This happens because industry often produces goods without consideration of demand and because their quality does not always meet the requirements of the customers." [135]

Even careful research of past consumer behavior and prudent forecasts concerning the same can only be tentative. One must be prepared to face unanticipated shifts in consumer attitudes and habits. Only wide assortment and considerable slack in each group of goods can reduce consumer disappointments and enable retail trade to perform its primary function satisfactorily. There would inevitably remain stocks unsold by the end of the

[133] Izvestiya, Oct. 3, 1962, p. 3.
[134] Pravda, June 12, 1962, p. 2.
[135] *Id.*, Aug. 22, 1962, p. 1.

period. This is a normal condition in a market economy but is regarded by the Soviets as waste, ideologically unpalatable.[136]

Contracts that skirt the difficult problem of assortment are largely meaningless, by reason of their unenforceability in this important respect. By basing deliveries on a superficially drafted contract the parties merely enable the *Gosbank* to authorize payments of purchaser's acceptances[137] and take a bow to the principle that all movements of commodities, in the execution of the national economic plan, must rest on contracts.

If a contract has been made with a purpose of ensuring not only timely deliveries and quality but also a carefully calculated assortment of goods, the law gives it teeth. There is a formidable array of legal sanctions for breach of assumed obligations. An organization defaulting in any one of a number of ways must pay the other party several kinds of stiff penalties *(neustoyka, penya, shtraf)* according to prescribed schedules, as well as compensatory damages to the extent that actual losses have not been covered by the receipts of penalties. Moreover, the payment of penalties does not release the obligor from rendering actual performance. And, since on top of all that, the organizations are duty bound to enforce and collect their claims,[138] the irresponsible obligors stand to lose large amounts of money and incur the wrath of superior authorities. Conversely, conscientious enforcers may find a short cut to riches. A high official of the Ministry of Trade of the RSFSR cites the good work of a Sverdlovsk department store which in 1959 brought more than 600 suits on grounds of poor quality alone, recovering in excess of one million rubles.[139] Although encouraged by the state, contract litigation on such a grand scale is not universally practiced. It is a time-consuming process demanding, under the present statute of the *Gosarbitrazh*,[140] the participation of responsible managers, in addition to the organization's legal counsel.[141] Litigiousness by managers is also in conflict with the need for maintaining friendly, informal contacts with their counterparts who are similarly situated and who would retaliate rather than cooperate were the tables turned. Furthermore, when breaches of contract are disclosed, it is not only the juristic person, the organization, which suffers. Managers and other officials are personally liable for nonperformance of the obligation. The laws in force provide for criminal,

[136] *Cf.* BUDARAGIN, *op. cit. supra* note 117, at 54.

[137] The requirement is found in Decree of Aug. 21, 1954 (U.S.S.R.) art. 25, 1 ZAK. AKTY NAR. KHOZ. SSSR 154.

[138] RAIKHER, PRAVOVYE VOPROSY DOGOVORNOY DISTSIPLINY V SSSR (LEGAL PROBLEMS OF CONTRACT DISCIPLINE IN THE USSR) 79-80, 88 (1958).

[139] Ivanov, *supra* note 128, at 8.

[140] A system of economic courts having jurisdiction over disputes between socialist organizations.

[141] See Friedman & Zile, *Soviet Legal Profession: Recent Developments in Law and Practice*, 1964 WIS. L. REV. 32, 70-71.

property (civil), and disciplinary liability.[142] This may be all the more reason for not sticking one's neck too far out by imposing, and at the same time assuming, commitments which are difficult to fulfill.

IV. Devices for Shaping Consumer Demand

A. Price Policies; Use Restrictions; Priority Sales; Advertising

The Soviets manage retail prices to achieve and maintain a rough balance between the stocks of consumer goods and the purchasing power in the hands of the people. They also manipulate the prices to influence the demand for individual groups of items. Characteristically, prices would be kept high on items whose use is discouraged (alcoholic beverages, tobacco, etc.) or nonessential (jewelry, various delicacies, etc.). Conversely, prices of necessities have been kept relatively low; some goods in this class are actually sold below cost.

Similarly, when some goods are in ample supply, far exceeding the current demand for them, their retail prices will be reduced either to deplete inventories or to avert excessive accumulation. Given the opposite trend, prices will be raised, even on prime necessities; witness the recent price increases on meat and dairy products. Except for the few instances of below-cost sales, Soviet retail prices, after allowing for the cost of production, producer's planned profit, and wholesale and retail rebates, leave a sizable variable element known as turnover tax. In 1960 its average rate to the total retail sales was approximately 40 per cent.[143] The function of the turnover tax is thus twofold: it constitutes one of the chief sources of revenue for the state, and simultaneously acts as a shock absorber in the up and down movements of retail prices. Until 1957-58 price administration was almost entirely vested in the union government. A 1958 decree empowered republic and local authorities to set retail prices in a limited way. By 1962 about 45 per cent of the entire volume of goods was sold at decentralized prices. However, the new policy is a mixed blessing. The fact that in different communities similar goods are sold at unequal prices "perplexes buyers and lays groundwork for abuses in the trade network."[144] I have made no attempt to look into these abuses. Probably the workers of retail trade situated in a low-price area buy the goods on their own account and ship them to a high-price area for private resale.

Since the postwar abolition of the rationing system, the Soviet Union has not resorted to use restrictions until recently. The perennial hardships

[142] *E.g.*, Edict of April 24, 1958 (U.S.S.R.), [1958] Ved. verkh. sov. S.S.S.R. text 202. "It seems a fair generalization that all Soviet managers are, *ipso facto*, criminals according to Soviet law." Granick, *op. cit. supra* note 112, at 43.

[143] Goldman, *op. cit. supra* note 109, at 86.

[144] Pavlov, *op. cit. supra* note 116, at 52-53.

of Soviet agriculture culminated in a serious food shortage in 1962-63. The massive wheat imports, extreme sensitiveness to foreign opinion,[145] hoarding, [146] emotional appeals "to show respect for bread" and "save every grain," [147] and programs for massive investments in agriculture all testify to the magnitude of the continuing problem. Bread is the foundation of Soviet diet. The demand for bread is inelastic; higher prices alone would not appreciably affect the consumption. In order to reduce the demand, the Soviets are waging a battle against wasteful use of bread. People are denounced for leaving half-eaten slices of bread on restaurant tables.[148] Stores are asked to limit the amount of bread sold to a single customer at one time.[148a] But the strongest action is being taken against those who feed bread or other cereal products purchased at state or cooperative stores to cattle or poultry. Since May 1963, minor violators are subject to fines of 10 to 50 rubles, imposed by the local administrative authorities. A new article, article 154-1, was added to the Criminal Code:

> "The purchase in state and cooperative stores of bread, flour, groats and other cereal products for the purpose of feeding them to cattle and poultry, or such feeding of bread, flour, groats and other cereal products so purchased, if the actor has already been administratively fined, or is doing it systematically or in large quantities—are punishable by either corrective labor for up to a year or deprivation of liberty for a term from one to three years with or without confiscation of the livestock." [149]

Other republics have enacted similar laws.[150] For purposes of enforcement, local soviets, the press, and vigilance groups organize forays into both sheds where private animals are kept and people's apartments. The investigators examine troughs and count loaves on kitchen tables.[151] The wrong which these laws punish is a subtle one. Obviously, there is no destruction of food stuffs involved, in the same sense as throwing away perfectly good slices and crusts of bread would be. Instead of being wasted, cheaper products are converted into more valuable forms. Meat and lard command higher prices than the cost of feed (including bread) that goes into their production. Evidently the offense is found in the fact that private individuals who happen to own livestock and poultry, rather than the state, are making

[145] *E.g.*, Izvestiya, Oct. 27, 1963, p. 5.
[146] Kazakhstanskaya pravda, Oct. 13, 1963, p. 3.
[147] Cina, Sept. 20, 1963, p. 1.
[148] Cina, Nov. 14, 1963, p. 4.
[148a] Trud, Sept. 29, 1962, p. 1.
[149] Edict of May 6, 1963 (R.S.F.S.R.), Sov. yus. No. 11, p. 7 (1963).
[150] *E.g.*, Law of July 25, 1963 (Latv. S.S.R.), Cina, July 28, 1963, p. 1.
[151] Cina, Sept. 19, 1963, p. 4; *id.*, Sept. 21, 1963, p. 4; *id.*, Nov. 30, 1963, p. 4.

economic decisions and pocketing the differential between the artificially fixed prices.

The demand for certain scarce items is not influenced by making them more expensive or imposing restrictions on their use but rather by exercising control over who gets them. In some cases stores which carry lines of this kind maintain waiting lists for prospective buyers. The merchandise is then sold in the order in which the customers' names appear on the list. For some articles coupons *(talony)* are issued by state and public organizations to selected persons, either entitling them to purchases outside the waiting lists or making the articles available exclusively to them. This device is simultaneously part of the system of rewards for meritorious service, with the coupons going to socialist labor heroes and other outstanding workers and the car becoming a symbol of cooperation with the system.[152]

In 1961 the Lithuanian SSR inaugurated a much praised system of selling automobiles only to persons recommended by factory and plant committees or collective farm administrations. The procedure was made applicable to sales of both new and used cars.[153] The power to screen the sales through state and cooperative stores, together with the tight restrictions on transfers of automobiles between private individuals,[154] enables the public organizations to determine, to a large extent, who in the Soviet society will own and drive automobiles.[155] There is concern over the fact that private automobiles are widely used to transport paying passengers and thus turned into sources of unearned income, contrary to the concept of personal property.[155a]

As long as a sellers' market prevailed in the Soviet Union, the disposal of goods was assured without much sales talk. The emergence of patches of a buyers' market has now awakened interest in techniques of consumer persuasion. Advertising Soviet style still lacks the swagger of Madison Avenue, but it has earned recognition as a legitimate economic endeavor and is growing. Moscow may well be the world's most signless metropolis, advertisingly speaking, yet in 1961 alone, 7,500,000 rubles were spent on advertising signs in the capital of communism.[156] Most of the signs are either public service announcements ("Beware of Fire") or propaganda slogans ("Glory to the Communist Party"). However, there are also signs that

[152] NOVAK [pseud.], THE FUTURE IS OURS, COMRADE 38, 188 (1960).

[153] Decree of April 25, 1961 (Lith. S.S.R.) arts. 1, 3, Sots. zak. No. 7, p. 85 (1961).

[154] See text pp. 227-29 *supra*.

[155] I am not quite sure whether this system of automobile sales is now used throughout the Soviet Union. See a broad statement indicating universality in ALEKSEYEV, GRAZHDANSKOYE PRAVO V PERIOD RAZVERNUTOGO STROITEL'STVA KOMMUNIZMA (CIVIL LAW IN THE PERIOD OF ALL-OUT CONSTRUCTION OF COMMUNISM) 220 (1962).

[155a] See note 10 *supra;* Edict of Aug. 3, 1957 (Arm. S.S.R.), Sov. yus. No. 1, p. 75 (1958); Case of Dronevich, [1960] Byul. verkh. suda S.S.S.R. No. 5, p. 8 (Plenum Supr. Ct. S.S.S.R.).

[156] Pravda, July 14, 1962, p. 6.

advertise goods and services, as well as a few newspaper and magazine advertisements and radio and television commercials having the same purpose. Again, much of the advertising that refers to goods and services is purely informational: announcements of shows, opening of new stores, or arrival of large shipments of goods. Individual retail stores sometimes advertise their superiority over comparable stores, by stressing wide selection of merchandise and "the best in service." Occasionally attempts are made to incite people to shopping sprees, much the same as stores in our country would stage sales to mark holidays and anniversaries. For example, shortly before the International Women's Day a newspaper would carry a half page of advertisements under a banner headline: "Comrade Men! Read and Keep in Mind! The 8th of March Is Approaching." Below, in one of the items the Central Department Store of Riga reminded the male population: "Do not forget to buy presents for your mothers, wives, sisters, daughters and [girl-]friends." Another would list the addresses of stores carrying jewelry, watches, table accessories, and specially prepared gift sets. A third would offer perfumes, colognes, and beauty creams, by brand name.[157] Promotion of specific products is becoming more common. Advertising is used to create and remold habits of consumption, for instance, by presenting the merits of new products ("Tomato juice is healthy").

In the final analysis, the task of socialist advertising is to serve the interests of economic planning. Certain parts of the plan are such that their fulfillment would actually be impossible without advertising. The consumption of a number of goods would decrease without the people being reminded of them through advertising. Turnover in some of the retail stores would drop because many consumers would spend their purchasing power elsewhere.[158]

B. Mail Order Sales

Mail order sales were first introduced in the Soviet Union on an experimental basis in 1924, but they did not catch on. Mikoyan is credited with having revived the experiment in 1949.[159] *Posyltorg,* within the Ministry of Trade of the RSFSR, is the mail order house for the entire country, except that in late 1959 the consumer cooperative system began operating its own setup especially for cooperative members in the virgin lands territories.[160] Th mail order service endeavors to bring driblets of the new affluence to inadequately supplied localities, in particular the remote corners

[157] Cina, March 6, 1963, p. 4.

[158] GOLDMAN, *op. cit. supra* note 109, at 195-96; Milwaukee J., Dec. 5, 1963, green sheet p. 1, col. 6; Goldman, *supra* note 124, at 84; Varga, *An Economic Explanation,* 4 ATLAS 26 (1962). Izvestiya, May 23, 1964, p. 3.

[159] PAVLOV, *op. cit. supra* note 116, at 132.

[160] GOLDMAN, SOVIET MARKETING: DISTRIBUTION IN A CONTROLLED ECONOMY 36 (1963).

of the land. The overwhelming majority of orders come from Krasnoyarsk and Khabarovsk Territories and Arkhangel'sk, Irkutsk, Chitinsk, and Vologda regions.[161] The existence of the service and the availability of goods are made known through newspaper advertisements, billboards, and radio commercials. Detailed information about the merchandise, prices, and the conditions of sale and shipping is published in illustrated catalogs listing several thousand items. Although the minimum size of an order has been set to exclude petty purchases, the service is nonetheless a convenience for the Soviet citizen. The state, on its part, derives principally two kinds of benefits: savings through a smaller number of retail trade outlets, and an opportunity for disposing of surplus stocks or, as the Soviets would put it, of "those manufactured goods which are in adequate supply." [162] By changing the contents of the mail order catalog the *Posyltorg* is able to tap latent demand in areas heretofore not reached by the retail trade network, and can deal successfully until the point of saturation is reached. For example, at one time surplus watches were a major component of the mail order sales volume. Today almost everyone seems to own a watch, so that scarcely anybody buys them even by mail.[163] The volume of sales has been growing. In 1961 more than 3,000,000 orders were filled in the amount of more than 70,000,000 rubles, or approximately twice as much as in 1955.[164] However, this is still only a tiny share—less than one-thousandth of the entire retail trade volume, so that it cannot really be said that the mail order service as of now can generate sufficient effective demand to enable suppliers to get rid of otherwise unwanted goods.

The *Posyltorg* is required to fill an order within 10 days from the day of its receipt. Sending the merchandise after the 10-day limit is a contract violation which makes the *Posyltorg* liable to the customer for any damages caused by late performance. Undoubtedly, in the overwhelming majority of cases it is impossible to prove any damages. However, if the delay has caused the customer to lose any interest in the merchandise due to changed circumstances, including acquisition of a substitute item, the customer can refuse to accept performance and demand damages instead. The damages, if any, will include an out-of-pocket loss incurred in placing the order. In addition, the customer may also claim a refund of the money sent in advance. The same would be true if the *Posyltorg* refused entirely to perform.[165]

Soviet legal writers take the position that a mail order catalog which contains all the necessary information on the basis of which a prospective

[161] PAVLOV, *op. cit. supra* note 116, at 133.
[162] PRAV. REG. GOS. TORG. SSSR 268.
[163] GOLDMAN, *op. cit. supra* note 160, at 194.
[164] PAVLOV, *op. cit. supra* note 116, at 132-33.
[165] PRAV. REG. GOS. TORG. SSSR 269-70.

buyer can act, is an offer to make a contract of sale. Consequently, the buyer's order (accompanied by a remittance of money) constitutes an acceptance.[166] Under the Civil Code section governing the formation of contracts where the parties are negotiating at a distance, a contract is concluded at the time of the receipt of the acceptance by the offeror.[167] This is a bit awkward. In theory, at least, there could be problems regarding the duration of an offer and thus the existence of an enforceable agreement. If the *Posyltorg* revises its catalog, will orders placed in reliance on the previous edition be considered valid acceptances? What if the item listed in the catalog is not available at all? I suspect, however, that this is strictly classroom law, that in practice such problems seldom arise, and that if they do they are not under Soviet conditions pressed to a litigation stage. In the absence of any evidence to the contrary, hypothesizing would be uncalled for.

Disputes concerning the quality of merchandise are handled in accordance with principles generally applicable to problems of quality. By way of a natural exception, the buyer, because of his absence, is not required immediately upon delivery to examine the merchandise for obvious defects. Delivery to pass the title is effected at the time the merchandise is turned over to postal or transportation authorities.[168]

C. Installment Credit Sales

Early in 1959 the trade organizations in several cities began to allow consumer credit on an experimental basis. Apparently the people responded appreciatively, and no untoward consequences of the "progressive" method were noted.[169] Heartened by the quick success, the Council of Ministers of the USSR on August 12, 1959, authorized[170] the union republics to give their unreserved blessing to installment credit sales of durable consumer goods. Although buying on time had been once in a while denounced as a bourgeois evil, the step was not without a precedent in the Soviet setting. In 1923-24 the RSFSR, Belorussian SSR, Ukrainian SSR and possibly other republics had adopted decrees[171] regulating retail sales on credit. As a matter fact, they were still on the books at the time of the 1959 enactment. However, the early decrees had grown out of a semimarket environment and had

[166] *Id.* at 269.

[167] CIVIL CODE art. 134.

[168] PRINCIPLES OF CIVIL LAW art. 30; PRAV. REG. GOS. TORG. SSSR 270; see text pp. 267-72 *infra.*

[169] Gribanov & Kabalkin, *Pravovoye regulirovaniye kupli-prodazhi s rassrochkoy platyozha (Legal Regulation of Installment Sales)*, Sov. gos. i pravo No. 8, pp. 103, 104 (1960).

[170] Decree of Aug. 12, 1959 (U.S.S.R.), ISTOCH. SOV. GRAZH. PRAV. 414.

[171] Decrees of Oct. 10, 1923 (R.S.F.S.R.), Nov. 26, 1923 (Bel. S.S.R.), Oct. 3, 1924 (Ukr. S.S.R.), cited in Gribanov & Kabalkin, *supra* note 169, at 104-05.

been adopted mainly to facilitate sales of tools and farm implement to peasants rather than of nonproductive goods to consumers in general.[172]

Installment credit has been paraded as "one of those instances in which the public interest of . . . [the] socialist state coincides with the personal interests of Soviet citizens." [173] The avowed purpose of the 1959 decree was to "create for the workers and employees the most favorable conditions for the acquisition of durable goods." [174] But a closer look at the rest of the provisions and Soviet own admissions indicate that the installment credit is first and foremost an instrument for marketing otherwise unsaleable inventories.[175] Any benefits that in the process redound to the consumer, though real, are purely incidental. The initial union decree listed only a few selected items which could be sold on installment basis, instead of giving blanket authority to sell anything durable.[176] While the enumeration included bicyles in general, it singled out one make of sewing machines, one make of outboard motors, two makes of motor scooters, the more expensive cameras, etc. The list was to be kept flexible. The Council of Ministers of the USSR delegated to the union republic councils of ministers the power "to modify the list and supplement it with other durable goods of which sufficient quantities are available." [177] As a result, the lists differ considerably from one republic to another.[178] In the RSFSR the Council of Ministers has further delegated the amending authority to the republic's Ministry of Trade,[179] as an agency best qualified to react immediately to changes in inventory accumulations. On the whole the nomenclature of goods sold on credit is constantly increasing, although some retail outlets, on their own initiative, refuse to sell some listed goods for which they find enough cash customers.[180] The rapid growth of the total volume of credit sales evidences the success of the device in reaching an otherwise untapped market. In 1960, the year after the adoption of the enabling decree, 396,-000,000 rubles' worth of consumer goods was sold on credit.[181] By the end

[172] *Id.* at 105.

[173] Kunik, *Dogovor kupli-prodazhi v kredit (Contract of Credit Sale)*, Sov. yus. No. 12, at 16 (1962).

[174] Decree of Aug. 12, 1959 preamble.

[175] Lokshin, *Za dal'neyshiy pod''yom kooperativnoy torgovli (For Further Improvements in Cooperative Trade)*, Sovetskaya potrebitel'skaya kooperatsiya (Soviet Consumers' Cooperatives) No. 3, p. 38 (1960). *Cf.* Gribanov & Kabalkin, *supra* note 169 (the view criticized as excessively "sales-oriented").

[176] While laws and writers all stress that only durable goods can be subject to installment sales, it is to be noted that clothing and footwear are included in that definition.

[177] Decree of Aug. 12, 1959 art. 1.

[178] YAZEV, PRODAZHA TOVAROV NASELENIYU V KREDIT (SELLING GOODS ON CONSUMER CREDIT) 7-9 (1960).

[179] Regulations of Sept. 4, 1959 (R.S.F.S.R.), ISTOCH. SOV. GRAZH. PRAV. 414.

[180] Gribanov & Kabalkin, *supra* note 169, at 106.

of 1961 the figure had trebled.[182] Statistics for the RSFSR show that installment credit is used mostly by people of lower incomes. It is also significant that goods for which there is a strong buyers' market (*e.g.*, watches) are purchased overwhelmingly (84.1 per cent) by people with monthly incomes below 100 rubles and hardly at all (2.8 per cent) by those in the higher bracket—over 151 rubles. By contrast, the sales of relatively scarcer items (*e.g.*, motorcycles) show a much less pronounced disparity between the two income groups (48.9 and 15.7 per cent, respectively).[183]

Quite apart from the limited selection of goods, the installment credit sales are wrapped up in a multitude of other restrictions. Some of them have been adopted perhaps for the sake of administrative simplicity. Others remind one of the most thorough efforts of a nineteenth-century monopolistic company store [184] to squeeze every possible advantage and safeguard out of the relationship with an incomparably weaker customer. At times the consumer interests have seemed to be in a danger of being smothered by all the other considerations. Initially credit sales were permitted "in cities" only.[185] The 1960 decree "On Measures To Achieve Further Improvements in Trade" [186] authorized the consumer cooperative system to extend credit sales to rural areas as well.[187] The sales are, however, inadequately organized outside the cities, and this method of trade is still nonexistent in the so-called settlements (workers', summer-house, resort), densely populated places of urban character which still have not achieved city rank. Soviet experts say that it would be perfectly possible to bring the share of credit sales up to 10 per cent of the total retail turnover by extending the law to settlements and by better organizing the sales in rural areas.[188] The RSFSR regulations make it clear that even in cities credit sales are to be conducted exclusively through stores specifically designated for that purpose. Moreover, not every customer who goes to a credit store can avail himself of the privilege. At first, installment sales were only for "workers and employees (among them service personnel of officer and noncommissioned officer rank in the regular armed forces) permanently employed in the city where the store is located." [189] Temporarily employed persons were

[181] Kunik, *supra* note 173, at 16.

[182] PAVLOV, SOVETSKAYA TORGOVLYA V SOVREMENNYKH USLOVIYAKH (SOVIET TRADE UNDER CONTEMPORARY CONDITIONS) 131 (1962).

[183] *Id.* at 132.

[184] I am indebted to my colleague, Professor Robert H. Skilton, for this felicitous comparison.

[185] Decree of Aug. 12, 1959 art. 1; Regulations of Sept. 4, 1959 art. 1.

[186] Decree of Aug. 8, 1960 (U.S.S.R.), ISTOCH. SOV. GRAZH. PRAV. 435.

[187] Art. 17.

[188] Pravda, Nov. 18, 1962, p. 4.

[189] Regulations of Sept. 4, 1959 art. 2.

excluded "because they might find it difficult to meet the payments." [190] Kazakh, Belorussian, Lithuanian, and Tadzhik republics still make both permanent employment and permanent residence in the same city preconditions to credit. This excludes a large number of potential buyers, as a good part of the urban labor force resides in suburban settlements. Even if credit sales were extended to these settlements, the commuters would still be unable to take advantage of the credit system because of their inability to satisfy both conditions at either place.[191] The omission of self-employed craftsmen, writers, pensioners, rank-and-file servicemen, and others was not perhaps extremely significant in terms of stored-up demand, but it certainly was an example of inequitable classification from a consumer standpoint. Much more striking was the denial of access to the new system to the rural residents who constitute roughly one-half of the Soviet population. One may wonder whether there had been a deliberate decision to shortchange the already under-supplied country dwellers or whether the shutout had been prompted by a reluctance to encounter unknown difficulties in collecting time payments from defaulting peasants. The circumstances under which new groups have been granted the credit privilege in the last few years suggest that the original restrictions were at least partly for the benefit of administration. In an article written shortly before the 1960 decree "On Measures To Achieve Further Improvements in Trade," two writers argued that "along with the gradual transition to monetary payments for labor on collective farms, and in the light of the growth of the output of consumer goods, a need arises to organize credit sales in rural areas." [192] When the policy change came it was explicitly made applicable to rural workers, employees, and collective farmers, who are members of consumer cooperatives and are not behind in their membership share payments.[193] Some republics now permit installment credit sales to pensioners. Commentators approve of this practice, stressing the reliability of the pensioners' source of income.[194] They also suggest inclusion of seasonal workers, if the repayment period is appropriately shortened.[195] Stores actually have no power to extend the credit method in their discretion to persons not covered by law, but some stores in Kiev, "taking into account concrete conditions and circumstances, sell goods on credit to students." Finally, in a few republics the law directly prohibits credit sales to minors. In some other places the question is unsettled. The critics of this particular limitation argue that the

[190] Gribanov & Kabalkin, *supra* note 169, at 106.

[191] Ospanov, *Dogovor roznichnoy kupli-prodazhi s rassrochkoy platyozhi (Contract of Installment Sale at Retail)*, Sots. zak. No. 9, pp. 23, 23-24 (1962).

[192] Gribanov & Kabalkin, *supra* note 169, at 106.

[193] Kunik, *supra* note 173, at 16.

[194] YAZEV, *op. cit. supra* note 178, at 17; Gribanov & Kabalkin, *supra* note 169, at 106.

[195] Kunik, *supra* note 173, at 17.

important question is whether the minor has a separate wage or salary. If so, he should not be denied the privilege.[196]

These provisions really add up to an attempt to establish rough credit ratings. They are rough because the risk is not appraised on basis of the status and past performance of an individual, but rather in terms of the position and performance of a large social group of which the individual is a member. However, the state does not stop at this. Several other safeguards individualize the case and come close to eliminating any residual risk left by the law's broad classification. For purposes of preliminary appraisal of the seller's risk in a particular case, the Soviets make use of a statement *(spravka)* issued by the prospective buyer's place of employment, certifying the worker's or employee's average pay. At the beginning, the law of the RSFSR required at least three-months' employment with the attesting organization immediately prior to the issuance of the statement.[197] This period was extended to six months in the spring of 1962, apparently with a view to tightening credit.[198] The statement, which is valid for 15 days, is treated as a document of major importance: it must be signed by the manager, deputy manager, or senior accountant.[199] By contrast, some lax employers issue signed and sealed statements, leaving the recipient to fill in the blanks. This liberty has been abused. A buyer through a consumer cooperative obtains a similar statement from his place of work and submits it, together with his cooperative membership booklet and an application for credit sale, to the chairman or deputy chairman of the cooperative association.[200] In those republics which permit credit sales to pensioners, the latter obtain statements of their pension income from the social security agencies.[201] The earnings figures contained in the statements help in determining the maximum amount of credit to be allowed. The Ministry of Trade of the RSFSR originally ruled that a person's credit purchases in any one year could not exceed his four-months' wages or salary.[202] In case of a collective farmer the ceiling is calculated by looking at his annual earnings, both in money and *in natura.* The limit on credit is set at one-third of this figure.[203] It is ordinarily less than his actual earnings for a four-months' period, because he derives additional income (oftentimes substantial) from his garden plot economy. The treatment of pensioners seems

[196] Ospanov, *supra* note 191, at 23. See also CIVIL CODE art. 9.

[197] Regulations of Sept. 4, 1959 art. 6.

[198] Decree of March 26, 1962 (R.S.F.S.R.), Sots. zak. No. 9, p. 79 (1962).

[199] Kabalkin, *Dogovor roznichnoy kupli-prodazhi s rassrochkoy platyozhi (Contract of Installment Sale at Retail)*, Sots. zak. No. 12, p. 65 (1960).

[200] Kunik, *supra* note 173, at 16.

[201] YAZEV, *op. cit. supra* note 178, at 17.

[202] *Id.* at 15.

[203] Kunik, *supra* note 173, at 16.

to be unsettled. A suggestion has been made to limit their installment credit to a month's pension.[204] In the RSFSR employers must not issue another statement until after the applicant's previous indebtedness on a credit purchase has been fully extinguished.[205] In the Armenian SSR a person may buy on credit only one item at a time, irrespective of its price. In those republics which do not have regulations of this type, the employers are expected to cease issuing new statements when a worker's or employee's obligations to stores become unreasonably high relative to his earnings.[206] In their total effect these restrictions save individual buyers from assuming excessive burdens. Overcommitment of private resources might, under Soviet conditions, lead to illicit money-making activities or induce shopping around for more remunerative work. The latter practice would only aggravate the already serious problem of high labor turnover.

After the buyer has made a downpayment of at least 20 per cent of the retail price and paid a "service charge" of 1 to 2 per cent calculated also on the total price rather than the unpaid balance, he signs an instrument authorizing his employer (or collective farm or social insurance agency) to withhold the balance from his pay in equal amounts, twice a month, over a period from 6 to 12 months. The amounts so withheld are transferred to the appropriate trading organization (seller) by the eighth day of each month.[207] There is, however, some pressure in favor of modifying the compulsory withholding feature. In at least two republics (Ukrainian and Latvian SSR) the buyer may elect a direct payment system: cash at the store or money order.[208] On collective farms an agreement is usually made as to how much will be withheld by the farm administration and what amounts will be paid directly by the purchaser. This is natural, because a collective farmer derives a part of his money income from sales of produce either distributed to him by the farm or grown on his own plot. Some say that pensioners should make all their payments directly. The advocates of the direct payment method contend that its wider use could cause the volume of installment credit sales to expand.[209]

Unless otherwise provided by law or contract, the title passes at the time the thing is delivered, which in the ordinary case is simultaneous with the downpayment. The transaction is not a conditional sale. The seller retains no security interest in the thing; his rights are purely contractual. Neither the union nor republic laws limit the buyer's power over the thing.

[204] *Ibid.*

[205] See note 198 *supra.*

[206] YAZEV, *op. cit. supra* note 178, at 16.

[207] Decree of Aug. 12, 1959 art. 2; Regulations of Sept. 4, 1959 arts. 3, 4, 8. In the RSFSR the repayment terms are set by law for each commodity. Kunik, *supra* note 173, at 17.

[208] YAZEV, *op. cit. supra* note 178, at 26.

[209] *E.g.*, Pravda, Nov. 18, 1962, p. 4.

He can sell it or give it away, at his pleasure. Of course, the transfer of ownership or the loss or destruction of the thing does not terminate the seller's right to collect the debt in full. It is possible though to write a new contract whereby a subsequent buyer assumes the first buyer's obligation toward the store and releases the former. Preliminary to a new contract of this kind, the second buyer must procure an earnings' statement from his employer and, in accordance with article 126 of the Civil Code, obtain the creditor's approval of the transaction.[210] Under the 1923 decree of the RSFSR, the seller retained a security interest until the indebtedness was paid off; the buyer could not sell the property, or give it away, or encumber it, or use it in a manner inconsistent with its purpose or tending to damage it. After a default on three installment payments, the seller was entitled to rescind the contract, demand the return of the thing and recover an appropriate compensation for its deterioration and use.[211] Today the closely controlled payment system, in combination with the Soviet citizens' general duty to work and an effective machinery for collecting civil judgments, actually makes a repossession feature superfluous.

The earnings' statement issued by an employer is informational only; it is in no sense a suretyship agreement. It is after the purchase that the buyer's enterprise or organization is obliged to withhold the necessary amounts, that is, where the direct payment method is not used. Whenever, for any reason, the employer ceases withholding, it is required to communicate this fact to the creditor. In addition, by signing the withholding authorization, the buyer himself has undertaken to report the same.[212] If the termination of withholding is due to the buyer's removal to another place of employment, the trading organization's position is somewhat impaired. In the scheme of the 1959 regulations of the RSFSR, the trading organization requested that the withholding authorization be forwarded to the buyer's new employer which thereafter was to act as a collection agent.[213] This procedure has now been amended to require the first employer to withhold from the departing worker's or employee's pay the entire unpaid balance, unless it exceeds the ceilings established by law.[214] The effect is essentially that of an acceleration clause. Here, too, one finds considerable experimentation in the several republics. Thus in the Armenian SSR a buyer who changes his job must pay the remaining installments directly. By contrast, the neighboring Azerbaydzhanis have elected an approach that affords a high degree of protection to the creditor. In case the original pattern is upset, they shift

[210] Ospanov, *supra* note 191, at 24.

[211] Gribanov & Kabalkin, *supra* note 169, at 105.

[212] Regulations of Sept. 4, 1959, art. 8; Annex to the Regulations, ISTOCH. SOV. GRAZH. PRAV. 416.

[213] Art. 8.

[214] See note 198 *supra*.

the risk to the buyer's initial employer. When the buyer moves away, the employer pays off the debt to the trading organization and becomes subrogated to its rights and subsequently can avail itself of the usual legal means for collecting the debt from the former employee.[215] The Kirghiz law goes as far as to require a debtor to liquidate his obligation before leaving for a different place of residence.[216] Complaints are heard that employers frequently neglect their duties and aggravate the debt-collecting process. As might have been expected, the solution is seen in stiffer punishments for the delinquent managers.[217] When a member of a consumer cooperative either leaves the cooperative system completely or transfers to another association, his indebtedness is collected by taking the amount owed out of his paid-in shares and dividends earned but not distributed.[218]

The question of a buyer's liability for late payment or nonpayment may arise in those cases in which the buyer has been making direct payments all the while or where such payments are imposed after the termination of a withholding arrangement. In the Ukrainian and Latvian republics the buyer has to pay the creditor organization a contract penalty calculated at .2 per cent of the amount in default for each day of delay.[219] The penalties are added to payments currently due. The statute of limitations apparently begins to run from the maturity date of each installment.[220]

According to Soviet sources, defaults on installment sales contracts are rare. They reached only .85 per cent for the entire country in 1960. The greater number of defaults is said to be associated with changes in employment. Quite a few others are attributed to employers' neglect in reporting their former employees' whereabouts, or issuing earnings' statements under circumstances permitting the applicants to overcommit themselves. Now and then a buyer's heirs fail to pay up.[221] In several union republics recovery of unpaid balances on time contracts is by an ordinary civil action in the people's court of the district or city in which the defendant resides. On the other hand, in some republics, including now the RSFSR and the Ukrainian SSR, the debt may be enforced in an *ex parte* proceeding before a notary by obtaining an endorsement of execution *(ispolnitel'naya nadpis')*. Execution on the debtor's property may be levied on the basis of this document. The Statute on State Notariat of the RSFSR provides: "A state notarial office shall issue an endorsement of execution: (a) whenever the documents

[215] Yazev, *op. cit. supra* note 178, at 27-28.

[216] Kabalkin, *supra* note 199, at 66.

[217] Gribanov & Kabalkin, *supra* note 169, at 109; Kunik, *supra* note 173, at 17-18.

[218] Kunik, *supra* note 173, at 17.

[219] Yazev, *op. cit. supra* note 178, at 33.

[220] Gribanov & Kabalkin, *Pravovoye regulirovaniye kupli-prodazhi s rassrochkoy platyozha (Legal Regulation of Installment Sales)*, Sov. gos. i pravo No. 8, p. 108 (1960).

[221] *Id.* at 109; Kunik, *supra* note 173, at 17.

presented, as a whole, establish the debtor's indebtedness to the person seeking to collect it, beyond any doubt." [222] The claimant-seller must present (1) the original contract, (2) a certificate from the debtor's employer to the effect that he has left, and (3) an extract from the debtor's account showing the amount of the indebtedness, attested by the seller.[223] A bona fide dispute over the existence of the debt or its amount, is within the jurisdiction of the courts.[224] Retailers have been complaining about the necessity of collecting debts by court action. This, they say, considerably "complicates" their work. They have been vocal in advocating the *ex parte* proceedings. Apparently, in response to their clamor, the RSFSR in 1960 switched over to the notarial method. However, regulations issued by the *Tsentrosoyuz* in 1962 ordered judicial in lieu of notarial enforcement.[225] One explanation for this inconsistency in attitudes might be found in the fact that cooperatives operate mainly in rural areas where the competence of the notaries is perhaps less adequate and informal proceedings in their offices lend themselves to miscarriages of justice. Of course, a debtor faces an enforcement action, whether judicial or notarial, only when the breach has been due to his fault. If, for instance, the collecting agent (employer) has failed to transmit the amounts withheld from the debtor's pay, the debtor is not liable. Under those circumstances the creditor would have to seek recovery from the employer.

D. Rental of Consumer Durables [226]

Rental service *(prokat)*, though not properly part of retail trade, has much to do with developing and satisfying consumer demand. It is not treated merely as a transitory expedient but, as I mentioned in the introduction, is regarded as a wave of the future. The rental system increases the utilization rate of consumer durables, thus making each item "socially more useful." Alekseyev stresses the educational potentiality of the system; it will help gradually to obliterate concepts such as "exclusively mine" and "exclusively yours." [227] In this connection, perhaps the most striking vision of things to come has been offered by octogenerian academician Strumilin:

> "The people themselves will throw away personal cars and dachas and individual [garden] plots like so much excess baggage when modern

[222] Statute of Dec. 31, 1947 (R.S.F.S.R.) art. 33, ZAKONODATEL'STVO O NOTARIATE (LEGISLATION ON THE NOTARIAT) 151 (1960).

[223] Decree of Nov. 12, 1962 (R.S.F.S.R.), summarized in Sov. yus. No. 2, p. 30 (1963).

[224] Gribanov & Kabalkin, *supra* note 220, at 109.

[225] Kunik, *Dogovor kupli-prodazhi v kredit (Contract of Credit Sale)*, Sov. yus. No. 12, pp. 16-17 (1962).

[226] See text pp. 257-62 *infra* on "Automobile Rental."

[227] ALEKSEYEV, GRAZHDANSKOYE PRAVO V PERIOD RAZVERNUTOGO STROITEL'STVA KOMMUNIZMA (CIVIL LAW IN THE PERIOD OF ALL-OUT CONSTRUCTION OF COMMUNISM) 231 (1962).

> boarding houses with all the conveniences spring up in the best and most picturesque locations, offering separate rooms, yachts, motor scooters for pleasure rides, helicopters for excursions, etc., and when excellent cars of all models and colors (just pick one to suit your taste!) are lined up in the public garages, just waiting for passengers. . . . "There will be plenty of everything in the public dining room or the apartment-house kitchen: Eat it or leave it alone as you please. Excessive clothes only clutter up the closet." [228]

As the Good Book says: "Your old men shall dream dreams."

Ordinary leasing agreements involving consumer durables were occasionally made in the earlier days, but it appears that not until 1957 was the public rental system recognized as a distinct institution requiring its own rules in derogation of the Civil Code.[229] Since then, the popularity of the service has grown. As of January 1, 1961, there were 2,081 "rent-all" centers in the country, not including sporting equipment counters at stadiums and parks of culture.[230] But considering the size of the country and the uneven distribution of the centers, the service is not yet generally accessible to the people.

The Principles of Civil Law refer to rental service in article 55, which states that "conditions and procedures" of such service shall be prescribed by laws of the union republics. The special rules, when enacted, are to displace the general provisions of the chapter on property hire (articles 53 to 55).[231] Article 55 further provides that "the councils of ministers of the union republics shall approve model contracts to govern various specific kinds of rental" and that "any departure from the terms of the model contracts, which limit the borrowers' rights, is void." Because of either inaction at the republic level or further delegation of the rule-making power, no uniformity of regulation has been achieved in any of the 15 republics. Since the centers are operated by many different masters (trade organizations, public service branches of local soviets, industrial enterprises, housing administrations, etc.),[232] the rental contracts are typically governed by diverse departmental regulations and local ordinances. The multiplicity of principles and rules perplexes both administrators and consumers. The critics of the present system say that the existing differences for the most part cannot be justified in terms of local peculiarities and should be done away with in the new civil codes.[233]

[228] Izvestiya, Aug. 30, 1961, p. 3, transl. in 13 C.D.S.P. No. 35, pp. 24, 25 (1961).

[229] Basic Rules of Rental of April 9, 1957 (U.S.S.R.), Istoch. sov. grazh. prav. 532.

[230] Petrishcheva, *Pravovyye voprosy bytovogo prokata (Legal Problems of Rental Service)*, Pravovedeniye No. 2, pp. 40, 40-41 (1963).

[231] Kommentariy 232-33.

[232] Kabalkin, *Dogovory prokata predmetov bytovogo obikhoda (Contracts Involving Rental of Articles of Everyday Use)*, Sots. zak. No. 9, p. 90 (1962).

[233] Petrishcheva, *supra* note 230, at 41.

The regulations of rentals are similar to those of installment credit sales in that they seem to be designed to give maximum protection to lenders. In fact, a fear that socialist property would be squandered by lenient rental centers has been one reason for demanding uniform and compulsory regulation at a higher level.[234] At present the authorities which promulgate rental regulations also issue lists enumerating articles available for rent.[235] Here centralization would be undesirable. A local body fully conversant with the conditions of local trade is no doubt better qualified to manipulate the rental lists with a view to influencing consumer demand for durable goods in the stores. The USSR regulations of 1957 extended the service to all adult citizens residing either permanently or temporarily "in the city (suburb) where the rental center is located."[236] Again, the exclusion of rural areas and urban-type settlements is puzzling. I have found no clear reference to a subsequent extension of the service, as has been the case of installment credit sales. To establish himself as a resident, a customer must present his domestic passport. A temporary resident may be required to leave a monetary deposit in the amount of the retail price of the borrowed item.[237] In some cities articles are rented, by way of exception, to nonresidents, if they make a deposit equal to 150 per cent of the retail price![238] The City of Leningrad Rules of August 22, 1960, are worried about borrowers who are not gainfully employed (except students in institutions of higher learning, armed forces personnel and pensioners). However, instead of being required to make prohibitive money deposits, they must find someone to sign a contract of guarantee *(poruchitel'stvo)* backing their performance. The guarantor must be a Soviet citizen, a permanent resident of Leningrad and gainfully employed.[239] A regressive rental fee is collected according to a government-established schedule. When no deposit is required, the fee must be paid in advance. Frequently, maximum use periods are set.[240] The agreed upon period can be extended upon notice to the rental outlet and payment of an additional fee, if necessary. If, however, an article is withheld without the lender's consent, the borrower may be charged double rental for the excess time. On the other hand, if the borrower returns the article ahead of the appointed day, the unused portion of the fee is not refunded.[241]

[234] Kartasheva, *Nekotoryye pravovyye voprosy bytovogo prokata (Some Legal Problems of Rental Service)*, Sov. yus. No. 4, p. 11 (1962).

[235] Kabalkin, *supra* note 232, at 90.

[236] Basic Rules art. 1.

[237] *Id.* art. 2.

[238] Petrishcheva, *supra* note 230, at 46.

[239] *Ibid.*

[240] *E.g.*, in Leningrad, household articles, sporting equipment, and musical instruments are rented for a maximum period of three months. *Id.* at 43.

[241] Basic Rules arts. 3, 4; Kabalkin, *supra* note 232, at 91.

When the rented property is damaged, some of the local regulations have little sympathy for the borrower. The rules of Moscow prohibit him from making his own repairs. Understandably, rental centers wish to control the quality of work and guard against attempts to conceal serious defects by superficial "fixing." Thus, in Moscow, when a customer returns a thing whose damage is repairable, he must pay the cost of the needed repairs according to a list of prevailing prices. By contrast, under the rules of City of Izhevsk, in the Udmurt ASSR, a customer who returns an article in a damaged condition must find a way to repair it at his own expense and, in addition, pay a double fee for each day the item is being repaired. Considering the shocking state of repair services in the Soviet Union, where it may take weeks, months, and even years to eliminate a minor flaw, such a rule, if enforced, is downright cruel. Indeed, the hapless customer might be wiser to claim total loss. In such a case, in Izhevsk the rental outlet would extract from him three times the depreciated value of the item, still quite an unsatisfactory alternative. He would be only a little better off in Aktyubinsk (twice the depreciated value) or Sverdlovsk (list price plus an extra month's rental). Characteristically, the local rules are much more unfavorable to the public than were the original USSR regulations of 1957. This evidences possibly not only local narrow mindedness, but also misuse of rental outlets to "buy" things. The USSR regulations of 1957 provided for payment of the depreciated value only.[242] But since June 13, 1958, the Ministries of Trade and Finance of the RSFSR have required their rental outlets to sue for either return of a rented article or one-and-half times its value.[243] If rental services are indeed used to shape consumer demand for goods in retail trade, the inflated value feature makes a great deal of sense. It is the scarce goods that are made available on rental basis. Being in short supply, they are apt to command high prices in a free bargaining situation. At ordinary retail prices the most desirable items would be rapidly withdrawn from rental outlets, the borrowers subsequently claiming their loss or total destruction. Of course, some articles might be highly desirable even at a 50 per cent premium. Perhaps it is necessary to impose a 200 per cent premium in Izhevsk to keep the goods within rental channels. A desire to "buy" things from a rental outlet may be intensified by another factor, too. Poor quality of consumer goods being a constant problem, a Soviet consumer might feel much safer in acquiring an item which he himself has tested for a while and found in working order. If, however, the law empowers a retail outlet to sue for actual performance (return of the article itself), the borrower is not free to render substitute performance (payment of money) without the lender's consent. Under this rule, a conscientious rental service should accept sub-

[242] Basic Rules art. 8; Kabalkin, *supra* note 232, at 91; Petrishcheva, *supra* note 230, at 47, 49-50.

[243] Kabalkin, *supra* note 232, at 92.

stitute performance only in cases in which delivery of the thing itself has become objectively impossible.

If not voluntarily settled, claims for damage to, or return of, rental property are brought in people's courts. The number of such suits is "quite considerable."[244] In the overwhelming majority of cases, the rental outlets are successful. A writer reports that none of the defendant borrowers has appealed an adverse decision.[245] On the other hand, rental outlets have not taken full advantage of article 36 of the Principles of Civil Law and article 117 of the Civil Code; their monetary recoveries, as a rule, have been limited to repair expenses only.[246] Criminal liability for deliberate failure to return a borrowed article arises only in those cases in which the customer, "by way of fraud or abuse of confidence," converts the property to his own use, without paying for it.[247]

E. *Automobile Rental*

"Rent-a-car" service *(prokat bez shofyora)* appeared in the Soviet Union along with the other innovations of the late 1950's. On March 23, 1959, the RSFSR Minister of Autotransport and Highways approved the first comprehensive rules to regulate the use of rented cars.[248] On October 6 of the same year, Khrushchev, fresh back from his American trip, came out strongly in favor of automobile rental service in his Vladivostok speech on consumer problems:

> "[I]t is not at all our aim to compete with the Americans in the production of large numbers of automobiles . . .
>
> "We will turn out a lot of cars, but not now. We want to establish a system for the use of automobiles that will differ from the one in capitalist countries, where people reason on the principle: 'The car may be lousy but it's my own.' We will make more rational use of automobiles than the Americans do. We will develop public taxi [rental] pools on an ever broader scale; people will get cars from them for necessary trips. Why should a man worry about where to park his car; why should he have to bother with it."[249]

[244] *Ibid.*

[245] Kartasheva, *supra* note 234, at 11.

[246] Petrishcheva, *supra* note 230, at 49.

[247] CRIMINAL CODE art. 93; Kabalkin, *supra* note 232, at 92-93; Case of Yefimov, Presid. Supr. Ct. R.S.F.S.R. 1960, [1961] Byul. verkh. suda S.S.S.R. No. 4, p. 44. But see the earlier case of Shahavelev, Presid. Lenigr. City Ct., ab. 1959, Sots. zak. No. 3, p. 86 (1960).

[248] The rules are cited in Levenson, *Dogovor prokata legkovykh avtomobiley (Contract of Automobile Rental)*, Sots. zak. No. 6, p. 64 (1961). Regulations of automobile rental are not the same in all republics. Moreover, several regions and cities have adopted their own rules. Krasavchikov, *Dogovor prokata legkovykh avtomashin (Contract of Automobile Rental)*, Sov. gos. i pravo No. 11, p. 74 (1962).

[249] Pravda, Oct. 8, 1959, p. 1, transl. in 11 C.D.S.P. No. 4, p. 3 (1959).

The draft of the 1961 Party Program promised that "output of automobiles for the population *(dlya naseleniya)* will increase significantly." In the final version, this innocuous phrase was changed very pointedly to read that "output of automobiles to serve the population *(dlya obsluzhivaniya naseleniya)* will increase." [250]

A Soviet *avtobaz* (rental station) is not overly anxious to put any comer into the driver's seat. Just as the pleasure of owning an automobile is bestowed only upon carefully selected persons, the thrills of driving, too, are parcelled out with circumspection. Naturally, the prospective borrower must have a valid driver's license. He must also reside and work in the town in which the rental station is located. In addition, he must secure from his place of employment a certificate indicating his privilege to use rented automobiles. Such certificates issue for limited periods (*e.g.*, one year in the RSFSR, Tadzhik SSR, and Georgian SSR; six months in Azerbaidzhan SSR) and thereby give employers an opportunity to review the applicant's deserts. Some local rules, such as those of the City of Odessa, permit rentals only to *peredoviki* (first-rate workers). It seems, however, that the ultimate decision to rent or not to rent is made by the *avtobaz* bureaucrats, who have the power to dishonor a perfectly good employer's certificate. A rental station keeps a card file containing detailed information about its customers. As long as a person has failed to meet his obligations arising out of a previous rental arrangement, another automobile is not rented to him. Some of the stricter rules provide that for a serious violation of the terms of a rental agreement (*e.g.*, involvement in an accident, damage to the automobile, use of the automobile to derive unearned income, systematic violation of the rules of the road) a person forfeits his privilege of renting an automobile *forever*. Apparently, this affects only the person's relations with that particular local rental station. If he moves to live and work elsewhere, his past transgressions stay behind, unless there exists some method by which other rental stations are apprised of the fact of disenfranchisement. Whereas Soviet commentators criticize the harshest aspects of the regulations, they support rigorous screening of prospective customers who are to be entrusted with an expensive piece of state property which, at the same time, is a dangerous instrumentality. As the final step before getting an automobile, the applicant must pass a special driver's test administered by the personnel of the *avtobaz*. This test, however, is not repeated in cases of subsequent rentals from the same station.[251] In all this, opportunities for red tape, favoritism, and corruption are unlimited.

Automobiles are rented for periods ranging from three hours to one

[250] Alekseyev feels that the amendment confirms his theory of gradual shrinkage of personal property ownership. ALEKSEYEV, *op. cit. supra* note 227, at 196.

[251] Petrishcheva, *supra* note 230, at 42-43, 48-49; Levenson, *supra* note 248, at 64; Krasavchikov, *supra* note 248, at 75.

month. In some republics longer periods are permitted with ministerial approval in exceptional cases. Rental charge is computed on the basis of both time and mileage. The borrower, in addition, pays for fuel and lubricants. By signing the rental agreement, he declares that he has examined the vehicle at the time of accepting it, and either has found nothing wrong with it or has informed the rental station of all discovered defects. It is abundantly clear that an ordinary person is ill-equipped to carry out a successful inspection. Obviously, he cannot see any hidden defects. An unreasonable contract term of this kind is likely to breed abuse. Some *avtobaz* personnel rent defective automobiles and cover up their own carelessness and mismanagement by shifting the blame to users. Since the borrower has expressly agreed to return the automobile in good working order, he must pay for all parts and labor needed to restore it to that condition.[252]

In the experience of rental stations, each rental automobile is damaged on the average 15 to 20 times per year. Consequently, many former users owe large sums of money to the rental stations. Showing concern for protection of the interests of the state, some rental station managers have suggested large security deposits; others, casualty insurance. Deposit requirements would surely cut into an already severely restricted number of users. Insurance would be far more acceptable, with the cost of the premiums shifted to the clientele. As a general proposition, a borrower is liable for damage to, or destruction of, the automobile only if the loss is attributable to his fault. In case of late return, he is, however, liable also for harm inflicted by circumstances beyond his control.[253] Some rental stations have adopted form contracts which extend borrowers' liability beyond these limits. When a third person has caused damage to the automobile while it was in the borrower's possession, the rental station can nevertheless claim compensation directly from the borrower, who then has a claim over against the wrongdoer. All disputes involving claims against borrowers are tried in the people's court of the city or district of the *avtobaz*. Despite efforts of some rental stations to calculate their claims in retail prices, the courts have held that since state organizations acquire automobiles at a special low price and carry them on books at this low cost figure, their recovery should be similarly limited (acquisition price less depreciation). Apparently, to fight the stripping of automobiles of scarce parts and accessory equipment, some local rules impose multiple liability for their removal. For example, in Baku, a borrower pays double the value of the missing item; in the Latvian SSR, he is assessed its fivefold value. Also, according to the

[252] Petrishcheva, *supra* note 230, at 43, 45; Levenson, *supra* note 248, at 64-65; Krasavchikov, *supra* note 248, at 65. For the most cogent critique of the present practice, see Sokolova, *Ob otvetstvennosti grazhdan, vsiavshikh legkovoy avtomobil' naprokat (On Liability of Citizens Using a Rented Automobile)*, Vest. Mosk. Univ. No. 3, p. 50 (1962).

[253] CIVIL CODE art. 121.

Latvian rules, the borrower who returns a damaged automobile is assessed both the cost of repairs and the income lost by reason of idleness, in accordance with the regular schedule of rental fees.[254]

Serious problems have arisen with respect to allocation of liability for damage caused to third persons. Article 90 of the Principles of Civil Law, corresponding to article 404 of the Civil Code, provides:

> "Organizations and citizens whose activity involves increased danger for those in the vicinity (transport organizations, industrial enterprises, construction projects, owners [*vladel'tsy*] [255] of automobiles) are obligated to compensate for damage caused by the source of increased danger, unless they prove that the damage arose as a result of an insuperable force or the intention of the victim himself."

The person (juristic or natural) whose activity is proximately connected with a source of increased danger is "in charge (possession) of the source of increased danger *(vladelets istochnika povyshennoy opasnosti).*" Identification of this person is important: whoever is in charge is liable for any harm done to others. Ordinarily, where an organization owns the source of increased danger, it is considered as being in charge thereof. Thus, a cab driver employed by a taxi park is not liable for injuries caused to others in the absence of his own fault.[256] For some reason, the rent-a-car situation has not been regarded as analogous. It has been argued by some that a rental station which turns an automobile over to a user pursuant to a rigorously drafted rental agreement is no less in charge than an organization whose vehicle is operated by one of its employees. Consequently, a victim should be permitted to proceed against the *avtobaz.* The "majority view" is diametrically opposite. Russian, Ukrainian, Armenian and other regulations, as well as the judicial practice of the RSFSR, take the view that the liability is the borrower's alone. On top of that, a provision of the Ukrainian regulations makes the borrower criminally liable, if the injury has been inflicted by reason of his fault. The Latvian SSR has taken a slightly modified position. Its regulations look to article 403 of the Civil Code (of the RSFSR) as a basis of recovery, thus making the borrower's liability hinge on fault. It is not clear whether the Latvian courts permit victims to hold the rental stations liable without fault under article 404. The "majority view" has been praised by righteous commentators as placing the loss where it belongs—on the real culprit, the driver; they feel strongly that no state money ought to be paid to the victim. This constant obsession with "safeguarding

[254] Petrishcheva, *supra* note 230, at 48-50; Kartasheva, *supra* note 234, at 12; Levenson, *supra* note 248, at 64-65.

[255] [Author's note] "*Vladelets*" is a bad term. In common usage it has the same meaning as "*sobstvennik*"—"owner." In a more technical sense it means "possessor." In article 90 the distinction is important.

[256] KOMMENTARIY 328.

the socialist property" and tendency to look for a single guilty individual make virtually impossible any rational analysis of distribution of risks. Some writers suggest making the borrower and the rental station jointly and severally liable, an approach "justifiable, first of all, from the point of view of the victim."[257] Indeed, in many cases accident victims obtain money judgments which, for some reason, turn out to be uncollectible. Something can be said also in favor of easing the burden of the borrower who, in the present scheme of things, can be well-nigh ruined moneywise.[258]

The Soviet Union knows of no automobile accident liability insurance. Occasional proposals for its introduction have been severely criticized. The Principles of Civil Law do not acknowledge this form of insurance,[259] and article 3 denies to the union republics the right to take initiative in the area of insurance. Objections against liability insurance are based mainly on assumed deterrent effect of delictual liability. We know enough by now to regard such assumption with much caution. I have not seen any Soviet writer try to analyze the idea that accidents are avoidable by the conscious efforts of a driver, in the light of article 90 of the Principles of Civil Law which recognizes as defenses only narrowly defined "insuperable force" and "the intention of the victim himself." Even "gross negligence" of the victim, mentioned in article 404 of the Civil Code, has been dropped from the new Principles. The opposition to liability insurance is thus really a matter of faith. For example:

> "The institution of liability insurance, so widespread in capitalist society, is principally and categorically unacceptable to socialist society and law.
>
> "It is unacceptable especially now when the Party Program calls for more vigorous educational work, for realization, within the lifetime of this generation, of habits and ways of communistic living . . ."[260]

It is a good guess that before long this bit of ideological nonsense, too, will be relegated to the memory hole. Czechoslovakia, Poland, and GDR are undisturbed by the alleged antisocial effect of liability insurance.[261]

[257] Krasavchikov, *supra* note 248, at 76-77; Levenson, *supra* note 248, at 65; Dobrovol'skiy, *Novoye v sudebnom praktike po delam o vozmeshcheniyi vreda (Recent Judicial Practice Concerning Compensation for Injury)*, Sots. zak. No. 8, p. 54, 59 (1960).

[258] Artyom'yev & Polovinchik, *Novyye vidy strakhovaniya podskazyvayet zhizn' (Life Suggests New Forms of Insurance)*, Sov. yus. No. 11, p. 3 (1961). Artyom'yev at the time was a Deputy Minister of Autotransport and Highways of the RSFSR.

[259] Arts. 78-82.

[260] Rakhmilovich, *O strakhovaniyi grazhdanskoy otvetstvennosti (On Liability Insurance)*, Sov. yus. No. 4, p. 21 (1962).

[261] Katanyan, *Dogovor prokata legkovykh avtomobiley (Contract of Automobile Rental)*, V. I. Yur. Nauk: Uch. zap. No. 17, pp. 118, 152-53 (1963).

V. Protection of Buyers' Interests

The discussion of this section assumes that production patterns have been determined, and that some goods are being channelled into the trade network and others are already awaiting final distribution. For a moment we are not viewing the individual as a dynamic "consumer" whose reactions can affect even the august national economic plan. Instead, we now focus our attention on the individual in his role as a humble "shopper" or "buyer" of things offered to him by a vast and impersonal trading system. A buyer is interested in doing his shopping conveniently and in a decent way, and in getting what reportedly has been produced to satisfy his needs. In other words, he is interested in the quality of facilities and service, and in seeing that the things he buys are really what they purport to be. He has a definite interest in the quality of merchandise. In these areas many of the more effective controls are not legal controls. This is not, however, entirely a Soviet phenomenon. The pervasiveness of extralegal controls in our own country's business affairs, and especially in consumer relations, is no secret. The striking thing about the Soviet system, therefore, is not the employment of these devices but rather some of their peculiarly Soviet forms.

A. Quality of Facilities and Service

The number of consumer trade outlets is still inadequate. The absolute volume of retail trade has increased considerably faster than the number of stores, catering establishments, and various service concerns (laundries, repair shops, gasoline stations). By stretching the existing facilities, the Soviets have managed to hold down costs of distribution, but only at the expense of the amenities of trade. Rural areas continue to be served mainly by simple, if not primitive, "general stores." Because of transportation problems, many people are practically dependent on a single store and must take both the goods and the service as they come. Where a large segment of the population, whether it be in a city or country, is dependent on a single store or a small group of stores, it is not at all certain that the store (or stores) will carry all the needs. While the monetary incentive system discourages stocking of unsaleable merchandise, it does not necessarily lead to stocking all those items that could be sold without any trouble. Store managers are reluctant to carry lines on which the percentage rebate is low. And in order to increase the volume of gross sales, they would rather stock and sell a few television sets and bicycles than simple things like hairpins and thumb tacks. Fresh vegetables might not be carried because of danger of quick spoilage. The belief is that in the absence of garden greens, the customers will purchase more potatoes, or macaroni, or similar worry-free products. If canned fish is obtainable, why stock much demanded herring with all the attendant problems of handling? When making proposals for the next planning year, the previous "consumption pattern" is cited to wangle an allocation of products good for the store. If supply of consumer goods is inadequate, even that which is sold obviously gives a distorted picture of what demand actually is. By reason of their virtual monopoly position some stores are able to go on slanting the information about demand indefinitely.

In recognition of the fact that economic stimuli alone, under Soviet conditions, do not assure balanced inventories of merchandise and proper trade practices at individual stores, Commissions of Societal Control were established in the late 1950's.[262] They were endowed with broad powers to gather facts and make proposals for the improvement of retail trade, public catering and everyday services. For this purpose the commissions may, among other things, conduct surprise inspections on the spot and obtain explanations from managers and sales personnel concerning poor assortment, bad physical layout, questionable sales practices, etc. In cities the commissions are attached to trade unions, in rural areas—to cooperative associations. Their accomplishments probably have been modest, once the initial effect of newness wore off. Usually crusades of this type soon become formalistic and before long turn into bureaucratic fossils. Some sort of *modus vivendi* is reached between the inspectors and the inspected. Not infrequently the inspectors simply join the vast circle of recipients of graft. When a control apparatus has outlived its usefulness, whether because of complacency or corruption, it must be either abolished or placed under a new untainted super-institution. The Commisions of Societal Control continue to exist in the area of trade, but they as well as similar inspectorates in other sectors of the Soviet economy, are now overshadowed by the Party-State Control Committee. The Committee was created in 1963 [263] as a control body to control all controllers and everyone else, too. The hope is that now the Committee will wage "the struggle against abuses, waste and pilfering and against inefficiency, bureaucracy and bribetaking." [264] Some informal control is exercised by the press. Newspapers often organize raids on various trading enterprises and report in detail their findings of deficiencies. The "hottest" exposés may contain extremely serious accusations and passages amounting to character assassination. The episodical nature of the press raids makes for both good and bad results: while the information gathered is probably quite trustworthy, it is far too sketchy to give the higher authorities a thorough and systematic account.

Shopping in the Soviet Union has always been closer to drudgery than delight. Notwithstanding recent improvements, the buying of things still requires perseverence and a great deal of luck. The buyer must be prepared

[262] Statute of July 11, 1958 (U.S.S.R.), ZHILISHCHNO-BYTOVYYE VOPROSY: SBORNIK POSTANOVLENIY I INSTRUKTSIY (PROBLEMS OF HOUSING AND EVERYDAY LIFE: A COLLECTION OF DECREES AND REGULATIONS) 225 (1960).

[263] Izvestiya, Jan. 18, 1963, p. 3.

[264] Pravda, April 5, 1963, p. 2.

to spend considerable time in drab surroundings and in contact with unpleasant people. The retailing methods are still inefficient and cumbersome. The so-called cashier *(kassa)* system (still widespread in Western Europe, too) is the accepted way of operating a store. The cashier system is a three-line ritual that facilitates checking and doublechecking on store personnel: "the unattended customer is not allowed to examine any commodity, the salesclerk is not allowed to take cash, and the cashier is not allowed to handle any goods." [265] However, behavior of the store personnel can cause more grief than the mechanics of retailing. The most often heard complaint concerns "chilly indifference" and even rudeness of the salespeople.[266] Possibly Soviet trade attracts not just average Soviet people (who are ordinarily quite meddlesome and easily plunge into petty quarrels) [267] but types who choose the occupation primarily because it offers illicit fringe benefits to the unscrupulous and the dishonest.[267a] Persons with such proclivities are perhaps even less suited to face an anxious and demanding public. There are untold opportunities for both lowly and ingenious crooks. In retail trade their schemes usually will not be so spectacular nor their rewards so lush as those of the grand operators in factories and wholesale organizations, but they will serve well to supplement a man's pay and improve his diet. Pilfering *(khishcheniye)* is part of the Soviet way of life. An American tries to recoup a portion of the government's take by cheating on his income tax; a Soviet citizen makes it his daily habit to stuff something into his pocket or handbag. "The scarcity element which predominates in Soviet society . . . must be assumed to have aroused intense anxieties about oral deprivation in the Soviet population which would serve greatly to increase the impact of the objectively real shortages which have been chronic in the system." [268]

Trade regulations provide for write-off of an assumed percentage rather than actual losses of products by spillage, evaporation, etc. In 1961 about 5,000,000 rubles worth of goods was written off in the RSFSR alone. In a delicatessen store the sales staff would be appropriating one-half liter of vodka out of every 1,000 liters and 2.5 kilograms of butter out of every 100 kilograms sold.[269] If the products are scarce, consumers as a group suffer.

[265] GOLDMAN, SOVIET MARKETING: DISTRIBUTION IN A CONTROLLED ECONOMY 132-33 (1963).

[266] Sov. Ross., April 7, 1960, p. 2; Izvestiya, Feb. 13, 1963, p. 3; Cina, Aug. 3, 1963, p. 1.

[267] Especially true of the large Russian population. Russians are generally expansive; they express their feelings easily and are given to impulse. Suppressed, pent-up feelings easily break out in the form of petty quarrels in routine face-to-face relationships. See BAUER, INKELES & KLUCKHOHN, HOW THE SOVIET SYSTEM WORKS 163-67 (1960).

[267a] The 1960 Congress of Consumers Cooperatives conceded that "people who want to live at the expense of society without giving anything in return still worm their way into the midst of cooperative personnel." Pravda, Aug. 22, 1962, p. 1, 4.

[268] BAUER, INKELES, & KLUCKHOHN, *op cit. supra* note 267, at 163.

[269] Izvestiya, Feb. 21, 1963, p. 4.

This may all seem to be within the law. Not so. When the write-offs are fictitious, a crime has been committed. One Krasintsev, the manager of a warehouse in Kalinin, made 15,733 rubles by writing up imaginary glassware breakage and pulled fifteen years for it.[270] Pilfering of socialist property is an extremely serious crime.[271] If the pilfering is on an "especially large scale," it may be punished by death.[272] Executions under this article have been common. Whether the scale of the effort will be gauged "especially large" depends on many factors, including the ruble value of the loot. Three organizers of "a large group of swindlers entrenched in the province delicatessen trust . . . in Dnepropetrovsk" were shot after "a search brought to light millions of rubles in cash and valuables in the possession of the swindlers."[273] In the celebrated *pirozhki* (small hot rolls with meat or vegetable filling) case, key persons in a Sverdlovsk restaurant reduced the fat content in each of the rolls from six to four grams, but continued charging the previous price. Investigation established that, in four years, the innovators had appropriated 125,000 rubles worth of foodstuffs (evidently for resale on the black market). This was sufficient to put two of the leaders in front of a firing squad.[274] Given equal amounts of appropriation, repeated acts involving small amounts apparently are dealt with more severely than a single act involving a large amount.[275]

The penalties are milder when the property loss falls on a buyer rather than the state. So, if instead of reducing the assets of the state by appropriaion of merchandise stocks, the dishonest retailer derives his gain from intentionally cheating by measurement, shortweighing, shortchanging, inflating prices, or selling a lower grade product at the price of a higher grade, he can be imprisoned for up to two years only; except that when such acts are committed on a "large scale" or by a person previously convicted of the same offense, the prison term may be increased to seven years, with or without confiscation of property.[276] According to two known judicial decisions, the line between "large" and "small" scales lies somewhere between

[270] Case of Krasintsev, [1963] Byul. verkh. suda R.S.F.S.R. No. 1, p. 15 (Crim. Div. Supr. Ct. R.S.F.S.R. 1962).

[271] CRIMINAL CODE art. 92 (the most commonly applicable article).

[272] *Id.* art. 93-1. "Pilfering" in English usually denotes petty stealing or filching. The meaning of "*khishcheniye*" is not so limited. Although I realize that "grand pilfering" may be regarded as contradiction in terms, I prefer the word "pilfering" because most taking of state property is on a small scale. The term has been used by others in this context, and it is more colorful than "larceny" or "theft," which I would use to translate "*krazha*."

[273] Trud, May 29, 1962, p. 4.

[274] Pravda, Feb. 10, 1963, p. 6.

[275] Case of Lyubavina, [1963] Byul. verkh. suda R.S.F.S.R. No. 4, p. 15 (Presid. Supr. Ct. Karel. A.S.S.R., late 1962 or early 1963).

[276] CRIMINAL CODE art. 156.

42 and 625 rubles.[277] A few years ago, a check of the retail trading outlets of Baku showed that twenty percent of the scales cheated the customer.[278] Marking and price tagging of consumer goods is very poor, permitting various abuses.[279]

A common practice is to conceal certain much desired and scarce goods and trade "under the counter." After the customer has made correct overtures, an agreement is reached to sell and buy the article at an amount in excess of the fixed price. Sometimes the article is displayed, but sale refused on the pretext of lack of certain necessary documents or instructions on price.[280] However, as soon as "good will" money appears in the prospective buyer's hand, the log jam breaks. Information concerning arrival of much demanded merchandise is priceless. As a matter of fact, in connivance with warehouse and transportation people, a special delivery of a single article to a retail store may be staged to enable a special customer to "chance upon" it. The legitimate part of the deal is concluded openly, before everyone's eyes. The other part of the bargain is carried out in privacy, at another place and time.[281] From time to time, of course, effective inspections uncover some of these transactions and, at least temporarily, disrupt the established "business." Since the seller pockets the buyer's money in return for favors connected with his official position, this form of misconduct is treated as bribery. The Criminal Code regards bribery as a most serious crime, in some cases bringing death to the bribetaker.[282] As a rule, arrangements of the kind described involve of necessity large numbers of people. All those who know, or might know, of the operations are entitled to a cut. It is axiomatic: "if you rob, do not forget to share [the loot] with your fellow man." [283] As a security precaution, inspectors, too, are enlisted.

> "After all, the most a member of the commission can get as a reward for reporting a store manager is some praise, but just a little effort invested in collaborating with the store manager can triple his monthly income. Show me the man who under these circumstances would prefer to be a socialist hero of labor and ruin the source of his best, truly socialist income." [284]

[277] Vol'fman, *Ugolovnaya otvetstvennost' za obman pokupatelya (Criminal Liability for Defrauding Buyers)*, Sov. yus. No. 2, pp. 18, 20 (1963).

[278] Pravda, Jan. 19, 1958, p. 2.

[279] Cina, July 18, 1963, p. 2.

[280] Radyanska Ukraina, Feb. 26, 1958, p. 3; Cina, June 8, 1961, p. 4.

[281] NOVAK [pseud.], THE FUTURE IS OURS, COMRADE 195-96 (1960).

[282] Arts. 173-74.

[283] Cina, June 8, 1961, p. 4. On the involvement of large conspiratorial groups, see Dremov & Gustov, *Prinimat' mery k likvidatsiyi khishcheniy v torgovle (Measures Should be Taken for the Liquidation of Pilfering in Trade)*, Sots. zak. No. 8, p. 46 (1963).

[284] NOVAK, *op. cit. supra* note 281, at 194-95.

When misdeeds of this sort are brought to trial, defendant's benches are normally occupied by whole "gangs."—It takes a collective to build a socialist system; it takes a collective to beat it.

Chapter seven of the Special Part of the Criminal Code treats the so-called "general" official crimes, that is crimes that can be committed in any branch of state administration, including the trade network. Besides bribery, the chapter includes abuse of authority (article 170), acts exceeding authority (article 171), failure to use authority *(khalatnost')* (article 172), and forgery in connection with official duties (article 175). Article 172, the successor of article 111 in the 1926 Code, could perhaps be applied to trade situations with considerable ease. "Failure to use authority" means failure to perform or poor performance of one's official duties, by reason of negligence or bad faith. It carries a penalty of imprisonment up to three years, or corrective labor up to one year, or dismissal from duties. Failure to secure a store against thieves and pilferers might be qualified as such a crime. Likewise, careless certification of incorrect accounts and other trade documents might come under article 172.[285] However, these broad catch-all articles are invoked very sparingly. Almost every Soviet administrator, at some time during his career, has offended against their sweeping provisions. Quite on the contrary, there is a lot of shielding of, at least, the more important officials by their brethren in other positions of authority. The following example is not at all unusual: When Aliyev, a high official in the Baku Trade Department was called before a party committee to answer serious charges of misconduct in office, he "quickly sensed the way the wind was blowing, repented immediately and with unusual fervor." He was let off with a warning. But this was not his first trouble. Some time before, while Aliyev was the Director of the Azerbaydzhan Trade Trust, waste and embezzlement in his department came to more than 2,500,000 rubles. Aliyev was merely reprimanded "for failing to wage a satisfactory struggle against irregularities, for employing questionable personnel and for conniving with swindlers." [286]

B. Quality of Merchandise

A story out of the Soviet Union tells of a buyer hard put to choose among several shirts. He finally picks out one, but confides to the salesclerk that he is not entirely pleased with its color. Don't let the color bother you, says the clerk, it will come off after the first washing anyway.

[285] 2 PIONTKOVSKIY, MEN'SHAGIN & CHKHIKVADZE, KURS SOVETSKOGO UGOLOVNOGO PRAVA: CHAST' OSOBENNAYA (A COURSE ON SOVIET CRIMINAL LAW: SPECIAL PART) 105-06 (1959).

[286] Pravda, Jan. 19, 1958, p. 2. But see Case of Barulina, 1959, [1960] Byul. verkh. suda S.S.S.R. No. 3, p. 46 (Presid. Supr. Ct. Latv. S.S.R.) (store manager who knowingly sold goods to speculators convicted of abuse of authority and complicity in speculation).

The poor quality of products is a disgrace to the Soviet economy. Added to a lack of ways and means for eliminating defects, it at times borders on disaster. Obtaining spare parts for producer goods presents a major problem for managers and their staffs. The need is even more neglected in the area of consumption. The cost in terms of time and energy wasted by a factory to hunt down a certain gear or by a teacher to find a tiny screw for the frame of his eyeglasses is incalculable. Furthermore, defects in machines and gadgets that are supposed to work constitute an interminable source of frustration. One can easily imagine the annoyance felt by a Soviet viewer whose set goes on the blink during a telecast on the next Seven-Year Plan. Repair services are few, understaffed, inadequately supplied and ill-organized. Corruption has not spared this nook of Soviet economic life either.

According to the Civil Code, a buyer is obliged to examine the merchandise on the spot for "obvious" defects, such as scratches in the finish of furniture, loose seams in ready-made suits and crooked heels on women's shoes. He must immediately report his findings to the seller, at the risk of losing his right to raise any objections later on. The rule unmistakably has been designed to guard against buyers who willingly acquiesce in a defect at first, then change their minds, as well as those who mar the merchandise while handling it themselves. Immediate discovery of "hidden" defects cannot be and is not required. Defects in the works of a watch or loose connections in a radio receiver are usually noticed only after some period of use. In these cases, the buyer must present his claims to the seller as soon as defects have come to his notice. A buyer who has thus in due time informed the seller has the right to claim either a substitute item of proper quality, or reduction in price, or rescission of the contract and recovery of all damages.[287] The Principles of Civil Law add a fourth option—elimination of the defects without expense to the buyer,[288] but in other respects retain the general approach of the Code: the buyer's recourse is to the seller (in most cases, the retail trade organization) rather than the producer from whom the seller acquired the thing; the buyer chooses the form of relief.

In practice, leaving aside a few exceptions, a buyer enjoys neither a right to proceed directly against a retail trade organization nor a choice of the type of relief. Disputes over quality are handled under departmental rules issued by the Ministry of Trade of the USSR on June 15, 1956.[289] These rules are inconsistent with the Code provisions and it is not clear on what (formal) authority they have been promulgated.

[287] CIVIL CODE arts. 195-98.

[288] PRINCIPLES OF CIVIL LAW art. 41.

[289] Rules for Exchange of Consumer Goods of June 15, 1956 (U.S.S.R.), ISTOCH. SOV. GRAZH. PRAV. 412.

The 1956 rules distinguish between goods the quality of which has been assured for a specified period of time and those which are not so guaranteed. If a buyer discovers any defects, within the guarantee period, he can take the article to a repair shop designated in the contract of sale. A faulty item is accepted by the seller for exchange only when either (a) the designated shop is unable to correct the defect for lack of skill or parts, or (b) when the item refuses to function properly more than twice during the guarantee period, notwithstanding efforts to get the problem corrected. A third alternative—returning the item for refund of money—is open to the buyer only after he has become entitled to get the thing exchanged and it appears that no replacement is available.[290] The procedure envisaged by the rules is not entirely unreasonable, but it breaks down in application. Significantly, when trouble first occurs, the retail store (seller) is in no way interested in helping, or obligated to help, its hapless customer. The buyer initially has to deal with a repair shop. A Soviet critic of the present system writes:

> "In some cases, the guarantee workshops are directly subordinated to producer plants, in other cases—tied to them by contract. In every case they act in the name and the interests of the plant.
>
> "Since it is not a party to the contract of sale-purchase, a guarantee workshop has no contractual obligations toward the buyer. It is interested neither in improving the construction of the article, nor in conscientious performance of repairs, inasmuch as the length of the guarantee period is unaffected by the number of repairs, and the shop is fully compensated by the producer plant. The mission of the guarantee shops is simply to employ all means to "prolong the life" of the article until the expiration of the guarantee period." [291]

Electronic goods have been especially plagued by poor quality. But, instead of trying to combat the crisis with the incentive weapons we discussed in the section on "Transmission of Consumer Demand to Producers," the government showed the white feather. On October 30, 1956, the Ministry of Trade of the USSR released a circular letter "On Procedure for Exchanging Defective Radio-Goods." The letter declared that the June 15 rules on exchange (for either a *new set* or *money*) were inapplicable in the event that supplies of suitable tubes, condensers, etc. had been exhausted, and that, in any event, exchange after two unsuccessful efforts to repair was permissible only if an authorized guarantee workshop certified that further repairs would be necessary! Thus a buyer's rights were made to depend on a self-serving statement of a manufacturer's agent.[292] Obviously, the short-

[290] Rules, *supra* note 289, art. 2.

[291] Moyseyev, *O pravovykh garantiyakh dobrokachestvennosti tovarov (On Legal Guarantees of Quality of Goods)*, Sots. zak. No. 10, p. 56 (1962).

[292] This system is described and severely criticized in *id.* at 57. See also Cina, Feb. 9, 1963, p. 4 (the case supports Moyseyev's analysis).

comings of the present method for adjusting buyers' claims are not due to retardation of the law. The Soviet system is capable of rewriting any doctrine in short order, if it so wishes. And, at any rate, it is the recent administrative regulations, not the traditional civil law institutions, that neglect buyers' interests by refusing to face the problem.

A buyer who has discovered defects in an item which is not subject to a guarantee ordinarily has a right to return it to the store for exchange or refund (if no replacement is available), within seven days. Some products are subject to special rules; *e.g.*, footwear.[293]

If the guarantor does not perform its part of the undertaking, the buyer may bring a civil action. There is a general six-months' statute of limitations. When a guarantee is longer than for six months, the statute of limitations is extended to coincide with the guarantee period.[294] I have found no discussion concerning selection of the proper party defendant. It seems that, under some circumstances, the action lies against the retail trade organizations. But can it ever be brought against a repair shop? Although the manufacturer would seem to be the proper party defendant, have any actions actually been brought against manufacturing enterprises? There might be some jurisdictional difficulties in the latter case. Suits against an enterprise must be commenced in the district where its executive organ is situated or where it has a local organ (branch), provided the suit arises out of a transaction concluded with the local organ.[295] Would an Estonian consumer have to travel to Irkutsk to sue a manufacturer there? Is a repair shop working for an Irkutsk factory its "local organ" for purposes of territorial jurisdiction?

Efforts to protect the buyer's interests in the quality of merchandise are already made before the goods reach sales outlets. Article 152 of the Criminal Code (replacing article 128-a of the 1926 Code) provides:

> "The release from any industrial enterprise, repeatedly or on a large scale, of products of bad quality or products which are incomplete or do not meet the standards and technical requirements, by its director, chief engineer or head of the department of technical control, as well as by persons who fulfill the duties of the aforesaid persons—
> is punishable by deprivation of freedom for up to three years or by corrective labor for up to a year, or by dismissal from the official position." [295a]

For purposes of this article, "products of bad quality" are products which cannot be used for the designated purpose at all. There is no basis for crimi-

[293] Rules, *supra* note 289, arts. 2 (note), 3.

[294] PRAV. REG. GOS. TORG. SSSR 159-60.

[295] CODE OF CIVIL PROCEDURE arts. 14, 27.

[295a] Approximately the same criminal sanctions are imposed upon the trade personnel who subsequently sell such products. CRIMINAL CODE art. 157.

nal prosecution if the goods merely have to be reclassified into a lower grade. "Incomplete" products lack spare parts, service tools, technical data (*e.g.*, operating and maintenance instructions), etc.[296] As I mentioned before, there are very few Soviet managers behind the bars for violating criminal statutes of this kind. An unsuccessful manager today is not likely to be faced with anything worse than a party reprimand, possibly followed by demotion. The occasional trials and convictions do not necessarily involve instances where waste has been extreme or the people most irresponsible.[297] It seems that in some cases the Party and the rest of the "business" community, for whatever reason, are not anxious to stand up for some individuals. These cases thus create an illusion that transgressions of this kind do not go unpunished. The procuracy, which bears overall responsibility for seeing that laws are obeyed, is not happy with nonenforcement, but its officials in the field do not seem to be able to overcome the local sentiments and pressures.[298]

Contracts between trading organizations and producers for delivery of consumer goods are supposed to contain detailed terms governing their quality. But quality requirements of some goods are deemed so fundamental that their definition has been transferred to the State Committee on Standards, Measures and Measuring Instruments attached to the Council of Ministers of the USSR. These requirements are known as "state standards" (*GOST*) and cannot, under any circumstances, be lowered by agreement.[299] In the event that the delivered goods do not meet the quality standards (whether established by law or by agreement), a trade organization is under a legal duty to reject the shipment and refuse to pay for it, and to demand a contract penalty amounting to twenty per cent of the value of the defective goods.[300] Since by law breaches of delivery contracts may not be compromised, violators should suffer great monetary losses and their failures should be noted by superior authorities. But enforcement of an organization's rights with respect to proper quality is tempered by the familiar reluctance to treat fellow organizations with the full severity permitted (and even demanded) by law. Besides, as we saw before,[301] many contracts are

[296] Vol'man & Shevchenko, *Otvetstvennost' za khozyaystvennye prestupleniya (Liability for Economic Crimes)*, Sov. yus., No. 7, pp. 10, 11 (1961).

[297] Case of Romanov, Sov. yus. No. 18, p. 21 (1960) (Crim. Div. Supr. Ct. R.S.F.S.R.) (release of 4,685 pairs of shoes valued at 400,000 (old) rubles, "over a long period of time"). In some instances administrative penalties are imposed as an inbetween measure. Pravda, Jan. 29, 1962, p. 2.

[298] See generally Gol'st, *Usilit' bor'bu s vypuskom nedobrokachestvennoy i nestandartnoy produktsiyi (The Struggle Against Poor Quality and Non-standard Output Should Be Intensified)*, Sots. zak. No. 8, p. 32 (1963).

[299] SHELESTOV, PRAVOVYYE FORMY BOR'BY ZA KACHESTVO TOVAROV (LEGAL MEANS IN THE STRUGGLE FOR QUALITY OF GOODS) 12-22 (1960).

[300] Decree of May 22, 1959 (U.S.S.R.) art. 58, ISTOCH. SOV. GRAZH. PRAV. 465.

[301] See text pp. 237, 239 *supra*.

drafted purely as a formality and do not create any enforceable obligations. The handling of guarantees on consumer goods also impairs the value of contract as a device for ensuring quality. A producer should be answerable to a trade organization for poor quality of guaranteed merchandise. However, under the present system, the trade organization does not have a chance (even if it wanted) to claim penalties from its supplier for defects that have appeared only in the course of use. Such claims cannot be presented because the trade organization is unaware of how the items are actually functioning: after the sale, the merchandise leaves the purview of the store, and the quality of the goods is watched over by repair shops which do not report to the retail stores.[302]

"Production mark" is a trademark with a peculiarly Soviet twist. The primary purpose of a trademark is to indicate origin. In a market economy a trademark is normally regarded as a valuable asset; it is displayed prominently on the holder's goods and jealously guarded against infringement. In the West it contributes to deliberate "individualization" of products. By contrast, the Soviet producer characteristically prefers anonymity, since his output is nothing much to brag about. As a result, in the Soviet Union the affixing of a production mark is compulsory and serves the interests of the state rather than the individual enterprise.

> "Production mark makes it easy to determine the actual producer of a product in case it is necessary to call him to account for the delivery of goods of bad quality. By reason of this, it is one of the most effective means in the struggle for the quality of products." [303]

VI. Extent and Function of Illicit Private Trade

We saw before that, as a general proposition, private trade has been a crime in the Soviet Union since the early 1930's. This offense against the Soviet state is known as "speculation." However, the wrath of the law is not directed only against individuals who deal "with a view to making a profit from conjectural fluctuations in the price" or individuals who enter "into a business venture involving unusual risks for a chance of an unusually large gain or profit." [304] The Soviet legal system outlaws the earning of ordinary profit by private persons. "Speculation" in Soviet context, therefore, is nothing but "purchase and resale of goods or other articles for gain." [305] The common Soviet "speculator" makes his living by charging a fee for services rendered: for finding scarce goods and bringing them to a clientele willing to pay a price that reflects the true state of supply and demand. If

[302] Moyseyev, *supra* note 291, at 57-58.

[303] Prav. reg. gos. torg. SSSR 118. See also Wiles, The Political Economy of Communism 176-77 (1962).

[304] Webster, Third New International Dictionary 2189 (1961).

[305] Criminal Code art. 154.

his activity involves any unusual risks, they are not due to economic conditions, but rather to the fact that the state has decided to suppress and punish private trade for reasons of its own.

"Even though the number of persons criminally prosecuted for speculation has significantly decreased over the recent years," writes a doctor of juridicial science, "speculation was and still is a dangerous crime." [306] The number of prosecutions is not publicized. This is in keeping with the Soviet policy of not releasing crime statistics. But even if their frequency were readily ascertainable, the actual extent of speculation would still be a matter of guesswork because of the problem of non-enforcement of law. Most speculators operate on a small scale. While their contribution to the welfare of the Soviet society is modest, their business is not particularly repugnant to the average Soviet citizen. Most Soviet citizens at one time or another have made use of speculators' services, and perhaps even dabbled in speculation themselves. We have read of the plight of a mother in search for a pacifier for her newborn baby, from Krasnodar to Krasnoyarsk.[307] We have been told of the despair of the men of Moscow, who were exhorted to remember their women with flowers on the 8th of March,[308] but were unable to find any in Moscow's flower shops. How much public indignation could then be whipped up against a man who suddenly appeared with a pocketful of pacifiers (even if he charged 100 or 200 per cent over the state price), or against a group of Georgians who flew twelve and a half tons of mimosa to Moscow to supplement a state supply of two and a half tons? [309] The illicit private trade meets demands left unsatisfied by the socialist distribution system. The only sensible way to fight the crime of speculation is to eliminate the environmental conditions in which it thrives. Suppose that speculation were eradicated before the governmental distribution had been put in order. As a result, some goods would be unobtainable at any price. How effective would be the principle of material incentive in the eyes of those workers and salaried employees who were now compelled to accumulate cash which they had intended to spend?

Some speculators have organized genuine enterprises that carry out far-flung operations. A staff of buyers scans all corners of the country in search for scarce goods. Transportation crews ship them to points of demand. Local sales personnel do the marketing. Some such enterprises, and even individual speculators, have substantial capital. It enables them to own automobiles. This is no doubt one reason why car sales are now so strin-

[306] Mitrichev, *Bor'ba so spekulyatsiyey (Struggle with Speculation)*, Sots. zak. No. 8, p. 28 (1961).

[307] Trud, Oct. 7, 1962, p. 4.

[308] See text p. 243 *supra*.

[309] *Operatsiya "Mimoza" (Operation "Mimosa")* Krokodil No. 9, p. 13 (1962).

gently regulated. Often air freight is used to rush supplies.[310] When an individual or a group of individuals engages in private trade on a fairly large scale, chances are that other criminal acts besides speculation are involved. Not infrequently, Soviet investigative authorities unearth private economic empires showing considerable vertical integration. The pilfering of state materials may constitute the first phase. A scarce product may then be manufactured either in a hidden unlicensed private shop or by using the facilities of a state plant. Distribution follows in the usual manner. Bribe money is used freely to close eyes, ears, and mouths. Nikolay Kotlyar, the "Soviet lipstick king," was a millionaire at the time he was shot. The description that the Soviet press gave of the villain's life was a story of an extraordinary success. It was probably calculated to arouse intense feelings of envy in the readers who then would become more prone to turn in speculators who manage to achieve today a standard of living not even dreamed up by the Party Program.

> "Kotlyar's Riga accomplices lived luxuriously. They had their own seaside *dachas* [summer houses] and automobiles and spent tens of thousands of rubles in cafés. The "lipstick king" himself eschewed night clubs, preferring to buy valuables—gold, diamonds, silver and lottery tickets—which he carefully hid away in vaults in his house.
>
> "In the evenings, after tightly closing the shutters, the Kotlyar family would gather around a table and start checking their lottery tickets against the lists of winning numbers. This was their favorite pastime. Kotlyar dreamed of accumulating more valuables." [311]

Admittedly some speculation is artificially generated and is not attributable to failures of the economic system. For instance, workers in trade organizations turn into speculators' accomplices by informing them what goods will be available and how to get them. Such practice obviously is "in restraint of trade" in that it creates a scarcity situation in state stores and forces consumers to buy on the black market. Thus, in evaluating the speculator's role in the Soviet economy, one should recognize that some of his activities are truly pernicious.

Article 154 of the Criminal Code distinguishes between three "degrees" of speculation. Ordinary speculation, that is, "purchase and resale of goods or other articles for gain," is punishable by deprivation of freedom for a period up to two years, with or without confiscation of property, or by corrective labor for a period up to a year, or by a fine up to three hundred rubles. Speculation can be committed only with direct intent; a person must be conscious of the fact that he is buying an article for resale at a profit. The profit motive is already crucial at the time of purchase. If it is lacking,

[310] Mitrichev, *supra* note 306, at 28; N.Y. Times, Sept. 18, 1960, p. 4, col. 1

[311] Izvestiya, Dec. 2, 1961, transl. in 3 ATLAS 135-36 (1962).

there is no speculation. Whether a profit was indeed made is irrelevant. In cases in which resale has not been proved, the court may, nevertheless, find from the entire evidence that the purchase was intended for resale for profit and designate the act as an attempt to commit the crime of speculation.[312] However, under article 15 the same criminal liability attaches for an attempt as for the completed crime, so that the distinction is relevant only for purposes of meting out punishment. In determining the punishment, the court can take into account the stage to which the criminal attempt had been carried and the reasons for its abandonment. When a man resells his motor scooter at a handsome profit, he puts himself at odds with the Soviet system, but he is not necessarily a criminal. If the craving for profit has overcome him only after the purchase of the machine, his state of mind is despicable, but not criminal. Even under the Leninist banner it is not a crime to drive a hard bargain. I pointed out earlier, though, that a profit-oriented executory contract might be unenforceable in courts as violative of socialist morality (a rule reminiscent of the civilian principle of *contra bonos mores*).

Speculation conducted either as a business or on a large scale is punishable by deprivation of freedom for a period from two to seven years, with confiscation of property. Speculation "as a business" will be found in those cases in which the speculator *systematically* buys and resells goods for profit, so that the income derived becomes either the basic or supplemental source of his subsistence. Whether the acts of speculation are "on a large scale" cannot be mechanically determined. The Soviet courts supposedly take into account the quantity of goods involved and their value and the amount of the profit derived. Where 495 needles (officially priced at 6 (old) kopecks and sold speculatively at 15 (old) kopecks apiece) were seized from the defendant, the offense was classified as petty speculation. On the other hand, a deal involving a single 4,000 ruble "Volga" car, resold at 5,500 rubles, was speculation on a large scale. Ordinary speculation was found where the defendant had in his possession various parts of wrist watches, including 4,930 watch hands (the largest number of a single part), in the total amount of 176 rubles, and the authorities marked 607 rubles of the defendant's money as having been acquired by criminal activity.[313]

Petty speculation is not specifically defined in the Code. The term undoubtedly covers transactions of extremely minor importance. As a matter of fact, petty speculation is considered a crime only if the person concerned has been previously guilty of speculation. It is punishable by deprivation of

[312] Yur'yev & Konstantinov, *Otvetstvennost' za spekulyatsiyu i zanyatiye zapreshchennym promyslom (Liability for Speculation and Engaging in Prohibited Crafts)*, Sots. zak. No. 7, pp. 50, 51 (1961).

[313] Romanenko, *Otvetstvennost' za spekulyatsiyu pri otyagchayushchikh obstoyatel'stvakh (Liability for Speculation Under Aggravating Circumstances)*, Sov. yus. No. 9, p. 8 (1963).

freedom for a period up to a year, or by corrective labor for a like period, or by a fine up to two hundred rubles with confiscation of property involved in the speculative transaction.

Activities of speculators are known to a great many (perhaps most) people. Thus the war against this form of criminal conduct could be waged successfully with the cooperation of the masses. But the law enforcers complain that people are reluctant to talk about these matters, a sad comment on the new Soviet man. In a case involving speculative sales of foreign made watches by the personnel of retail stores, evidence could be secured only by means of getting Moscow University law students to pose as bona fide customers. The prosecution got its witnesses, and the students a field exercise in entrapment. The media of mass communications have been enlisted in the campaign against speculation. Newspapers and broadcasters are urged to reveal the names of speculators to the people. However, such reports, lest they be regarded as announcements in furtherance of illicit trade, must, if possible, be accompanied by caricatured likenesses of the speculators and details of their sordid lives.[314] Recently, the RSFSR Statute on Comrades' Courts was amended to expand the jurisdiction of these informal, quasi-judicial bodies. They will now have the right to decide first-offense cases of petty speculation.[315]

[314] Mitrichev, *supra* note 306, at 29-31.

[315] Izvestiya, Oct. 25, 1963, p. 3.

THE SOVIET LEGAL PATTERN SPREADS ABROAD

BY JOHN N. HAZARD *

I. Introduction

MOSCOW'S "FRIENDSHIP UNIVERSITY" is teaching Soviet law to the Africans and Asians in its classrooms.[1] The course is not an option designed to permit the curious to expand their knowledge of Soviet culture by examining its law. It is a compulsory subject for social scientists, taught as an instrument of social revolution.

Indoctrination of foreigners in the principles of Soviet law is not new. Well before the arrival of former colonials in Moscow, Eastern European law students mingled with Soviet youth at the Law Faculty on ulitsa Gertsina. Many of these returned to their homelands as assistants to the communist leaders intent upon fashioning a legal system that would achieve for their countries what Lenin had achieved for Russia. At the 1958 congress in Warsaw devoted to sharing of views on socialist legality,[2] these men appeared behind the name plates for several of the Eastern European states, and their Russian wives, courted during their student days at the Moscow Law Faculty, circulated among the Western delegates during the receptions.

During the 19th century young scholars from Latin America and Eastern Europe congregated in Paris to learn the civil law. And centuries earlier their counterparts had travelled to Bologna to sit at the feet of Inerius, but the pilgrimages were not so purposeful. There was no government agency in earlier times devoting its attention to granting scholarships, selecting the most militant activists, and propagating a faith. The U.S.S.R.'s program has been characterized by what was absent at Bologna and Paris. It is a conscious effort to spread the Soviet system to other lands. It is a manifestation of Soviet faith that the Russians under Lenin's leadership found the road to social salvation, and it is the duty of his heirs to extend to others the same opportunity. Law, as one of the principal instruments of

**JOHN N. HAZARD, A.B. 1930, Yale University; LL.B. 1934, Harvard University; certificate, Moscow Juridical Institute, 1937; J.S.D. 1939, University of Chicago; Professor of Public Law, Columbia University, New York City.*

[1] The Vice President of the short-lived People's Republic of Zanzibar was described by a woman claiming to have been his Moscow wife, as a graduate of Friendship (Lumumba) University. N.Y. Times, Jan. 20, 1964, p. 6, col. 3.

[2] For the proceedings of the congress, see Polska Akademia Nauk, 21 Cahiers de l'Academie Polonaise des Sciences, *Le Concept de la Legalité dans les Pays Socialistes*. Colloque de l'Association Internationale des Sciences Juridiques, Sept. 10-16, 1958 (Warsaw 1961).

social change, must be disseminated together with the Marxist doctrine that is its motivation.

Since the revolts in Poland and Hungary in 1956 the Soviet tutors have shown more tolerance of variation than they exhibited previously. When the People's Democracies were created in the wake of German retreat at the end of World War II, it was appreciated, as communist doctrine had long declared through the programs of the Comintern, that societies in the newly acquired countries would have to be weaned by degrees from their old ways. Stages of development were envisaged, but progress was to be relatively swift toward achievement of the Soviet model.[3] Stalin is reputed to have told Jan Masaryk of Czechoslovakia that he hoped the Czechs would profit by Soviet mistakes. No one seems to have thought that the new communist-oriented states would be required to move deliberately through every stage of Soviet development experienced during the preceding 30 years. They were expected to move swiftly, skipping some of the stages and avoiding some of the pitfalls, notably the too-speedy collectivization of the peasantry. Yet, the pattern was made clear by Russian advisers, as Tito of Yugoslavia later revealed when he protested in 1948.[4] Stalin was the director, and the new states were expected to follow his lead and to introduce the policies and the legislation effecting those policies as quickly as he thought necessary.

The revolts of 1956 provided the warning, and it was accentuated by Mao Tse-tung's support of the Poles. The U.S.S.R. could no longer push without careful regard to local sensibilities. Gomulka and Kadar had to be permitted to elaborate their own road to socialism and eventually communism.[5] There would be advice and occasional pressures from Moscow, but Mao Tse-tung would be free even of these. Communist inspired programs were being initiated, but the period of Soviet domination was over. No longer were all of the law books in law faculties translations from the standard Russian texts. No longer did Polish and Hungarian law professors wait for signs from Moscow of lines to be developed before they published their articles. They dared to innovate within the framework of Marxist theory as they understood it, although in subsequent reviews of their books in Soviet periodicals they found themselves criticized and "corrected."

The role of law as a principal instrument of social change has been understood by Marxists since the early days of the Russian revolution. Lenin's oft-repeated statement that "a law is a political instrument, it is

[3] Program of the Communist International 1928, published in BLUEPRINT FOR WORLD CONQUEST 147-245 (1946).

[4] For an account of Stalin's relationship to diversity in the People's Democracies, see BRZEZINSKI, THE SOVIET BLOC—UNITY AND CONFLICT ch. 3, especially 58-64 (1960).

[5] See *id.* ch. 12.

politics"[6] was said with regard to a Norwegian law, but it became a slogan of all revolutionary jurists. Through legislation the Communist Party put into effect its program for Russia, and through the courts its members improvised in exercise of their "socialist consciences" when there was not yet a statute to guide them.[7] Marxist doctrine that law is but superstructure on an economic base emphasized the proposition that legislatures cannot achieve the good society in a single act or code. Statutes can but prepare the way by speeding the social change which is dictated in the main by the progress of invention and industrial evolution.

For a time during the late 1930's, law's potential as a tool of social development seems to have been minimized, only to be reasserted after Stalin's intervention in the linguistic controversy which reemphasized that superstructure can influence base.[8] Since then, the role given law as an instrument of social change has been fully manifest by communist leaders and this provides added reason for its inclusion in the course at Friendship University.

What part of the Soviet experience must be copied to achieve the goal? Since 1956, and indeed since Stalin's death in 1953, Soviet Communists have not required slavish adherence to the Soviet model. A Soviet textbook has given the essentials.[9] They fall into three categories: political, economic, and ideological. In the political sphere the authority of the toiling masses must be established in the image developed in the U.S.S.R., namely under leadership of the workmen and their vanguard, the Communist Party. In the economic sphere private capitalist property must be liquidated and an end put to employment by private employers. In the ideological sphere the Marxist-Leninist view of world developments and the working out of a cultural revolution must be accepted.

Expanding these points the author indicates that politically the Communist Party must lead in establishing a new state, must create links between the workers and peasants and other strata of the toiling masses (this means the intellectuals), must develop a social democracy, liquidate prejudices between races and peoples of different ethnic origin, protect the new state from attacks from within and from abroad, and create brotherly solidarity with the working class of other countries in the form of proletarian internationalism.

Economically, the liquidation of private enterprise requires the replacement of it by public property in the principal tools and means of production

[6] Lenin, *Concerning a caricature of Marxism and concerning "imperialist economism,"* 23 SOCHINENIYA 36 (4th ed. 1949).

[7] The history of the early period is set forth in HAZARD, SETTLING DISPUTES IN SOVIET SOCIETY: THE FORMATIVE YEARS OF LEGAL INSTITUTIONS (1960).

[8] The philosophical portent of the 1950 discussion on linguistics is set forth in MARCUSE, SOVIET MARXISM—A CRITICAL ANALYSIS 156-59 (1958).

[9] INSTITUT PRAVA AKADEMII NAUK SSSR, GOSUDARSTVENNOE PRAVO ZARUBEZHNYKH SOTSIALISTICHESKIKH STRAN (PUBLIC LAW OF FOREIGN SOCIALIST COUNTRIES) 3-4 (1957).

and also the introduction of economic planning, and an improvement in the standard of living.

No one of these points can be meaningful to friend or foe unless the history of the Russian revolution and the subsequent years when the U.S.S.R. stood alone as the only communist-led state is familiar. It is this history, and the manifestation of policy in political tracts and the laws enacted to implement policy that has to be taught to Asian and African students in Moscow if they are to understand the program that is being recommended.[10]

From the point of view of Soviet teachers the political and economic organization of the U.S.S.R. is still something to be emulated in some detail if a proletarian state is to emerge, although the demand that it be exactly in the image of the U.S.S.R. has been modified. No longer is self-confidence what it was in 1920 when the leaders of the Communist International wrote to the shop stewards in England. At that time and in response to questions as to whether the English in their revolution would have to adopt forms developed in Soviet Russia, the Comintern spokesmen said:

> "Our English comrades in their sixth question wish to know what other forms of Soviet government are possible in other countries. We can say nothing definite. It is necessary to admit theoretically the possibility of variation of forms depending upon the varying economic structures of the different countries in a state of revolution. It must, however, be said that the experience of the development of the world revolution until recently has given no indications of the realisation of this theory."

Then follows a final sentence which seems an afterthought to soften the blow, for the authors wrote, "It is the opinion of the Communist International that it is not its concern to indicate the exact form in which revolution is to develop." [11]

The Soviet legal system is now familiar to comparative lawyers outside the U.S.S.R. Its fundamentals have been set forth in the papers presented in this special issue. The question now posed is whether practice in communist-led states across Soviet borders has demonstrated that People's Democracies may go beyond the Soviet pattern of legal relationships and still be accepted by the original Communists as doing what is necessary to achievement of a society which can justly be called "communist."

[10] This history is currently set forth in a textbook translated into English as HISTORY OF THE COMMUNIST PARTY OF THE SOVIET UNION. (Rothstein ed. Moscow 1960).

[11] The questions and answers appear in THE I.L.P. AND THE 3RD INTERNATIONAL 44 (1920). This booklet contains the questions submitted by the Independent Labor Party delegation to the executive of the 3rd International and its reply, with an introductory statement by the National Council of the I.L.P.

II. Restructuring the Public Law

The public law presents an appropriate starting point in accord with the Soviet textbook's selection of the political component as the first element of a proletarian revolutionary program. Soviet public law has incorporated since 1918 the concept of monopolization of organized political power in a single political party. For 18 years after withdrawal of the Left Socialist Revolutionary Party from Lenin's coalition government in the spring of 1918, the Communist Party ruled alone in the new Russia under what might be called a concept of "convention." In 1936 this convention was incorporated in the constitution in a somewhat vaguely worded article on the right of association.[12] Citizens were granted the right, but limited to association in the Communist Party. In discussing the proposals for a new Soviet constitution, Soviet authors emphasize that in the next document the party's role must be stated even more affirmatively.[13]

All of the People's Democracies have followed the Leninist concept of a "vanguard party," although China, Poland, and Yugoslavia have established variations. The Polish People's Republic in its 1952 constitution guaranteed the right of association without limitation of political activity to a single political party.[14] In practice the Communist Party shares power with two parties, one representing the peasants, the Peasant Party, and the other the petty bourgeoisie and intellectuals, the Democratic Party. In addition there is an "interest group" designed to give representation to the Roman Catholic elements. This variation on the U.S.S.R.'s pattern preserves the multiparty structure and is said to represent the continuing class differentiation of Polish society. Still it is under effective Communist Party direction, since the number of seats available to each party is determined by party leaders meeting in advance of election rather than by the voters themselves, and in the allocation, the Communist Party, which in Poland bears the name of United Polish Workers' Party so as to indicate its union with the old Socialists, retains for itself the preponderant majority.

The Polish party situation is said to include only parties in power. It avoids the concept of parties in opposition.[15] In practice this effect is achieved by causing the minor parties to meet with the Communists to prepare a single slate of candidates from all parties. The persons on the slate run unopposed so as to cause the election of persons representing a mixture of interests corresponding to the Communists' concept of what is appropri-

[12] Art. 126.

[13] Romashkin, *A new stage in the development of the Soviet state*, Sov. gos. i pravo No. 10, p. 31 (1960). Translated in Hazard & Shapiro, The Soviet Legal System pt. 1, 33 (1962).

[14] Art. 72(2).

[15] Rozmaryn, LaPologne 93 (Vol. VII of Comment Ils Sont Gouvernés (1962)).

ate to make state organs representative of the class character of the regime. The Soviet Union's pre-1936 method of keeping hostile elements from gaining representation was to exclude nonworking classes by restricting the franchise. The Polish political scientists say that their system provides other guarantees against ousting of communist leadership, permitting maintenance of an electoral system without restriction on the right to vote.

The Chinese People's Republic has introduced something of the same system, for there exist in addition to the Communist Party the following parties: The Revolutionary Committee of the Kuomintang, to reach some former officials of Dr. Sun Yat-sen's party; the China Democratic National Construction Association, to attract former private business interests; the China Democratic League, to appeal to former bourgeois intellectuals; and the Taiwan Democratic Self-Government League, designed to appeal to native Taiwani. The groups provide the Communists with a means of attracting non-Communists to the program, and their value to the regime is demonstrated by the fact that their expenses are paid by the Communists.[16] As with Poland, the representation from the minority parties is calculated in advance by the Communists so that the majority of the Communist Party cannot be threatened.

Both the Polish and Chinese systems are devised to overcome the early hostility experienced by the Soviet leadership from Socialist Revolutionaries and Mensheviks who resisted, even to the point of attempted assassination, the Communist Party's assumption of monopoly power. The new formula leaves no doubt that the Communist Party is in all People's Democracies the vanguard as Lenin said it must be, and as the Soviet authors declare also that it must be if the system is to be Marxist-Leninist in its inspiration. Yet the Polish and Chinese variations give room for some criticism of communist-inspired policies. Support of miniority parties provides a measure of the Chinese and Polish political sophistication in that Chinese and Polish Communists have seen the advantage of constructive criticism from outsiders so long as it cannot attract a following of sufficient size to threaten Communist Party leadership. Lenin and Stalin missed this opportunity.

The French Communist Party in early 1964 indicated that the Chinese and Polish method of rule through multiple parties under communist control has become its preference for the future.[17] The one-party system of the U.S.S.R. has been decried as a product of Stalin's mind. The French Communists promise a place for the Socialists in whatever the future may offer. If this program is accepted by other communist parties, it may spell the end of communist conceived one-party political systems and the adoption generally of the Polish and Chinese approach.

[16] Peter S. H. Tang, 1 Communist China Today: Domestic and Foreign Policies 166-83 (2d ed. 1961).

[17] *French Reds Offer New Party Rules*, N.Y. Times, Jan. 17, 1964, p. 5, col. 3.

The Yugoslavs have provided another variation. The constitution of 1963 states the Communist Party's preeminent position in precise terms in its preamble:

> "The League of Communists of Yugoslavia, initiator and organizer of the People's Liberation War and Socialist Revolution, owing to the necessity of historical development, has become the leading force of the working class. . . . Under the conditions of socialist democracy and social self-government, the League of Communists, with its guiding ideological and political work, is the prime mover of the political activity necessary to protect and promote the achievements of the Socialist Revolution." [18]

Without organizing other parties the Yugoslav Communists have sought to unite with themselves on a somewhat broader base citizens not prepared to join the party. They created in 1953 a Socialist Alliance of Working People of Yugoslavia, which is said to have embraced "just about everybody and everything" [19] and to have had the task of putting communist ideas into action and of transmitting them back to the party.

The variations in China, Poland, and Yugoslavia demonstrate what can be permitted in communist minds in the way of providing to the public an opportunity to join with political aims, but they are clearly only variations on the Leninist theme. In no case has the vanguard position he sponsored been abandoned. The first requisite of a Marxist-Leninist system is leadership by Communists organized in a party dedicated in accordance with principles elaborated by Lenin in 1905 to leadership drawn solely from militant revolutionaries and bereft of mere sympathizers. Public law's task is to preserve that position.

Human rights have been treated in all communist-led countries in accord with similar thinking. Primary emphasis is placed upon what have been called the economic rights, with such strong emphasis upon the "right to work" that throughout the new states of the world, whether communist-led or not, this right cannot be omitted from constitutions. It was stated even in the Universal Declaration of Human Rights adopted by the United Nations, although some of the established Western states thought that to guarantee such a right was but propaganda. To the Communists, it has special importance because it not only appeals to the masses of persons who are either unemployed or fear unemployment, but also because it suggests that a socialist-planned economy alone provides assurance that there will always be employment. Thus, the Polish Constitution declares that the right to work means the right to employment, and that this is ensured by the social ownership of the basic means of production and by other measures

[18] Preamble, § VI.

[19] Hoffman & Neal, Yugoslavia and the New Communism 179 (1962).

now accepted as typical of a communist-led society.[20] The Yugoslav Constitution of 1963 is more cautious, however, with the guarantee of the right to work, for although it guarantees the right, it places upon the community only the burden of providing "ever more favorable conditions toward the realization of the right to work." [21] This formula was proposed by groups in the United States at the time of adoption of the Universal Declaration of Human Rights as being all that a free enterprise society could promise. These experts said that where the state is not the entrepreneur in a position to create jobs as it wishes, even at the risk of featherbedding, it cannot give an absolute guarantee of employment.[22] Yugoslavs, having less state enterprise and planning than other of the communist-led states, seem to have been doing the same kind of cautious thinking.

The civil rights of speech and press are generally treated in constitutions of the People's Democracies as they have been treated in the constitution of the U.S.S.R. Thus, the Polish Constitution guarantees these freedoms in the same language as the 1918 Constitution of the Russian Republic, stating that these rights are ensured by making available paper and public buildings to effect these freedoms.[23] Unlike the draftsmen of the first Soviet constitution, however, the Poles include no express limitation on use of the freedoms to the advancement of socialism, but they may be implied by the obligation placed by the constitution upon all citizens to respect the rules of social intercourse.[24] This cannot mean permission to speak or write in favor of a return to capitalism. This has been made clear by a Polish authority, who has written:

> "We find in numerous other dispositions of the constitution the idea that political rights and liberties are the result and the function of the political and social regime, and that they must serve the interests of the working people, and that from this fact their imminent limitation is in the inadmissibility of their utilization (in the spirit of the Constitution, therefore—of their abuse) contrary to their origin and their purpose for existing." [25]

In this statement is expressed the basis of all political thought on civil rights with the People's Democracies, and it follows Lenin's original concept incorporated *expressis verbis* in his 1918 constitution.

As to the structure of the state apparatus, greater variation has emerged in spite of the Russian views of 1920 that experience had demonstrated that

[20] Art. 59.

[21] Art. 20.

[22] See Shotwell, *The Idea of Human Rights*, 1946 INT'L CONCILIATION 551, 554, (1946).

[23] Art. 71.

[24] Art. 76.

[25] ROZMARYN, *op. cit. supra* note 15, at 337.

the "soviet" form was to be preferred. The principal characteristic of the "soviet" form was derived from the circumstances of its emergence in 1905. It came to life as a representative body of factory workmen to coordinate and direct the merging opposition to Tsarist policies, and most particularly to lead massive strikes. Again in March 1917, it reappeared as a nucleus for antigovernment opposition from working class elements and sympathetic intellectuals. Peasants and soldiers were added to the soviet in 1917, but the major characteristic of 1905 was preserved. It was an association of the "have-nots" drawn from the working classes of factory and field and led by fiery intellectuals determined to achieve drastic revision of society.

From the moment of Lenin's return to Russia in April 1917, the soviet became his principal mass instrument of revolution. After achievement of power, it was continued as the nucleus of the state apparatus, retaining its class character by excluding from the franchise and from holding office anyone who employed labor or gained his living as a merchant. Not until 1936, when the number of such excluded persons had been reduced by taxation to less than three per cent, and at the moment when Stalin's constitution prohibited all further employment of labor, was the franchise opened to all, and the soviet made representative of all the people. In Lenin's eyes it was a school of government as well as the formal instrument of government, and seats on the soviet at the local level were to rotate swiftly. Cohesion and policy direction came, of course, from the Communist Party's representatives within each soviet, and the ordinary workmen and peasants and intellectuals drawn into the apparatus of the soviets were executors rather than initiators of policy.

The pattern developed by the Russians was introduced generally into the People's Democracies after the war,[26] and it was not until Tito's ejection from the Communist Information Bureau in 1948 that experimentation began. Yugoslavs now date their system from 1950 and claim it to be "unique in the annals of political and economic organization." [27] Local government is the focal point of this change. In sharp split with the Russian system of centralization of decision making in the capital, leaving for local soviets only the implementation of centrally taken decision, except for policy making on matters of local economic and cultural concern, Yugoslav Communists have devised a pattern giving to local government considerable autonomy. The basic unit is called an *opshtina* or commune. In this unit was created by a General Law of 1953 on People's Committees, followed shortly by the 1953 Constitutional Law, a government in the form of a committee.

[26] Jones, *Polish Local Government Reorganized on Soviet Model*, 10 AM. SLAVIC & EAST EUROPEAN REV. 56 (1951). Includes translation of law of March 20, 1950.

[21] HOFFMAN & NEAL *op. cit. supra* note 19, at 212, quoting from Djordjevic, *Status and Role of the Executive Organs During the First Stages of Yugoslavia's Political and Constitutional Development*, 1958 INT'L SOC. SCI. BULL. 262.

All authority other than that specifically delegated to the federal and republic governments was transferred to this unit.[28] In 1955 the system currently in operation was put into effect in evolution of the 1953 provisions.

After their "October" in 1956, the Poles likewise sought to broaden their local government base to overcome what they had found to be the excessive bureaucracy of a centralized system of Russian type.[29] By law of January 25, 1958, the jurisdiction of the local councils was enlarged and their position reenforced. They were given almost the totality of economic and administrative authority of the state, the central authorities retaining only such powers as were explicitly named in legislation. These were the right to direct the mines, foundries, great industrial complexes, and railways, but the local councils were given the right to direct their own local police. High schools also remained under central direction, as did certain museums and theaters. Centrally directed agencies were, however, required to "concert" their programs with local councils, and to make reports. The 1958 law remains in force.

The internal functioning of the councils is similar to that of the local soviets in the U.S.S.R. The major work is done in standing commissions, and members of these commissions may be, as they are in the U.S.S.R., not only deputies to the council but outsiders so long as they do not exceed one-half of the commission's members. Further, each council is within an hierarchy of superior councils, as is the case in the U.S.S.R. As in the U.S.S.R., each is directed by a presidium, which serves as a steering committee.

The presidium is a joint organ of the local council and of the Council of Ministers of the Republic, and the latter under the 1953 law must approve the choice of president for the provincial (*wojewod*) and large city councils, while presidents of county councils have to be approved by the Chairman of the Council of Ministers. Still lower councils have to submit their choice for president of the presidium to the presidium of the provincial council for approval. Higher councils may suspend the presidents and presidium members from their functions if they engage in illegal action or act contrary to the essential policy line of the Polish state.

Additionally, as in the U.S.S.R, there is supervision of activities of executive departments of councils by the next higher department engaged in the same activity until the minister is reached at the very top level. Polish scholars, like their Soviet counterparts, refer to this as "dual subordination," although the Poles claim that vertical subordination is not hierarchical, but a limited right fixed by law to surveillance and not direction of activities. It is the right of suspension prior to possible ultimate veto by still higher authorities rather than the right of initiative.

[28] *Id.* at 224.

[29] Rozmaryn, *op. cit. supra* note 15, at 224-76.

From the Polish and Yugoslav experience, it is evident that the U.S.S.R.'s traditional pattern of state structure, characterized by centralization of authority, both in making policy and directing its execution, has been subjected to critical review. The center maintains control in the new states, but the local authorities are given increased authority, especially in the economic field. Whether this is a decentralization may be debated, for the Khrushchev government in 1957 began a similar process with creation of the *sovnarkhozy*, but these were different in conception. Khrushchev expressed lack of confidence in local soviets, and later reinforced his view by eliminating them entirely from agricultural direction, while the Poles and Yugoslavs express confidence in local government but feel it necessary to retain some controls lest they upset important policy lines adopted at the center.

III. The Economic Base

While the role of public law in creating monopoly leadership in the Communist Party and in establishing a state structure that will assure majority representation to the working classes is obviously the key to establishing a Marxist-Leninist legal system, this is only the beginning. The attention of Communists is immediately thereafter focused on what the theory calls the "base," namely the economic structure. It is here that civil law plays its role, because it is the law defining property relationships on which Marx rested his analysis of all societies.

The Soviet model is uncomplicated and unequivocal on the law of property. Instruments of production must be state owned. Since 1918, the land has been solely owned by the state, and since 1930 industry, except for the small shop of the artisan, has been state owned. Soviet property law is built around these principles.

Until the Second World War it seemed likely that other states brought under communist leadership would adopt the same position. The Mongolian People's Republic, which was the only state other than the U.S.S.R. prior to the war to be directed by Communists, followed the Soviet pattern in detail as to the treatment of property, although its economic conditions were wholly different.[30] Mongolia was a nomadic country without industry when Communists gained control. State ownership of land could stir little opposition so long as the herdsmen were permitted to roam the range, and there was no class of industrial owners to oppose nationalization in principle. Under such circumstances there was no strong force requiring compromise, and the Leninist pattern of land nationalization and state ownership of industry could be adopted promptly.

[30] See Ginsburgs & Pierce, *Revolutionary Law Reform in Outer Mongolia: A Study in the Impact of Soviet Legal Doctrine on a Backward Society*, in 7 Law in Eastern Europe 207-52 (Szirmai ed. Leyden 1963).

Quite a different situation existed in Eastern Europe after the war. Peasants had long owned their own farms in many of the countries concerned. Only a small percentage had tilled land as tenants on great estates. For these tenants nationalization of the great estates was popular, but it would have been another thing to take from well-settled peasant owners of small farms their family plots, as Lenin had done in his second land decree of February 19, 1918. In consequence, not a single People's Democracy in Europe since the war has followed Lenin's pattern, and even in the Far East the communist-led states of North Vietnam, North Korea and China have refrained from taking title to land. The communist leaders have preferred to disarm peasants politically by other means. This has been done primarily through organization of collective farming associations of various types on land that remains legally the property of the members, although in practice its use is planned by the state.

The major exceptions to the scheme of control through collectivization have been Poland and Yugoslavia in Eastern Europe, and China in Asia. The Poles and Yugoslavs have retreated from early plans to collectivize use and currently permit peasants to continue their established pattern of family farming. The Poles seem to expect eventually to move in the direction of collectivization when opposition has been dissipated, but the Yugoslav Communist Party program no longer even looks to complete collectivization. A scheme has been developed under which farmers have to utilize their private farms in accordance with the plans of the district, but the farms will remain privately owned and operated.

The Chinese experiment with communes provides a variation at the other extreme, which has been denounced by Khrushchev as too radical. Although land is legally privately owned in China, peasants have been pushed to join communes and pool their land. Thereafter, they can identify nothing as their own, including their tools of production and the household property. The Russians experimented with this form of ownership and operation in the 1920's, but it was abandoned in 1930 with the drive for collectivization.[31] Stalin had concluded that it was not workable for most of his people.

There is no longer even the faintest dream in the U.S.S.R. that the agricultural commune will be the operating pattern of the future. The U.S.S.R. has been moving steadily in the direction of "state farms" organized as public corporations engaged in agriculture. This is the Soviet program, already well on the way to realization in communities around the large cities and in the "virgin lands" of Central Asia. It may also be the future for Rumania, which has 100 per cent collectivization in agriculture at the present time, although it has not moved in the direction of state farms except for certain highly technical agricultural operations.

[31] WESSON, SOVIET COMMUNES (1963).

Industry as a major resource was subjected to nationalization in the U.S.S.R. less swiftly than the land, but not for want of desire to bring it all into state ownership. The civil war of 1919-1921 wreaked havoc, and Lenin introduced his New Economic Policy to cope with shortages by extending the period of compromise with capitalism for a period of years. Beginning with 1928 the compromise was over, and every pressure was used to make private enterprise unprofitable through heavy taxation. In 1936 it was banned by constitutional provision against the employment of labor. Only the individual artisan or the group of cooperating artisans could thereafter produce. Since 1960, the cooperators have been absorbed by state industry, except in the service trades. The U.S.S.R.'s pattern has been one of short-lived compromise with private enterprise for so long as necessary to establish a satisfactory state producing system. Once this has been achieved, the Marxist concept of ending private ownership of producers' goods has been put into effect.

For a time after the war the Soviet experience of a period of compromise with capitalists followed by their liquidation seemed the pattern for the People's Democracies. Private enterprise was permitted to continue to function but subject to heavy taxation and heavy restrictions on labor policies. Cooperatives were favored for the individual artisans. Only the Chinese made a point of continuing to work with what they called their "national bourgeoisie," who in contrast to the "international bourgeoisie" were capitalists without ties to international capital.

The pattern of the People's Democracies with regard to industrial property is being copied from the experience of the U.S.S.R. Each Communist Party has introduced a preliminary period rather like Lenin's New Economic Policy, during which cooperatives are favored, but in which small private producers and shopkeepers are tolerated.[32] Were it not for some voices in Poland which suggest a permanence for current policy, and limitation of state ownership to commanding heights, a prognostication that all People's Democracies would follow the Soviet pattern to monopoly of distribution and production in the state would not be risky. What the Polish voices may accomplish has yet to be learned. They are not echoed even in Yugoslavia, which is looking to state-owned industry as its goal. It seems unlikely that the Polish moderates will be listened to by present Polish leadership.

"Personal" property is a concept which the Soviet theorists have developed to support a system of property incentives to production by wage earners. All of the People's Democracies have developed the concept and divide property into categories, one of which is "personal property." By this is meant nonproductive privately owned property. In the Marxist-

[32] See Przybyla, *Private Enterprise in Poland Under Gomulka*, 17 Am. Slavic & East European Rev. 316 (1958).

oriented mind this type of property cannot provide the base for political power strong enough to unseat communist leaders, and it can provide the production stimulus required to achieve the abundance necessary to eventual distribution in accordance with need.

While all of the People's Democracies follow the Soviet lead in recognizing the existence of a category of personal property, there is variation in what can be placed within it and how it may be utilized. Generally it is not limited to clothing, furniture, and personal belongings, but includes dwelling houses, barnyard animals, and artisans' production tools. Only in China has the category lost meaning in the communes where nothing is personally owned. With the recognition of the category the rules of civil law as they have been known to the Romanist system generally since the Code Napoleon apply. But the U.S.S.R. has introduced limitations on disposition so as to curb what is interpreted to be the obtaining of "unearned income." Since 1932 the pursuit of the profession of merchant has been a crime, and a long line of court decisions has sought balanced application of the criminal code to individual cases of sale of personal property. Generally sale is forbidden as speculation if the property was acquired with the intention of resale in the near future, while it is permitted if sale occurs from family stocks that have become surplus with changing needs.

The People's Democracies have taken various positions on this score. Those that have not banned private enterprise naturally permit the conduct of a merchant's trade, although a strict licensing system is employed to limit its expansion and to tax it. Polish cities have special districts in which private shops function legally and with apparent profit to their owners. Just as with private production, it can be presumed that eventually the People's Democracies will follow the example of the U.S.S.R. and tax the private merchant out of existence. Perhaps he will even be declared criminal as the state becomes capable of meeting the desires of its citizens for consumer goods. There may be resistance in Poland on the ground that the state has no need to absorb such enterprise and, in fact, can benefit by eliminating from its own worries the problem of catering to whimsical personal tastes.

Inheritance has been a debated issue in the Marxist-inspired systems. The Soviet policy makers decided with the New Economic Policy that it had to be permitted to obtain maximum benefit from the property incentive system introduced in 1922. Even though the N.E.P. was taxed out of existence and finally outlawed by the criminal code, inheritance was saved from abolition. At that moment Stalin decided to abandon all thought of egalitarian pay scales in favor of differentiated pay to encourage production, and such a system seemed to require inheritance as well. Inheritance remained in somewhat narrower scope than in the Romanist countries generally, but with the passage of time even the limitations established on the circle of heirs and the persons who might be named as legatees in a will were removed. Today, Soviet inheritance law includes no restraints. It is justified as an inseparable part of the rights of personal property and distinguished from the law of bourgeois states not by its provisions but because of the absence of privately owned productive property to pass by inheritance.

The People's Democracies have followed the Soviet lead. No one has questioned the desirability of this institution.[33] Of course, in those countries which still support a measure of private enterprise, there would be no reason to question its suitability so long as the property incentive is retained, but no one looks to its abolition when private enterprise is no more. Only in China with the communes does it lose significance in practice, because there is no personal property to be inherited, but outside the communes it retains full vigor and is recognized in the law.

The Chinese position presents another contrast which may lead eventually to considerable variation from the Soviet pattern. The Chinese Communists believe in attempting to achieve something of an egalitarian pattern in wage distribution. Managers of state industry are not paid such premiums over the workman's wage as is the case in the U.S.S.R. and in the other People's Democracies. This fact has led Soviet critics to question whether Chinese industry can claim properly to have introduced the Soviet concept of *khozraschyot*, or business-type accounting designed to determine costs. The Soviet system of business-type accounting, introduced in 1923 on an experimental basis in state industry in an attempt to achieve efficient use of resources, has been accepted in all of the People's Democracies as necessary to the operation of state industry. To facilitate its use all state industries in the U.S.S.R. and in the People's Democracies have been established on the pattern of the public corporation, to which are assigned determined amounts of the state's property as resources and for which full accountability is required. Within this system has developed the concept of the supply contract in which relations between the public corporations are made precise in implementation of the state economic plan. On the basis of these contracts disputes are taken before specialized tribunals for resolution and the assessment of damages and the payment of penalties.

Property has become within this framework a means of measuring efficiency through the balance sheet and the profit and loss statement. Costs are set with relationship to the result, except in industries of such vital national concern as to require subsidization. To the Russians costs must reflect the real value of resources, including human resources, and so managers must be paid at rates much higher than the bench workman be-

[33] For symposium treatment of the subject in Eastern Europe and China, see 5 LAW IN EASTERN EUROPE, (Szirmai ed. Leyden 1961).

cause of what they contribute in value to the whole. When the Chinese refuse to recognize this factor, they are in Russian eyes upsetting the whole concept of efficiency measurement through business-type accounting.

While all of the People's Democracies recognize the necessity of maintaining tribunals to hear disputes between public corporations over performance of supply contracts, not all maintain the type of tribunal developed by the U.S.S.R. Yugoslavia had such a tribunal when it first adopted its communist-led system, but after the split of 1948, it initiated a commercial court which has far more limited functions. Instead of attempting to resolve the dispute so as to obtain production, the new court contented itself with assessment of damages as would any court. This change was inaugurated to accompany deemphasis upon detailed centralized planning, which Tito thought to be creative of a bureaucracy that would make more trouble than it avoided.

China likewise has no state arbitration in the U.S.S.R. pattern. Disputes over contracts between public corporations go before the Financial and Economic Commission in the area to which both parties are subordinate, and, if they are from different areas, to the national Financial and Economic Commission. This much sounds like the Soviet system, but then comes the difference, for if the decision is "ineffective," the parties may go to court, presumably to obtain damages alone without thought of resolution of the dispute in a manner salvaging as much production as possible.

A word as to the law governing relations between public corporations is in order, for the People's Democracies have not agreed on what to call it. For Soviet legal specialists it has become the "civil law," although it is recognized that special features of flexibility in the interest of performance must be permitted. For the German Democratic Republic, the law is a branch of law separate from the civil law and called "economic law," to demonstrate its special function in aid of plan performance. Some of the other People's Democracies have also wished to make this distinction, but Soviet persuasion to maintain a unified system of civil law which includes the law of public corporations has been so strong that the Soviet attitude has generally prevailed.[34]

IV. The Ideological Front

The ideological acceptance of Marxism-Leninism is the third element of concurrence necessary between communist-led states, if the outline established by the Soviet textbook used as the guide for this paper is

[34] The implications of this dispute and its resolution appear in Hazard, *Has the Soviet State a New Function?*, 34 Pol. Q. 391, 394-96 (1963).

to be followed. Until Tito's explusion from the Communist Information Bureau in 1948, it seemed unlikely that the interpretation of Marxism-Leninism established by Communists of the U.S.S.R. would be challenged. After 1948 Tito's interpretation was treated as heresy and was looked upon with such hatred by Stalin that everything was done short of war to unseat him. Still he survived and lived to compose his differences with Stalin's heirs when Stalin had gone, but not until the threat to Soviet determination of orthodoxy from the Chinese became so great that even Tito's defection seemed mild. It is currently the Chinese who present the challenge on the ideological front, and the challenge requires examination because it affects the role of law in a communist-led society.

The split between the Communists of the U.S.S.R. and China dates from 1957. Up to that time Chinese policy as it related to the role of the state and law followed the Soviet model. China was far behind Soviet development, but its leaders seemed to be moving in the direction plotted by the Soviet leadership. In the legal field this meant preparation of codes of law and abandonment of the features written into law to preserve flexibility. After Stalin's death, in company with the Russians in post-Stalin society, the Chinese program called for increasing predictability in the law and for "stability."

Soviet leaders in advising the Chinese gave the impression of having forgotten that they had drafted codes only with the adoption of the New Economic Policy in 1922, except for domestic relations and employment relations. Perhaps they thought that their experience after 1922 had proved that even with a codified system of law enough flexibility could be preserved to meet unexpected situations. At least Stalin's passion for security had been satisfied with the codified system he inherited from Lenin, for he found that ample provision had been made by the draftsmen of 1922 for flexibility in application of the codes. In the criminal code there was a provision permitting application of definitions of crime by "analogy," and the civil code opened with an article permitting a judge to refuse to apply a substantive provision of the code in the event that its strict application would in his view defeat the social and economic purpose for which it had been enacted.

Each of the People's Democracies of Eastern Europe followed the Soviet pattern of codification. Few found it necessary to abrogate the prewar codes so as to introduce a period like that between 1918 and 1922 in Soviet Russia when Soviet judges improvised with the guidance of only a few statutes enacted without systematization. Poland abrogated the pre-world-war I German, Austrian and Russian civil codes but kept its inter-war civil legislation (code of obligations, commercial code, and labor laws) in force. A 1950 statute on general principles was enacted to guide the courts in applying the inter-war legislation. Judges were directed by this statute to apply the inter-war legislation but to set it aside if its provisions contradicted the principles of social intercourse in the People's State.[35] Most other People's Democracies did likewise, and many have continued to move slowly in drafting new codes of their own to replace the prewar documents.

China created the surprise. When the Chinese People's Republic was proclaimed in 1949, the old Kuomintang codes were abrogated *in toto,* as Tsarist codes had been abrogated after a brief period of experimentation with their use in Soviet Russia, but a codification commission was set to work to prepare new codes. Text books were introduced in the Peking Law School which followed in structure the pattern of a code, and suggested that the applicable law was essentially that of a Romanist codified system.[36] Soviet textbooks were translated and soviet codes discussed as models.

The surprise came in 1957 at the time now revealed to have been the moment of first tension between Soviet and Chinese Communist leaders. Chinese judges were dismissed in large numbers and replaced with men untrained in law. The codification commissions no longer met. Stability as it had been developed in the U.S.S.R. after Stalin's death was decried as unsuitable to China's situation, which was said to call for "flexibility." [37]

The movement does not seem to have been a retreat after a too-hasty start to a position like that which existed in Soviet Russia between 1917 and 1922, when judges were improvising in search of a law suitable to a new society. During the early Soviet period the Commissar of Justice had evidenced his expectation that systematization would occur, for he wrote articles for judges exposing good and bad decisions, and suggesting what were the principles that were emerging. He was leading in the direction of codification. The Chinese have evidenced no such desire. No judicial decisions are published systematically even in summary form to guide the courts. Judges are directed in each case to discuss the problem with local Communist Party officials, giving the impression that decisions are based on expediency rather than principle. What distinguishes the Chinese situation from the Soviet is the lack of apparent desire to regularize the judicial function, to lead courts in the direction of stability and codification.

[35] The cases have been collected and analyzed in an unpublished paper prepared by Dr. A. W. Rudzinski of Columbia University's Research Program on Communist Affairs.

[36] The legal and constitutional history of the Chinese People's Republic has been described and compared to the legal system of Romanist states in Engelborghs-Bertels & Dekkers, *La République populaire de Chine, cadres institutionnels et réalizations* (Vol. 1, L'HISTOIRE ET LE DROIT (1963)).

[37] Documents relating to the transition have been collected by Jerome A. Cohen and reproduced in a classroom manual entitled, PRELIMINARY MATERIALS ON THE LAW OF COMMUNIST CHINA (University of California, Berkeley, 1961).

The question facing legal sociologists at the moment as they examine the Chinese development is whether the Chinese Communists have really moved in a new direction, or whether they are but prolonging the formative stage of their jurisprudence beyond the number of years required by the Russians to get on their feet. Even to determine the question of direction, it may also be necessary to consider the influence of Chinese tradition upon what would seem necessary to Chinese communism as a legal system.

It is a notable fact that all of the People's Democracies of Eastern Europe as well as the U.S.S.R. itself are built upon a legal tradition that can be called Romanist.[38] All have long been "code States," and none has had experience with the common law method of developing law. Under such circumstances, development of codified law in the service of Marxist-inspired socialism may have been inescapable, with the result that the Soviet legal system has come to be a codified legal system, and not some other type. The Chinese may be thinking in other terms because Chinese experience with a codified system was short-lived. It began only in the 1930's, well after the 1911 overthrow of the Manchu dynasty, and its effectiveness was limited in large measure to urban centers and to the features of social relationship springing from modern industrial and commercial needs.[39] The traditional Chinese concepts of conciliation and lack of rigidity in law may have started to reemerge in 1957 as compatible with a legal system designed to foster a Marxist-inspired policy. If so, the Chinese pattern need not be considered to be as much of a departure from the Soviet model as it would seem to be on the surface. It would be only a cultural variation without ideological overtones.

One other ideological feature of contrast between the U.S.S.R. and China requires stating. It emerged in the exchange of letters during the summer of 1963 between the Soviet and Chinese Communist parties.[40]

The Chinese attacked the declaration in the Soviet Communist Party's Program of 1961 that the stage of the dictatorship of the proletariat has been passed, and that the U.S.S.R.'s political system had become that of the "state of the entire people." To the Chinese there can be no such thing as the state of the entire people, for until the state has withered away, it must remain a dictatorship of the proletariat.

This dispute has ramifications for law. To the Soviet theorists, the criminals of 1964 in the U.S.S.R. are not class enemies but wayward work-

[38] For a summary of the background, see Slapnicka, *Soviet Law as Model: The People's Democracies in the Succession States,* 8 NATURAL L. F. 106 (1963).

[39] The pre-communist history and principles of Chinese law are set forth in ESCARRA, CHINESE LAW: CONCEPTION AND EVOLUTION, LEGISLATIVE AND JUDICIAL INSTITUTIONS, SCIENCE AND TEACHING (Browne transl. 1961).

[40] The letters have been translated and printed in 15 C.D.S.P. No. 8, p. 3 (1963).

men. They cannot be class enemies because in accordance with the Marxist definition of class, they provide no contrast with all other citizens. They are wage earners and not owners of means of production. To the Chinese the embezzlers of state property, the murderers of Soviet policemen, and the gangs of rapists make themselves class enemies by virtue of their acts. The consequences of the difference in approach are to be found in the way in which trials are conducted, not in the penalties prescribed. Both communist parties believe in the severest punishment for offenders of the type mentioned, but the Soviet party currently supports in its program of stability a system of legal procedure designed to determine material or absolute truth. The Soviet jurists in treating their criminals as wayward workmen rather than class enemies take the position that they must be given protection against conviction if they are innocent. Hence, there must be a burden of proof on the prosecutor as the significant element in realization of the concept of presumption of innocence, which Soviet jurists accept even though they are not as yet willing to write it *expressis verbis* into the code. They also believe that the citizen should know in advance what is to be treated as criminal, and so they have abolished the concept of punishment by analogy.[41]

The Chinese reject both of these positions. They decry the concept of presumption of innocence as bourgeois, and they have, in effect, the freedom of action provided by the concept of analogy, since they have no criminal code defining crime. They rely on isolated statutes and the interpretation of the concept of crime by the individual judge in consultation with the Communist Party representative as expediency may seem to require.[42]

Again, the outsider can but speculate as to whether the difference between the Soviet and Chinese Communists is based upon conflicting ideological principles or whether the Chinese are but slower to establish their regime and so require a longer period than did the Russian Communist before they can act on other than crisis lines. One might think that the latter explanation was unlikely in view of the vehemence with which the Soviet position is criticized as violative of Marxist-Leninist principles, but Communists in all countries have traditionally polemicized their arguments. A strongly stated ideological position can be changed when circumstances no longer require its maintenance. It is not impossible that a China with ample food, steadily improving living standards, and no fear of foreign armies or subversive agents might move on to the Soviet position and accept Soviet interpretation of what Marxism-Leninism requires as criminal law and procedure.

[41] The current trends in the U.S.S.R. are set forth in Berman, *The Dilemma of Soviet Law Reform*, 76 HARV. L. REV. 929 (1963).

[42] The Chinese position is set forth in an article to be published in 1964 by the AM. J. COMP. L. written by Lin Fushun and entitled *Communist China's Emerging Fundamentals of Criminal Law*.

V. Conclusion

The Soviet legal pattern has become the model for Eastern European Communists, and in some measure for those of Asia as well. From the point of view of Soviet policymakers there is no reason why their pattern should not provide the model for Africa and Latin America also. To be sure, the sharp edges of the model have been blurred as leaders with political experiences different from those offered by Tsarist Russia have entered the communist camp. The blurring has been even greater when the culture patterns within which the law was applied were Asian rather than European. Still, the model has been recognizable, and perhaps even strengthened by the blurring, for it would of necessity have met resistance had it been forcibly applied without change to peoples that shared no common culture.

The model has been seriously challenged by the Chinese since Stalin's death. Mao Tse-tung has challenged basic principles, and his voice is strong. In the light of the Chinese challenge, dissemination of the Soviet model acquires increased significance. If Communists in Southeast Asia, Africa, and Latin America accept the Soviet model, they can be presumed to have forged an additional bond between themselves and Moscow. If they reject the Soviet model in favor of the Chinese variation, Soviet leadership of all Communists is threatened. Schooling has been demonstrated to play its part in preparation of future communist leaders and in their orientation toward the Soviet or Chinese pattern of thought and practice. Is it any wonder that Soviet law and the political doctrine on which it rests are being taught to potential revolutionaries in Friendship University? Law has become a key weapon in the Soviet arsenal with which the Communists of the U.S.S.R. hope to influence the future of the world.